# Bringing Krishna Back to India

# Bringing Krishna Back to India

## *Global and Local Networks in a Hare Krishna Temple in Mumbai*

CLAIRE C. ROBISON

OXFORD
UNIVERSITY PRESS

OXFORD
UNIVERSITY PRESS

Oxford University Press is a department of the University of Oxford.
It furthers the University's objective of excellence in research, scholarship,
and education by publishing worldwide. Oxford is a registered trade mark of
Oxford University Press in the UK and in certain other countries.

Published in the United States of America by Oxford University Press
198 Madison Avenue, New York, NY 10016, United States of America.



Library of Congress Cataloging-in-Publication Data
Names: Robison, Claire Catherine, author.
Title: Bringing Krishna back to India: global and local networks in a
hare krishna temple in Mumbai / Claire C. Robison.
Description: New York : Oxford University Press, 2024. |
Includes bibliographical references and index.
Identifiers: LCCN 2023043755 (print) | LCCN 2023043756 (ebook) |
ISBN 9780197656457 (hardback) | ISBN 9780197656471 (epub) |
ISBN 9780197656488
Subjects: LCSH: International Society for Krishna
Consciousness—India—Mumbai. | Hinduism—India—Mumbai—21st century.
Classification: LCC BL1285.832.M86 R63 2024 (print) | LCC BL1285.832.M86 (ebook) |
DDC 294.5/512—dc23/eng/20231026
LC record available at https://lccn.loc.gov/2023043755
LC ebook record available at https://lccn.loc.gov/2023043756

DOI: 10.1093/9780197656488.001.0001

Printed by Integrated Books International, United States of America

MIX
Paper
FSC FSC® C183721

# Contents

*Note on Translation and Transliteration* vii
*Acknowledgments* ix

Introduction: The Novelty of Traditionalism: Tracing Global Networks in Local Hindu Revivalism 1
Revivalism and Revising Religion 8
Revision as Crossing and Dwelling 14
Hindu Traditions and Transnational Religion in Urban India 17
ISKCON and Religious Globalization 21
Finding Krishna in the City of Dreams 24
Entering the Space 30

1. New Religious Movement, Old Religious Movement: Historicizing a Transnational Organization 38
Early Gauḍīya Vaiṣṇavism 39
New Orthodoxies and a Global Mission 44
In the West but Not of the West 56
Taking a Hit: The Liability of Transnationalism 61
Bringing Krishna Back to India 65

2. Global and Local Networks in a Neighborhood Temple: ISKCON Chowpatty, Mumbai 71
Entering the Radha Gopinath Temple 75
The Demographics of Local Devotees 82
Local Networks, Transnational Ties: Forming an Indian ISKCON Community 87
The Counselling System: Reproducing Idyllic Community 92
The American Swami at the Heart of an Indian Temple 97
*The Journey Home:* Completing a Global Circle of Krishna *Bhakti* 102
Becoming a Local Orthodoxy 109

3. Crossing Over: Entering the Devotional Family 114
Outside the Looking Glass 115
Becoming Religious in the City 118
"You Cannot Keep Your Feet in Two Boats" 122
It's Always Easier for Brahmins 125
But Can You Become Brahmin? 130

Choosing a Path: The *Brahmacari* Ashram or the Marriage Board 136
"She Tells Us What to Do and We Listen": Everyday Religious Kinship 142

4. Ancient Answers to Modern Questions: Revising Religion 150
Finding Answers in ISKCON 152
From Vedic Texts to PowerPoints 155
The Science of God 163
The Systematic Gītā: A Quiz and Its Champions 174
Managing Doubts, Practicing Certainty 177
ISKCON Has Arrived 182

5. *Bhakti* and Its Boundaries: Enacting a Religious Nation 187
Charting a National Heritage of Hindu Devotion 188
Performing Pan-Indic *Bhakti* on Stage 198
India Rising: Representing the Indian Nation 203
The Others of the *Bhakti* Body Politic 215
The Blurred Boundaries of Religious Nationalisms 224

6. A New Traditionalism in the City: Transforming Local Culture 230
Claiming Culture, Revising Culture 234
Contesting Western Modernity 237
Making "Universal Religion" Local 243
Saris in the City 250
"Phir Bhi Dil Hai Hindustani" 254

Conclusion: Producing a Religious Modernity in Urban India 261

*Notes* 267
*Selected Bibliography* 293
*Index* 311

# Note on Translation and Transliteration

The translations of Hindi and Sanskrit passages, unless otherwise noted, are my own. I have used diacritics for historic figures and technical terms from Indian languages, but I have opted not to employ them for contemporary proper nouns, terms that frequently appear in English (yoga, guru), and to ease pronunciation in some cases (Krishna, *rishi*). The transliteration of Sanskrit terms generally follows the system adopted by the *Journal of the American Oriental Society*, with exceptions explained in the case of modifications common in contemporary Indian usage. The transliteration of Hindi terms and dialogue follows the Library of Congress system for the Romanization of Hindi letters and contemporary usage prevalent in the community with which my study is concerned. When citing direct quotations and primary source material, I have followed the author's conventions in spelling and diacritical marks. In cases of conflicting spellings, I have opted for simplicity and accessibility.

# Acknowledgments

This book is the result of over a decade of research and writing, supported by many wonderful, generous people who have helped it to manifest along the way.

First, I want to thank the devotees of the ISKCON Chowpatty community, who graciously shared their time and lives with me over the span of my research there. To begin, Radhanath Swami Maharaja was wonderfully generous in welcoming me into the temple community. As he said in our initial interview soon after my arrival: "you have an unlimited passport and full freedom to speak to anyone and to go anywhere on the temple property . . . except inside the *brahmacari* ashram!" I am glad to say I followed those appropriate parameters. At that initial meeting in late 2012, Radhanath Swami also introduced me to Amritanaam and Krishnanaam Prabhus, who became my *de facto* local parents and generously introduced me to many of their friends and fellow devotees. They invited me to join them on trips to the Govardhan Ecovillage, a pilgrimage to Kerala and Tamil Nadu, and many other outings. Those became some of the most rewarding experiences during my time in the community and the source of many anecdotes written in this book. Along with other devotees, they warmheartedly folded me into their lives and helped my research develop through candid conversations and unwavering kindness.

A number of devotees opened their homes to me as a guest, and I am grateful for those many meals and gatherings. I cannot name everyone here, but among those I came to know best, Sita's friendship and enthusiastic spirit were always a joy. Manasvini and Mrs. Gandhi were fabulous travel companions and fearless guides, and Parampurush was an unparalleled trip leader. Tulsi Manjari, Radharani, Labanga, Reena, Sushila, Brajsaumani, Brajeshwari, Rupa Manjari, Akshata, Radhika, Rasrani, Tejal, and others all shared vivid personal perspectives on religion and life in Mumbai. Parijata, Braj Kumari, and Priyesha were candid and inspiring in the time we spent together. Sri Nathji, Krishna Chandra, Radha Gopinath, and Gauranga were generous with their time, given their busy schedules. Shubha Vilas was a thoughtful visionary, Gopinath Prasad a kind interlocutor, and Purushottam always a welcoming presence at the temple. These devotees all exemplified the virtues of humility and selflessness that are prized in the community. At the highest level, Radhanath Swami was boundlessly gracious, always a joy to be around whenever he was present. I am also grateful for the formal interviews and informal discussions I was able to have with other senior gurus and teachers in ISKCON, including Indradyumna Swami, Jayadvaita Swami, Rukmini Devi, and Anuttama Prabhu. And the chance visits of Saudamani, Vraja Lila, Gopal Lila, Susan, and Gita Priya punctuated my time with valued companionship and good humor.

But, without my academic gurus and mentors, this project would not have proceeded as smoothly. My doctoral advisor Barbara Holdrege and ethnographic advisor Mary Hancock were both invaluable guides throughout my research and while I revised my work into a book manuscript. Doctoral committee members Juan Campo and Mark Juergensmeyer were important intellectual guides during my project's development. The Religious Studies department at the University of California, Santa Barbara, could not have been a more supportive and life-affirming place to complete my graduate work. I benefited from the open, generous spirit of the department and its networks of informal mentorship. Thank you to Rudy Busto for workshopping my prospectus and to Greg Hillis, who helped map out this project idea at its inception and offered enthusiastic support along the way. My work was financially supported by Religious Studies Department at UCSB, and language fellowships from the South Asia Summer Language Institute (SASLI) and the American Institute for Indian Studies (AIIS) supplemented my research skills.

As I crafted my doctoral research into a book manuscript, I received valuable help from colleagues, mentors, and friends. I am particularly indebted to John Cort for combing through an early draft of the entire manuscript and guiding me through the process of contacting a publisher. Clark Chilson offered feedback on my book proposal that helped shape my thoughts about the project. I benefitted from the direction of Joyce Flueckiger, Tulasi Srinivas, and Brian Hatcher during an AIIS Dissertation to Book Workshop at the Annual Conference on South Asia in Madison, Wisconsin. And in the years that I developed my research, colleagues and friends in my campus communities were wonderful interlocutors. At UCSB, conversations with Scott Marcus, Bhaskar Sarkar, Mark McLaughlin, Kerry San Chirico, Rohit Singh, Joel Gruber, and Shalini Kakar helped me formulate my ideas. Academic mentors and senior colleagues, including Antoinette De Napoli,

Hanna Kim, Paula Kane, Anna King, and Jeanette Jouili, were great sources of support along the way. And I am deeply grateful to Jessica Starling, Joshua Urich, and Vineet Chander for their crucial feedback that helped me cross the finish line.

At Oxford University Press, thank you to Cynthia Reed, who accepted this manuscript and ferried it through uncertain times during the pandemic. The valuable feedback of my anonymous academic reviewers helped me clarify my arguments and improve the final version. Finally, thank you to Chelsea Hogue, Lavanya Nithya, and the editorial staff who saw it through to its completion.

This work was greatly enriched by many conversations with close friends, including my coven: Mayumi Kodani, Hareem Khan, Shayla Monroe, and Pawan Rehill. Lynna Dhanani, Zamira Abman, and Stefanie Schott helped me develop and refine my ideas at different stages. On the ground in Mumbai, Jacob Hustedt helped me get my sea legs, Arjuna Desai supported many nights of engaged conversation about religion and life, Mario da Penha and Sarover Zaidi were always inspiring company, and Dilip D'Souza and Vibha Kamat provided generous hospitality and neighborly friendship.

Finally, the care of family members has been invaluable during this project's development. The intellectual and personal inspiration of my parents gave me the foundational tools for an intellectual life, guided my interest in taking religion seriously, and set my direction toward India before I was even born. Countless conversations with my partner and his support over the years helped formulate what was most meaningful to me in this project and in life, and the unparalleled beauty and sweetness of my son, Mirza Ali, put everything into perspective.

# Introduction: The Novelty of Traditionalism

## Tracing Global Networks in Local Hindu Revivalism

One January evening in the Tilak Nagar neighborhood of Mumbai, elaborate festival tents filled a large park, encircled by blocks of concrete apartment complexes. The low-key, middle-class neighborhood was transformed into an event space. White satin fabric draped the perimeter walls, and glossy posters advertised the logos of local technology companies alongside the name of the Hindu temple that organized the festival. As commuters walked home from the train station down the lane, passing corner groceries and wayside shrines, neighbors came out to see the festivities. Rickshaws and private cars idled at the entrance, ferrying guests in formal saris and well-ironed kurtas. Groups of visitors filed through the entrance gate, where jasmine garlands hung lavishly on both sides of a red-carpeted pathway.

The scene evoked an ornate wedding, also held in the winter season when the nights are cooler and the social season flourishes. But this was part of a five-night "Rath-Yatra gala" hosted by the local International Society for Krishna Consciousness (ISKCON) temple of Chowpatty, South Bombay.[1] Like ISKCON communities globally, Mumbai's devotees celebrate the Rath Yatra as their largest annual public festival. On the culminating day, well-coordinated groups parade chariots of Vaiṣṇava deities through the streets of Dadar and neighboring Hindu-majority neighborhoods, winding toward a park reserved for stage performances and a free vegetarian meal. Although rooted in the centuries-old temple traditions of Puri in the Eastern Indian state of Odisha, the Rath Yatra is celebrated in Mumbai by several nights of organized stage programming, ranging from the religious lectures of ISKCON swamis, messages from local political leaders, and Bollywood celebrity appearances. Local corporate sponsorships endow it with a glossy, camera-ready atmosphere.

*Bringing Krishna Back to India*. Claire C. Robison, Oxford University Press. © Oxford University Press 2024.
DOI: 10.1093/9780197656488.003.0001

A local friend joined me to walk around the festival grounds before dinner. Shoaib, who grew up in Calcutta, had encountered white American Hare Krishna devotees (a commonly known name for ISKCON members) as a young boy, as they were handing out pamphlets about their mission at Calcutta's bookstores and cafés. He recalled visiting their center once in Mayapur on a family trip, driving down the dusty roads to the rural settlement several hours south toward the Bay of Bengal. As a child, he was amazed by how many Americans were living austerely in that remote Bengali countryside, and he was later surprised to learn that the term "hippy" was not a synonym for all Westerners.

Given all this, Shoaib was immediately intrigued by this gathering of middle-class Indian families and young couples strolling through the well-appointed festival grounds to the main stage. "Where are all the Americans?" It was a sentiment familiar to me by now, after taking multiple friends to ISKCON temples, where they expected to find groups of white Americans in ill-fitting saris and *dhoti*s and would instead find well-organized congregations of Indian families dressed in designer saris, suits, and even sometimes jeans.[2] As a journalist with a keen eye for analyzing religion and history, Shoaib shared my curiosity in how much the community has changed over the course of its five decades in India. ISKCON's global spread provides a vivid example of how profoundly a religious tradition can transform through the growth of new practitioner communities and cultural settings. Contrary to their long depiction in India through hyper-visible Western followers, ISKCON's Indian devotees presented themselves instead as guardians of Indian heritage, stylized through recognizable nationalist tropes. Not only West Bengal but a panoply of Indian states were represented in government-sponsored craft stalls and regional dance performances on the main stage. Spanning India's diverse linguistic and cultural regions, these displays depicted a consonant thread of Vaiṣṇava Hindu heritage throughout the subcontinent, tracing the boundaries of the modern nation-state from the politically dominant Uttar Pradesh to the northeast borderlands of Assam and Manipur. In this quiet neighborhood, named after the twentieth-century nationalist politician Bal Gangadhar Tilak, the curated festival conveyed a clear message: ISKCON devotees are not only Indian, they seek to *represent* India in their religious image.

This curation of Indian national heritage as, implicitly, devotional Hindu religious heritage is notable due to its purveyor: a transnational religious organization known historically for *not* being Indian. But early American

ISKCON devotees in Mumbai saw their mission as "bringing Krishna back to India." That evokes a remarkable agenda of transnational Hindu revivalism directed toward the site of the world's most Hindus—a phenomenon some may label as a complex instance of cultural imperialism.[3] But this mission-driven approach was guided by Bhaktivedanta and continues to be central among Indian devotees decades on, now with more local nuance. Today's Krishna revivalists seek not only to promote their religious traditionalism in Indian cities but also to "bring Krishna back," in a trendy sense, in public culture. This involves remaking public space as devotional space, bringing Krishna into spaces normally coded as secular, such as MTV-sponsored music festivals and college campuses. Therein, ISKCON media and missionizing efforts portray Krishna and the religious messages of Vaiṣṇavism as the solution to problems that people face in careers, relationships, and families. This fusion of piety with public culture has gained ISKCON a status in mainstream media outlets as a posh religious destination for the display of piety among Mumbai's film industry celebrities and business tycoons. The mission of "bringing Krishna back" thus seeks to remake India through religious revivalism as it also reshapes Hindu traditions to fit a contemporary urban context.

And this remaking of modern space extends into devotees' personal lives. Once one joins ISKCON, old communal structures of the natal family, with inherited ritual traditions and informal religious practices, are refigured. Their notion of Hindu tradition centers on a philosophical system with defined bounds of orthodoxy and orthopraxy, diminishing inherited religious practices not centered on Krishna. Here, an emphasis on adopting Krishna *bhakti* practices as a personal choice grounded in educational attainment—learning tools for personal growth and spiritual fulfillment—frames religious dedication through modern sensibilities. In many contemporary ISKCON productions, the early-modern Sanskritic textual corpus of the Gauḍīyas is channeled into guidance for healthy relationships and stress reduction through a new spin on practices of asceticism and devotion. In this sense, ISKCON's traditionalism forges a religious Indian modernity—resonating with other religious modernities across the globe.[4] Grounded in an institutional systematization of Hindu traditions and guided personal formation through training in Vaiṣṇava etiquette and *sādhana* practice, the adoption of Gauḍīya traditions also reflects broader trends among Indian religious groups to couch religious attainment in the language of educational rigor and professional success.[5]

This study considers the growth of this consummate transnational religious network in the megacity of Mumbai. My research centers on the Radha Gopinath temple, known commonly as the Chowpatty ISKCON temple community due to its location in the seaside neighborhood of Girgaon Chowpatty. Now one of four ISKCON centers in the metropolis, this temple community has been at the vanguard of normalizing ISKCON's Hindu traditionalism in an elite Indian context within the country's entertainment and finance capital. The community comprises around six thousand members from diverse Indian backgrounds—particularly Gujarati, Maharashtrian, North Indian, and South Indian. Within ISKCON's multi-guru authority structure, their religious leadership team stems from an American-born guru, Radhanath Swami, who has led the community since the early 1990s.[6] Originally viewed within Mumbai as a "foreigner's Hinduism," ISKCON Chowpatty (hereafter, Chowpatty) has gained respect from conservative Hindu groups who share their postcolonial anti-Western, anti-secularist ethos. But at the same time, Chowpatty's devotees orient themselves toward Mumbai's "Westernized" publics, and many move in global corporate circles, embracing diverse technologies of modernity in industry and business. They thus provide a valuable case study of a Hindu community in an interface with urbanization, globalization, and transnational networks in India.

More broadly, my study considers the influence of transnational religious organizations, which are increasingly the source of people's knowledge about their inherited religions, effectively remaking and standardizing what have been historically varied, fluid traditions. The power yielded by large religious organizations also impacts people's political orientations and social views, shaping electorates and family norms alike. These transformations of religion often occur in tandem with migration and urban mobility. Alongside globalizing economic trends, urbanization and interurban migration over the past few decades have not only remade India and its economy; they have also remade how (and whether) people practice religion. For Indians who now routinely move across the country to megacities like Mumbai or Delhi for education or work, ties to local kinship networks and family temples are often replaced by new social networks. Amid these increased migrations of people and ideas, transnational religious organizations have become influential in mediating Hindu traditions to urban publics. Contemporary Hindu organizations present new visions of religious traditions—distilling their ideas online, through popular book series, or on college campuses. Like the Sathya Sai International Organization and the Mata Amritanandamayi

Mission, ISKCON often couches Indic practices in terms of spirituality and wellness, and they develop a strong public-facing focus on humanitarian projects, heading off widespread public suspicion in India about the accumulation of wealth at historic temple complexes with models of religious community that emphasize contemporary values of social engagement.

However, ISKCON pairs its modern branding practices with assertions that it represents a traditional *paramparā*, a lineage of teachers mediating a textually centered orthodoxy. This interpretation of Hindu traditions foregrounds Vaiṣṇava *bhakti*, or the devotional worship of the god Viṣṇu and his *avatāras*—including Krishna (in Sanskrit, Kṛṣṇa) and Rāma—collectively one of the largest strands of Hinduism. ISKCON founder, the Bengali *saṃnyāsin* A. C. Bhaktivedanta Swami, centered his theology on the statement that Krishna is the Supreme Personality of Godhead, a frequent articulation in his work.[7] This places Krishna at the center of a devotional Hindu worldview and acts as an interpretative device to measure other religious and cultural practices. Although this discourse is grounded in asserting its traditionalism, ISKCON's teachings often overtly critique adherents' inherited Hindu traditions, offering an interpretation of these expansive and diverse traditions that centers Krishna as supreme. To this end, its educational structures challenge devotees to measure family traditions against their new religious community's practices, relinquishing those that are not complimentary. This is markedly different from an understanding of Hindu traditions as embedded in one's natal family and community—a novel traditionalism.

ISKCON is not entirely the product of modern times. While it has been studied in the Global North almost exclusively as a Western New Religious Movement (NRM), in India it draws on recognizable premodern religious sources. Its teachings and practices are grounded in the sixteenth-century Bengali *bhakti* tradition called Gauḍīya Vaiṣṇavism, which envisions the deity Krishna as the supreme divinity. However, from its centralized missionary focus to its regulated formal membership, its model of religious belonging is palpably modern. ISKCON was registered as an official society in 1966 in New York by Bhaktivedanta Swami and described as "Krishna consciousness" for his countercultural Western audiences of the time. Bhaktivedanta drew on the global missionizing agendas of nineteenth- and twentieth-century Bengali teachers who sought to spread their traditions to wider audiences in India and the West, themselves responding to the condescending logic of European Christian missionary agendas.[8] As a true global missionary, he was keen to spread Krishna *bhakti* not only to the West but to all lands, and to that end he directed disciples to develop communities in every continent. Throughout the 1970s, he supported missionary work in the former USSR that has led to some of the most vibrant devotee communities outside of India today, in Ukraine and Russia, which are home to eleven and twenty centers respectively as of 2023. His followers distinguished themselves through forging new temples and centers for devotees abroad, including in Africa, Asia, and Latin America. These efforts led to prominent devotee communities in, for instance, South Africa, Kenya, and Brazil, which alone is home to eleven temples and a total of forty-four ISKCONs projects.[9] In addition to this global spread, Bhaktivedanta foregrounded missionary work in India from 1970 onward, considering Mumbai the "gateway to India," and he worked with his American disciples to establish a temple there in a symbolic return.[10]

Although he was one of many gurus in his lineage, Bhaktivedanta came to occupy an unparalleled centrality in ISKCON's religious culture and theological self-understanding. Guru-centered lineages are commonplace in Indian religions, but ISKCON's institutionalization and even legislation of Bhaktivedanta's primacy is mediated through internal edicts governing membership. Bhaktivedanta's centrality is balanced with a model of multinodal religious authority, however, in which numerous disciples in his lineage act as "initiating gurus," accepting their own disciples within ISKCON's parameters. Beginning with eleven appointed in 1977 at Bhaktivedanta's passing, ISKCON's gurus today total ninety-seven, and they reside throughout the world, connected through shared institutional adherence.[11] Debates over authority and ownership have led to community schisms and—in some Indian cities—court battles over lucrative temple property. This distinguishes members of the organization from many often far-less-institutionalized Hindu groups. ISKCON's grounding in community legislation and conformity in matters of ritual and belief reflects Bhaktivedanta's upbringing amid the British bureaucratic regime in late colonial Calcutta. This rationalizing context, to draw from Max Weber's use of the term, compelled a profound reframing of Hindu traditions to mirror the institutionalized structures of modern bureaucracies, complete with legislative governing bodies (for ISKCON, the GBC or Governing Body Commission). At the same time, this tightly legislated organization is centered on the cultivation of devotional affects through systematic education and training—a very modern combination of the aspiration for personal transformation and its mediation through a bureaucratic system.

Although ISKCON is an NRM in the sense of it being a modern institution, ISKCON has gained broad traction in India precisely because it has developed its public image as a custodian of premodern Hindu traditions. In molding this image, ISKCON's members navigate, on the one hand, widespread impressions in India that ISKCON temples are bastions of Western converts—and the wealth, tourism, and moral decadence that entails in the popular imagination—and, on the other, a deepening affiliation with Hindu traditionalist organizations, including Hindu nationalist parties' religious agendas in India's public spheres. The support of many temple leaders for the greater place of Hindu religiosity, vegetarianism, and cow protection in the contemporary Indian state means that Western-born temple presidents or international donors have, tellingly, not been subject to the Modi government's attacks against "foreign organizations," including Amnesty International or Greenpeace, in recent years. By contrast, ISKCON's temples in urban India provide vivid places for the melding of urban aspirations for globalized markers of success and traditionalist Hindu lifestyle norms—a combination popular throughout many monied Hindu communities.

Through Indian devotees, the organization has managed to position itself as an increasingly central player in India's Hindu public spheres, wielding vast economic assets, political influence, and—more recently, in Mumbai—a curated, posh identity endorsed by corporate leaders and Hindi film stars. Indeed, members of the most prominent business families in the metropolis—Mafatlal, Piramal, Ambani—have been connected to the Chowpatty ISKCON temple and its resident guru, Radhanath Swami, reflecting its standing in the city. Despite this, to date there has been little scholarship investigating the influential place of ISKCON in contemporary urban Indian settings, although their missionizing programs are arguably having an outsized impact on how many young Indians view Hindu traditions due to the prominence of their workshops at college campuses and workplaces and their growing social media presence.

This has political ramifications, due to many members' support of the soft Hindu right that bolstered Prime Minister Narendra Modi's 2014 election and the Bharatiya Janata Party's return to mainstream Indian politics. But it also has religious ramifications. Their missionizing networks frame their message in terms of revival and reform, seeking to *educate* Hindus about *authentic* Hindu traditions, and their media products have remarkable currency in urban Hindu communities beyond the boundaries of ISKCON's membership. Much of this education, although it often encourages members to break with their family traditions and adopt a new religious practice, is presented in a language of reinstating tradition. ISKCON devotees globally describe their decision to adopt Krishna consciousness as a return to the practices of an idyllic Vedic past. In India, devotees describe their practice as a return to Hindu rituals that members view as having been lost or corrupted over the past generations through the influence of Western-style modernity in Indian cities. To encompass these characteristics, I depart from the categorization of ISKCON as an NRM within a North American context to describe ISKCON as a revivalist religious organization within India, since it seeks to affect a revival of premodern religious texts and practices recognized as traditions of the majority. The terms revivalism and revising religion offer a window into understanding how elements of both new and old, global and local, operate in this religious traditionalist group.

## Revivalism and Revising Religion

Despite historic associations with Christian movements in early-modern Europe and the American Great Awakenings, revivalism is a term central to understanding trends in many religious communities over the past two centuries, as the growth of print media and later online media have enabled the widespread circulation of ideas about the ideal character for one's religious practice. Revivalist religion is a central form of being religious today and a growing trend throughout the world over the past few decades, from Evangelical Christian groups in the United States and Brazil to the Tablighi Jama'at in South Asia or the Muslim Brotherhood in Egypt. Although these groups differ in theological content and social ethics, they converge in their shared interest to reform the lived religious practice of adherents in their communities, through focus on a perceived revival of an earlier, purer, "traditional" form of being a good Christian, Muslim, or Hindu.

As Peter van der Veer has noted, "immense ideological work" goes into the project of "traditionalism," requiring a transformation of previous and existing discursive practices in the name of revival.[12] A positivist sense of an essentialized Indian cultural or religious "tradition" has been perpetuated by a range of thinkers over the past several centuries, including both Orientalists and Indian gurus, emerging from the multidirectional flow of ideas during the colonial period. As David Washbrook writes, the lens of Western modernization itself provided a certain gaze through which to conceptualize the character of Indian "tradition" as a static and conservative "other," in contradistinction to the self-flattering understanding of European modernity as dynamic and liberal.[13] While the terms "Hindu renaissance," "Hindu revivalism," and "neo-Hinduism" have been widely used to describe Hindu groups that have developed since the nineteenth century, those terms often convey implicitly that British colonization comprised a definitive break between traditional and modern India.[14] Scholarship over the past several decades has sought to dismantle the qualitative value judgments in describing Hindu formations through the bifurcated categories "tradition" and "reform," centered on before and after the British colonial period, or the "revival" of a lost golden era.[15] But these terms have their own vernacular lives in Hindu communities today.

In this study, I highlight the potency of discourses of revival and reform in contemporary urban Hindu communities—and their underlying supposition of the need to change or "purify" existing religious practices.[16] ISKCON's revivalism in India reflects the multidimensional development of Indian modernities—developing from the legacy of colonial institutions, the formation of nation-states, and the rise of neoliberal globalization, but also equally from the growth of Asian megacities, aspirations for the creation of urban enclaves, and nostalgia for premodern lifestyles amid industrial fatigue. As these vectors shape contemporary public discourse in India, they are also reflected in ideas of what comprises Hindu tradition and particularly how Hindu traditions should relate to the realities of modern life.[17] This is at times a conscious discourse in communities themselves; ISKCON *sannyasi* and scholar of religion Tamal Krishna Goswami calls for the categories of tradition and traditionalism to be rescued from being fossilized, as the theology of Krishna *bhakti* tradition was itself harnessed by Bhaktivedanta as a modality of change.[18] Cognizant of this, I label ISKCON's identity in Mumbai as traditionalist and revivalist in the sense that it is ideologically grounded in the project of reinstating or reviving Indian religious and cultural identities that it locates in precolonial origins. At the same time, it also embodies new structures of organization indicative of its place in contemporary society.[19]

Traditionalist or revivalist notions of religion are never made in a vacuum. ISKCON shares important characteristics with a range of Hindu groups that crystallized from the mid-nineteenth century onward. These include attempts to standardize the historically decentralized and various Hindu traditions through shared participation in print and now digital media communities, the formalization of religious communities through models of bureaucratic organization drawn from civil society organizations of colonial-era India, the development of a notion of a unifying pan-Indic Hindu heritage, a sense of urgency to purify or reform contemporary Hindu practices with reference to an idyllic Hindu past, and shared orientation toward remaking Hindu traditions for global audiences.[20] And yet, for many religious traditionalists, the adoption of modern means of communication and organization is coupled with an overt suspicion toward Western and secularizing ideologies of modernity.[21]

Beyond this, however, religious revivalism revises the stories we tell about our families, regions, cultures, and histories. Although employing the language of return, it ironically remakes us as new, profoundly modern individuals, distinguishing us from more proximate pasts by linking us to a hallowed, idealized image of the past that we are compelled to revive in the present day. To become religious in a revivalist group also means to adopt new moral geographies,[22] to cross over into a new relationship with one's surroundings in industrialized cities, which are often juxtaposed as antithetical to a traditionalist lifestyle. These shifts in perspective are taught, not inherited. Although religious revivalist movements often have strong missionary orientations and seek converts, some of the largest revivalist movements over the past two centuries specifically target people who have been raised in their broad religious traditions already. Internal missionizing aims to reshape the way people see their own traditions, often abandoning their family practices and local, cultural understandings of religion to adopt the systematic and often more rigid, textually based approach of the revivalist group. This also recasts what is meant by religious belonging: it is no longer tied to birth and upbringing primarily but to personal choice. To relearn one's own religion in this way—excising those aspects of lived practice and family background that do not fit—positions one within a new web of networks, shifting from those defined through family lineage and regional background, to those defined by voluntary, shared membership in an organization and adherence to its norms.

Although this study is focused on one religious organization and the development of a temple in one Indian city, my guiding questions are grounded in a fascination with revivalist movements' current popularity around the world. What motivates people who grew up in secular or non-observant homes to adopt profound religious piety in their lives? What does it mean to become devout in a cultural space dominated by depictions of religion as old-fashioned, extremist, or—at best—harmless but irrelevant? When social norms are trending in Indian cities toward more assertively liberal norms of gender and sexuality, what draws people to join religious groups that promote conservative, traditionalist social norms, apparently limiting their ability to inhabit more flexible spaces? What is at stake when the adoption of new religious norms creates friction with one's own family and broader society? And how might these choices change the way we view globalized and local religion?

I pose these questions not in search of sociological, quantitative, or cognitive behavioral answers, but as an ethnographic exploration into what motivates people in one transnational revivalist organization—and by extension, to point toward an exploration of contemporary religious revivalism in the Global South and beyond. Religious identity today intersects with the realms of personal choice, community belonging, and nationalist discourse. The popularity of transnational organizations such as ISKCON shows how trends of religious and cultural globalization can be discursively conservative, not only liberal. Their growth in urban India, particularly, demonstrates that local religion today is increasingly shaped by transnational networks—from migration patterns that introduce one to new temple communities, to the media platforms that become one's source of information about religious traditions.

In this study, I link the intention of reviving to acts of revising and invoke several connotations of the related terms revising and revisioning to highlight their agentive and interpretative properties. Revivalist groups do not mediate passive absorptions of tradition but rather creative innovations in a modern context. The rhetoric of a return is, in fact, an act of revisioning, an interpretation of what is authentic among the myriad models of past traditions. And the modality of education and training is central to ideas about how to revise one's religion "correctly," that is, according to understandings promoted by the revivalist group. Through acts of revisioning the past and oneself, the process of revising religion is made personal, shaping one's relation to family and local cultures.

In North American English, the verb revise carries primary connotations of re-examining or returning to a subject, involving an emendation or a perceived process of correction. Even in religious communities designated as conservative or orthodox, discourses of fidelity to texts or community structures inevitably involve an agentive, interpretative process by each new generation of practitioners. As Tulasi Srinivas has shown, even those most imbued with the designation of orthodox authority—brahmin temple priests—are in fact engaged in constant processes of creative reconceptions of Hindu rituals, toward the aim, in Srinivas's analysis, of generating wonder in new urban environments.[23] And, as shown in Deonnie Moodie's study of Kalighat in Kolkata, even the most iconic historic temples are in continuing states of innovation, reflecting the changing social and political norms around them.[24] Although acts of interpretation weave through all religious expressions, the rhetoric involved in religious traditionalism—that it represents an original or authentic way of being religious—often obscures its essential work of revision as curation, or the choice of which aspects of the past count as valid, authentic, or correct according to the lens of interpretation. This inherently involves innovation in practice, a departure from much that came before it, even if couched in the notion of a return to a purer past. The notion that religious traditions are *always* being interpreted—and never existing in a vacuum of purity separate from cultural contexts and human influence—is controversial to some conservative religious groups. But the reality that living religion involves a continual process of recasting and adaptation is not anathema to all revivalists. ISKCON devotees are familiar with Bhaktivedanta's assertion that Krishna consciousness should be adjusted to fit *deśa-kāla-pātra*, or the "place, time, and context" in which one is interpreting religious injunctions. Indeed, evaluating how to adopt a lifestyle that developed in premodern Bengal while living in a contemporary megacity involves an array of alterations that occupy many conversations among devotees, engaging them in acts of cultural as well as linguistic translation.

ISKCON's revivalist ideas are grounded *not* in an idealization of common Hindu practices but rather a critique of them and, instead, the conviction that a lost, more authentic Hinduism that must be recovered through formal learning before it can be embodied.[25] In this regard, my analysis will also engage with the British usage of revise as "to reread or to study, particularly in preparation for an exam." This valence illumines the role of educational modalities in this contemporary form of religion. ISKCON's centers internationally have foregrounded models of education and training in their approach to community formation. This includes classes that guide devotees through systematic scriptural study in a scholastic mode, such as Bhaktivedanta's development of the Bhakti Śastri course, which leads students in a directed study of core Gauḍīya Vaiṣṇava scriptures through his translations and textual commentaries. This extends to adult education modules that draw on self-help trends, such as courses on stress management and relationship building, which are mainstream in India as well as North America. And a focus on systematic educational modalities in temple programming mirrors the structure of higher education and coaching classes also prevalent throughout urban India.[26] In ISKCON's Mumbai communities, educational and training components have reached new heights through the tightly knit Spiritual Counselling System that weaves together the several thousand devotees through biweekly meetings and individual sessions centered on training each aspirant in the lifestyle and behavior of an ideal Vaiṣṇava devotee. The centrality of educational approaches to engagement with religion is also on full display at ISKCON Chowpatty's scripture-based quiz competitions, such as the Gita Champions League, and the PowerPoint-based courses that comprise the community's recruitment of new members on college campuses and office environments throughout the city.

For Hindus and others raised in Hindu-majority India, the act of revisioning Hinduism in a traditionalist mode involves looking again at a ubiquitous religious tradition but through the language of a return to or discovery of a more authentic understanding of oneself. This connection between the way we view collective pasts and our own identity resonates with the related term "re-visioning," developed by the feminist writer Adrienne Rich, which connotes an agentive reconstruction of personal identity through reassessing the past. Rich describes the concept of re-visioning as an "act of looking back, of seeing with fresh eyes, of entering an old text from a new critical direction," grounded in a quest for self-knowledge that reconsiders "the assumptions in which we are drenched."[27] Although Rich developed the concept as a tool for feminist literary critique, it has since acquired broader intersectional applications. I evoke this perspective to analyze dynamics among religious revivalists in the Global South, elucidating their personal adoption of piety in resistance to a perceived hegemony of Western modernity as a form of revisioning religion—in this case, as the assertion of a religious modernity in contrast to what they see as corrosive secularizing norms. Revisioning is not simply an intellectual exercise, but a form of agency that manifests in visible change and has material stakes.[28] For ISKCON devotees in Mumbai, revisioning their relation to a religious past entails revisions of daily life in the present, made visible through the adoption of traditionalist Indian dress in contrast to most Mumbaikars around them and, for some, abandoning lucrative careers built on years of hard-earned success in India's competitive education system to adopt a life of renunciation at a temple ashram. Accordingly, I will center my analysis not just on ISKCON's revivalist teachings and practices but also on the aesthetics and social stakes of revival, assessing how certain material forms—including choice of dress and lifestyle changes—become central grounds for asserting a new religious identity and reimagining aspirations for the future.

The work of a traditionalist community in urban India involves creative acts of revisioning individual pasts, family histories, and broader cultural and national notions of belonging. It also involves navigating friction with family and society through their adopting markers of difference, including distinct conservative clothing and dietary regulations. Nonetheless, many devotees conveyed to me that "these practices were common earlier but have been lost in recent generations," thus the revival of a lost orthoprax heritage. This assertion provides a powerful interpretative tool to encode their adopted religious norms with a unique value, fortifying themselves against criticism for their rejection of family and community norms. In these ways, revivalism engenders change in an individual's religious and social identities, as one crosses into a new identity altogether.

## Revision as Crossing and Dwelling

Although rooted in an idealization of premodern local cultures, revivalist religions today are often transnational in composition, importing ideas of the local that then have the potential to transform it. Contemporary religious traditions broadly are honed through a complex web of local communities, globalized media production, and transnational authority structures.[29] In the case of ISKCON, this is immediately visible in the itineraries of its global development and its multiethnic, international range of gurus who mediate ISKCON's institutional norms and practices to their local communities.

To illustrate these processes, my examination draws on Thomas Tweed's theorizing of religion through the themes of movement, relation, and position. Tweed developed these ideas to depict migrants' religious practice in diaspora, highlighting how practices both are brought over and come to dwell in novel forms. He applied the terms "crossing" and "dwelling" to describe both geographic and cultural shifts in their religious practice.[30] For transnational migrants, religious practices and regional identities are reshaped through the processes of migration itself and building a home in new lands. But aside from international migrations, transnational networks—and their dynamic movements of people and ideas—are now characteristic of urban lives in general. For ISKCON devotees globally, a network of pilgrimage sites in Northern and Eastern India serves as the sacred center of their tradition. This places Indian devotees at the geographic center of the transnational organization's devotional imaginary. But even though Indian devotees articulate their religious choice as a return to old traditions, their commitment is often developed through contact with ISKCON centers abroad, gurus of non-Indian descent, and a desire to reject contemporary urban Indian cultures. This connotes the adoption of a view of local tradition that is mediated through global channels and ultimately premised on changing local cultures in the name of revival. Moreover, inter-urban migration patterns and attendant shifting social networks figure into the religious identities of Indian devotees in Mumbai, as many residents of the city are recent migrants from across India who arrived for work opportunities or to attend college. Many Indians among the middle and upper classes from which ISKCON draws its base have also lived and studied abroad in London, Singapore, New York, or Toronto before settling in Mumbai. In some cases, their first encounter with a formalized study of Hinduism is through ISKCON temples abroad. Fittingly, the Hindu tradition they have adopted has itself migrated and been reshaped by its transnational spread, from India to the North America (and later Europe, Africa, and beyond) and then back to India. These transnational networks woven into the experiences and religious lives of Indian devotees convey that religious revival today is often a process marked not by literal nativism but by a complex interaction between global networks and transregional personal histories.

Geographic and cultural crossings are also woven into the fabric of urban life. Mumbai has often been called a city of migrants, and migration threads through the family histories of many Indian devotees. For those who are first- or second-generation migrants to Mumbai, settling in the city involves crossing out of a social identity supported by familial networks in small-town Kerala, Karnataka, or Bihar. As the children of employees in India's large multinational corporations or national industries, several devotees described their childhoods in stages, as their families relocated from Surat to Calcutta to Delhi, or Chennai to Goa to Mumbai, over the course of two or three generations. Acclimating to life in Mumbai particularly is marked by crossing into its vibrantly multilinguistic and regionally diverse communities, where old caste and class lines can be muted through the attainment of professional markers of success and urban anonymity. Yet many members describe feeling cut off from their family and regional backgrounds. In response, ISKCON's systematic institutionalized structures offer a new home—even a new concept of family. As Shail Mayaram notes, transnational religious organizations can provide new forms of community for those in countries undergoing major economic and demographic transitions, providing new boundaries and a new language of politics (indeed membership in a new political constituency) for migrants to rapidly growing urban centers.[31] Through these movements—of people to the city and into a new religious community—joining ISKCON engenders new forms of dwelling. These range from one's choice of nuclear family, daily lifestyle, and modes of behavior, to ways of inhabiting public space that differ distinctly from many devotees' upbringings.

Tweed draws attention to the kinetic power of religion to produce movement, change, and the means of crossing over to new realities. The global networks that inform ISKCON's revivalism transform local religion through devotees who join the organization. The systematic, commodified form of Hindu identity mediated through ISKCON reorients practitioners to conceive of Hindu traditions as monotheistic and centered on the devotional worship of Krishna rather than the vernacular plurality of worship of gods and goddesses, family deities, and regional spirits, which comprise many Hindu religious traditions. Accordingly, the process of joining ISKCON for many Indians includes crossing over to a new way of conceiving their own regional and religious history, even without the experience of transnational migration. Thus, alongside one dislocation—forging a new identity outside of one's ancestral home—devotees also choose to undergo another process of crossing, through joining a transnational religious organization that refigures their relationship to familial religious traditions, creating new kinship structures among devotees from different regional and class backgrounds across India and beyond.

But to be devoutly religious in Mumbai's middle-class and upper-class spaces is often to be set apart from mainstream cultural trends, and many ISKCON members described to me that they fell out of friendships and took some heat from their families—at least at first. For the Indian Hindus and Jains who join ISKCON, revising religion involves revisioning oneself and one's social community through choice rather than birth-based ties. Members' diverse upbringings are reconfigured into a shared culture of

Vaiṣṇava *bhakti*. Therein, new symbolic spaces for dwelling are fashioned, as practitioners are guided to redefine their relationship to the city through the networks of ISKCON temples and community gatherings. Positioned in this new community, they move away from social networks defined through natal language, religious background, and *jati* (or *jāti*, birth-based class)—which in prior generations may have formed one's closest social circles—to those defined through shared membership in a transnational organization. Therein, chosen membership in a religious group, reinforced through mentorship systems and systematic education and training modules, reshapes devotees' notions of family, religion, culture, and nation, forming a distinctively modern religious individual.

## Hindu Traditions and Transnational Religion in Urban India

While I situate my study in relation to contemporary religious revivalism, it also highlights the transnational character of Hinduism in practice. Hindu traditions have been often conceived as primarily tied to birth or ethnic background. This obscures the prominent role of migrations, transregional politics, and missionizing in their development, particularly in relation to contemporary Hindu traditions. Although rooted in origins in the Indian subcontinent, Hindu traditions have a millennia-long history of transregional spread throughout South and Southeast Asia. Over the past few centuries, prominent numbers of Hindus have migrated to Africa, the Caribbean, and the Global North, due to colonial networks and more recently globalized education and employment opportunities. Many Indian-origin families now span two or more continents, and this flow of people is mirrored in a global flow of ideas and practices such as yoga and meditation.

Transnational migration patterns impact religious authority structures, and this has led to a widening global conversation on who represents Hindu traditions—ethnically, socially, and doctrinally. Through the growth in global missionizing trends among guru-led organizations such as Transcendental Meditation, 3HO International, or Sri Sri Ravi Shankar's The Art of Living, Indian gurus have become fixtures in the globalized religious marketplace. The formation of transnational Hindu organizations and their discourses of Hindu traditions have also been dialectic processes, forged by diaspora communities, Indian and non-Indian practitioners, and cultural formations in India and abroad.[32] And over the past few decades, transnational organizations have become central curators of discussions about the character and content of Hindu traditions in popular culture in ways that are fundamentally changing the way people view their own religious traditions. Accordingly, scholarship on Hindu diasporas has grown alongside studies of transnational and multiethnic Hindu communities. As recent studies have shown, a transnational context is not only incidental to contemporary religious practice, rather it fundamentally shapes individuals' experiences with their religions and understanding of history.[33] Building on this work, my research highlights negotiations between the global and the local in urban India and how local religion today is in ongoing dialogue with transnational contexts.

Religious traditions are fundamentally shaped in public arenas, and Hindu communities' modes of public representation convey discourses about religion's place in contemporary societies.[34] Gayatri Spivak has drawn attention to the dynamic between the dual functions of representation, "speaking of" and "speaking for," in that any attempt to speak for a particular group involves the production of images and representations associated with that group.[35] The importance of engaging—and indeed, curating—representations of Hindu traditions gains significance for contemporary devout Hindus in an urban center such as Mumbai where there is a rapid urban movement away from the lifestyles of earlier generations. As John Zavos discusses, these representations become moments for the construction of community and ideas about that community's culture and tradition. There, we can examine representations of Hindu traditions not just in terms of their "right of representation" but also to contextualize the images of Hindu traditions they produce.[36]

My analysis unpacks what it means to join ISKCON in urban India through examining ISKCON's discursive processes of producing Hindu identity. ISKCON-produced media allows one to trace how notions of contemporary Hindu identity are shaped. Their media productions are often steeped in debates about defining ("proper") Hindu traditions and what place those traditions have in the contemporary world. For ISKCON devotees, the role of representing the Gauḍīya tradition in their daily lives and, by extension, representing Hindu traditions in public forums, is guided by carefully controlled messaging.[37] They are, after all, a missionizing organization. Indian devotees seek to appeal to an array of publics, from pious middle-class traditionalists to ardently secular, "scientific-minded" college students and corporate professionals. The Chowpatty devotees who are involved with producing and marketing forms of ISKCON-related media are keenly aware of the different publics to which they speak, ranging from Gauḍīya Vaiṣṇava temple-based publications, to the development of their Ecovillage that hosts American yoga teacher-training groups annually, to corporate seminars on themes such as "Stress Management" and "Meditation for a Modern Lifestyle" for Mumbai's business elite.[38] By packaging ISKCON's Gauḍīya tradition as at once conservative and in sync with cosmopolitan circles, they underscore the community's place as representatives of Hindu devotionalism. At the same time, they also align with popular "self-help" discourses prevalent among Mumbai's middle and upper classes, providing spaces to discuss "the journey within" alongside temple lectures on Vaiṣṇava scriptures.

These articulations of religious tradition are shaped by complex trajectories of influence. One might recognize resonances with Protestant-inflected institutionalizations of religion in ISKCON's Counselling System and pedagogical framework.[39] Indeed, manuals such as Stephen Covey's 7 Habits for Highly Effective People have been influential in ISKCON's educational development over the past decades.[40] In a local Indian context, these globalized influences resonate with the popularity of self-help books that speak to business and leadership aspirations through religious narratives. Walk into any mainstream Indian bookstore and you will see that Hindu mythology has become a focus for self-help literature through the work of writers such as Devdutt Pattanaik. Meanwhile in the workplace, meditative practices have become integrated into corporate wellness culture.[41] ISKCON's articulations of Vaiṣṇava Hindu tradition are situated in relation to these broader currents, merging with local concerns for educational rigor as well as the prominence of globalized wellness terminology in religious settings.

But alongside the growth of globalized wellness culture, the place of Hindu religiosity in urban India has been undergoing transformations in recent years, as India experiences a growth of public religious conservatism.[42] As Meera Nanda asserts, "Globalization has been good for the gods."[43] In the liberalization and globalization of India's economy, a surge in popular religiosity among the burgeoning Hindu middle classes has impacted public institutions and shaped the character of the flow of new wealth. In addition to luxury vacations, many upwardly mobile middle classes spend their money on pilgrimages and contributions to local religious institutions. Nanda ties this rise to a "state-temple-corporate complex" that she notes is replacing the ideologically secular public institutions of the Nehruvian era—demonstrated by the fact that both the Bharatiya Janata Party (BJP) and the Congress Party have overseen a dramatic increase in state patronage for organized Hindu rituals, yoga camps, temple tourism, and land endowments to religious organizations. This meeting of Hindu religious space and state interests can of course take many forms, as Mary Hancock has discussed in relation to the development of government-sponsored heritage preservation initiatives in Tamil Nadu.[44] However, through these matrices of religious spaces and state funding, a new Hindu religiosity emerging in both the private and public spheres.

Since Narendra Modi's election as prime minister in May 2014, a push toward the "Hinduization" of India's public spheres has manifested in diverse displays, from debates over school textbook content, to the growth of anti-conversion laws, to continued attempts to convert historic sites connected to India's Muslim heritage to Hindu nomenclature and control. Academic and independent press coverage has emphasized the religious chauvinism enabled by Modi's Bharatiya Janata Party (BJP) and its ideological affiliates such as the Rashtriya Svayamsevak Sangh (RSS) and student organization Akhil Bharatiya Vidyarthi Parishad, which perpetuates notions of a *savarna* (or *savarṇa*, upper caste) Hindu as the ideal national subject and compels other groups to shape themselves in relation to that hegemonic norm.[45] With the Sangh Parivar in a privileged place of political decision-making under Modi's BJP government, the interests of India's conservative Hindus are now articulated from the center of power, promoting idealized notions of *rām rājya* as the model for India's governance and attacking those, particularly from religious minority backgrounds who are presumed to oppose it. Support for the BJP has developed in tandem with a strong drive toward developing India into a privatized, neoliberal, "business-friendly" state, grounded in economic and nationalist aspirations for India's postcolonial rise on a global stage. This pairing has arisen since India's move away from a Non-Aligned, socialist-leaning state and toward a privatized, capitalist economic model in the 1980s and early 1990s.[46] Profiles of extremist right-wing actions often do not make visible the broad middle-class base that has enabled Modi's rise and the BJP's renewed popularity in urban India, although the former often guides the way religious discourse enters and sustains currency in public discourse.

My study of ISKCON in Mumbai provides an ethnography of an Indian community that shares with many in India's Hindu middle and upper classes an interest in remaking the Indian nation-state through increased religious influence. But the dual nature of ISKCON—as representative of both traditional Hindu culture and global networks—appeals particularly to many urban professionals. Popular agendas for both India's economic growth and the inculcation of Hindu religious ideals in the political sphere happen to coincide with concerns of the ruling BJP: namely, "good governance" based on brahmanical Hindu ethics, the promotion of vegetarianism and cow protection, and the centering of Hindu character in public and governmental spaces in contrast to secularizing models.[47] Hindu nationalist agendas thus seem to echo through devotees' mission to revise Indian public spaces in their religious image, as increasingly prominent, if unlikely, purveyors of Hindu traditionalism in India's public spheres. But here, calls for the greater presence of Hindu *dharma* in Indian public life are delivered not through political protests but through evening courses in private halls and in air-conditioned temple facilities. Moreover, many would describe political alliances as secondary to their agenda of popularizing Vaiṣṇava *bhakti*, which is after all delivered via a thoroughly international, multiethnic organization with prominent branches in Ukraine and Ghana as well as India and the United States. This is not a nativist message opposed to the structures of globalism. Rather, it is thoroughly transnational and cosmopolitan in its history and practice.

## ISKCON and Religious Globalization

Just as the term "Hinduism" has conflicting genealogies and referents, leading many to describe Hindu traditions only in the plural, so too "globalization" is a term misleading in the singular.[48] Globalization is multidirectional, and the widespread diffusion of ideas, products, and cultural forms is not necessarily a homogenizing force; rather forms acquire new meanings in local reception.[49] While globalization is often uneven, economically and in the production and circulation of knowledge, Tulasi Srinivas has argued that the unequal playing field created by histories of colonialism and the structure of capitalism has led to an obscuring of myriad processes of cultural globalization. And this imbalance can be rectified by recognizing the development of cosmopolitan cultures outside of Western Europe and North America.[50] Spheres of economic, cultural, and religious globalization often intertwine in ways that upend notions of the West as "center" and Asia as "periphery," accompanying Asia-centric exchanges of religion, culture, financial capital, and media.[51] A focus on globalization as marked by capital and labor flows obscures transnational operations of religious movements that transform local communities, while a focus on nation-states obscures the centrality of cities and grassroots groups in those transregional networks.[52] My research builds on these interventions to demonstrate how the workings of transnational religious groups can illumine a fuller understanding of how globalized currents—as imports and exports—have affected the articulation of local traditions.

ISKCON in urban India reflects trends in globalization, as its networks promote transnational links between people, resources, and media that have developed in a complex itinerary between the Global North and Global South. After Bengali founder Bhaktivedanta Swami developed its institutional character in North America and Western Europe in the late 1960s, devotee communities expanded to Africa, Asia, Latin America, Eastern Europe, and former Soviet states particularly from the 1970s onward. This resulted in the growth of a remarkably diverse network of followers with shared institutional training and social norms. And yet, most scholarship on ISKCON has tended toward sociological examination of North American ISKCON communities, implicitly coding membership as a phenomenon among predominantly white middle classes.[53] ISKCON has been placed in a modern-day pantheon of NRMs, discussed in college classrooms alongside Scientology and the Branch Davidians, with some characterizing ISKCON as an American import to transnational locales and as a "fast religion" analogous to the global spread of American "fast food."[54] Even in popular culture, ISKCON continues to be affiliated with an implicitly white-coded West. In the Swetshop Boys' 2016 album *Cashmere*, hip-hop duo Riz Ahmed and Himanshu Suri underscore this racialized dynamic in their ode to "Zayn Malik": "you out of place like a brown Hare Krishna."

Coding ISKCON as American had an effect not only on how it was originally received in India, but also in Soviet Russia and 1980s Bosnia. According to one report, residents of Sarajevo sought to move away from the Soviet power structure and toward American culture by embracing ISKCON as an "American movement."[55] In such globalization, the branding and reproducibility of religion as a consumer package echoes an economy of religion at work.[56] Perceived affluence and connection to American networks of wealth have even led to the appropriation of the ISKCON name by aspiring entrepreneurs in India, prompting lawsuits about the usage of its brand name. In one case in Ahmedabad's High Court, a property development company that erected an "ISCON" shopping mall and apartment complex was taken to court for trying to capitalize on connotations of international prestige in the institution's name.

Although recent studies have noted ISKCON's growth among Indian diasporas in Western cities such as New York and London, a continued centering of devotees from the Global North obscures its multiethnic and international composition.[57] ISKCON today is a world away from its early growth in 1960s American counterculture.[58] It has moved from, in the words of Thomas J. Hopkins, "a small intimate community of disciples dependent on the inspiration and physical presence of a charismatic leader" to a transnational organization with multiple nodes of authority.[59] Recent studies have begun to highlight the organization's global presence and its multiple faces in different cultural contexts.[60] But little focus has been given to Indian devotees, although they now constitute the majority of many ISKCON congregations both in India and abroad.[61] How does the choice to join an international organization with roots in in North America affect their relation to Hindu traditions—and their view on "tradition" broadly? White Americans have played a dominant role in ISKCON's management, disproportionate to their per capita membership since ISKCON has been established as a transnational organization with centers in India and elsewhere throughout Asia, Africa, and South America since the early 1970s. But the global face of ISKCON has changed, and devotees internationally are just as likely to be Indian, Ukrainian, Ghanian, or Taiwanese. Their religious belonging speaks to a form of religious globalization that is multidirectional and marked often by transnational networks within the Global South.[62] In India particularly, ISKCON communities enjoy an unprecedented level of political and business connections to urban elite establishments and are reframing the meaning of ISKCON in their local settings.

Indian devotees are arguably the new center of ISKCON globally—both numerically and geographically. Their prominence showcases how religious traditionalism is shaped by global networks and in turn reshapes local, lived religion, displaying the full-circle globalization of a religious tradition. Drawing on Aihwa Ong's reframing of globalization to decenter our tendency to focus on the West as the center of *gravitas* for global economy, I depict ISKCON's growth as a truly transnational organization not bound by a center of *gravitas* in the West but rather operating polynodally through multiple centers of development and regional authority. In urban India today ISKCON functions as a form of Hindu traditionalism that seeks to decenter a Westernized secular modernity through developing a religious Indian modernity.[63] Their religious networks also align with global flows of business and industry in ways that center Asian capital, a central node of contemporary globalization.[64] In ISKCON Chowpatty, for instance, key donors include some of the most prominent figures in India's economy, many at the helm of Indian multinational corporations. Through organizing seminars in India and abroad to promote ideas from the Bhagavad Gītā as a template for contemporary business ethics and arranging speaking events for temple *brahmacaris* at multinational financial institutions, they yield influence in corporate cultures to promote ISKCON's teachings.[65] Additionally, major temple projects in India receive transnational donations and pilgrimage revenues from international devotees who trace their religious customs to India. Through these channels, Indian devotees partake in the interlocking nature of transnational networks of religion, culture, and finance that recast the itineraries of globalization.

## Finding Krishna in the City of Dreams

On the Arabian Sea in the Western Indian state of Maharashtra, Mumbai vies with Delhi as India's largest commercial and cultural center. It is the economic capital of India, the center of Bollywood (the Hindi cinema industry), and the political capital of Maharashtra. Although known in the Global North as a center for corporate outsourcing, Indian cities are prominent sites for multinational corporations that hold significant power internationally, including the Tata Group, Infosys, and Mahindra. But many city dwellers experience the deprivations of neoliberal development. Indian ISKCON communities navigate these paradoxes between their religious aspirations and urban realities. Rejecting the glimmer of a laissez-faire "city of dreams" image that the city of Mumbai holds for many Indians, local devotees aspire to revive an idyllic Vedic heritage *in* a modern Indian city.[66] Parallel to contemporary religious groups, ISKCON positions itself as an antidote to a vision of late modernity as cultural loss and hedonism.[67] Yet ISKCON's revivalism is also propagated in urban contexts reshaped by global networks, complicating the notion that their traditionalism is rooted in an isolated local context free from external influence.[68] In myriad ways, ISKCON's development in India has been shaped by Mumbai's varied cultures and that is reflected in the Chowpatty temple community.

Mumbai (historically Bombay) is a relatively modern city by Indian standards, developing during the past few centuries. Unlike many ancient Indian urban centers, Bombay was built predominantly by ethnic and religious minorities. In the early twentieth century, Bombay's public institutions were established by Parsi merchants, Iraqi Jewish mill owners, Goan and Mangalorean Catholics, and Gujarati Muslim businessmen. For over a century, skilled workers from across the country have moved to the metropolis for employment opportunities, and traditional boundaries between regions, castes, and religions have often become blurred. Accordingly, it is often dubbed India's pre-eminent cosmopolitan city.[69] Sunil Khilnani likens Bombay's place in postcolonial Indian imagination to be "a totem of modern India itself."[70] Often called "not a city but a state of mind,"[71] it is also a city known for relatively looser social restrictions, partly due to the presence of the Hindi film industry but also the interweaving of many religious and regional cultures—none with preeminent power. In his *City Adrift: A Short Biography of Bombay*, Naresh Fernandes notes: "Among the truths Bombay holds to be self-evident is the fact that it is cosmopolitan."[72]

The word cosmopolitan has a specific meaning in India. It denotes not only the presence of multiple languages and regional cultures but also the presence of multiple religious and caste groups and their intermingling through, for instance, intermarriage and shared residences—taboos throughout much of the country today.[73] This cosmopolitanism is reflected in local religious traditions rooted in the landscape of the city, many of which claim diverse and eclectic roots.[74] But for many residents, including those at the helm of higher education, business, or the entertainment sector, religious piety often seem outmoded or even coercive. Although home to strict and exclusivist religious communities—the Bohras, orthodox Parsis—the city is also by shaped by the continual flow of new migrants, who forge lives outside the bonds of family and community networks in their ancestral homes. As Gyan Prakash asserts: "If the idea ever needed confirmation that the modern city is a place for forming a human community based on chance encounters and fabricated ties—not prior family and kin links—you will find it in Bombay."[75]

But amid continual waves of migration and changing political norms, urban religious hybridity has jostled with socially and politically conservative Hindu communities. While Bombay has historically represented the consummate cosmopolitan city in public imagination, the ethno-religious nationalism of the city's Shiv Sena (a right-wing Marathi nationalist political party founded in 1966) has vied to replace this with a regional Hindu cultural dominance. When the Shiv Sena rose to power in the 1970s, they decried the city's supposed takeover by North and South Indian immigrants and sought to claim Bombay for a Maharashtrian Hindu populace.[76] Launching aggressive, sometimes violent campaigns, they sought to revision it as a regional Maharashtrian city, home to "sons of the soil." They succeeded in 1995 in renaming the city Mumbai, after a Marathi Hindu goddess, but as Fernandes writes:

> Under most circumstances, the erasure of a colonial identity would have been welcomed by everyone. But coming as part of the Sena's campaign of hate, the rechristening of the city as Mumbai is still remembered for what it is—a refutation of Bombay's inclusive history. Disconcertingly, the Sena had seduced a globalized city to aspire to provincialism.[77]

This perspective reflects why many locals continue to refer to their city as Bombay, pitting ideological contestations between *Bombay*'s cosmopolitan inhabitants and *Mumbai*'s champions of Maharashtrian Hindu identity. Against this background, the 1992–1993 riots in Bombay targeting Muslim and non-Maharashtrian residents are framed by many residents as a rupture, imposing a coercive ethnic and religious identity on the city that emphatically defies such parochialism.[78]

Aside from these cultural tensions, Mumbai also encompasses stark economic disparities. Almost half of the city's population (many recent rural migrants) live in informal housing, including corrugated shacks and "lean-to" structures. Yet ambitious images of luxurious gated communities fill billboards and construction-site banners throughout the city and its developing suburbs, reflecting sharply different urban experiences.[79] In a context of rapid urbanization and transregional migration, public culture is a contested terrain, existing in multiple forms through India's many regional languages and multilingual spaces, as well as abundant religious, political, and class diversity.[80] This yields multiple public spheres, heightened by new forms of media, especially with the rising influence of social media.[81] The media production of middle-class Hindu publics, for instance, is often distinct from that of middle-class Muslim publics in the same city, and newspapers in English, Marathi, Urdu, Hindi, and Gujarati circulate throughout the city's diverse neighborhoods. Language also denotes class and power, with English both a lingua franca amid India's vast linguistic diversity and a marker of middle- and upper-class educational achievement.

Although Mumbai exemplifies modern secular life in the public imagination, religion remains front and center in urban India, and the city is interwoven with temples, *dargahs*, churches, and wayside shrines. As William Elison notes, many view their neighborhoods as inhabited and demarcated by local gods and guardian spirits.[82] Glitzy high-rise condominiums in Lower Parel and posh seaside restaurants in Bandra coexist with devout mothers donating a few rupees to feed a temple cow by the side of the road in Sion or pilgrims processing along the seaside walkway to Haji Ali *dargah*. But many people now inhabit religion in new ways that reflect an urban economy of choice and individuality. Especially for younger generations whose aspirations are shaped by the technology and global business economies, leading a life centered on austere piety stands in stark contrast to goals of career advancement and experiencing fulfilling personal relationships. Aspirations for a life guided by personal attainment and romantic love are not tied to predetermined hereditary roles.

Even beyond major life ambitions, religious piety bristles against popular ways of being young in the city. What would be the likelihood of friends who meet for drinks and a late-night meal of Chicken Lollipop and Prawns Koliwada on a Friday night, perhaps at a beloved local dive bar like Janata in Pali Hill, suddenly donning saris and abstaining from meat and alcohol? Would they forsake their night out to rise at 4:00 a.m. for morning prayers? That would be as dissonant as the choice to abandon an upwardly mobile career in accounting at a competitive firm amid the gleaming high-rise office buildings of Lower Parel to move into an ashram and dedicate one's working hours to temple service. But these are choices made by those who adopt the mode of religious life promoted by ISKCON, against the tide of the surrounding city. And this very centrality of *choice* connects their decision to cross over into a religious revivalist group, with its attendant conservative worldview, to other more liberal choices one may make in a globalized urban context in which family ties and hereditary identities are already loosened. The choice to adopt a conservative traditionalist identity also implies that religious communities and identities are potentially fluid, tied to individual rather than hereditary determination—a decisively different way of conceiving Hindu traditions than through family and *jati* alone.

Since Mumbai is viewed as India's most cosmopolitan, liberal city, in the discourse of ISKCON members it is also the most challenging place to promote Hindu traditionalism. Yet, although diverging from secularist imaginaries, I situate their choice to adopt a new religious traditionalist

**Fig. 0.1** A woman walks outside the front entrance to the ISKCON Chowpatty temple as a newly built high-rise apartment building looms in the background, 2015. Photo by the author.

identity as a form of modern cosmopolitanism. As van der Veer has argued, traditionalist cosmopolitanisms are no less globally networked and modern in their development. Albeit challenging to those who view their city as inherently liberal, they represent creative agency in relation to new social environments.[83] Members of the Chowpatty ISKCON community hail from an array of Indian regional backgrounds, particularly Gujarati and South Indian, mirroring the city's diverse ethnic makeup and particularly those regional groups who have been targets of the Shiv Sena. As inheritor of a religion that is both Indian and global, developed locally with a community base that embodies histories of migration to the city, the temple's structure is encoded with the character of a modern metropolis (Figure 0.1).

Moreover, devotees in Mumbai also fuse together two segments of the city often at loggerheads: the globally oriented elite and devout middle-class Hindus. Within this divide, ISKCON Chowpatty provides a third space for its members: a religiously conservative community that is globally oriented. And this articulation of Hindu traditionalism mirrors the sensibilities of its urban adherents. ISKCON's growth has developed in tandem with the migrations of Indian technology and business specialists to Mumbai and their development of the city's global economy. This is a space marked by class privilege, providing a rarified temple experiences that many describe as an oasis from the chaotic city outside. Befitting the temple's monied South Bombay address, most religious programs are recorded for professional distribution by the temple's media department and higher education is a prerequisite to enter the *brahmacari* ashram. But alongside its posh status, temple members often noted that Chowpatty provides a space for newcomers to Mumbai to negotiate their migration away from traditional family homes and to balance their modern, urban context with the maintenance of their Hindu religious and cultural roots. Countless Chowpatty temple lectures address the tension between Mumbai's urban setting and the nostalgia to return to Hindu religious roots lost in the shuffle of a globally poised urbanism. In this regard, the concerns of Chowpatty's business and technology rich community parallel the defining features of post-1991 Indian public culture: specifically, the pairing of economic liberalization with development of strong Hindu civic identities. Accordingly, ISKCON's media products formulate a streamlined urban Vaiṣṇava identity, seeking to rival the entertainment industry and secular lifestyles in the city. This new traditionalism is defined by urban contexts reshaped by global migration, as an American-born leader like Radhanath Swami takes the role of Hindu guru in India. Mumbai's urban spaces have thus both disrupted traditional religious identities and created room for new religious configurations to claim traditions as their own. In these arenas, Chowpatty's temple community is not only *in* but quite crucially *of* the city.

## Entering the Space

This project is the result of my longstanding interest in the ways that religious communities transform as they spread across regions and cultures. As a curious teenager wandering around to temples and monasteries in the Washington DC area in the early 2000s, I came to spend time at the ISKCON temple in suburban Maryland through a circle of friends, some of whom were second-generation devotees, people raised in the community. In contrast to Martin Luther King's long resonant saying that the United States is most racially segregated on Sunday mornings, I found remarkable racial and national diversity at ISKCON gatherings. I also saw people make serious changes in their lives based on adoption of a religious tradition that was Indian in origin but mediated by teachers who had grown up in Chicago, Lagos, or Durban. Although I originally planned to focus my graduate studies on early modern religious networks in North India, I became increasingly interested in how the inheritors of those early modern traditions are practicing religion in urban India today.[84] There is perhaps no more vivid, albeit provocative, example of this than ISKCON. That compelled me to focus on the organization I already knew well in a new light, particularly to explore its "full-circle globalization" and development in India.

In my ethnographic research for this book, I took a multi-sited approach to express how religion is practiced between private and public spaces, as well as through transnational networks of family and religious community.[85] Though centered on the Radha Gopinath temple complex in Girgaon Chowpatty, South Bombay (Figure 0.2), my research extends to the homes and public spaces frequented by devotees. This focused but flexible approach reflects the elastic nature of the temple community itself. The community is, on the one hand, centered at the temple. Devotees commute from all over Mumbai and beyond to attend festivals and programs there, while a core team of roughly one hundred *brahmacari*s and a small group of families live on site and tend to daily maintenance and administration. But both renunciant and congregational members have developed communities outside of Mumbai, referred to sometimes as "satellite centers." These extend Chowpatty's community networks and ethos to other regions of Maharashtra. The most established of these are the ISKCON temple in Pune, developed largely by congregants affiliated with Chowpatty and Radhanath Swami's mentorship in its early years, and the Govardhan Ecovillage in Wada, in a rural part of Maharashtra's Thane district. Also included are the

**Fig. 0.2** Evening visitors take *darshan* of Radha Gopinath and the presiding temple deities, 2015. Photo by the author.

ISKCON temples in Aurangabad, Nashik, and Nigdi, and the community's Bhaktivedanta Hospital in North Mumbai, which is a popular place for employment. Neighboring ISKCON temples in Juhu and Navi Mumbai also connect devotees across Mumbai's metropolitan area, and many regularly travel back and forth between them. On a smaller scale, there are communities of followers throughout Mumbai's ever-expanding metropolitan area who identify the Chowpatty temple as their center of religious authority, attending large festivals whenever possible, but whose daily religious lives are centered on neighborhood-based Counselling groups, a prominent feature of Chowpatty's congregational structure.

My multi-sited ethnographic approach participates in a movement toward locating the practice of religion not only in the official spaces of temples and ritual performances but equally—in some cases most vitally—amid ordinary life, in homes, city streets, and informal gatherings. Herein, the stories devotees tell about their own religious formation and the interactions that occur outside of central rituals—what Elizabeth Pérez has called micropractices—convey the character of religious traditions as they are handed down and also modified, as living bodies of tradition rather than fossils.[86] Such an approach also highlights the trajectory of religious traditions, revealing how they are given form by the histories of migration embedded in their members' lives and their creation of new communities. I approached my ethnographic research as a study in vernacular religion, or religion as lived in the everyday and taking shape in a particular locality, rather than frozen in a classical or orthodox form.[87] I find this particularly important for the study of conservative communities that style themselves as orthodox, to impart that vernacular or lived religion does not exist in opposition to discursive constructions of orthodoxy. Rather all religious traditions are negotiated in daily life, by practitioners both at the center and the margins of a given community.[88] My approach to conducting ethnography is also informed by Tweed's assertion that all theories are itineraries, embodied travels that represent sightings, underscoring that a living religious community will change throughout time and depending on one's vantage point.[89] In this, I consider my analysis to be not definitive in relation to a diverse and evolving urban Indian temple but rather to illuminate the texture of lived religion at a confluence between local lives and transnational communities, as these strands of the local and global co-constitute how religious traditions are seen and practiced in Mumbai.

During my initial months of research, I lived in one of Chowpatty's guest houses on the temple grounds, alongside other guests from abroad and in proximity to the few resident women of the community. During several return trips, I lived in apartments in the residential neighborhoods of Santa Cruz and Bandra, both a train ride away, which afforded the valuable perspective of viewing ISKCON in relation to the broader city outside. Over the course of a collective twelve months of research between 2012 and 2015, I amassed over eighty interviews and developed relationships with a range of devotees and their families, many of whom generously welcomed me into their homes and shared their time and experiences with me.[90] I also accompanied temple groups on pilgrimage to regions of North and South India, including an annual pilgrimage to Vrindavan in Uttar Pradesh, and a tour of Vaiṣṇava temples in Kerala and Eastern Tamil Nadu. My flexible, multi-sited approach enabled me to encompass these varied experiences.

My primary research languages have been English and Hindi, but I have also drawn on Sanskrit and Bengali in textual analysis of the tradition's scriptures. My ethnographic data draws from regular attendance of daily religious programs while a resident at the temple and, later, visits to several ISKCON temples, public venues, and private homes throughout the metropolitan area. My analysis also engages with a range of ISKCON's media productions and events—including public festivals, live dramatic performances, and literature produced by the temple. Since a major feature of ISKCON's media presence is online, I also incorporate information from online forums, including temple websites, affiliated devotee websites, and social-media pages. Chowpatty's online media presence spans YouTube, Facebook, Instagram, ISKCON Desire Tree (a temple audio and video archive), and a host of websites maintained by temple-based offices for media and communications. In addition to public-facing online media, e-counselling services and devotee chat forums are password protected and linked to membership credentials, providing private spaces for community discussions. I was able to follow these conversations to some extent but have chosen not to include information in this study that is not either publicly available or published with all participants' consent. I have also changed most individuals' names and obscured identifying details to protect their privacy. For individuals with prominent public profiles, I have retained their names for coherency when referring to media productions or public statements.

In successive chapters, I weave my ethnographic work alongside historical analysis of ISKCON's development, internationally and in India, and analysis of media products produced by and relating to Indian ISKCON communities. To understand where ISKCON Chowpatty fits into the contemporary Hindu religious landscape of Mumbai, this study will begin by examining the processes that led to the formation of a transnational, multiethnic Gauḍīya Vaiṣṇava tradition in the first place. This includes the formative shifts in late colonial India that provided the impetus for a global Gauḍīya missionary imperative. This history is integral to understand the process through which what was once deemed an "American" Hinduism became localized in Mumbai over a few brief decades. Chapter 1, "New Religious Movement, Old Religious Movement: Historicizing a Transnational Organization," leads the reader through a historical summary of the Gauḍīya Vaiṣṇava traditions from which ISKCON derives, contextualizing the development of this transnational religious organization with a focus on the local and transregional networks at each major step in its formation. Beginning in sixteenth-century Bengal, I follow Gauḍīya Vaiṣṇavism's transregional development in early modern India and institutionalizations of Gauḍīya traditions in the context of colonial Bengal. I discuss the growth of a Gauḍīya global missionary imperative during the colonial period as a precursor to A. C. Bhaktivedanta Swami's establishment of ISKCON, its transnational spread, and its subsequent re-importation to India as a highly systematized form of Gauḍīya Vaiṣṇavism, an example of a globalized religious traditionalism.

Chapter 2, "Global and Local Networks in a Neighborhood Temple: ISKCON Chowpatty, Mumbai," introduces the ISKCON community based in South Bombay neighborhood of Girgaon Chowpatty, where I conducted my primary ethnographic research. It lays out the history and formation of the community, its authority structure centering on the American-born Radhanath Swami, and the temple's urban context. This chapter also analyzes the ways Chowpatty's Indian devotees have localized ISKCON's transnational systems through the development of their Counselling System, a structure for community organization and devotee care. The transnational history of their religious organization and its contemporary global networks distinguish Mumbai's devotees from their Indian neighbors. However, they also exemplify trends in urban Hindu communities toward a disinvestment in traditional kinship networks and realignment along transregional networks and interurban migration patterns, which signal broad changes in the production and reception of religious knowledge in urban India.

Now that ISKCON has "arrived" in India, completing a full circle in the organization's global spread and a place within Mumbai's Hindu public spheres, what kind of Hindu traditions do they convey to local audiences, and what can this tell us about transformations of religious identity in urban India? The remaining chapters analyze how ISKCON's institutional structures seek to revise Indian devotees' notions of family, religion, nation, and culture.

Chapter 3, "Crossing Over: Entering the Devotional Family," focuses on members' narratives of joining ISKCON, which revises their relationships to regional and family-based forms of the Hindu and Jain traditions in which most devotees were raised. Building on Tweed's theory of religion, I depict their processes of joining ISKCON as acts of crossing over to a new identity distinct from regional and religious backgrounds, sometimes heightened by devotees' recent geographic migration to Mumbai. Chowpatty's ISKCON community provides a systematic, institutionalized framework for members to be fitted into new religious lifeways, adopting a brahmanically inflected Krishna *bhakti* that also creates novel approaches to dwelling in the city. This framework shifts prior social and familial bonds with newly forged religious networks—including Chowpatty's Counselling System, the *brahmacari* ashram, and the Marriage Board—that offer models of religious kinship in their place.

Chapter 4, "Ancient Answers to Modern Questions: Revising Religion," explores the curated educational processes that guide Indian devotees through the shifts in doctrine and ritual praxis they must make to adopt this modern, institutionalized form of Hinduism. This chapter examines the forms of religious education at the helm of ISKCON's engagement with potential new members among Mumbai's publics, particularly the Chowpatty temple's repertoire of courses and exams. I argue that recommitment to a religious heritage through ISKCON refigures that heritage as something gained through a discrete process of education and training, rather than family customs, that parallels contemporary Indian coaching culture. This process aims to replace the uncertainties of modern urban life with the conviction of representing a lineage that can "answer all one's questions" through imparting the "science of God" and the "systematic Gita." Therein, ISKCON's religious messages reflect an indigenization into local idioms of Hindu religiosity, including aspirations for religious organizations to display a rational basis in educational rigor and to channel economic success.

Chapter 5, "Enacting a Religious Nation: Bhakti and Its Boundaries," analyzes how membership in ISKCON Mumbai's religious community relates to broader political orientations and ideas about the Indian nation. With reference to Chowpatty's pilgrimages, public festivals, and dramatic performances, I trace a pan-Indic Vaiṣṇava *bhakti* imaginary that maps a Vaiṣṇava religious heritage onto the modern Indian nation. Therein, I assess both who is included in this national imaginary and who is performatively excluded, often through representations of Indian history. Such processes of mapping and drawing boundaries render ISKCON's *bhakti* imaginary distinctly political, in conversation with contemporary discussions about the role of Hindu identity in the Indian nation state, echoing desires among India's devout Hindu middle classes to ground the nation in a dharmic idiom.

Chapter 6, "Transforming the Local: A New Traditionalism in the City," focuses on how Mumbai's devotees navigate their adopted religious lifestyle alongside other desires and personal commitments, grappling with what it means to fit their religiosity into the cultural landscape of a modern city. Tensions center on notions of ISKCON's ideal culture as expressed in Bhaktivedanta's foundational writings and through their embodied transnational community. Resident guru Radhanath Swami is viewed as a representative of Indian culture, devaluing his Western roots to embody Hindu traditionalism. Meanwhile, many Indian aspirants find it difficult to embody ISKCON's dictates on culture, as many spaces within the city and activities among friend and family groups are deemed too influenced by Western modernity and not conducive to devotional life. I follow everyday conflicts, from debates about vegetarianism and wearing saris to negotiating non-binary gender identities amid temple norms. ISKCON's elastic understanding of culture enables instances of remarkable social mobility, through deterritorializing notions of "Indian culture" and "the West," but also produces tensions over how to live as a devotee in a contemporary Indian city.

My conclusion considers ISKCON in India today as a form of religious modernity, grounded in revising religion through refiguring devotees' relation to family, religion, nation, and culture. This transformation of ISKCON as a globalized religious organization demonstrates that local, lived religion in urban India today is intertwined with transnational networks even alongside rhetorics of traditionalism. And ISKCON's global development and growth in India alert us to four characteristics of this style of urban Hindu revivalism: (1) a realignment of Hindu religious identity from shared regional and linguistic-specific traditions to personal choice, separating religious practice from one's family background; (2) the development of a discourse that mediates Hindu traditions through a systematic, organizational model grounded in idioms of training and education, casting these traditions as discrete and reproducible systems to be learnt in modern educational venues; (3) a reconfiguration of Hindu authority structures, detaching the category of guru from a hereditary model to encompass individuals from a range of caste and ethnic categories as mediators of middle class Hindu identity, including the indigenization of non-Indian practitioners into the highest levels of authority; and (4) the assertion that Hindu traditions provide a critique and alternative to Westernizing cultural globalization that should be packaged and exported globally. In this religious modernity, inflections of globalization and transnationalism are utilized to dismantle the Westernization that has generally undergirded them.

In reframing categories that are at the core of how Hindu traditions are understood and practiced, ISKCON's Indian members are reconfiguring how urban Indian aspirations relate to global networks, promoting a return to local tradition that is mediated through a transnational organization. Through a return to tradition, as an aspiration for devout religiosity within India's urban spaces, they also affect a radical break with tradition, as family and hereditary practices. And here, a distinctly urban form of Indian religious belonging bears the marks of both a globalized religious economy and postcolonial desires to revive a religious past in the modern city.

# 1

# New Religious Movement, Old Religious Movement

## Historicizing a Transnational Organization

The past, like other cultural constructions, changes as we attend to it.
—A. K. Ramanujan[1]

When one enters the ISKCON temple grounds in Chowpatty today, murals grace the inside courtyard that depict the early development of the Gauḍīya tradition in sixteenth-century Bengal, and a small museum space occupies the left side of the courtyard, containing dioramas and placards detailing Bhaktivedanta's twentieth-century odyssey to America and the early days of the Hare Krishna movement there. Ascending the sandstone steps to the temple room, visitors pass by a long hallway with depictions of each guru in the lineage that links ISKCON to Gauḍīya teachers of the past. Contemporary globalization processes underlie ISKCON's style of urban religion in India, but these are not the starting point for the movement of people and ideas that formed its traditions. ISKCON traces its roots to a Bengali Vaiṣṇava tradition centered on the saint Caitanya (1486–1534), known as Gauḍīya Vaiṣṇavism, which came to develop into one of the region's most prominent Hindu traditions, popular throughout what is now West Bengal, neighboring Eastern Indian states, and much of Bangladesh.

The codification of that tradition in ISKCON owes as much to its founder, Bhaktivedanta, and his interpretation of religious trends from his upbringing in early twentieth-century colonial Calcutta and the social context of his development of the organization in the countercultural world of 1960s America. But its rituals and doctrines are grounded in Gauḍīya roots, articulated through an emphasis on membership in an unbroken lineage of religious authorities and orthodox integrity. Due to ISKCON's positioning as an

*Bringing Krishna Back to India*. Claire C. Robison, Oxford University Press. © Oxford University Press 2024.
DOI: 10.1093/9780197656488.003.0002

inheritor of premodern Hindu traditions, urban Indians who join the organization understand themselves to be partaking in this heritage from India's precolonial past. To provide a foundation for examining how ISKCON taps into the new appeal of the old, in this chapter I will trace the formation of the Gauḍīya Vaiṣṇava traditions from which ISKCON draws it roots and the transnational missions that developed among nineteenth- and twentieth-century Gauḍīyas, which laid the groundwork for ISKCON's transnational Hindu traditionalism.

## Early Gauḍīya Vaiṣṇavism

Krishna's identity is linked to the Braj region of Uttar Pradesh in North India, but since the early centuries of the Common Era he was celebrated throughout many parts of the subcontinent. Cast in many roles, he appears as wise teacher, beloved deity, and trickster cowherd in Hindu texts ranging from the pan-Indic Mahābhārata epic, the Harivaṃśa and the Vaiṣṇava Puranas, and the vernacular poetic compositions of Āṇṭāḷ as far south as Tamil Nadu from the ninth century onward.[2] Traditions of Krishna worship had been present in Bengal since at least the twelfth century, when Jayadeva wrote his *Gītāgovinda* at the court of Lakṣmaṇa Sena.[3] The late medieval Bengali poets Caṇḍidāsa and Vidyāpati continued the tradition of Krishna *bhakti* in their compositions. Thus, Krishna was revered as a central devotional figure in many parts of India by the sixteenth century—a deity who was both depicted as reveling in breaking norms and revered by the brahmanical elite.

In the late fifteenth and early sixteenth centuries, the Bengali scholar and mystic Caitanya inspired the development of a new tradition of Krishna devotion that drew on medieval Vaiṣṇava precedents to develop distinctive theological and ritual traditions.[4] His followers—many of them educated brahmins affiliated with local courts—embarked on prolific writing projects and infrastructural developments, and secured extensive courtly patronage to build and subsidize a network of Krishna temples throughout North India. Through their knowledge of Sanskrit and familiarity with popular courtly genres of literature, they developed a prolific body of work that promoted a devotional Vaiṣṇavism through *rasa* theory and poetics, dramas (*nāṭaka*), and hagiographical texts connecting Krishna as the supreme divinity to the saint Caitanya. The latter came to be enshrined in Gauḍīya orthodoxy as a divine descent (*avatāra*) who introduced new heights of devotion to Krishna through a fusion with the female figure of the *gopī* Rādhā as both exemplary devotee and feminine aspect of the divine. In the late sixteenth and early seventeenth centuries, a growing community circulated this corpus of literature in both Sanskrit and vernacular languages, particularly Bengali. These early Gauḍīya texts also laid out a distinct set of ritual and meditative practices that served to demarcate the community from other contemporaneous Vaiṣṇava traditions.[5]

This Gauḍīya orthodoxy was outlined through the works of Rūpa Gosvāmin, Jīva Gosvāmin, the other "Gosvāmins of Vṛndāvana," and their followers. Numerous hagiographic records derive from these early generations, such as Kṛṣṇadāsa Kavirāja's late sixteenth-century Bengali hagiography of Caitanya, the *Caitanya Caritāmṛta*.[6] These works provided what Joseph O'Connell termed a "soft institutional structure," which existed in relation to a range of interpretations of theology and practice, from brahmanical purists and temple families to tantric *sahajiyās* and Bauls, whose identity straddles Bengali Vaiṣṇava, Muslim, and even Buddhist heritage. Sanskritic scriptural literacy was not a hallmark of all Gauḍīya communities, many of whom were rural, non-elite agriculturalists. Nonetheless, a foundational text-based identity allowed for reproduction across regional boundaries, facilitating transregional followings beyond the reaches of Bengal into Odisha, Manipur, Assam, and Tripura, Hindi-speaking regions of North India and eventually, through the patronage of prominent Rajput rulers, in Rajasthan and across North India.[7]

Early Gauḍīya hagiographies center on charismatic men, while women are venerated as family members and, occasionally, as religious teachers. Despite the historical presence of female and mixed-gender guru-disciple lineages, orthodox Gauḍīya communities have often institutionalized models of succession through male lineages, in temple posts and guru-disciple relationships.[8] Early Gauḍīyas both articulated their religion in the language of orthodoxy but also traversed some caste and class lines. Conflicts with local brahmanical communities are memorialized in early hagiographies around the issue of challenges to caste-determined religious hierarchies. Nevertheless, discrete acts of rebellion from brahmanical norms recorded in early hagiographic literature sit alongside an overall brahmanically inflected Sanskritic orientation, which is underscored in the strict lifestyle prohibitions laid out in extensive praxis manuals. In the style of brahmanical temple custodianship, lineages of Gauḍīya gurus and *pujārins* (temple priests) have historically been centered on family lineages, as in the Radha Raman temple of Vrindavan. Moreover, Gauḍīya texts largely adopt the framework of the *varṇāśrama-dharma* system, the brahmanical Hindu division of society into four *varṇas*, or social classes (*brāhmaṇas*, *kṣatriyas*, *vaiśyas*, and *śūdras*[9]) and four *āśramas*, or stages of life (*brahmacārin*, *gṛhastha*, *vānaprastha*, and *saṃnyāsin*[10]) that derives from the religio-legal texts known as the Dharma Śāstras, compiled in the early centuries of the Common Era.[11] In this regard, David Lorenzen's categorization of the Gauḍīya Vaiṣṇava tradition as *varṇadharmī*, or accepting the normative brahmanical social structures and injunctions of *varṇāśrama-dharma*, is widely applicable.[12] Yet it does not consider the array of interpretations expressed by Gauḍīya groups in different historical periods, particularly in Gauḍīya scriptural commentary and hagiographies such as the *Caitanya Caritāmṛta* and the *Caitanya Bhāgavata*, wherein social categories are often inverted to present the highest models of spiritual attainment as irrespective—or in explicit opposition to—elite gender and caste identities.[13]

The Gauḍīya tradition encompasses a vast literary and philosophical corpus. This literature includes Sanskrit *śāstras*, scriptures, which form its theological backbone. The Bhagavad Gītā and Bhāgavata Purāṇa, prominent texts for many Vaiṣṇava traditions, are ascribed central orthodox status, supplemented by a vast and ongoing commentarial literature. The Gauḍīya theological system developed by Rūpa Gosvāmin and Jīva Gosvāmin established a hierarchical assessment of different notions of divinity that placed Krishna at the pinnacle.[14] ISKCON's assertions of Krishna's preeminent place, at the top of a religious taxonomy that encompasses other Hindu and non-Hindu notions of religious truth, partakes in this philosophical lineage and serves as a demarcating line from other Hindu groups in the present day. Additionally, the Gauḍīya canon includes hagiographic literature about Caitanya and his early followers, Sanskrit works on scholasticism and *kāvya*, and hybrid texts such as Rūpa Gosvāmin's *Bhaktirasāmṛtasindhu*, Jīva Gosvāmin's six-volume *Bhāgavata Sandarbha*, and Gopāla Bhaṭṭa's *Haribhaktivilāsa*, which lay out Gauḍīya theology and *sādhana*, personal ritual regimens understood as devotional practices through providing a template for the development of *bhakti* along with lists of injunctions and prohibitions.[15] In practice, this textual orthopraxy existed alongside a robust range of Gauḍīya practice in North and Eastern India, which incorporated Sufi, *tantra*, and local non-elite religious traditions on a grassroots level.[16]

In Indian religious traditions broadly, literature has been tied to oral and performative contexts. As Philip Lutgendorf explains in his *Life of a Text*, a devotional text in North India is experienced through temple-based recitations and staged performative renderings of its narratives. In Bengali Vaiṣṇava communities, texts have been mediated in both Sanskrit and widely spoken vernacular languages through similar performative traditions.[17] Multidimensional engagement with religious stories has included dramatic performances, from the *rāsa-līlā*s of Vrindavan to the *kathakaḷi* performances of Kerala.[18] In the Gauḍīya tradition, dramatic performances have often centered on the *līlā*s, divine activities, of Krishna.[19] Religious dramas in a vernacular idiom (*jātrā*s) also attained widespread popularity in Bengal, affecting modern genres of India performance arts. As we shall see, these various styles of religious performance arts have contemporary analogues in ISKCON's Indian communities in a revisioned form.

These traditions developed through networks of Bengali speakers in the historic Gauda region, which sits today near the West Bengal-Bangladeshi border. Caitanya was Bengali speaking, as were the tradition's first theologians and most Caitanya's early hagiographers within the century after his passing, including Vṛndāvana Dāsa and Locana Dāsa. According to accounts of the tradition's development, early followers were directed on missionizing trips throughout and beyond Bengali-speaking regions.[20] As Gauḍīya devotionalism expanded, later hagiographies were composed in Sanskrit and Odia, and both brahmanically oriented literature and vernacular literature available to multiple classes and castes were produced. Outside of Bengal and Odisha, the region of Braj—including the pilgrimage city of Vrindavan—became a principal locus of Krishna worship for Gauḍīya Vaiṣṇavas in the sixteenth century. Gauḍīyas claimed a central place in Vrindavan's religious topography alongside contemporaneous Krishna *bhakti* groups, most notably the Puṣṭimārga or Vallabha *sampradāya*. Influential Gauḍīya theologians who relocated from Bengal to the broader region of Braj lived, wrote, and established centers of worship there while also maintaining links with communities in Bengal and Odisha through pilgrimages and travel. Ascetic traditions still found among the *bābājī*s at Radha Kunda and throughout Braj were developed in this period.

Early Gauḍīya writers shaped the distinctive identity of the tradition in Sanskrit, as their language of communication for developing *bhakti śāstra*s, commentaries, and supplemental works, and they engaged with elite genres of literature that were prevalent in courtly settings of the time.[21] This Sanskritic religious culture endowed Gauḍīya literature with a brahmanical prestige, as seen in the *Bhaktirasāmṛtasindhu* of Rūpa Gosvāmin, which engages with *kāvya* traditions and with aesthetic traditions stemming from Bharata's *Nāṭya Śāstra* and Bhoja's *Śṛṅgāra-Prakāśa.*[22] Gauḍīya elites also drew on ritual and devotional traditions from South India, Odisha, and Braj to formulate their articulation of Vaiṣṇava *bhakti.*[23] The notable early Gauḍīya Gopāla Bhaṭṭa Gosvāmin hailed from a brahmanical Śrīvaiṣṇava family in Śrīraṅgam in the Tamil-speaking regions of South India. He brought a Śrīvaiṣṇava influence to the development of *mūrti pūjā*, worship of the ritual images of Krishna and his *avatāra*s, that early Gauḍīyas standardized in accordance with Pāñcarātra Āgamas.[24] The community further expanded through courtly patronage networks, and through Rajput patronage Jaipur developed as an important center for Gauḍīya activity in the seventeenth century.[25] The signature architectural style of Gauḍīya temples in Vrindavan synthesized styles of both Rajput and Mughal patrons with Bengali architectural influences.[26] This regional heterogeneity blended a multilingual textual corpus, including scriptures, dramas, poetry, prayers, and songs, into the liturgical life of the tradition.

The Gauḍīyas developed a missionizing focus from their first generation, seeking to bring new members into the fold through the production and circulation of literature and *sādhana* practices.[27] The *Caitanya Bhāgavata*'s prophecy that the "name of Caitanya" will spread to "every town and village" evolved in Narahari Cakravartin's circa seventeenth-century *Bhaktiratnākara* to an imperative to spread Caitanya's devotionalism, and devotional missionizing is enshrined in the heroic narratives of the early Gauḍīya leader Narottama Dāsa and others in Bengal.[28] Caitanya himself promoted his religious teachings in Braj, Varanasi, and Gaya, as well as throughout Andhra Pradesh and Tamil Nadu, and he later settled in Odisha for the last twenty-four years of his life. As networks of early devotees secured patronage to establish Gauḍīya temples throughout North India, a transregional Gauḍīya tradition was born.

As Stewart has discussed, early Gauḍīyas' regional and transregional identities were also solidified through pilgrimage, *yātrā*. The *Caitanya Caritāmṛta* describes annual *yātrā*s made by Bengali Gauḍīyas to Odisha to see Caitanya and participate in the Rath Yatra (*ratha yātrā*) festival of Jagannātha.[29] Pilgrimages to Vrindavan were inaugurated, with pilgrimage routes mapped and established by Nārāyaṇa Bhaṭṭa, a Gauḍīya who arrived in Braj in 1545 from Madurai. Bhaṭṭa also composed the *Sāmānya Praghaṭṭaka*, a Sanskrit manual devoted to general rules and rites of pilgrimage.[30] Throughout the sixteenth and seventeenth centuries, with the establishment of transregional networks of Gauḍīya communities between Bengal, Odisha, and Braj, pilgrimage would take place in several directions, as described in Narahari Cakravartin's *Bhaktiratnākara*.[31] In the mid-seventeenth century, Gauḍīya elders such as Jāhnavā Devī also strengthened ties between the growing communities in Bengal and Braj through annual pilgrimage and festival events.[32] Although this provided opportunities for transregional exchange, Gauḍīya communities overall existed in local spheres, distinguished by regional guru lineages and ritual practices.

These early precedents for transregional religious networks, however, were repurposed by Gauḍīya gurus in the twentieth century, who highlighted traditions of text-based and mission-oriented Vaiṣṇavism in their own endeavors over against European Christian missionary efforts in India. Today, the transregional religious networks recorded in Caitanya's hagiographies take on new resonances for Indian devotees, many of whose families trace their religious orientations to Vaiṣṇava traditions from Gujarat, Rajasthan, or Karnataka. These resources aid contemporary devotees in Mumbai in celebrating a range—albeit selective—of their families' religious traditions alongside their adoption of ISKCON's institutional identity, framing their new religious identity as a revival of a lost heritage in both broad and deeply personal terms.

## New Orthodoxies and a Global Mission

Previous studies have documented that Gauḍīya Vaiṣṇava communities prior to the late nineteenth century were largely decentralized.[33] Until this time, as Fuller notes in relation to Bengal, Gauḍīya *akhāṛās* (monastic schools) and itinerant *vairāgins* (renunciants) existed throughout mostly rural regions with no central organizational body.[34] The demographic composition of Gauḍīyas in nineteenth-century Bengal ranged from peasants in the countryside, sharing a social status similar to neighboring Muslim peasants, to a middle-class population in towns and cities, including Calcutta.[35] Rough census records indicate that by the late nineteenth century up to one-third of the Bengali Hindu population were affiliated with the Gauḍīya tradition, but it is likely that religious identities were rarely exclusive. While some socially prominent businessmen in Calcutta identified as Gauḍīya, census data suggests that Gauḍīya communities flourished primarily in rural areas and among lower castes.[36]

Following the incorporation of Bengal, Odisha, and Bihar into the East India Company's control in 1772, Bengal became the first region of India to experience British rule and a central site for both colonial culture and indigenous reactions to it.[37] British political and cultural influences forged new links between India and the rest of the world, displacing old visions of transregionalism with new notions of a transnational economy and an intellectual dialogue directed toward Europe. Educated in the British system and familiar with both European and Indian cultural preferences, the Bengali elite—known as the *bhadralok*—experimented with new religious and cultural identities that could render their religious traditions on equal footing in conversation with European ideas. In the process, they foraged older forms of community for frameworks of transregional and, later, national coalescence. Creating organizations that competed to speak both to and for Hindu traditions, groups like the Brahmo Samāj began to develop their ideas in global scope through the growth of print media and the increased transnational flow of people, ideas, and goods that characterized the colonial era. Concomitantly, after the East India Company Act 1813, European Christian missionary organizations in Indian cities purveyed their brand of institutionalized religion, providing a new model of religious organization to Hindu communities that were previously organized more loosely around family and neighborhood traditions and whose members practiced at home as much as in public spaces.

In the developing civil society among English-educated elites, characterized by registered societies and institutions that engaged with growing print publics, a formalization of religious communities occurred alongside categories developed in the colonial production of knowledge. In conversation with the developing notion of "world religions" under Max Müller, print media reflected a notion that religious communities represented a homogeneous heritage that had been passed down seamlessly through the ages and was rooted in unifying cultural histories.[38] The coalescence of manifold local traditions into the broader world religions category of "Hinduism" grounded religious discourse in the manner of *Religionwissenschaft*, in which discrete religious systems were analyzed in the language of developing social science disciplines.[39] Poised behind intellectual trends in the "science of religion" or comparative religion, as it later developed, was a notion popularized by Müller of a "natural religion" common to all humankind, publicized in writings and lectures alongside his concept of a Vedic Golden Age in order to encourage Vedic studies and to inspire a "reinvigoration" of (Hindu) India.[40]

The writings of modern Gauḍīyas reflect this intellectual context, alongside the trend throughout the late nineteenth and early twentieth centuries of viewing religions in a qualitative taxonomy. Therein specific religions, grounded in historical, delimited forms, were contrasted with a theorized "universal religion" that exists purely beyond the limitations of the former. The tensions surrounding who represents "Hinduism" and how it relates to "universal religion" reflected the strategies of Christian missionaries in late colonial Bengal who often missionized under the guise of comparative religion.[41] However, for late colonial Hindu intellectuals—including Vivekananda, Dayananda Sarasvati, and Paramahamsa Yogananda—this articulation of religious comparison provided, by contrast, a means to advance one's own doctrinal positions over others, to "talk back" to the often patronizing scholarship and suppositions held about Hindu traditions in the Anglophone academy.

In this context, religious intellectuals such as Dayananda Sarasvati framed Vedic Hindu religion as *sanātana dharma*, the "eternal" or "timeless" *dharma*, conceived to be superior to world religions—a trend that continues to undergird contemporary Hindu doctrinal formulations. This vision has gained ground in post-Independence India, even as grounds for claiming a legal status separate from religious institutions.[42] Gauḍīya publications adopted the appellation *sanātana dharma* and began to reframe formative their theological taxonomies to describe their tradition as above and beyond categories like "Hindu" or "Muslim."[43] Certainly, the themes of an underlying religion superior to sectarian traditions, and the articulation of a universalist religious truth, also weave through early modern North Indian *bhakti* history, as in the poetry of Kabir and Guru Nanak. In colonial Bengal, however, as Gauḍīyas began articulating their tradition as a universalist heritage that transcended sectarian religious categories, they also retained a sectarian lineage, designating their tradition as a Vaiṣṇava *sampradāya*.

The rethinking of Gauḍīya traditions in the modern era would have a substantive effect on how Gauḍīya communities themselves were conceptualized. By the 1870s, as shown by Varuni Bhatia, various members of the Bengali *bhadralok* began to reconfigure the image of Gauḍīya Vaiṣṇavism and its related material culture.[44] Bhaktivinoda Ṭhākura, a Bengali civil service officer, became one of several prominent Gauḍīya writers in *bhadralok* circles of the time.[45] While proselytizing activities were not a prominent characteristic of the nineteenth-century Gauḍīyas, North Indian elites had experimented with developing institutionalized forms of Vaiṣṇavism, and some *bhadralok* Gauḍīyas adopted the new model of voluntary civil society associations and a concomitant use of print media in parallel to organizations like the Ārya Samāj. In affiliation with Sishir Kumar Ghosh and others, Bhaktivinoda circulated his thoughts on Gauḍīya theology and history through his *Sajjanatoṣaṇī* journal, published between 1884 and 1904.[46] *Sajjanatoṣaṇī* issues documented Bhaktivinoda's *nāma-haṭṭa* programs, missionizing initiatives in rural Bengal and Odisha focused on creating and expanding a standardized, institutionally centralized Gauḍīya community.

In place of decentralized authority structures, Bhaktivinoda proposed the reproducible group structure of *nāma-haṭṭa*, drawn from his experience living and legislating among rural communities in the course of his civil service. *Nāma-haṭṭa* groups, he suggested, could be governed by *pañcāyat* systems that delegated each member a specific role and set of responsibilities, repurposing a model of community governance to link coreligionists in loosely connected local hierarchies. Alongside from this local restructuring, Bhaktivinoda organized the Viśva Vaiṣṇava Rāja Sabhā, "World Vaiṣṇava Association," in Calcutta in 1885, which sought to unite Vaiṣṇavas across India through theological commonalities, developing a model for urban bourgeois intrareligious connectivity.[47]

As I have argued elsewhere, Bhaktivinoda's *nāma-haṭṭa* program set the stage for the later institutionalized structures of ISKCON through its foregrounding of the Gauḍīya missionary imperative and emphasis on reproducing a romanticized notion of rural Gauḍīya communities.[48] In this development of a new Gauḍīya orthodoxy, Bhaktivinoda rejected many established Gauḍīya hierarchies, such as the hereditary *gosvāmins*, and he engaged in polemic efforts against what he saw as heretical Vaiṣṇava groups. While most scholarship on modern Gauḍīya traditions focuses on the institutionalized successors to Bhaktivinoda's reforms—specifically the Gauḍīya Mission and ISKCON—many Gauḍīya communities were written out of the orthodox tradition at this time, including Bauls and *sahajiyās*.[49] Bhaktivinoda's son and religious successor, Bhaktisiddhanta, would later classify these traditions as "*apa-sampradāyas*," or those "outside of" or "inferior to" the Gauḍīya *sampradāya*, in tandem with imagining a new orthoprax community.[50] Bhaktisiddhanta particularly sought to minimize the *tantra*-influenced Gauḍīya traditions in his *maṭhas*, condemning practitioners of the sexually oriented *rāgānugā sādhana* practices and foregrounding the ascetic-oriented practices of *vaidhī-bhakti* in a form acceptable to both *bhadralok* and Victorian British sensibilities. Bhaktivinoda's written systematization of an orthodox Gauḍīya community thus provided a template for missionizing followers seeking to replicate this notion of ideal Gauḍīya community.[51] Inherent in this systemization, perhaps in response to colonial critiques, was the notion that Vaiṣṇavism exemplifies a rational theological system that is also systematically reproducible.

These new lines of orthopraxy constituted a disjunction from previous modes of community identity among many Gauḍīya populations of Bengal, whose religious identity was often fluid in relation to the region's other prominent religious traditions, including *tantra*, Śaktism, and Sufism. Yet, in the course of his civil service postings, Bhaktivinoda was also deeply impacted by the Bengali rural landscape, which served as an inspiration for his romanticist urban intellectual revisioning of the Gauḍīya tradition. Bhaktivinoda's approach was, in fact, not the first Gauḍīya romanticization of the pastoral context of Krishna worship. This was also foundational for the elite sixteenth-century *gosvāmin*s, who traveled from courtly Bengal to rural Vrindavan and formulated what A. Whitney Sanford vividly describes as a "defanged notion of the forest and villages of Braj," centered on worship of Krishna and a subsumption of rituals oriented toward local goddesses and forest spirits (*yakṣas*).[52] In Bhaktivinoda's case, this elite gaze was directed toward celebrating "simple" *bhakti* practices, including *bhajan* and *kīrtan*, of Bengali Vaiṣṇava villagers, in line with the rural romanticism of many intellectuals in the late nineteenth and early twentieth centuries. As Bhatia discusses, *bhadralok* Gauḍīyas forged links between the countryside and the urban center of Calcutta by emphasizing the centrality of villages to Bengali cultural life, coupling a reverence for rural religious practices with a modern civil society organizational framework.[53] This pairing of missionary aspirations and emergent cultural nationalism lay the groundwork for modern institutionalized Gauḍīya Vaiṣṇavism.

During the same years that Bhaktivinoda was conceptualizing a reorganization of Bengal's Gauḍīya communities and speculating about the possibility of its global reach, Swami Vivekananda was becoming a spokesperson for Hindu traditions abroad. Through founding the Ramakrishna Mission in 1897—conspicuously named in resonance with the Christian missions to Bengal—Vivekananda made lengthy visits to England and America throughout the 1890s to teach and popularize Vedānta, one philosophical strand of Hindu traditions.[54] This idea of articulating Hindu philosophy on a global stage led Bhaktivinoda to make similar attempts and to inspire his son, Bhaktisiddhanta Sarasvati, to establish a global mission. After his father's death, Bhaktisiddhanta took the helm of the Viśva Vaiṣṇava Rāja Sabhā, which became known as the Gauḍīya Mission in the 1920s, and opened monastic centers known as the Gauḍīya Maṭh.[55] These innovations centered Gauḍīya identity not in shared community heritage but strictly delineated orthodox and orthoprax markers, including the standardization of guru-disciple structures through the governing oversight of an institutional Mission, and the introduction of standardized practices and vows undertaken upon formal entry, or "initiation," into the *saṅgha*. Additionally, a profound step in the new global aspirations of the Bhaktivinoda-Bhaktisiddhanta lineage was the decision to missionize to Europeans and accept non-Indian Gauḍīyas into the tradition—a move inextricable from the European colonial presence in Bengal and, indeed, a fittingly symmetrical rejoinder to it.[56] This transnational turn in defining the Gauḍīya community increasingly marketed Gauḍīya Vaiṣṇavism as a discrete system that could be adopted by anyone anywhere.

Bhaktisiddhanta outlined his institution's official aims in a 1920 *Sajjanatoṣaṇī* article, presenting a charter in the style of contemporary colonial-era civil-society organizations but linking these explicitly to institutions in the Gauḍīya past.[57] Resonant with the job descriptions and institutional structure of the *nāma-haṭṭa* as described in Bhaktivinoda's *Godruma Kalpāṭavī*, this charter created the bureaucratic basis for modern institutionalized Gauḍīya organizations by dividing religious authority structures into management teams and committees (*maṇḍalī*), including a Śrī Krishna Caitanya missionary (*pracāra*) committee; an investigative committee, "responsible for evaluating the character of a candidate before assigning a service in the movement"; a polemicist committee, "responsible for the rational defence of *bhakti* against opposing arguments"; and a devotional practice committee, "responsible for the maintenance of ancient sacred places, the building of new temples."[58] This list conveys the corporatized structure of the revisioned Gauḍīya tradition, in which membership is formed and monitored by a managerial body, and personal religious practice, observance of community rituals, and a missionizing agenda are deeply intertwined. It sketches the outlines—from a mission-centered identity to a focus on "arguing" *bhakti* against opposing ideologies—of what would become distinctly modern institutional Gauḍīya concerns.

Bhaktisiddhanta worked to broaden a transregional Gauḍīya presence through the opening of *maṭhas*—consisting of temples (*mandirs*) and ashrams (*āśramas*), facilities for resident *brahmacaris* (*brahmacārins*) who maintained the temple space and allocated its resources. By the time of his death in 1937, he and his followers had established sixty-four *maṭhas* throughout India and smaller centers in Burma, Germany, and England. He connected these centers through circulated publications of Gauḍīya Maṭh-sanctioned newspapers and journals, as well as the creation and distribution of commentaries on classical and early modern texts in the increasingly regulated Gauḍīya canon.[59] Although deeply concerned with delimiting orthodox practice in this new institutionalization of the Gauḍīya community, Bhaktisiddhanta also popularized an idea of *yukta vairāgya*, "skillful means" or "engaged renunciation."[60] This enabled the use of modern machinery—including cars and printing presses—even by those who like Bhaktisiddhanta had taken vows of renunciation. This was controversial among many of his renunciant Vaiṣṇava peers, who saw the use of technology as a dangerous compromise with respect to the emphasis on asceticism in the ethos of the *saṃnyāsa āśrama*.

Bhaktisiddhanta's decision to reformulate caste hierarchies drew even more controversy. Unlike other members of the *bhadralok* or nationalist leaders like B. R. Ambedkar, Bhaktisiddhanta did not advocate for an abolishment of caste. Remarkably, the assertion of Vaiṣṇava universalism did not prevent either Bhaktivinoda or his Gauḍīya successors from asserting the continued importance of *varṇāśrama-dharma*. Rather, as Bhaktivinoda advocated for the universal recognition of the principles of *bhakti*, Bhaktisiddhanta argued for a potential global application of *varṇa* and *āśrama*.[61] This approach was consonant with that of Dayananda Sarasvati and later Mohandas K. Gandhi in their own respective refiguring of Enlightenment-era universalist categories within the context of Hindu traditionalism. Gandhi termed *varṇa* (commonly, *varna*) as a "universal law" for ordering society, a "unique contribution from Hinduism to the world," and depicted the ideal *varṇāśrama* as "in its origin . . . a wholesome custom that promoted national well-being" distinct from the present-day "corrupt" or "distorted" caste system.[62] Bhaktisiddhanta likewise reframed *varna* in an individualist framework based on personal character and occupational inclination rather than on birth-based designations.

Such views were particularly contentious among the Vaiṣṇava brahmins to whom Bhaktisiddhanta proposed them in his iconic 1911 speech,

"Brāhmaṇa o Vaiṣṇava."[63] But on this basis of reframing caste categories, Bhaktisiddhanta introduced a Vaiṣṇava *saṃnyāsa* initiation ritual, drawing on established patterns of the Daśanāmī *saṃnyāsa* lineage to establish an institutionalized Vaiṣṇava renunciation lineage. He also formulated for his followers a *brāhmaṇa* (brahmin) initiation, designed to be bestowed on anyone, regardless of caste or gender, based on one's allegiance to live in accordance with brahmanical lifestyle ideals, as laid out in Vaiṣṇava literature, and to practice Gauḍīya *sādhana*.[64] This opened the door to a democratized capacity to read and write official commentaries on Gauḍīya texts, eroding a brahmanical male monopoly—a change the writer Rashsundari Debi heralded in her own life a century earlier.[65] In a milieu of challenges to the caste system, then, modern institutionalized Gauḍīya Vaiṣṇavism navigated a course of both universalism and traditionalism, encoding new comparatively egalitarian norms into the fabric of a brahmanically inflected lifestyle. ISKCON practices, following Bhaktivedanta, would further expand this in a global context.

The Gauḍīya mission outside of India dramatically developed through the efforts of A. C. Bhaktivedanta Swami, the founder of ISKCON. Bhaktivedanta was born as Abhay Charan De into a devout Vaiṣṇava *subarna banik* merchant community in Calcutta. In 1920, he refrained from claiming his bachelor's degree at Calcutta's Scottish Church College to join the Gandhian movement.[66] However, later that year he met Bhaktisiddhanta at the Gauḍīya Maṭh in Calcutta. Bhaktisiddhanta dismissed the nationalist cause as a distraction from what he taught as the goal of life, pursuing Krishna *bhakti*. To follow his teachings, Bhaktivedanta distanced himself politically from Gandhianism, although his later writings remained aligned with Gandhian views of Indian civilization and critiques of Western modernity. He married, had children, and worked for a pharmaceutical company for several decades while gradually developing a missionizing campaign.

From its inception, global Gauḍīya missionizing both adopted the language ("preachers," "mission," "sermons") of Western Christian missionary networks but was intent on shifting the balance between center and periphery in the networks of globalization developed by the British colonial government. Echoing Gandhi's own inversions of colonial pretensions to dispense the most advanced civilization, Gauḍīya missionizing centered the colony, India, as the source of civilizing missions and a new form of religious globalization to the metropole and adjacent cultural regions. By the 1930s, prominent disciples of Bhaktisiddhanta, headed by Swami Bhakti

Hrdaya Bon Maharaja, undertook mission trips to England and Germany. Bhaktisiddhanta especially promoted efforts to spread the Gauḍīya mission in English, the language of the colonial administration and the colonial metropolis. Bhaktivedanta eventually sought to fulfil Bhaktisiddhanta's directives through the establishment of an active English-medium periodical entitled *Back to Godhead* in 1944 and, later, translations of the Bhāgavata Purāṇa and other Vaiṣṇava texts. For Bhaktivedanta, this agenda centered on missionizing to an English-educated Indian elite as much as to those beyond India's shores. In this sense, Bhaktivedanta also sought to shift modern cultural dynamics within India itself, addressing in English what he saw as the troubling adoption of Western lifestyle choices over Indian traditions. In his elderly years, after retiring from his pharmaceutical business and adopting a lifestyle of a *saṃnyāsin—sannyasi* in contemporary usage—in 1959, Bhaktivedanta devoted his time to training a core of dedicated disciplines and creating an organization (at first, the League of Devotees in Jhansi) to propagate Gauḍīya teachings.[67] After finding a lack of traction in India, however, expanded his mission to the United States, leaving the port of Bombay just a few days before his sixty-ninth birthday.[68] The institution that Bhaktivedanta developed there, in New York, was registered separately from the Gauḍīya Maṭh and named ISKCON, an acronym for the International Society of Krishna Consciousness.

ISKCON, formed in New York in the countercultural setting of 1966, became the first large-scale Gauḍīya missionary success.[69] Developed largely through an American and European convert base, Bhaktivedanta's ISKCON stressed fidelity to its Bengali roots but also formed distinct structures, rituals, and idioms as it expanded on American terrain. Bhaktivedanta's choice of the United States as his missionizing destination, rather than the colonizing power, England, may reflect the growing status of the United States as the preeminent English-language world power in its post–World War II ascension.[70] Like Bhaktisiddhanta upon founding his Gauḍīya Mission, Bhaktivedanta accompanied the registration of his society in July 1966 in New York with a formal set of agendas, known in shorthand as the "Seven Purposes of ISKCON." These include the following aims:

> to systematically propagate spiritual knowledge to society at large and to educate all peoples in the techniques of spiritual life . . . To propagate a consciousness of Krishna as it is revealed in the *Bhagavad-gītā* and *Śrīmad Bhāgavatam* [Bhāgavata Purāṇa] . . . To erect for the members, and for

> society at large, a holy place of transcendental pastimes, dedicated to the personality of Krishna . . . [and] with a view to achieving the aforementioned purposes, to publish and distribute periodicals, magazines, books and other writings.[71]

This formalization of a Gauḍīya community as a "registered society" and the bestowal of official aims for its membership conveys a merging of the templates for civil-society groups in colonial Calcutta with the religious content of Bengali Vaiṣṇavism. In this bureaucratized form, ISKCON shifted the transnational discourse developed by Bhaktivinoda and Bhaktivedanta into radical realization. In North America and later Europe, Bhaktivedanta developed communities of followers who adopted the rituals and precepts he taught, melding selective ideas about brahmanical culture and Hindu religiosity into residential communities populated largely by middle-class youth.[72] Dressing styles included an insistence that women wear saris and men wear *kurtas* and *dhotis*, seen as traditional attire befitting religious services. Alongside attire, cuisine, gender norms, and daily rituals were also standardized among international ISKCON communities to the extent that daily services in an ISKCON temple in Tokyo may be virtually identical those in Los Angeles or Mumbai. Charles Brooks, who researched the still largely American-run ISKCON temple in Vrindavan in the 1980s, deemed this emulation of idealized brahmanical characteristics a form of Sanskritization, as per M. N. Srinivas's famous formulation.[73] Indeed, this Sanskritization blends ISKCON's unique mixture of Indian transnationalism and multiethnic membership; a gateway not only for non-brahmanical Indians but also those of non-Indian ancestry to adopt the language and lifestyle of brahmanical Vaiṣṇavism as markers of authenticating religiosity.

In formulating this institutionalized Gauḍīya community, Bhaktivedanta tailored regulations from Bhaktisiddhanta's Gauḍīya Mission for his American followers. For instance, Gauḍīya practitioners measure their chanting of the Hare Krishna mantra, a central aspect of Gauḍīya *sādhana*, on a *mālā* (a strand of prayer beads, generally 108 in number). Bhaktivedanta reduced Bhaktisiddhanta's instituted *sādhana* requirement from sixty-four rounds of *japa* daily to sixteen, to accommodate American work schedules. But he adopted Bhaktisiddhanta's institutionalized two-tiered practice of *harināma* initiation and *dīkṣā* (or *gāyatrī*) initiation for his primarily Western disciple base.[74] He also standardized a set of disciplinary precepts or regulatory practices, referred to in ISKCON as the "four regulative principles": vegetarianism and abstinence from intoxicating substances, gambling, and extramarital sex.[75] These practices are still undertaken as vows at the time of ISKCON initiations. Though today there is an increased allowance for different levels of commitment within the broader ISKCON *saṅgha*, insider identity is clearly demarcated through these lifestyle markers, and formal membership through the maintenance of the *sādhana* and the regulative principles is seen to connect contemporary practitioners to Gauḍīya forbearers and co-religionists globally. These forms of discipline find parallels in other modern Vaiṣṇava-oriented Hindu communities,[76] but they also underscore a correlation between a broadening socio-ethnic base and increased institutionalized boundaries around Gauḍīya identity from Bhaktisiddhanta to Bhaktivedanta.

As Bhaktivedanta became the central figurehead for ISKCON, his ideas about what constituted essential practices and correct ideas came to occupy unparalleled centrality for ISKCON followers. A longer lineage of guru succession is reproduced in visual form in ISKCON literature and on temple altars worldwide, resonant with broader devotional Hindu visual culture,[77] but Bhaktivedanta also inhabits a singular place theologically and visually in ISKCON temples. A standardized, life-sized statue of him sits at the back of each temple, facing the direction of the altar. It is bathed and clothed in saffron *sannyasi* garments, as well as offered food and *āratī* daily, reflecting a similar reverence shown to *mūrtis* on the altar. And, although ISKCON shares with the Vallabha and Swaminarayan traditions of Gujarat an assertion that the ultimate deity is Krishna, ISKCON's explicit subordination of other popular Hindu deities to the status of "demigods" further demarcates their philosophical identity from the general Hindu fold. Bhaktivedanta often emphasized his identity in a lineage he called the "Brahma-Madhva *sampradāya*," connecting to one of the four Vaiṣṇava *sampradāya*s, or "sanctioned lineages," while also accusing other popular gurus of lacking a specific *paramparā* or *sampradāya*.[78] In this sense, Goswami describes him as a renewer rather than a founder of a religion.[79] Accordingly, Bhaktivedanta's ISKCON explicitly diverged from many transnational guru movements through its emphasis on maintaining brahmanical cultural forms, a Gauḍīya scriptural orthodoxy, and strict ritual and lifestyle practices.[80]

The religious life of ISKCON temples centers on the worship of *mūrtis* (sacralized images) of Krishna and his divine companions through *pūjā*, *kīrtan*, and elaborately choreographed offerings traced to the *śilpa śāstras*.[81] ISKCON centers observe a systematized array of Gauḍīya temple-based rituals. Through the celebration of Vaiṣṇava festivals and elaborate morning services that engage members in a systematized form of Rūpa Gosvāmin's five central practices of *vaidhī-bhakti*, ISKCON's centers seek to develop an insulated environment where devotional communities are formed in sharp distinction from the purportedly materialistic life outside. In tandem with this orthopraxy, Bhaktivedanta foregrounded an ethic of *bhakti* as "devotional service," which entailed developing an attitude of *sevā* (service) toward others. While *sevā* is a popular aspect of many modern Hindu groups, Bhaktivedanta was keen to distinguish his notion of *sevā* as service within a theistic Vaiṣṇava worldview, preserving generational and gender-based hierarchical distinctions in promoting a traditionalist idea of Indian culture.

Despite this traditionalist Hindu orientation, ISKCON became a symbol of American 1960s counterculture, often associated with drug use, free love, and hippie aesthetics.[82] Bhaktivedanta capitalized on the growing Western interest in Indian religions, and his initial missionizing efforts were received by young American and British countercultural audiences. In turn, the early ISKCON community received the support of counterculture giants including George Harrison and Allen Ginsberg. Harrison would become a lifelong practitioner of Gauḍīya *sādhana*, extending the path charted by the Beatles for public and celebrity interest in Indian gurus.[83] In his missionizing, Bhaktivedanta foregrounded an intersection among Krishna *bhakti* practices, music, and consciousness-altering experiences. After opening his first ISKCON center at 26 Second Avenue in New York, he inaugurated ISKCON's second center in January 1967 at a storefront in Haight-Ashbury. New followers organized events like the "Krishna Consciousness Comes West Mantra-Rock Dance" at the Avalon Ballroom in San Francisco, which drew an all-star line-up featuring the Grateful Dead, Moby Grape, and Big Brother and the Holding Company, with Allen Ginsberg introducing Bhaktivedanta.[84] Yet, as Rochford has noted, early ISKCON devotees aligned themselves with their countercultural American audiences through the messaging that chanting Hare Krishna provided a natural high and alternative to drugs.[85]

For practitioners, ISKCON could not have been further apart from the laissez faire hippie cultural era with its concern for rigidly mandated orthopraxy. Bhaktivedanta further demarcated his organization—and conveyed its roots in late colonial Bengal—through establishing a parliamentary-style management structure for the organization. In 1970, Bhaktivedanta instituted the Governing Body Commission (GBC), a committee of ten (explicitly male) members, to ensure the cooperative functioning of the organization and to serve as the institution's guardians of orthodoxy in perpetuity.[86] Upon Bhaktivedanta's passing in 1977, the GBC led the institution based on a legal identity Bhaktivedanta outlined for them in writing, including the supervision of the group of originally eleven male "initiating gurus" (that number has skyrocketed to ninety-seven as of 2023) who act as Bhaktivedanta's successors. GBC cabinets were initially dominated by those who had taken vows of renunciation but now also include *gṛhastha*, or lay, members. The guru system has evolved significantly since then, but the GBC remains the gatekeeper in delimiting lines of orthodoxy and orthopraxy in ISKCON internationally, issuing declarations in the "ISKCON Laws" made available to followers online and throughout temple communities.[87]

This level of institutionalization provides a corporatized layer to the ISKCON community, yet one also aimed at ensuring the stability meant to supersede a single charismatic figure. Through this parliamentary-style organizational "governance," practices of ISKCON communities transnationally are regulated, though norms do diverge slightly in accord with local leadership and cultural contexts. This translates today, for example, into often greater opportunities for public leadership for women in ISKCON's North American and Western European communities than in many Indian and Eastern European communities, based on the surrounding cultural precedents and how interpretations of Gauḍīya tradition have been instituted on a local scale. However, regional cultural differences are not monolithic. As of 2023, for instance, the international organization remains in a several-decade impasse over whether women should be allowed to initiate disciples. While broad support was given by ISKCON representatives from countries in the Global North and resistance expressed from a coalition of leaders in ISKCON's India Bureau, some of the most vehement opposing leaders are senior white Western-origin *sannyasi*s, while prominent GBC support has also been voiced by several Indian gurus.[88] This multiethnic diversity of opinions on how to develop the organization can be lost in homogenizing discourses of Indian and Western culture, yet those can still guide internal discussions.

## In the West but Not of the West

In 2016 ISKCON celebrated the fiftieth anniversary of Bhaktivedanta's registration of ISKCON in the United States. A memorial issue of the institution's *Back to Godhead* periodical reflected on Bhaktivedanta's first American disciples as the post-war generation and the first generation to grow up watching TV.[89] Bhaktivedanta's main audience in the first years of ISKCON—young, mostly white, middle-class Americans—asserted their break from mainstream American society with a rhetorical rejection of capitalism and post-industrialized modernity, characteristic of 1960s counterculture. As one American follower wrote in the introduction to a collected volume of Bhaktivedanta's works:

> For one acquainted with the spiritual wisdom of India, the ideal life is not a fast-paced competitive run through a self-serve consumer paradise. There is a higher measure of success and happiness than the number of high-gloss gadgets, baubles, and thrills one can zoom through the check-out counter with—before Time runs out.[90]

This comment is emblematic of a sense in many early devotees that a return to a pre-industrialized lifestyle carried the promise of greater existential contentment.[91] This reflected a broader contemporary movement toward Indian spirituality and away from perceived American materialism and capitalist greed, dichotomies also prevalent in the membership of other contemporary transnational Hindu organizations[92]—and resonant, compellingly, with the early twentieth-century idealisms of Gandhi and Bhaktivinoda.

As Anna King notes, ISKCON defines itself in essentialist terms, in terms of not only what it is, but what it is not.[93] Bhaktivedanta combined his bold undertaking of the Gauḍīya mission to "the West" with a disdain for the culture he viewed to be prevalent there. He conceptualized his mission as an attempt to liberate fallen Western souls, striking a parallel to the mixture of religious zeal and cultural superiority that European missionaries brought to India several centuries earlier. Aboard the Jāladūta steamship that carried him from Bombay to New York on his first trip to America in 1965, Bhaktivedanta wrote a series of poems describing the arduous voyage. At nearly seventy years old when he boarded, he suffered cardiac issues throughout the journey, which underscored his religious motivation for undertaking a mission in his elder years.[94] As he appealed to Krishna to guide him, several of his verses depict those whom he expected to meet and his notion of what America must be like, which formed the basis of his mission to the fallen:

> Most of the population here is covered by the material modes of ignorance and passion. Absorbed in material life, they think themselves very happy

> and satisfied, and therefore they have no taste for the transcendental message of Vāsudeva [Krishna]. I do not know how they will be able to understand it. . . . I wish that You may deliver them. Therefore, if You so desire their deliverance, then only will they be able to understand Your message.[95]

As the Philadelphia-based ISKCON guru and intellectual William H. Deadwyler (Ravindra Svarupa) notes, Bhaktivedanta referred to America as an *ugra sthān* ("terrible land") and did not hesitate to call his mission a "cultural conquest" of what he termed a degraded "cat and dog society."[96] This negative essentialization of Western culture is further encoded into ISKCON's ritual practice in its most basic form: the *praṇāma* mantra that Bhaktivedanta composed to highlight his mission. Recited in Sanskrit by all participating ISKCON members during their daily prayers and at the outset of ritual undertakings, this mantra's standardized English translation in ISKCON prayer books reads: "I offer my respectful obeisances unto His Divine Grace A. C. Bhaktivedanta Swami Prabhupāda . . . You are kindly preaching the message of Lord Caitanyadeva and delivering the Western countries, which are filled with impersonalism and voidism."[97] The focal point on Bhaktivedanta's mission as "*paścātya-deśa-tārine*," or "one who delivers the West," employs philosophical terminology from the Vedāntin tradition, "*nirviśeṣa-śūnyavādi*," to equate the proposed Western "worldview" with followers of Śaṃkara's Advaita Vedānta and Indian Buddhists, early ideological opponents of the Gauḍīyas.

Many late colonial Indian intellectuals seized on the juxtaposition that Vivekananda popularized between the material wealth of the West and the spiritual wealth of the East. Drawing on colonial-era imperialist and Orientalist constructions of East and West as separate civilizational zones, Gandhi reproduced this in *Hind Swaraj* ("Indian Self-Rule"), in which he critiqued the colonial premise—that the British were bringing a superior civilization to India—by promoting an idealized, uniform Indian civilization in juxtaposition to a decadent Western civilization. He writes: "The tendency of the Indian civilization is to elevate the moral being, that of the Western civilization is to propagate immorality . . . It behooves every lover of India to cling to the old Indian civilization even as a child clings to the mother's breast."[98] Coming out of this milieu, Bhaktivedanta's declaration that his writings were "meant for bringing about a revolution in the impious life of a misdirected civilization" appears in the preface to each published volume of his English-language commentaries to the Bhāgavata Purāṇa. On the opening night to his first major festival program in Bombay in 1971, he titled his lecture "Modern Civilization Is a Failure, and the Only Hope Is Krishna Consciousness."[99]

Paradoxically, Bhaktivedanta's intellectual formation within the Western-style educational system of Calcutta's Scottish Church College was inextricability tied to global flows of knowledge in the production of "East" and "West." Even in his denunciation of Western modernity, Bhaktivedanta often paraphrased a Gandhian maxim, itself drawn from a Wordsworth sonnet, that advocated for "simple living and high thinking" to characterize his own mission.[100] Yet in conversations with his followers, Bhaktivedanta frequently denounced Western societies, critiquing everything from feminism to American social-welfare departments and modern transportation systems, to modern forms of government, both capitalism and communism.[101] Bhaktivedanta instead promoted a return to an agrarian economy and self-sufficient rural communities, drawing on colonial-era tropes of the idyllic Indian village that have become a widespread imaginary in India's urban middle classes.[102] Communities started by Bhaktivedanta's followers in West Virginia (New Vrindaban), Pennsylvania (Gita Nagari), and Watford, England (Bhaktivedanta Manor), modeled the importance of self-sufficiency, organic farming, and cow protection—agendas now promoted by Indian ISKCON agricultural centers. However, Bhaktivedanta adopted the symbolic terms of modernity, particularly grounding his descriptions of the Gauḍīya tradition in terms of "science," "rationality," and "progress," such as referring to Krsna *bhakti* as the "science of the soul." Therein, couching the Gauḍīya tradition in the language of science, ISKCON publications by Bhaktivedanta and his followers set up a dichotomy between Western science and Vedic science—a discourse that has become central to Indian ISKCON communities today.[103]

The missionary orientation promoted by Bhaktisiddhanta and Bhaktivedanta brought print media into the center of their institutionalized Gauḍīya communities. In Bhaktisiddhanta's extensive utilization of colonial Calcutta's growing print media culture, he deemed the printing press *bhāgavat yantra*, "God's machine," for its ability to spread the Gauḍīya message of *bhakti* to unprecedentedly large audiences.[104] Bhaktivedanta in turn grounded ISKCON in a strong print-based orientation through his focus on translations and commentaries on Gauḍīya texts, enshrining the publication and distribution of Gauḍīya literature as his seventh and overarching "purpose" when registering ISKCON as a society. The direction of this print-media flow was to disseminate Vaiṣṇava ideas about religion and history throughout diverse non-Indian populations, as well as English-speaking Indians. Throughout the 1960s and 1970s, he translated Sanskrit and Bengali Vaiṣṇava texts into English, which were in turn later translated by followers into myriad European, African, and Asian languages. To print his publications, he founded the Bhaktivedanta Book Trust (BBT) in Los Angeles in 1972. Many early ISKCON temples were funded by selling his books—a mission-based approach to spreading religious knowledge that will be all too familiar to anyone who encountered ISKCON devotees at American airports throughout the 1970s and 1980s. Devotees are encouraged to participate in the distribution of Bhaktivedanta's publications, referred to in shorthand as "book distribution," or *shastra daan* in Hindi. The primary books to be distributed are Bhaktivedanta's translations of the Bhagavad Gītā and the Bhāgavata Purāṇa, as well as his commentaries on aspects of Gauḍīya Vaiṣṇava philosophy.

This literary focus, coupled with the daily philosophical lectures that Bhaktivedanta normalized in temple settings, the educational courses he instituted in his centers,[105] and the regulative powers of the GBC that he established, ensured that ISKCON developed as an organization centered on a *siddhānta*, philosophical system, alongside its ritual repertoire and culture of social relations. Bhaktivedanta encouraged his early American followers to enhance the experiential dimension to their religious practice by performing dramas based on Gauḍīya scriptural narratives. While these casual productions are not conversant with *nāṭya śāstra* conventions, they echo the multisensory orientation and concern for aesthetics encoded in early Gauḍīya literature and Indian *bhakti* literature broadly.

The transnational development of ISKCON began with temple communities in New York, San Francisco, and Boston, and expanded next to Montreal, London, and Amsterdam. From these early temples, Western devotees developed ISKCON missions to Eastern Europe and the Soviet Union, sub-Saharan Africa, Australia, East Asia, South America, and the Middle East. Today, some of the largest ISKCON communities are in Russia, Ukraine, and South Africa.[106] But particularly after A. C. Bhaktivedanta Swami had established bustling centers in North America and Europe, he strove to take his accomplishments back to Indian soil, both to prove to his co-religionists that "making Westerners into Vaiṣṇavas" was possible—and to connect his followers to the land from which their new religion came. From 1970 onward, Bhaktivedanta shifted his transnational focus to developing centers in India, specifically designating three sites for future temple complexes: the Gauḍīya pilgrimage centers of Mayapur in Bengal and Vrindavan in Uttar Pradesh and the cultural and business hub of Bombay in Maharashtra. Under his guidance, American and European ISKCON devotees moved to India and assumed the roles of ritual specialists, religious teachers, and temple managers. Bhaktivedanta also introduced his Western followers to the temples of Braj and Gauḍīya festivals held there during the autumnal lunar month of Kartik (*kārttika*) and the midsummer Guru Purnima.[107] By the mid-1980s, ISKCON had become an integral part of the cultural scene of Vrindavan.[108] In subsequent decades, ISKCON transitioned from a renunciation-based movement with a largely European-American convert-based population to congregational communities with increasing populations of Indian origin.

## Taking a Hit: The Liability of Transnationalism

Before increased Indian demographic majorities within ISKCON, the international nature of the organization raised questions about authenticity among Indian Hindu communities: can a globalized religious group represent a Hindu tradition, when those traditions are often tied to ethnicity, caste, and family heritage? Is ISKCON an indigenous Indian tradition or a "foreigner's Hinduism"? Can an American guru be a genuine religious leader? When Bhaktivedanta first returned to India with his Western disciples, he described them as a spectacle—his "dancing white elephants"—to persuade Indians about the need to hold onto their religious heritage and not to abandon it in pursuit of Western modernity.[109] While those dancing white elephants did create a stir in Mumbai and elsewhere, the notion of American Hindus garnered both attention and ridicule. Accordingly, ISKCON's transnational profile has worked as both cachet as well as liability in India.[110] ISKCON's early development through transnational, multiethnic actors impact this reception, and Indian ISKCON members, ironically, are often tasked with offering responses. Thus, in contrast to more ethnically homogenous Hindu communities, ISKCON does not need to prove that it is global to its urban Indian audiences. Rather, it has been stigmatized for being *too* global.

When the first American ISKCON followers attempted to start a temple in the leafy northern seaside suburb of Juhu in 1970s Mumbai, they were met with public controversy. Spurred on by the popular 1971 Dev Anand film

*Hare Rama Hare Krishna*, negative stereotypes of the movement viewed it as a dangerous, drugged-out perversion of Hindu spirituality, conflating it with hippie subcultures that were hyper-visible in India and Nepal at the time. This cast a long shadow on ISKCON's reputation, as the Westerners draped in saris at ISKCON temples seemed interchangeable with those wandering high on the streets, often clueless about the cultural norms surrounding them. This tongue-in-cheek representation persists today in public-culture nostalgia. At trendy mall stores in Mumbai or Ahmedabad, one can pick up a retro poster or drink coasters depicting the film's upright male hero as he looks on in concerned horror at his wayward Indian sister, drugged out in bliss among her Western hippie friends. Local Indian devotees mentioned the long-term negative effects of this film—especially its headlining song, "Dum Maro Dum" ("take a hit"), which beckons the listener to join the Hare Krishnas and a general mélange of Western hippies in Kathmandu in chanting *bhajans* and smoking marijuana. Five decades after its release, the film still registered as a popular impression, even among a group of secular twenty-somethings I met on a plane on their way to Goa to celebrate a destination wedding. Upon hearing about my research, they immediately turned to the film and were able to collectively sing the full chorus of "Dum Maro Dum" accompanied to knowing laughter. ISKCON in India did indeed take a hit from these early public culture representations, just not in the manner supposed.

The introduction of an Americanized Hinduism was also suspect in Cold War–era India, which, though Non-Aligned, leaned left. Suspicions against ISKCON and its members cropped up in Bombay's newspaper articles throughout the 1970s, 1980s, and 1990s, some purporting to expose ISKCON leaders as undercover CIA agents or merely to ask if this was all a "hippie stunt or an elaborate leg pull?"[111] Others, following later abuse controversies in ISKCON's *gurukula* boarding schools in Vrindavan, merely pointed out that: "Of late, the International Society of Krishna Consciousness, ISKCON, has been in the public consciousness for all the wrong reasons."[112] Suspicions aired at the time reflected a concern from many Bombayites over Western political and cultural expansionism in the postcolonial period, as well as weariness over the growth of high-powered Hindu guru movements in public life. These two separate concerns have both affected ISKCON's local reception in the city.

In October 1970, the first substantial group of American ISKCON followers arrived to join Bhaktivedanta in Bombay to attend the Sādhu Samāj, a gathering of *sādhus* from across India, on Bombay's Chowpatty beach. They performed *kīrtan* at public *pandal* (marquee-based) festivals and gave public lectures in English and Hindi. A *Times of India* article on October 10, 1970, reported: "A group of Americans, including women with babes in arms, belonging to the International Society for Krishna Consciousness (ISKCON) has been moving around Bombay during the past few days chanting Hare Krishna." The reporter mused:

> Can the materialistic West, or at any rate, a microscopic part of it, have turned at last to embrace the spiritualism of the East? I met several of the Kirtan-chanting Americans. . . . and was at once struck by their sincerity and utter surrender to the cult they have adopted. The Vaishnavas of Mathura could not be so guileless, I thought, as this band of Bhakti enthusiasts.[113]

Narendra D. Desai, who was to become one of Chowpatty's primary donors and trustees, met Bhaktivedanta on this trip when the group visited his family home. His father, Dharmsinh Desai, a politician (later elected to the Lok Sabha, Indian Parliament) and successful businessman, was also a devout Gujarati Vaiṣṇava and would invite visiting Vaiṣṇava *sādhus* for religious home programs, but this was unusual. As we sat in the temple's restaurant awaiting a lunch of woodfired pizza, Desai described in vivid terms his initial reaction:

> I was sort of aloof, I didn't want anything to do with these guys. So, I was shocked when they came to our house. In the garden, people were sitting there—some were dancing, some were playing music. And I said: "What will the neighbors think? And what are these guys doing?" Prabhupāda [Bhaktivedanta] was totally in ecstasy, singing and playing the harmonium. . . I used to stay behind and stand in a corner. My father appreciated Prabhupāda and serving the Vaiṣṇavas and everything, but I thought it was all bogus.

Nonetheless, Bhaktivedanta received support from elite and influential Mumbaikars like Dharmsinh Desai—and a great amount of curiosity from Bombay's Hindu public.

Bhaktivedanta and his band of American devotees organized public events at Bombay's Cross Maidan field in early 1971. In preparation, followers placed posters throughout the city and a billboard at the Victoria train station, the site of the most foot traffic on a typical workday. According to the estimates given by newspapers at the time, several thousand people attended the festival programs each day, taking in the religious lectures (*pravacanas*) of Bhaktivedanta and the chanting and dancing by his white American followers.[114] This program series also attracted a young American spiritual seeker who had been traveling through India and studying with *sādhus* throughout North India. Richard Slavin, who would later be initiated by Bhaktivedanta as Radhanath Swami and come to lead the Chowpatty ISKCON community, met Bhaktivedanta and the ISKCON followers for the first time at these festivals at Cross Maidan.

Bhaktivedanta was keen that ISKCON's presence in Bombay reflect the international character of his mission. Following the Cross Maidan festival, he composed a letter to a group of his Indian followers, outlining his intent to:

> [establish] in this most auspicious city, a unique International Krishna Conscious Training Centre, where hundreds of persons from abroad may be educated in the Vedic way of life, while at the same time Indian boys and girls may be trained up for *pracāra* (preaching) work in foreign countries.[115]

A small temple space was established in a rented flat in the Cumbala Hill neighborhood, and public *pūjās* began to *mūrtis* fashioned for that space.[116] In that same year, Bhaktivedanta registered the Indian chapter of the International Society for Krishna Consciousness in Bombay under the Societies Registration Act of 1860 and as a Trust under the Bombay Public Trusts Act of 1950. He incorporated ISKCON Bombay as the main branch of ISKCON in India, making all other Indian ISKCON centers its legal branches—an arrangement carried out to this day, though not without contestation.[117] This centrality of Bombay to ISKCON's incorporation in India thus cast it as the center for ISKCON's urban development.

The well-attended 1971 Cross Maidan festivals initiated a series of newsprint debates. Several *Times of India* articles detailed the religious practices and lifestyle changes of these young American Vaiṣṇavas and were met by letters to the editor debating how to categorize white American Vaiṣṇavas in India's Hindu hierarchy. Some writers suggested that American devotees be categorized as *śūdras* in their adopted religion because of their non-Indian ethnic origin, family dietary habits, and past occupations.[118] Others scoffed at the notion that Hinduism could be a "proselytizing religion like

Mohamedanism or Christianity," but defended the American followers in India as "sincere spiritual aspirants."[119] Still others questioned the romanticist ISKCON depiction of rural Vrindavan as a utopia by venturing: "Churning milk Gopi-fashion is no way to attain spiritual bliss!"[120] One senses the quizzical tone, humored but unimpressed by Americans trying to popularize their newly adopted Arcadian religion in a cosmopolitan Indian city. Disparaging suggestions about the qualifications of ISKCON devotees to represent Vaiṣṇava traditions were met with aggressive responses by some of Bhaktivedanta's leading American followers.[121] Well versed in the philosophy he taught them about the precedence of lifestyle over family or *jati* in determining an individual's *varna*, their responses conveyed a conviction that they were engaged in "bringing Krishna back" to India, working to complete a process of the globalization of the Gauḍīya Vaiṣṇava tradition.

## Bringing Krishna Back to India

The provocative irony of white Americans claiming to represent a Hindu tradition for Indians is summed up in the title of a 1971 magazine article written by the American-born Giriraja Swami (Glenn Teton), who later went on to lead the organization's first Bombay temple in Juhu. The article, "Krishna Returns to India," lays out this idea, expressed in tropes of the spiritual East and materialistic West drawn from Bhaktivedanta's writings. Giriraja wrote: "Indians are very anxiously observing the example of the West, desirous of becoming materially advanced like the Westerners," while "the West is disgusted with so-called material happiness and is now looking to India for spiritual guidance." In this context, he identified Bhaktivedanta as "a real source of transcendental knowledge and a respectable representative of Indian spiritual culture. He has given to the West what no other *yogi* has: the spiritual bliss of personalism, Krishna *prema*."[122] In this dichotomy, modern Western life is attested to be lacking in a way that can be remediated only by India's (implicitly Hindu) spiritual culture. Therein, the author positions ISKCON followers, led by Bhaktivedanta, in the place of missionaries—in this case, carrying the message of Krishna *bhakti back* to India. Another *Back to Godhead* article by the American *sannyasi* Jayadvaita Swami, published four years later in 1975, further describes ISKCON's missionizing in India as: "not a question of teaching something completely new; it's a question of reviving something which is not very dormant. We say that Krishna consciousness is the dormant God consciousness within everyone. But here it's not quite as dormant."[123] In this regard, the American followers of Bhaktivedanta not only sought to spread Krishna *bhakti* abroad and asserted that Americans could practice Hindu traditions but proclaimed that they were engaged in "bringing Krishna back" to India—self-consciously working to complete Bhaktivedanta's mission of the globalization of Gauḍīya Vaiṣṇavism.

Proclamations that this message needs to be brought back to an India rendered wayward by a perceived influx of modern aspirations—and that ISKCON's message of Krishna *bhakti* will "correct misconceptions" about Hindu traditions within India—gloss Indian culture and tradition as inherently religious and Vaiṣṇava. Although reflecting Bhaktivedanta's missionizing tone as conveyed throughout his ample writings and lectures, these proclamations were delivered by devotees who would be classed as white Westerners in an India still adjusting to its postcolonial nationhood. Ironic resonances with Western missionaries of the past would not have been lost on readers. Nonetheless, this Western missionary agenda was not to *import* a religious tradition but to *revive* one, and alongside that, to condemn his own cultural background: an about-face of the contours of colonial-era civilizing missions. Yet, by bringing this tradition *back*, ISKCON followers revise the location and content of Hindu traditions themselves, affecting a religious revival that reconceives channels of authority and the "ownership" of traditions themselves. While suspicions about ISKCON have lingered among many Indians until the present day, Indian ISKCON members have adopted this translational history in their own narrative of Gauḍīya history in India. For instance, in a recent Mumbai edition of *DNA*, a brief and unblinking announcement of ISKCON's fortieth anniversary in India—seemingly copyedited by an Indian devotee for its media release—described that Krishna devotees celebrated the event through *harināma* chanting (melodic chanting in public procession, popularized by Caitanya in sixteenth century Bengal) and glossed the activity as having been "re-introduced in India by founder Swami Prabhupāda in Mumbai."[124]

But the contestation over whether Bhaktivedanta's non-Indian followers could be accepted into Bombay's Hindu public spheres developed dramatically in the organization's years, heightened through a land dispute over the property acquired in 1971 for ISKCON's first temple in Juhu, then a far-flung northern suburb of the city. Now one of the city's elite neighborhoods, Juhu is home to luxury shops and the beachfront villas of Bollywood film stars.[125] Bhaktivedanta christened the undeveloped property "Hare Krishna Land," evoking the theme park-inspired attractions he hoped to create on his temple properties.[126] A temple ground-breaking ceremony was celebrated in March 1972 and another series of high-profile *pandal* programs that December were attended by then-mayor of Bombay, R. K. Ganatra.[127] But the devotees faced a protracted legal battle with the prior landowners that stretched throughout most of the decade and threatened their presence in the city.[128] Although they faced stiff public opposition, the help of early local supporters drawn from elite professional circles, such as respected politicians like Desai and members of the Juhu chapter of the Lion's Club, bolstered their connections. Also, a strategic alliance with members of the Vishva Hindu Parishad (VHP), the Jan Sangh party, and—according to internal histories—even Bal Thackeray, head of the Shiv Sena himself, enabled ISKCON devotees to effectively make the case in the court of public opinion that they were a Hindu community under threat of destruction by corrupt municipal forces.[129] The Juhu temple resumed construction and opened in January 1978. For some locals, suspicions lingered, and the Juhu temple continues to encounter conflicts with its neighbors over its ongoing expansion projects.[130]

Nevertheless, ISKCON now encompasses four centers throughout the greater metropolitan area and is firmly established as a marker of the Juhu neighborhood itself. Highway traffic signs on Mumbai's Western Expressway direct one to the property, and both the Juhu and Chowpatty temples fluctuate within Trip advisor's top ten "Things to Do" in Mumbai, joining the historic Śrī Siddhivināyak temple in Prabhadevi, the Bandra-Worli Sealink bridge, and the Mount Mary Church in Bandra. ISKCON has marketed its temples as spaces for both recreation and education, for Mumbai's publics and for transregional tourist and pilgrimage markets.

This movement—from the imposed identity of a "foreigner's Hinduism" to the asserted identity of local Vaiṣṇava community—involved several spheres of change. The deployment of modern technology and mass-communications systems by guru organizations for the purposes of propaganda and publicity has been well documented in recent scholarship.[131] In the case of ISKCON, since the early legal conflict over ISKCON Juhu, sophisticated public-relations offices developed on both temple properties.[132] In a strategic rejoinder to the negative depictions of ISKCON in film and print media, members of ISKCON Juhu and later ISKCON Chowpatty developed communications and public-relations teams that sought to offer positive local depictions of their communities through sustained engagement with Mumbai's media outlets. Beyond this, the organization has gradually shifted toward predominantly Indian-born Hindu devotees who have increased connections with Hindu communities, developed charitable projects throughout Mumbai and rural regions that have yielded public accolades, and become a reliable public presence—along with their famed free vegetarian meals—at annual festivals held in some of the city's prominent public spaces.[133]

Through Western devotees and local Indian devotee networks, Bhaktivedanta "re-imported" his institutionalized Gauḍīya Vaiṣṇavism to India. Due to this history, ISKCON's name still retains an aura of transnational affluence, but on the ground ISKCON is now composed of largely Indian congregants and their managerial structures. In these communities, class status and educational levels diverge widely across rural and urban lines and between regions. Many Bengali Gauḍīyas who have affiliated with ISKCON's Mayapur center still belong largely to rural, agrarian communities. However, outside of Bengal, ISKCON is largely associated with urban affluence, and Mumbai's devotees include middle-class and upper-class professionals, many of whom hail from Indian Institutes of Technology (IIT) and medical-school programs.

But ISKCON's transnational, multiethnic character still shapes local temple cultures. Pilgrims from Estonia, Germany, Iran, or Japan may travel through the two major Gauḍīya Vaiṣṇava pilgrimage sites of Vrindavan and Mayapur in any given week. In Vrindavan, Russian devotees are known for their prominent pilgrimage numbers and employment in the local ISKCON hospitality industry, leading to the fascinating local nickname of "Ruskon" for the organization. The ISKCON Mayapur center also includes a prominent percentage of non-Indian residents, many of European and North American descent, who have lived in India for decades. And ISKCON's international presence in India has included transnational funding networks. In early meetings over how to fund the construction of ISKCON's Juhu temple, Bhaktivedanta suggested drawing from his books' publication profits in the United States.[134] While India's ISKCON centers today are overwhelmingly subsidized by local Indian donors, several non-Indian devotees—including an heir to the Ford Motor Company—have been prominent donors for ambitious building projects.

However, aside from transnational financial flows, the interweaving of Indian communities with non-Indian gurus presents a novel step in the development of transnational Hinduisms, beyond the de-ethnicization of Hindu traditions in diaspora contexts.[135] While most Indian ISKCON centers are led by an Indian guru and management team, several North American–born gurus hold positions of managerial and religious authority. The Japanese-Canadian Bhanu Swami serves as a resident guru in Chennai and GBC zonal secretary for South India, while the white American Jayapataka Swami has long guided ISKCON management teams based in Mayapur, and the British-born Bhakti Vikas Swami, known as one of ISKCON's arch conservatives on issues of gender and culture, leads the temple in Baroda, Gujarat. Among these Western gurus in India, Radhanath Swami acts as the senior religious leader of Chowpatty, Mumbai. ISKCON *sannyasi*s of diverse ethnic and national origins—from Nigerian to Ukrainian—also travel frequently between Indian ISKCON centers, lecturing and visiting temple communities in annual trips, their identity as non-Indians mediated through the prism of their adoption of the *sannyasi* dress and lifestyle. In this regard, they parallel the numerous Indian *sannyasi*s who lead other ISKCON centers in India, conforming to the centralized institutional regulations set out by ISKCON's literature and enforced by its GBC. Demographically this means that an ISKCON center in Vrindavan would be as multilinguistic and multiethnic as a Catholic pilgrimage center in Assisi; that is, this community has become interwoven by transnationalism even in its local pilgrimage sites.

A range of Gauḍīya communities still exist prominently in Bengal and throughout North India—in some cases in open antagonism to their transnational step relation. But ISKCON's influence in representing Gauḍīya tradition is propelled by its cultural and economic capital. Conversely, through its growth in India, ISKCON's visual-media and worship practices have influenced contemporary Hindu visual culture and religious formations beyond their institutional scope. Artistic representations of Rādhā and Krishna by early Western ISKCON devotees have become popularized in mainstream Hindu public spheres through calendar art, religious poster styles, and television serials.[136] These portrayals have impacted the iconography of Krishna and Viṣṇu-Nārāyaṇa on a pan-Indic scale.[137] ISKCON's codified *āratī* worship and elaborate *mūrti* and altar decoration styles have affected modes of Vaiṣṇava religious worship in Vrindavan and India's larger urban centers.[138] And ISKCON's influence seems even to have broadened some Indians' understandings of who can be seen as a brahmin and a Vaiṣṇava.[139]

These forms of influence are notably polynodal and multidirectional. For instance, a greater normalization of ISKCON communities in Europe and America led to their impact on the Religious Education curriculum in British secondary schools, prompting Mallory Nye and others to propose an "Iskconization" of British Hindu communities.[140] Since the 1990s, many ISKCON centers in North America and Western Europe lost momentum among convert populations as they gained strong community bases among Indian immigrants.[141] Contributing to these shifts, ISKCON temples in London and Washington DC now host weddings and cater events for local Hindu communities, serving as religious anchors for families seeking Hindu temples in diaspora. Indeed, outside of India, the organization's transnational character and congregation-oriented institutionalization can be assets for diaspora populations.[142] Accordingly, Rochford asserts that shifts in institutional rhetoric—from an early countercultural, renunciation-oriented message to a family-centered, congregation-based model of community and toward Indian-origin demographic groups—constitute ISKCON's process of "Hinduization."[143] In these dual processes, of the Hinduization of ISKCON and the Iskconization of religious knowledge about Hinduism in various forums, many influential ISKCON voices today are of Indian origin, be they in India, South Africa, or the UK.

It is to this fundamentally transnational, but also now locally Indian, religious identity that I will now turn. How does membership in a transnational religious organization refigure local notions of religion and culture—and even family and nation—for its Indian followers? And what can this reveal about the nature of local, lived religion in India today?

# 2

# Global and Local Networks in a Neighborhood Temple

## ISKCON Chowpatty, Mumbai

> Well, yes, my mother . . . Fortunately at that time mother and dad were not staying with us, so they didn't really know so much about what we were doing. By the time they found out, it was too late!
>
> That talk came about when I took initiation. My parents were flabbergasted, you know: "how could you take initiation from an American," you know? "How can an American be your guru? You were born in a high caste brahmin family and you're getting initiation from an American?" That was something that my mother found particularly hard to digest.
>
> - Sachin, chartered accountant and temple counsellor

> A *gora* [white] swami and his autobiography saw the swish set of Mumbai show up in full strength.
>
> "Swami's Tale," *Outlook Magazine*, 2009

As I sit tucked away near the back of the temple room one Sunday afternoon, visitors are guided through red-roped brass posts in line for *darśan*, and volunteers signal to guests to clear space as more newcomers arrive. Those seated shift their floor mats and bags forward in unison so as many people as possible can score an open space on the temple floor to settle in and join the *bhajans*, led by a group of *brahmacaris* near the altar. Surrounding me on the women's side of the temple, sitting cross-legged in tight rows, the guests' attire speaks to several segments of the temple's diverse community. Posh ladies who are driven down in private cars from their sea view apartments in Malabar Hill showcase designer *salwar kameez* and hand-loomed saris.

*Bringing Krishna Back to India.* Claire C. Robison, Oxford University Press. © Oxford University Press 2024.
DOI: 10.1093/9780197656488.003.0003

In their naturally dyed blockprint patterns and richly textured breathable fabrics, they are the ones whose families support the temple's major projects and liaise with the corporations that sponsor temple festivals. They sit alongside women dressed in much more affordable synthetic saris, some lined with metal *zarī*-work borders, many carrying knockoff handbags from the Fashion Street Market on MG Road or Bandra's Linking Road stalls. The knockoffs have the added benefit of being plastic rather than leather, saving the ethical burden accrued by their pricier counterparts in formal shops. Most of the temple's visitors are not heirs to a coveted South Bombay apartment and reach the temple via the Mumbai local from the city's working-class suburbs. Among the many thousands who commute on the trains every day are also the middle-class matrons who take the train from Mumbai's expanding residential suburbs of Borivali and Mira Road. Dressed in understated cotton saris and tidy braids, they form the backbone of the organizing teams for temple programs and festivals. Their day-to-day support—through money, time, and professional expertise—keeps the temple running smoothly and expansively.

Aside from differences in fabric and price tag, all these outfits signal an understanding of the religious atmosphere of this particular temple, where even *salwar kameez* were considered too non-traditional until the mid-aughts and the jeans, dresses, or shorts commonly worn on the streets of South Bombay would feel starkly out of place. Nonetheless, the character of the neighborhood is reflected inside the temple walls as well. On that Sunday afternoon, children, families with their elderly relatives, teenagers, and young adults from a wide spectrum of ages and backgrounds dot the temple floor. A middle-aged, self-assured Gujarati man approaches the altar in an ensemble evocative of Mumbai's cultural mélange, an immaculately starched white *kurta* and camouflage cargo shorts. One can almost hear the voice of his wife echoing in the ether: "are baba, at least put on a *kurta* before you go to the temple!" From the righthand side, slim woman darts to the front of the crowd, donned in sleek, black athletic gear, her dark brown salon-styled hair pulled back into a loose ponytail. As we chat near the altar, she tells me that she often gives a quick *praṇām* to the *mūrti*s after her daily jog along Marine Drive. She weaves in and out of the silver-haired devout South Indian women near the front, in tissue-thin silk saris and tightly plaited braids, who stoically sit through the full three-hour Sunday temple service from start to finish. Four teenage girls from the junior college down the road, wearing skinny jeans and tight animal-print tees in complementary shades, walk in and stand huddled together for a few moments, with folded hands near the altar before walking out in a pack. Students frequent the temple during the weekdays, for a quick samosa in between classes or to offer a prayer before exams. Behind them, mothers and daughters arrive and sit down in pairs in their best Sunday saris, cordially greeting the families already there.

The neighborhood of Girgaon Chowpatty, which gives rise to the temple's informal name, stands adjacent to one of the most popular weekend spots for Mumbaikars for generations Chowpatty Beach. Nestled on the coast of South Bombay, this is one of the city's most famous locales, with historic cinema houses, gymkhanas, and long-standing Parsi cafés dotting its leafy lanes next to new, imposing luxury apartment buildings and Starbucks locations. A short two blocks from the temple—down Grant Road and left at Ramabai Marg—the busy intersection opens out to Chowpatty beach itself, and the long promenade of Marine Drive leading on toward Colaba teems with visitors on an afternoon stroll to admire the ocean views and panoramic city skyline. Since most Chowpatty devotees commute to attend the temple services, arriving from inland neighborhoods throughout the greater metropolis, the Sunday program serves both as a religious function and a family outing for many to spend their one full weekend day near Chowpatty beach.

On any given Sunday evening, vendors offer snacks from small carts on the sand, while families and friends meet to fly kites. Couples dot the stone boundary wall, gleaning rare moments of privacy while hiding in plain view. Adjoining Marine Drive, which spreads out from there to the iconic "Queen's Necklace" seaside promenade, the beach provides a welcome expanse of calm sea and views of the city stretching out in either direction. To the left, toward Nariman Point, the art-deco apartment buildings evoke the glamour of classic South Bombay. Local coffee houses and small cinemas dot the side lanes where the jazz clubs of the 1940s established the cosmopolitan, liberal character of the neighborhood and the city at large. Newer, upscale international hotels raise the skyline upward, electronic dance music wafting from their rooftop bars, while the iconic Pizza By The Bay, with its panoramic windows and pithy billboard offering commentary on the contemporary state of Indian politics, holds its ground as a marker of the city's comedic and resolutely unpretentious character. To the right, the neighborhood winds up in leafy lanes and wide walkways to the affluent Malabar Hill. Beyond the Babulnath Shiva temple, one of the lone historic temples of the neighborhood, the Parsi Tower of Silence is hidden inside a shroud of tall banyans next to one of the city's premier parks, the Hanging Gardens, with its manicured flower beds and winding paths another prominent destination for early evening strolls and taking in views of the city.

Although mostly known as one of the city's premier weekend destinations, Chowpatty Beach is also a center for religious festivals throughout the year, most notably Ganesh Chaturthi and Ram Lila performances. The neighborhoods surrounding Chowpatty are home to a diverse population of Parsis, Hindus, Jains, Muslims, and Christians, with longstanding Gujarati, Konkani, and Marwari communities. Built on a tapestry of cosmopolitan communities and ardently multilingual, this neighborhood has also occasionally served as a flashpoint for tensions in determining the character of the city—most colorfully when Shiv Sena activists, protesting the rise of Gujarati Jain and Hindu populations and their strictly "pure veg" restaurants, protested by stuffing the pungent local fish, Bombay duck, into their mailboxes.[1] This neighborhood historically accommodated a range of residents, although in recent decades property values have risen so much that even the local tailor down the lane can no longer afford to live where his grandfather opened shop. He now commutes by train from Andheri every morning.

ISKCON's temples in Indian cities encompass an array of regional and religious backgrounds, shaped by the patterns of migration and patterns of diversity that comprise the cities themselves. Those who join ISKCON in urban India are not merely adopting a novel religious identity but also seeking to revive a lost orthodoxy, to become religious *again*, to "bring Krishna back." They speak of rejecting the normalization of secular modernity and reintroducing Hindu traditions in an urban context—but also of making those traditions relevant, streamlined to accommodate the aspirations of Indians today. Though religious conservatism often sits fundamentally in contrast to Mumbai's local urban cultures, Mumbaikars who join ISKCON reflect the growth of transnational religious organizations in local Indian contexts by joining a fundamentally transnational, multiethnic Hindu religious organization—a fact that resonates most strongly in Chowpatty through the presence of Radhanath Swami, the community's resident guru (born as Richard Slavin in Chicago). Therein, new urban topographies exchange birth-based identity markers for new community networks of coreligionists from diverse regional, religious, class, and family backgrounds. And in the process, devotees construct new notions of home and family through the networks of the temple community. In this chapter,

I will introduce the Chowpatty community. Behind their elite demographics and status as a temple for Mumbai's "swish set" lies a remarkable history of their formation, full of unexpected itineraries along the way.

## Entering the Radha Gopinath Temple

To begin, let us return to the temple room, packed as usual on a Sunday afternoon. As we listen to the lecture from the *brahmacari* on the dais, a steady line of visitors walks back and forth from taking *darśan* at the altar. *Kīrtan* and *bhajan*s are sung throughout the day, and *darśan* and *pūjā* follow the punctual norms of ISKCON temples, beginning with the first *āratī* at five o'clock every morning and concluding at nine o'clock in the evening. The altar, custom-built in the Vrindavan style by a legendary craftsman from Braj, houses the *mūrti*s three niches gilded in gold-leaf. Hardwood floors inlaid with semiprecious stones cover the floor, and Rajasthani-style carved wooden balconies line the upper levels of the hall, providing viewing points and sitting niches for visitors. Beside the main temple room, two halls flank either side and serve as seating areas on Sundays and on festivals, when the carefully managed crowds spill out of the temple room. From these side rooms, live video footage of the altar and lecture dais is broadcast on television screens, and live streams of temple events are also uploaded on community websites. Translations of English lectures into Hindi or Marathi are accessible via the temple's media services through headsets rented at the guest services desk. Every Sunday and during festivals, Counselling groups take turns volunteering in *sevā*; they cook the Sunday feast meal, direct the crowds at each temple room entrance, and clean up after the whole affair. To the right of the temple, on the women's side, the large adjoining hall also serves as the daily garland-making center, where a dedicated team of elder women and young women in between college semesters gather each morning from eight o'clock until noon creating elaborate garlands to be placed on the *mūrti*s for the following day's *pūjā*. Resident *brahmacari*s cook three meals a day for visitors and temple residents in the expansive temple kitchen. They take pride in its cleanliness and healthfulness, showcasing that all spices and the *atta* flour used to make *chapatis* are ground on site to maximize purity and nutritional value. An elaborate operation, the temple kitchen feeds between several hundred and several thousand people daily.

Fig. 2.1 A view from the center of the temple room, packed with visitors for an evening festival, 2015. Photo by the author.

When I talk about the temple space with both Chowpatty's devotees and guests, the term that comes up repeatedly is the English word "opulence." Many see it as a place that exudes opulence, and the altar is at the center of this. It is a picturesque space: its hardwood floors are inlaid with *maṇḍala* designs made from Greek-sourced stones in vibrant blues and greens. Arabesques are carved into thick walnut-wood wall paneling, interspersed with hand-painted murals and commissioned paintings of Krishna's *līlās*. Translucent dome skylights display blue and white cloud motifs, filtering in natural light, while a discreet air-conditioning system keeps the temple uncommonly cool, even during crowded festivals (Figure 2.1). As in all standard ISKCON temples, the *pujārīs*—temple priests—ritually bathe, dress, and elaborately ornament all seven large *mūrtis*, including Radha Gopinath (the iridescent marble forms of Rādhā and Krishna that are the central attraction on the main altar), Caitanya and Nityānanda (founding figures of the Gauḍīya tradition), and Śrī Gopāla (a replica of Rajasthan's Śrī Nāthjī form of Krishna, who stands to the right with his hand poised above his head to remind his devotees of his superhuman feats in Vrindavan, such as the lifting of Govardhan hill). Aside from these main *mūrtī*s, small statues of recent Gauḍīya *ācārya*s (teachers in Bhaktivedanta's lineage) fill the lower tier of the altar space, which sweeps down to an inlaid marble fountain and carved teak wood divider.

For ISKCON Chowpatty, the creation of this aestheticized world not only insulates its visitors from the chaos of the modern city but also communicates the content of the idyllic "spiritual world" of Krishna—developing a topography for a world that, for Gauḍīyas, is envisioned as existing on a plane transcendent to the "material world" and is the destination of all *bhakta*s. The temple's walls are ornamented with hand-painted murals and gem-encrusted portraits depicting the *līlā*s of Krishna and his *gopa*s and *gopī*s, cowherd residents of Vrindavan. This world is pastoral, jovial, characterized by song and dance, and—unlike our present world, according to Gauḍīya ideas—it is untouched by the sufferings of disease, old age, and death. The refined materials used to depict these idyllic pastoral scenes make vivid this elevated realm, while also communicating urban affluence more than rustic rural settings. In this sense, the temple's material culture reflects the aspirations of a cosmopolitan and distinctly elite Indian religious aesthetics.[2]

The temple experience for visitors produces a calm that is rare to find in Mumbai's public spaces, and its immaculately maintained interiors contrast with many of the city's other Hindu temples. The temple compound breathes luxury—not ostentatious wealth but careful design, sophisticated aesthetics, and meticulous maintenance (Figure 2.2). This imbues the space with the sense of being an oasis within an urban metropolis not always known for control and cleanliness. The main courtyard and all inside spaces are kept freshly mopped and tidy throughout the day. After guests deposit their shoes at the storage counter, they are met by volunteer greeters and invited into the reception area to receive information about the temple programs and events. Indeed, the tranquility and orderliness of the temple complex render it as somewhat liminal, in between a public space and a private space. However, it is also intentionally insulated, through security checkpoints and bag checks, alongside the distinctive attire and demeanor that distinguishes temple devotees from the city outside. Once inside the protective space, however, one can amble throughout the compound for hours—chanting in the temple room, meeting old friends in the courtyard or for a meal at Govinda's, shopping for devotional items and new book releases at the temple store, or just taking some time to refocus after a long workday.

Fig. 2.2 The temple complex provides an oasis for visitors amidst Mumbai's bustling downtown, 2013. Photo by the author.

Despite the carefully cultivated sense of calm space pervading the temple space, neighbors in this old wealth locality initially resented the all-too-audible pre-dawn worship services and frequently amplified *bhajan* programs. Over the years, various neighbors filed lawsuits related to sound pollution and property infringement, contesting the gradual expansion of the temple complex.[3] Devotees responded with the language of revival: since they are there to infuse a much-needed religiosity into the neighborhood, their neighbors should respect that endeavor. If loudspeakers broadcasting morning *bhajans* dominate the soundscape, all the better for those who can be purified by hearing. Nonetheless, steeled from the experience of early legal troubles in Juhu, an elder team of followers was already assembled when the first lawsuit was filed. Led by an established high court advocate who is also an ISKCON devotee, the temple administration often succeeded in settling out of court.[4] Meanwhile, temple residents strove to improve relations with their neighbors through invitations to festivals and the liberal distribution of desserts and even full meals to their doorsteps, building personal bonds and continuing ISKCON's reputation for abundant free vegetarian food.

Yet, still this demarcated temple space provides what many members described as an oasis from the bustle of the city with its traffic and overcrowded streets. As a woman, I noticed it was also a notable break from the low-level sexual harassment that often characterizes women's experiences of public space in India. The men on Chowpatty's grounds, regardless of social or marital status, displayed a cordiality for women on the property that is not only grounded in the often-discussed norms of Vaiṣṇava etiquette, *sadācāra*, but also reinforced by ideas that the devotee community is bound by kinship-styled networks. In this sense, this oasis space is also a performance ground, providing an opportunity for its members to practice and embody an idyllic religious community (Figure 2.3). Resonant with what Lise McKean has noted in relation to the temple complexes of many modern guru movements, it presents visitors with "the spectacle of institutionalized spirituality."[5] Crisply attired in ironed saris and *kurta*s and speaking in polite tones, devotees display an ethos of *sevā*, religious service. This is grounded in the codes of Vaiṣṇava etiquette elaborated in the training manuals given to each aspiring member.

This atmosphere of controlled conduct in the spiritualized topography of the temple mirrors the focus on training and education in the community's organized activities.[6] The development of an ideal Vaiṣṇava self is at the heart of ISKCON Chowpatty's community, through "training" to cultivate *bhakti* as devotional service—that is, as devotional self-humbling and active *sevā* to a personal deity. In addition to standard ISKCON temple rituals, a particular focus on ethical conduct is highlighted in Radhanath Swami's communication of Gauḍīya precepts. The values of humility, service toward others, and devotion to Krishna are emphasized and often contrasted to a "ritualistic approach" to religion. The hallmark scriptural verse that supports this reading of the Gauḍīya Vaiṣṇava tradition is the third verse of the *Śikṣāṣṭaka* prayers attributed to Caitanya and found in the *Caitanya Caritāmṛta*: *tṛṇād api sunīcena, taror eva sahiṣṇunā, amāninā mānadena, kīrtanīyah sadā hariḥ*.[7] The Swami's direct translation, quoted pervasively in his lectures and writings, is as follows: "One should be more humble than a blade of grass, more tolerant than a tree, ready to offer all respect to others and expect none in return. In this way, we can chant the holy name of the Lord constantly." Chowpatty's early morning service, the five o'clock *maṅgala āratī*, augments the standard set of ISKCON prayers by including a group recitation of the full eight Śikṣāṣṭakam verses at the closing of the ceremony each day, standardizing these prayers and their ethical aspirations in the liturgical life of the community.

Fig. 2.3 Baskets of flower petals, prepared by temple volunteers for days in advance, are prepared for the temple's annual Flower Festival, 2013. Photo by the author.

A focus on becoming a good Vaiṣṇava is reiterated throughout daily temple lectures, specialized monthly programs and retreats, the print and audio media distributed through the Radha Gopinath Media Services office, and in regular email listserv messages. Newcomers to the community are taught about "proper" codes of conduct in publications such as the "Manual for Vaiṣṇava Etiquette" and "Grhastha Manual," which dictates a set of strict lifestyle norms and regulations within marriage based on Vaiṣṇava scriptural commentaries. Available for purchase in English and Hindi at the temple store, these manuals are often referenced when "training" new members in the community. This ideal conduct is also cultivated for display at public festivals throughout the city and in the frequent dramatic performances organized by temple congregants. Concurrently, regular Counselling group sessions and the daily output of audio and print media provide ongoing instructions on how to better manifest the values of humility, selflessness, and service in one's present life. This is paired with a strong focus on each member maintaining prescribed daily *sādhana* standards, including the chanting of sixteen rounds of *japa*, a mantra-based meditation that requires around two hours daily of focused concentration.

This ordered atmosphere sends undeniable class signals. Some of the young women who volunteer weekly at the temple's educational facilities assure me that this is not a "typical temple." Jayati, a teacher in her early thirties, sitting among several other volunteers chatting and ordering Govinda's pizza to the office one day after class, specifically contrasted the "dirty and uncared for" condition of many temples with "some Hindi-speaking guru up on the dais who doesn't know what he is talking about" with ISKCON's English-medium classes that are provided to a well-educated community who values cultivating a "family-like" community over the "transactional" framework they identify in other Hindu temple settings.[8]

The ordered temple atmosphere is also maintained through a formal demarcation of space, enhanced after a series of threats to Hindu temples in the early 2000s prompted the installation of formal security stations to screen all guests entering ISKCON temple compounds.[9] Additionally, a kind of screening of one's intentions is also a part of joining or crossing into the community as a devotee. Shivan, a member of the temple's accounting department, whose headquarters sits alongside the marble staircase leading up to temple room, cautioned: "sometimes we're seeing the phenomenon in ISKCON that people are coming in because they're getting a free meal, and then they see the opulence of ISKCON and they want to get a share of that opulence. And then they do all sorts of illegal, wrong things to accumulate money." To avoid these motives, he tells me, the system of joining the community stresses integrity and "real renunciation"—that is, the engagement of one's medical or engineering degree, for instance, in the *sevā* of the temple community through its charitable hospital and humanitarian outreach projects. Training, seen as the development of the self toward the goal of love for Krishna and humility and *sevā* toward other living beings, is thus valued in both religious and class registers. Describing the *brahmacaris* resident at the temple, a temple manager with a background in finance conveys to me that: "they are people who have been trained, who are extremely intelligent," and their training continues, in the ethos of "real renunciation," through the guidance of the temple's educational programs.

In public discourse, the Chowpatty community posits itself as a representative of Hindu traditionalism, intoning a promotion of Hindu values, religion, and culture. Yet the community also breaks from a strict brahmanical interpretation of Hindu traditions with its ideals of inclusivity regarding caste and ethnicity, grounded in Bhaktisiddhānta's reinterpretation of the categories of *varṇāśrama-dharma* to refer to practices over birth. ISKCON Chowpatty is a strongly missionizing community; through lectures and outreach programs, core members of the temple community strive to spread their message of Krishna *bhakti* to Indians of all caste backgrounds, as well as non-Indians. However, inclusion in this community also involves an adoption of many conservative brahmanical cultural norms, including dress codes and gender-based regulations, that have become standardized within ISKCON communities. This stands at odds with ISKCON Chowpatty's placement in the historically liberal South Bombay area—long known for its night clubs and cinemas, historic jazz scene, and an array of fusion restaurants serving wines from Maharashtra's burgeoning vineyards. The neighborhood is also within a mile of one of India's largest red-light districts. In this setting, ISKCON Chowpatty represents the assertion of a type of Hindu traditionalism that is both formed by and asserted over against Mumbai's urban landscape, and patronage of the temple positions one in a community set apart from much of the city outside.

However, the demographics of the temple community also vividly reflect the city's historic and contemporary patterns of transregional migration. Gujarati and Telugu are spoken alongside English and Hindi, as the temple's devotees reflect the demographic diversity of Mumbai. In that sense, although symbolically set apart, this ISKCON community is also deeply emblematic of a profoundly local form of religion in urban India today—grounded in the development of utopic enclaves as well as publicized humanitarian projects, both meant to offer alternatives to urban realities outside, it is traditionalist but grounded in cosmopolitan, urban congregations and globalized religious networks.

## The Demographics of Local Devotees

On any given day, one will find individuals and families coming together, sometimes across three generations, and a remarkable variety in age among those attending temple services. The temple's managerial core encompasses diverse regional and linguistic backgrounds, from prominent Gujarati business families to the descendants of Sindhi Partition refugees and to South Indian computer engineers who came to the city to attend college. But across regional backgrounds, many of the temple's devotees share both a *savarna*

Hindu or Jain identity and family histories of migration, either in their generation or in the living memory of their parents or grandparents, as people moved to Mumbai's growing metropolis to partake of the increased centralization of economic opportunities in India's urban centers.

According to the temple's member database, over 5,800 individuals are listed as active members.[10] Common surnames display regional-origin diversity. The most common are Shetty, Singh, and Patil—mainstays, respectively, of Karnatic, North Indian, and Maharashtrian Hindu communities and groups with broad socio-economic parallels, including occupational histories in business and bureaucracy. Other prominent surnames in the community include Sharma, Gupta, Jadhav, Patel, Mehta, Thakur, Shinde, Yadav, and Iyer. The regional diversity denoted by these surnames reflects the patterns of migration augmenting Mumbai's status as the largest metropolis in Western India, as the city is a nexus for newcomers from along the coast and in neighboring inland states. While ISKCON members' decisions to join the community are often related to finding a new community in their adopted city, ISKCON's Krishna-centered worship also finds regional analogues among Vaiṣṇava traditions from Gujarat, Maharashtra, Karnataka, Andhra Pradesh, and Hindi-speaking regions of North India, appealing to this broad demographic range of Mumbai's inhabitants.[11] Ironically, one of the least represented regional identities among Mumbai devotees is Bengali, attesting to the profound shift ISKCON has made in modern India away from the tradition's regional origin.

The balance of the temple community is in an urban, upper-caste, and highly educated demographic group. The temple managerial core is run by a team of business professionals, chartered accountants, and CEOs from successful Mumbai business families, as well as *brahmacari* graduates from India's top engineering and technology schools. Several devotees communicated a subtle confidence in the upper-caste background of the majority of the temple's congregants. While this matches the prominence of brahmanical and merchant *jati* surnames in temple records, those documents also record a noteworthy number of surnames classified by the Indian government as Scheduled Caste (SC) or Other Backward Caste (OBC). Encompassing a range of *jati* backgrounds, the temple community does, however, tend to reflect an upwardly mobile urban middle class. Giving a rough estimate, one chartered accountant who works on the temple's Financial Team estimated that roughly 80–85 percent of the temple's congregants fall into the category of middle to upper middle class, while 15–20 percent could be categorized as lower middle to lower class. A frequent acknowledgment of high-caste and education status in casual conversations speaks to several orientations: a continuing value placed on upper-caste status, even within a religious community that ideologically rejects caste-by-birth identities, and an assumption of the upwardly mobile value of membership in the community itself, based on appraisals of its greater balance toward an upper-caste, educated demographic composition.

This corroborates with what one would expect after spending time at temple programs and is also confirmed by the educational levels reported in the community's database, which details a prominence of higher educational attainments. As of 2013, around 40 percent of those registered in the temple database had completed bachelor's degrees, at least 210 completed an MA, and twenty-four held PhDs. The highest-ranking professions comprised corporate and business management, engineering and the information-technology sector, healthcare, education, and accounting and finance. Most married women in the congregation do not work outside the home, although many spend significant time organizing temple-related programs. However, many prominent women do work as doctors, dentists, educators, administrators, and chartered accountants, while some possess their own practices, and a number have continued their careers after motherhood.

Alongside its balance toward elite urban groups, since the mid-2000s the temple management has increased missionizing to people from diverse socio-economic strata, particularly through the "village-based preaching" in conjunction with their developing Govardhan Ecovillage. Although the unmistakable stamp of urban wealth remains in those efforts by Chowpatty's well-educated and well-heeled strategists, a self-critique of caste and social divisions is a frequent refrain at temple programs. In lectures, Radhanath Swami often enjoins devotees to relinquish their attempts to be the "master" and strive instead to be the "servant of the servant." In a frequently retold story, one day during the devotional dancing and singing at a temple *kīrtan*, a prominent businessman is said to have started dancing with his driver in a wave of abandon. That led to roars and claps of approval from those encircling them on the temple floor. The memory of this elision of caste and class categories in a moment of devotional expression is repeated often in Radhanath Swami's lectures, a refrain that speaks as much to the beauty of the moment as to its rarity. The day-to-day power dynamics underscored by the unequal relations of India's informal domestic labor sector sit stubbornly beside the stress in Chowpatty's temple lectures on transcending birth, caste, and regional backgrounds in the higher goal of attaining the qualities of humility and Vaiṣṇava *sevā*.

Despite the presence of older generations, the most prominent age group in temple membership records is between twenty-one and thirty-eight years of age. This mirrors the temple's media products, which are particularly aimed toward the city's youth, a missionizing strategy that parallels early ISKCON communities in North America.[12] Despite a young demographic, the community is taught to uphold conservative gender demarcations, and events are nearly always segregated spatially into male and female sides. The gendering of space is heightened in the temple complex by the pervasive presence of temple's *brahmacari* monks who are the main residents of the property. Men account for almost 60 percent of the community, a balance likely also related to the orientation of the temple's missionary activities. Although Chowpatty is a largely lay congregation, the roughly one hundred monks who reside on the temple grounds perform most daily rituals and maintenance work. Keeping strict *brahmacari* vows, most refrain from speaking with women outside of limited professional contexts, thus their active missionary programs throughout the city cater primarily to other men. These audiences consist of students at colleges throughout the city at which *brahmacari*s give talks and courses, the monthly Prerna festival and ISKCON Youth Services (IYS) activities that cater to young men, and those whom *brahmacari*s approach in public trains and sidewalks on their frequent outings to distribute ISKCON literature throughout the city. While there are also organized venues for women to express interest in joining the community—particularly through the Journey of Self Discovery course and seminars organized on the temple site—young women as a group are not sought out in the same way that young men are by the active *brahmacari* preaching force. This has become a point of critique, and the occasional female student who decided to sit in on male-oriented classes spoke of a palpable sense of being out place.

Temple programs that are tailored to women include the Gopal's Fun School afternoon classes, organized by married women volunteers and advertised to mothers who send their children to the temple's Sanskrit classes. Additionally, the monthly Chetana program for teenage girls is also attended by mothers and grandmothers who accompany their younger relatives. Speakers are senior devotee women, and the promotion of their religious and professional qualifications mirrors these dual qualifications among JSD teachers. Moreover, the binary division of programming, with requisite gendered assumptions about professionalization and domesticity, breaks down in highly elite spaces, particularly in the "corporate preaching" programs in which an elite group of women and men are involved in marketing self-help-style courses to business professionals at work. Additionally, any greater weight toward male membership is apparent neither from the community's large festivals nor at the weekly Sunday program, where women occupy their full half of the temple room and gather at every location throughout the courtyard to catch up with friends and share a meal. The balance toward male participation is, however, more prevalent in the daily morning services. Because only a fraction of the congregation attends these early morning gatherings—given busy working schedules and family responsibilities—in the months I attended them regularly, the distinctly small space allotted to the women's section reflected a predominantly male monastic orientation.

But outside of this monastic core, the congregation includes individuals and families, in nuclear households and intergenerational homes. And centrally, the temple's administration and networks are often centered on married couples. Many devotees met their spouses through temple networks rather than traditional family arrangements and speak glowingly of the "inter-caste" marriages supported by the temple community. However, I was told a frequent problem for women who become interested in ISKCON is that their husbands (and in-laws) do not share their enthusiasm. ISKCON's Gauḍīya identity is underscored through extensive dietary restrictions, and married couples are encouraged to restrict their sexual lives as much as possible, striving toward an ideal of engaging in sexual intercourse only for procreation. These strict lifestyle norms make commitment to the community a tall order. Several women related how they must negotiate their personal Gauḍīya practice in the face of indifference or sometimes antagonism from their husband and in-laws, as in many Indian families a wife still moves into her husband's family household at marriage.

Aside from divergences of membership between a husband and wife, an important site of membership split is intergenerational—most devotees joined as individuals. This carries long-term ramifications for the demographic of the congregation. In thirty years, will the community be composed of children of those who joined over the past two decades, or another generation of converts who choose to join as adults? For parents who hold deep convictions about the need to practice ISKCON's practices strictly, it can be devastating if children do not continue that practice as well. Yet the pressure to carry on the zeal of a generation of converts does not come naturally to those raised within a liberal-leaning city, especially if this religion prescribes a restricted lifestyle set apart from one's peers. Accordingly, while the Chowpatty congregation is undoubtedly family-based, a full family's membership in the congregation cannot be assumed. Rather, the temple's networks span across individuals and families connected through a common bond of commitment to ISKCON's devotional community more than birth-based identities.

## Local Networks, Transnational Ties: Forming an Indian ISKCON Community

While most congregants now commute across town to the temple for their visits, the temple was originally developed by young members of Gujarati and Punjabi business families in South Bombay who had previously attended ISKCON's Juhu temple. Although they hailed from elite, established Bombay families, their membership in a transnational religious group charted unexpected itineraries in their religious lives and the history of the temple they founded. Around 1986, this handful of families began their own informal, home-based ISKCON programs in the Malabar Hill and Grant Road neighborhoods not far from the present temple property. The home of one Gujarati businessman who began supporting ISKCON in the 1980s—a sprawling apartment building partitioned into floors for each section of the family—became a center for the daily morning programs. This was a more convenient location for those who lived and worked in the historic city center, particularly when Mumbai's notoriously congested traffic can routinely make the thirteen-kilometer trip up from South Bombay to Juhu into a one-and-a-half hour commute each way.

However, soon an institutional reason to develop a separate center cemented this change. Through ISKCON networks, the families involved in this South Bombay center became affiliated with a new "preaching center" opened by an ambitious ISKCON guru from North America, Kirtanananda Swami. Kirtanananda was among the earliest followers of Bhaktivedanta and the first disciple to receive the sannyas order of renunciation in 1967. After Bhaktivedanta's passing, he was one of eleven men appointed to serve as the next generation of gurus. However, Kirtanananda's leadership of ISKCON's "New Vrindavan," an insular commune in rural West Virginia, became notorious for its restrictive atmosphere and legal scandals. He was eventually excommunicated by ISKCON's managerial body, the GBC, in March 1987.[13] Remarkably, all transnational communities affiliated with him, including centers throughout India and Africa, shared in that institutional expulsion, and this included the small group of Indian business families in South Bombay. They were suddenly barred from attending programs at official ISKCON centers, like those at Juhu, unless they renounced any affiliation with Kirtanananda. In this singular episode of strange bedfellows, the fate of a small group of aristocratic Bombay business families was tied to a group of mainly white American converts in a commune in rural West Virginia through their shared institutional connections to an American *sannyasi*. Some Indian devotees visited the West Virginia commune during this period, even adopting the unconventional norms introduced by Kirtanananda Swami. This included replacing the saris and *dhotis* introduced to ISKCON followers by Bhaktivedanta Swami with brown Franciscan-style monks' robes for both men and women, as an attempt to indigenize ISKCON's renunciatory ethics in a shared monastic religious vocabulary alongside traditions of the Christian West. While this might have held symbolic resonance for American Catholic converts, it was a remarkable prescription for Indian devotees from Mumbai.

As these innovations were introduced to South Bombay via fiat from West Virginia, Kirtanananda himself rarely visited or had direct contact with these Indian followers. Rather, in 1986 he sent Radhanath Swami—a young American *saṃnyāsin* who had already spent years in India—to manage the Bombay community locally. In a twist of fate, Radhanath had met Bhaktivedanta at South Bombay's Cross Maidan festival grounds in 1971 and later joined ISKCON in Vrindavan. In that sense, by leading the Bombay community, Radhanath Swami was returning to a place already significant to him and a history that would be later memorialized through Chowpatty's own public festivals at the same Cross Maidan grounds.[14] Ironically, I was told by several of Chowpatty's elder congregants, Radhanath Swami was the only person among the Indian congregation at that time who refused to don the Franciscan-inspired monks' robes, insisting instead on wearing his saffron *dhoti* and shawl, the traditional attire of the Hindu *daśnāmī* renouncer lineages that has been adopted by Gauḍīyas since Bhaktisiddhānta's early twentieth-century reforms. Thus, this early community of Bombay's Indian devotees wearing monks' robes during their temple rituals began to take local religious guidance from an

American *sannyasi* wearing the traditional saffron robes of a Hindu ascetic. The complex layers of ISKCON's transnational religious development were woven further together.

This little-discussed period of Chowpatty's early history may partially explain a proclamation I heard from a number of Chowpatty members: that Radhanath Swami teaches them "true Indian culture," imparting to them "more than they knew growing up in India."[15] But the excommunication impelled the small group of Indian devotees to find a suitable temple space of their own. Among them were members of eminent South Bombay business families who possessed good opportunities for property acquisition. The Mafatlal and Desai families in particular, through generations of industry and philanthropic investments, had deep ties to local civic service projects. Narendra D. Desai, also known as Srinathji, inherited from his father a trusteeship in the Lady Northcote Hindu Orphanage (LNHO) located in Girgaon Chowpatty, two blocks from the ocean and the sprawling, picturesque Marine Drive.[16] The Lady Northcote property was divided into units and rented to commercial tenants. The original small allotment on the orphanage property was surrounded by a tutoring school and a sewing workshop. The white marble *mūrti*s of Radha Gopinath were formally installed in that temple room in 1988, and gradually the space belonging to the temple expanded so that today it encompasses a majority of the city block, spanning several buildings and courtyards, while the orphanage has been relocated to the temple's rural property, the Govardhan Ecovillage.

With the temple space established and the *mūrti*s installed, the group began recruiting more members. By the early 1990s, new members began joining and changing their lifestyles in accord with the temple's norms. As in ISKCON's early communities in Europe and North America, these enthusiasts were nearly all in their twenties or early thirties. Many came across the temple while attending college at the nearby University of Bombay (now Mumbai), and many remain the administrative core for at the temple and its affiliated projects, such as the Bhaktivedanta Hospital in North Mumbai. As the group became disaffected from Kirtanananda, Radhanath Swami took an increasing role as their religious teacher, and in the early 1990s, he re-established links with other Indian ISKCON communities through several American ISKCON *sannyasis*. After a successful joint pilgrimage to Mayapur in 1994, the Chowpatty community was invited to rejoin ISKCON, now with Radhanath Swami as their official leading guru. Devotees were re-initiated by him, cementing that relationship, and from this point onward, many members tell me, the growth of the community into its present-day successes began.

By the late 1990s, the tight-knit group blossomed into an ever-growing congregation, and today the majority of Chowpatty's community joined after the early 2000s. But everyone in the community participates symbolically in this early history, as it is reiterated in temple lectures, annual festivals, and informal conversations. Discussions about what the community stands for—what its principles are—are often expressly linked to this early development. This origins story provides a regenerating narrative to tie the community together and reiterate their grounding both in ISKCON and in a particular local history. Their history of isolation produced what some devotees describe as a "self-sufficient character" that lasted, even after their re-absorption in the transnational organization. The people who today remain most of Chowpatty's central administrators, donors, and respected elders already formed the tight-knit group so often referenced in members' oral histories. In fact, while the allure of a transnational religious network is frequently suggested as a reason for Indian interest in ISKCON, Chowpatty's inner managerial structure speaks more to local structures of religious legitimation. The temple's main donors have developed among networks of Mumbai's Gujarati business communities, who have long occupied a central status in the city's development, and many prominent *brahmacari* teachers hail from South Indian brahmin families, often seen as traditional religious authorities for brahmanically oriented Hindus. These patterns of demographic distribution parallel well-established networks of power, but they were channeled into the unique image of the temple itself. As Chowpatty grew into prominence in ISKCON's global network of temples, devotees became an increasingly visible face of the organization, drawing thousands from Mumbai to the annual pilgrimage to Vrindavan and developing a recognizable "brand" among devotees worldwide.[17]

In tandem with familiar patterns of patronage and religious authority, the community also created alternative social structures for its members, forming social bonds distinct from those in their secular contexts outside. Arushi, who attended the historic Mumbai University about a mile down Marine Drive in Colaba, described the atmosphere of the temple community when she joined in 1993 as that of a group of very close friends. As we sat on a futon in her breezy living room, sipping *nimbu pani* among an array of vibrant plants lining the window ledge that overlooked a sunny courtyard below, she reminisced about the easy access they enjoyed to their guru Radhanath Swami in the temple's early years. They would sit for long afternoons in his rooms, talking and listening to others present their queries, and receiving his guidance on various aspects of their lives. Arushi likened that period to a kind of intensive personal training. This initial group, including the first couples who set up the temple infrastructure, were all in either college or medical school, and as Arushi described, they became fast friends, providing a sense of family to each other when their college friends could not comprehend their decision to become so religious.

The sense of community engendered in this early formation replaced circles of friends from college and professional environments and continues to do so to this day. Members chart their commitment to the community through their distancing from friends "outside." As one young couple reflected, when they started to become more "serious" in Krishna *bhakti*, undertaking the rigorous *sādhana* practices prescribed in the community, they also stopped drinking alcohol and going out to restaurants, due to their adoption of a strict vegetarian diet. This consequently left them with less time and less inclination to spend time with their old friends. As Sona put it: "It wasn't a conscious effort, it just happened automatically . . . because our interests are not so common now." But by contrast, many community members were keen to tell me about relatives or friends who had also joined or at least "become favorable." Sona told me with a clear sense of accomplishment about her sister who is "already a devotee and she's very strong and staunch," and her mother who has begun the daily chanting of several rounds of the Hare Krishna mantra on *japa* beads.

While new members are emphatically encouraged by elder members not to cut off family relations, membership in ISKCON reshapes one's relationship to both one's family and religious traditions as much as it is also asserted to be a revival of Hindu religious traditions in Mumbai's secular landscape. Due to the disjuncture with social life outside the conversative temple community, supportive social structures are offered in parallel temple events, including regular meetings for teenagers, young married couples, and retirees. But perhaps the most intriguing religious counterpart to the social structures of modern life is the core institutional structure of the Chowpatty temple: its Counselling System.

Therein, joining the community—officially committing to its lifestyle injunctions and *sādhana* prescriptions—is regulated by a formal relationship with a counsellor drawn from the senior ranks of the temple community. Through counsellor-counselee relationships, members gain access to employment and housing networks, financial support in times of need, children's education through the community-run and state-accredited Gopal's Garden elementary and secondary school, a range of adult education programs, and easy access to professional health services through the community's Bhaktivedanta Hospital. The benefits of "joining" also include a day-to-day social network, in which there is always an event to attend and always an opportunity deepen connections to other devotees. This institutional belonging can parallel—and even replace—bonds of family and friends, transforming a massive, chaotic city like Mumbai into a network of local communities. And, as temple networks stretch far beyond the South Bombay temple complex into individual neighborhoods throughout the city, they link the small-scale origins of the temple to its present, city-wide expansions.

## The Counselling System: Reproducing Idyllic Community

Today in the bustle of a Sunday program, squeezing past visitors lined up to take *darśan*, share a meal with family, or meet a friend from across town, chances are you may not know most of the people alongside you (Figure 2.4). And yet, when devotees talk about what sustains their commitment to this religious community, it is often the cherished relationships. Friendships can reiterate caste and regional parallels—someone with the surname Iyer may be more familiar with other Iyers in the community and South Indians generally. Or you might recognize the familiar faces of members who joined around the same time and attended the same introductory temple classes. But, most likely, you would be closest to members from your counselling group, divided into quadrants based on Mumbai's urban geography and often, through shared language and neighborhood, implicit class lines.[18] In keeping with this modern traditionalism, these cherished relationships are systematically maintained.

The "Counselling System" is formalized in the basic documents that lay out the temple's community structures and procedures.[19] Despite the connotations of this English word, ISKCON's usage of it does not refer to a system of professionally trained therapists advising others in one-on-one confidential sessions billable to a healthcare plan. Rather, the system centers on religious mentorship and encompasses the formal supervision of devotees' religious practices (Do they chant their required sixteen rounds of *japa* daily? Are they abstaining from meat and alcohol?) and confidential discussions of how to cultivate central religious values given weight in the temple community (such as humility and an attitude of *seva*). Most directly, the Counselling System owes its logic to an extension of the hierarchy of the *guru-śiṣya* relationship. It began as a pragmatic extension of the guidance early Chowpatty devotees enjoyed accessing through frequent group *darśans* with Radhanath Swami. As the community grew larger and individual time with the guru became less accessible, Radhanath Swami encouraged elder members to implement this as a structure to provide everyday guidance to each new devotee who joins the community. Not merely perfunctory relationships, they are rather linked to major decisions in life, as devotees would consult counsellors when trying to decide whom to marry or how to handle major personal struggles.

The Counselling System is detailed in the internally circulated temple publication, "A Report on the Social Development Programme at Radha Gopinath Temple," written in the late 1990s by several temple administrators to provide a written record of its development. This source also serves to record a type of internal mission statement, providing a glance at how the Chowpatty administration understands the development of its community.[20] Therein, its premise is grounded in emotional fulfillment:

> Our devotees require fulfillment in their social environment in order to continue to strive for spiritual perfection. That satisfaction will be found in loving, caring, and honest relationships among sincere devotees. There must be faith in the exemplary behaviour of our leaders, adherence to the regulative principles of *sādhana bhakti*, and confidence that our society [ISKCON] will provide protection at every stage of life. No sincere devotees should have reason to doubt that the Society will provide a secure future for them and their families.[21]

On a pragmatic level, as the brainchild of temple guru Radhanath Swami, the system also grew out of a moment of profound discontent within ISKCON's development, to steer away from some of the negative and frankly abusive trends encountered amid the hyper-centralized authority structure of early ISKCON communities, including the New Vrindavan of the 1980s. Temple-produced literature speaks of the need to counteract an over-emphasis of missionary outreach at the expense of community development, implicitly marked as a mistake of early ISKCON communities and a much-discussed cause of large-scale disaffection of ISKCON members transnationally.[22] This informs the discourse of community propounded by Radhanath Swami and other Chowpatty members, which emphasizes the holistic care of each individual congregant and explicitly strives to value personal religious well-being over material contributions to the mission. In that sense, this community structure is promoted as a solution to institutional mistakes of the past. This echoed a changing valuation of the ideal devotional life throughout ISKCON internationally, as a group of lay and monastic devotees formed a "Devotee Care Committee" in the early 2000s to place more emphasis on members' emotional and physical needs.[23] As late as 2012, this committee gave annual reports to the GBC on the progress of changing missionizing behavior to inculcate, as Radhanath Swami worded it, "people over projects." Therein, Chowpatty's Counselling System and other congregation-based outreach programs have even been explicitly defined as "Emotional Care,"[24] engaging the language of wellness in a fresh articulation of Gauḍīya institutional structure.

In this community, however, care is connected to training. The successful growth of a counselling group is linked to a commonly repeated goal that every member should receive "systematic training in Krishna Consciousness."[25] This emphasis relates to both the missionizing imperative of ISKCON's congregational structure and the idea that community is maintained through systematic and ongoing education. A focus on the centrality of "training" to religious life can be traced to the writings of Bhaktivedanta; however, this trend is also traceable to a broad early twentieth-century Indian concern with rigorous training as a sign of the physical and social strength underlying Indian cultural institutions (and a consequential rebuttal of colonial assertions otherwise). Additionally, in pairing a focus on human relationships and individual emotional fulfillment with a highly systematized formula for religious participation, the Counselling System conveys that *bhakti* is a rational, scientific process—something that can be reproduced systematically given the proper environment and variables. This confidence in its reproducibility forms the backbone of Chowpatty's soft power in affiliated ISKCON temples in Pune, Nigdi, Aurangabad, and at the Govardhan Ecovillage in Wada, Maharashtra, in which the Counselling System has also been instituted.

This highly systematized approach to congregational development, although echoing earlier models for modern Gauḍīya community, is most explicitly grounded in an engagement with popular wellness terminology.

Employing rubrics of holistic care of the body, mind, and spirit, the articulation of a Vaiṣṇava *saṅga* as a counselling group appropriates and seeks to supersede the structures of modern secular life from it take its cues.[26] This religion is not the informal, decentralized Hinduism of many people's upbringings, but a systematic process for personal transformation, the very contours of which are steeped in modern ideas about the efficacy of a "scientifically" provable religious practice and its reproducibility as a marker of efficacy. Even the community's advocacy of holistic care and the importance of individual supportive relationships in the cultivation of a religious life are highly institutionalized. Regulating one's actions, and ideally desires, through a reproducible model of mentorship offers the promise of spiritual and psychological contentment for each person and, broadening out, a fulfilling religious community. In drawing from popular contemporary language of individual fulfillment and community harmony, the counselling system also roots itself in principles of marketing drawn from broader neoliberal trends of personal development, locating individual fulfillment as the product of an efficient, reproducible system.

**Fig. 2.4** At the weekly Sunday program, guests spill into the adjoining halls, 2015. Photo by the author.

But the Counselling System also serves many practical uses for the community. In busy, time-strapped Mumbai, smaller groups maintain personal relationships and interconnectedness. They keep people involved, cared for, and accounted for, and they provide variegated spaces for community members at different levels of their involvement, including new members, long-time members, children, and teenagers. For those who recall nostalgically the family-like atmosphere that drew them to join ISKCON while at Mumbai University or IIT, the Counselling System enables small-scale reproduction of that connectivity amid growing community spread out over one of India's largest cities. It also nuances networks of religious authority. In ISKCON congregations, the formalized reception of religious knowledge occurs through print media and multimedia temple productions. However, the Counselling System as a tool of community organization systematizes religious authority as a personal, one-on-one relationship. Like Bhaktivinoda's *nāma-haṭṭa*, it creates a fluid Gauḍīya authority structure alongside expanding congregations. In this new formation, authority is modeled on an institutionalized family-like structure. Each "counsellor" is generally a husband-wife unit, chosen by temple authorities based on their seniority within the community and shared commitment to mentoring. This centers a heterosexual married couple as the locus of authority—rather than on the individual male preachers, either *brahmacari*s or *sannyasis*—that have been central to the public face of authority in modern Gauḍīya organizations. Counselling is also directed toward a new order of recipient: people who are already committed to the Gauḍīya tradition but who seek ongoing religious formation.

As much as this model has been informed by globalized wellness discourses, it has in turn influenced ISKCON communities transnationally.[27] The system is advertised in media consumed by global ISKCON audiences and has also expanded to online networks. As of July 2015, an e-Counseling service was advertised through the community's audiovisual media hub, "ISKCON Desire Tree," that offers the opportunity for a "Live Chat with ISKCON Desire Tree e-Counselor for Spiritual Guidance" in English and Hindi. Separate counselors for men and women are available for consultation between ten o'clock in the morning and ten o'clock in the evening (India time) daily.[28]

Herein, religious guidance and the relationships that sustain religious communities are presented as a reproducible system, a product that can be commodified in diverse modern landscapes through adherence to certain principles of community care and training. The system also segues into Chowpatty's missionizing efforts. According to *brahmacaris* involved with the college-based BACE (Bhaktivedanta Academy of Culture and Education) courses, the Counselling System works in tandem with their systematic recruiting measures in neighborhoods bordering colleges and universities throughout the Mumbai metropolitan area. Additionally, several lay members who grew up in Maharashtrian cities outside Mumbai—including Satara, Nigdi, Nashik, and Kolhapur—also mentioned to me that they had begun small ISKCON centers complete with counselling networks back in their towns, which they visit periodically to hold *nāma-haṭṭa* programs. This urban-to-rural mediation of ISKCON-style religiosity is also developing in tandem with ISKCON's medical services in small towns and rural areas of Maharashtra through the humanitarian work of the temple-affiliated Bhaktivedanta Hospital. In this way, a systematized religiosity of the city is mediated to smaller urban centers through the sons of the soil themselves. But this systematized formation of Hindu traditionalism remains profoundly transnational in its character.

## The American Swami at the Heart of an Indian Temple

From the sea of blond heads at the annual Yoga Festival in Rishikesh to massive Holi festivals now held in places such as Washington DC and Salt Lake City, Utah, Hindu communities are navigating new global trends of interest in their religious traditions, buoyed by the active missionizing efforts of transnational religious groups.[29] Beyond an increasing interest in Hindu traditions within North America and Europe, Chowpatty's Radhanath Swami represents another significant trend: Western converts who have assimilated into Hindu communities in India and have garnered enough acceptance to become Hindu religious leaders of their own repute.[30] Although the Chowpatty temple congregation and *brahmacari* monks are Indian, the North American heritage of their presiding guru imbues the community with an inherently transnational character.

The spectacle of a non-Indian guru can be read through abiding racial hierarchies, which also circulate among transnational religious communities. The visuality of a white Westerner at the helm of a predominantly non-white community may convey a sense that whiteness retains a privileged power and authority, even in postcolonial contexts in which markers of Westernization or modernity are rejected. The legitimating power of whiteness can indeed be perpetuated even in predominantly non-white communities and in relation to the promotion of non-Western religious or cultural traditions.[31] Zareena Grewal's work on Muslim moral geographies highlights the role of white American Hamza Yusuf (born Mark Hanson) in promoting a view of Muslim-majority countries as an utopian archive of tradition, which Grewal argues "single-handedly altered the religious imagination of thousands of mosque Americans" in the 2000s through his popularization of a rural Mauritanian *sheikh* as a "living fossil."[32] As many religious communities shift their demographic distribution globally, even those historically linked to particular geographic and ethnic groups are now navigating multiethnic dynamics as a feature of their local communities.

At the same time, perceiving racial groups in ISKCON along a binary of white Western and brown Indian both erases the presence of many devotees (including ISKCON's own founder) and often assumes an ethnic heterogeneity within nation-states. Chowpatty's temple guest houses regularly fill with devotees from places as diverse as the Ukraine, Taiwan, and South Africa, providing links across geographic and cultural boundaries through shared membership in ISKCON. Indian and British *brahmacari*s of multiple ethnicities have cycled between ISKCON's Mumbai and London ashrams (such as the British-born Jay Shetty). ISKCON temples in India—Chowpatty included—are also increasingly shifting toward local, Indian-based leadership among *sannyasi*s, *brahmacari*s, and temple presidents. Amid these international networks, Radhanath Swami's own life story forms an important part of Chowpatty's community history, as retold at countless programs and lectures, including with cameo appearances by his family and friends who fly from Chicago and Los Angeles as guests during the temple's event-packed season in December and January. This all weaves his Jewish American roots into the "family-centric" history of the Chowpatty community itself, developing unlikely alliances between them.

Radhanath Swami was born and raised as Richard Slavin in an upper-middle-class suburb of Chicago. His parents, descendants of Eastern European Jewish immigrants to the East Coast, grew up during the Depression, and the hardships they faced figure into his retelling of family history. Although his family had periods of financial uncertainty, he generally experienced the mid-century suburban stability that was so symbolically shaken by the rise of hippie culture in the late 1960s. After a stint of enrollment at Miami Dade College, he traveled to India in 1970 as a young man in search of a spiritual path and went on to spend several years traveling among the circuits of yogis and aspiring spiritual seekers in North India. There, he adopted the lifestyle of an itinerant Hindu *sādhu* and, after studying with several gurus and yogis throughout his travels, committed to the Gauḍīya path in 1972 under Bhaktivedanta Swami. He knew Bhaktivedanta to be the founder of the well-known and controversial ISKCON and is candid about the reservations he had regarding the organization. However, through his acceptance of Bhaktivedanta as his guru, he too became an ISKCON member. He took the official lifelong monastic vow (*saṃnyāsa*) in 1982 and has since lived by the traditional codes of conduct and the cultural behavior of a Hindu mendicant, from the style of his clothing to his social interactions. Since the early 1990s, he has been based in Mumbai as the spiritual guide for the Chowpatty community, acting as initiating guru for most devotees and advisor to their expanding religious and humanitarian ventures.[33]

This transnational fabric at the heart of Chowpatty's community complicates and transforms the religious landscape of both the United States and India. Some of Chowpatty's devotees have made informal pilgrimages to the Swami's childhood home in Chicago, while his Jewish American upbringing—including lessons he derives from the family values of his mother and father—are woven into the narrative of the Chowpatty community history in lectures and informal conversations. These interconnections between family and community became clear during an evening gathering after a historic Vyāsa Pūjā, or birth anniversary celebration held for a guru, in December 2014. Chowpatty members had successfully organized this event to celebrate Radhanath Swami at South Bombay's iconic Cross Maidan festival ground, a site of great symbolism to his followers as it was the location where he met Bhaktivedanta, by chance, in 1971. During the day, the festival ground filled to capacity at 5,000 and the crowd heard from long-standing ISKCON members who read letters of dedication and gratitude to their guru. Fellow ISKCON *sannyasīs*—Indians, South Africans, Americans—also conveyed their own affection, conveying an atmosphere of institutional legitimacy for this local temple event. In addition, Radhanath Swami's father, younger brother, and a close childhood friend had all flown out from the United States for the occasion. After this large gathering, an elite group of around one hundred followers gathered at a senior member's mansion for a more intimate evening gathering. Several couples sat around a projection screen close to the far side of the large rectangular living room, surrounded by rows of devotees spread out on couches, chairs, and floor mats, extending all the way back to the hallway. A few couples who had joined the community as university students in the 1990s began to present a slideshow of Chowpatty's early days, including shots of trips to chant *japa* and sing *kīrtan* on the city's beaches. Images of early *yātrās* (pilgrimages), taken when the community still numbered only in the hundreds and everyone knew one another well, captured groups of friends huddled over lunch and giggling together or posing casually on a beach with grins and arms around each other's shoulders.[34] Radhanath Swami's younger brother Larry performed an instrumental piece on the flute, while his close childhood friend Gary Liss—now a toned physical therapist in Malibu—jokingly reminisced over their travels and mutual search for religious meaning in the early 1970s. The devout members of this elite circle of Chowpatty followers attentively looked on from the couches and floor mats spread across the marble-floored living room, as the lines between guru and friend, family and community, became hazy in their overlaps.

The links between community and family, and comical moments therein, have been particularly strong for Chowpatty's most senior devotees. The prominent temple donor and board member Narendra D. Desai relayed some instances of these interwoven family links over *dosas* at Chowpatty's Govinda restaurant one afternoon.[35] Desai, whose father introduced to the family to ISKCON when he invited Bhaktivedanta to their family home in Mumbai in 1971, completed his PhD at the University of Pennsylvania and took over his father's business, APAR Industries, in his twenties. He was one of the first devotees to meet Radhanath Swami's parents, Jerry and Idelle Slavin, when he was in Chicago for a business trip in 1993. According to his retelling, Mr. Slavin asked him, incredulous: "Why would a Ph.D. want to study under a person who only went to one semester of college? Why would a multimillionaire want to be the student of someone who hasn't had a bank account since 1969 and has nothing in his name? And most of all, why does a person whose family has been devotees of Krishna and Hindus for generation after generation want to be the student of a Jewish boy from Chicago?" Dr. Desai replied, "I can't answer your question. I can tell you so many things that you will not understand. You have to come to India to understand." These memories were relished during later visits to Mumbai by Mr. Slavin, a retired car-dealership and small-business owner whose ancestors came to the United States in the early twentieth century to escape anti-Semitism in their native Lithuania. He recalled with surprise and affection the first trip he and his wife took to Mumbai to see the religious community that their son had somehow amassed in India. After years of disappointment at their son's choice to abandon a discernible career path in preference for life in an ashram, Jerry Slavin reported being shocked and finally gladdened to see the many "respectable" middle-class and upper-class Indians of Mumbai—many businesspeople like himself—taking religious guidance from his own son.

Such memories are recounted at Chopwatty's public and private events. Through this collective retelling of both Radhanath Swami's life story and the brighter points of Chowpatty's early community history, a narrative is woven together that incorporates both of these histories—North American and Indian, individual and communal—into the notion of what the community is today. On that Vyāsa Pūjā evening, the Swami recounted a story he tells frequently. When he was around eight years old, he forgot to buy his mother a birthday present. As he returned home from school that evening, he decided that the best he could do was to sneak into the backyard and pick a rose from the garden. When he gave it to his mother, instead of being disappointed in the ad hoc gift, she smiled and said, "It's the thought that counts." In the expansive modernist living room in monochromatic shades of white, crowded rows of followers sat on sofas and floor mats as Radhanath Swami went on to discuss how the gratitude and selflessness that his mother and father taught him are at the bedrock of the core values he now tries to teach his followers in the Chowpatty community. He stressed that his early life in a suburb of Chicago informs his orientation as a guru in Mumbai and his teachings about ideal Vaiṣṇava behavior. In this unexpected way, models of piety drawn from life in a hardworking family of mid-century Jewish immigrants to the United States are repurposed and tied into the ethical framework of a Hindu revivalist community in India.

The negotiation of multiple cultures in Radhanath Swami's identity as a Gauḍīya Vaiṣṇava guru offers him a cultural cachet, but his religious authority both in India and in the United States is inextricable from his embodiment of the standards and norms of a Vaiṣṇava *sādhu*. Despite his unconventional origins for a Hindu guru, he has acted as a spiritual advisor to many of Mumbai's wealthiest business families and has become acquainted with India's political leaders due to the networking of his Indian followers. While conducting my research between 2012 and 2015, he was invited to lead religious programs at the homes of the city's most preeminent business families, including the Ambanis, the Birlas, and the Piramals, as well as the Mafatlals and Desais, who are founding members of the Chowpatty temple. He accepted invitations to attend high-profile governmental events alongside other Hindu leaders, such as a reception for President Obama at the Indian presidential mansion, Rashtrapati Bhavan, after India's 2015 Republic Day celebrations. His persona as American and Anglophone, yet also Vaiṣṇava and grounded in the monastic tradition in India, enables him a particular hybrid identity. Although the legwork of the Chowpatty media production and publicity teams is done by dedicated Indian *brahmacaris* and laity, the visual culture of Chowpatty's media products often highlight their resident guru. In ISKCON's articulation of a multilingual, globally oriented Vaiṣṇava traditionalism, he is the emblem of Chowpatty's message and central speaker at many major annual festivals. Rather than playing down his non-Indian origin, the temple's media producers highlight him as an example of the universal applicability and transnational appeal of their religion.

Through the image of Radhanath Swami as a Vaiṣṇava *sādhu*, ISKCON Chowpatty proclaims two key assertions: that brahmanical Vaiṣṇava—and by extension, Hindu—identity is attained through practice, not birth, and that the religious tradition they mediate is practiced by *choice*, palatable even to Westerners as the culmination of their search for meaning in the contemporary world. These dynamics were particularly palpable during the publication of Radhanath Swami's autobiography, *The Journey Home*, in India in 2009 and the several years of book releases and publicization that ensued, a key period in increasing elite visibility for the temple community. Translated into regional Indian languages and sold at bookstores throughout India, this autobiography of an American swami exemplified a significant crossing of ISKCON's religious messages into mainstream Hindu public cultures.

## *The Journey Home:* Completing a Global Circle of Krishna *Bhakti*

ISKCON's devotees internationally are known for missionizing through distributing books and pamphlets about their teachings in public. Chowpatty's temple *brahmacaris* and some lay devotees partake in ISKCON mainstays, such as book distribution, daily throughout the Mumbai area—on public trains, in heavily trafficked urban spaces, and at universities. A devotee may approach individuals or a pair of friends to ask a leading question such as, "Are you interested in learning more about yoga?" or "Do you know about the goal of human life?" This may then segue into a discussion about how one can learn more about Bhaktivedanta's teachings from the books on display, including his translation of Bhagavad Gītā and small paperback volumes based on conversations with early followers. Every morning after Chowpatty's first temple service—the five o'clock *maṅgala ārati*—a *brahmacari* announces the number of books distributed by each volunteer the prior day, which is met with a small, ritualized cheer by the early-morning program attendees. Book-distribution activities culminate in the annual December "Christmas marathon," begun by Bhaktivedanta Swami in the United States in 1972 but still called by that name informally even among Indian ISKCON devotees in a majority Hindu setting. The distribution of ISKCON's print media is also linked to Chowpatty's extensive internet presence.[36] Lay donations are channeled toward this missionary activity, and online updates convey stories of recent distribution efforts in Maharashtra and Gujarat and advertise opportunities to engage in "*shastra daan*," or "giving scriptures"—through sponsoring the distribution of Bhaktivedanta Swami's books. *Shastra daan* promotional materials describe this as humanitarian work and celebrate that books are distributed free of charge in rural areas and donated to public institutions such as "libraries, schools, hospital waiting rooms, and government offices." The distribution of Gauḍīya literature thus both spreads Gauḍīya religious knowledge as a form of public charity and benefits the patron as an act of *sevā*.

This focus on distributing religious literature has expanded in Chowpatty through unique temple-produced publications. While Chowpatty's publications center on a personalistic Krishna *bhakti* strictly tied to Bhaktivedanta's scriptural commentaries, they now also publish new genres, including self-help-style manuals employing principles drawn from Hindu scriptures, as well as literature centered on the life and teachings of Radhanath Swami—in particular, Radhanath Swami's autobiography, *The Journey Home: Autobiography of an American Swami*, published with Mandala Press in the United States in 2008 and then with India's Jaico Publishers in 2009.[37]

In his remarkable autobiography, Radhanath Swami guides the reader through several years of his religious search as a young man, which develops throughout his travels in Europe, the Middle East, and, finally, India. Like many Americans in his Boomer generation, he was attracted to the asceticism and spirituality of Indian gurus. His interest led him to prolonged study—first under a succession of yogic teachers in the Himalayas and later under the spiritual direction of gurus in Vaiṣṇava *bhakti* traditions. And yet, in an inversion of Paramahamsa Yogananda's classical *Autobiography of a Yogi*, here the journey of personal religious formation is not an Indian yogi detailing his training and experiences in childhood before embarking on a global mission to spread his teachings to the West but rather an American traveling to India and ultimately finding his *home* in Hindu devotion.

This description of a personal process of "crossing and dwelling" (drawing from Tweed) blends geographic movement with religious meaning, as the reader travels with Radhanath Swami through a series of miraculous experiences and a stunning series of chance meetings that punctuated his journey to an eventual meeting with Bhaktivedanta Swami in Bombay in 1971. His life narrative situates his development of Krishna *bhakti* as a series of personal realizations, linking revelatory experiences to the range of gurus and regional *bhakti* traditions he encountered throughout his wanderings as a *sādhu*. Within the autobiography, his characteristic focus on the basic values of humility, service toward others, and devotion to Krishna cast the Gauḍīya tradition in an ecumenical form that, like the proclamations of *sanātana dharma*, downplays sectarian distinctions. While Vaiṣṇava texts, particularly the Bhagavad Gītā, are mentioned, the text departs from the scholastic tone of most ISKCON publications to emphasize a broad-based spirituality, depicted as shared by the various teachers Radhanath Swami encounters throughout his journey. The Swami encourages the reader to seek out "one's own essential spiritual nature," in whichever tradition he or she is following, in contradistinction to an overt missionizing tone.

While noting his own religious formation as a disciple of Bhaktivedanta Swami and *sannyasi* in ISKCON, he also situates the book broadly as an outcome of treasures received from "the people of India, both the saints and the ordinary people. They have blessed my life with Krishna, my beloved guru, and endless opportunities to serve them and share this blessing with the world."[38] In the book's afterword, the Swami describes, from the perspective of a successful leader of a religious community, how he returned to make his permanent residence in India in 1986 in downtown Bombay. He depicts his work as "a service to my guru and to the beautiful people of India . . . in establishing several temples as spiritual educational centers, *ashrams* to cultivate pure living, and a hospital."[39] And the journey ends in a reflection of the completeness of melding of his natal home with his found spiritual home, when his parents visited him in India for the first time in 1989 and "fell in love with the Bombay devotees, who have remained some of their dearest friends." This connection was cemented by his family's request for his mother's ashes to be scattered in the Ganges after her death, which took place in 2004, as "the mother of my physical birth and a mother of my spiritual birth have united."[40] As in the in the chapter section above, the tone of this widely distributed book melds the transnational origins of Radhanath Swami with the local identity of his Mumbai temple community.

*The Journey Home*'s release was closely linked to Chowpatty's networks. Working with Jaico Press, Shubha Vilas (then a resident *brahmacari*) founded an in-house press, Tulsi Books, to facilitate the distribution of the autobiography and anticipated future works, with the aim of managing their distribution to mainstream bookstores.[41] While in India between 2012 and 2014, I found *The Journey Home* at major bookstores in Mumbai, Ahmedabad, and Lucknow, spanning a geographic and cultural range far beyond ISKCON's typical distribution. Meanwhile, Chowpatty's managerial networks coordinated extensive press coverage, coupled with endorsements from local celebrities and businesspeople who take personal guidance from Radhanath Swami. An eminent business power couple, Swati and Ajay Piramal, managed the promotion the book, and a number of household names from Bollywood and cricket fame endorsed it on television and radio.[42] The book premiered with a Mumbai book launch hosted by Swati Piramal and events led by actress Juhi Chawla. In addition, prominent business leaders Yash Birla, Hrishikesh Mafatlal, and N. D. Desai, as well as artist Nawaz Modi Singhania, endorsed the book on stage at the National Centre for the Performing Arts in Mumbai in August 2009. The event was advertised in local English and Hindi news media, with photographs of businesspeople, fashion designers, and actors in the audience.[43] As *Outlook*'s glitterati section put it: "A *gora* [white] swami and his autobiography saw the swish set of Mumbai show up in full strength."[44] The book's release thus became an event in high-society Mumbai, promoting the affiliation of celebrities to Radhanath Swami and, by extension, ISKCON.

After its English release, the autobiography was translated into Hindi as *Anokha Safar*, "A Unique Journey," and later into Marathi, Gujarati, Telugu, Bengali, Tamil, and other regional Indian languages—largely by teams of *brahmacari*s in the Chowpatty ashram, into their mother tongues. Continuing the arc that Bhaktivedanta began with his translation of Gauḍīya texts from Bengali and Sanskrit to English, *The Journey Home* came to symbolize a full-circle translation of ISKCON's religious worldview back into regional Indian languages, through the medium of an American swami. While within Mumbai, the publicization of *The Journey Home* took place largely through English-language news media, but throughout the rest of the country, Telugu, Gujarati, and Hindi newspapers featured stories on the regional translations of *The Journey Home* and Radhanath Swami's teachings throughout 2010 and 2011.[45]

The Ahmedabad-based Gujarati *Divya Bhaskar* advertised the Gujarati Book Launch event with a large image of Radhanath Swami, eminent Gujarati-origin businessman Hrishikesh Mafatlal, and Narendra Modi holding a stage-prop cover of *The Journey Home* in Gujarati.[46] This image conveys a nexus of religious, economic, and political power grounded in Hindu Gujarati identity, with Radhanath Swami remarkably promoting the place of Vaiṣṇava religious tradition. Kannada news publications in Bangalore released similar pieces in January 2010, following the release of the Kannada translation. Therein, photos of local notables posed with prop book covers alongside proclamations on Hindu *dharma*, such as in Bangalore's *Prajavani*, entitled: "India's Strength is in the Hindu *dharma*." The most elaborate regional media focus was in the Hindi *Prabhat Khabar*, distributed in Bihar, Jharkhand, and West Bengal. *Prabhat Khabar*'s longtime managing director, K. K. Goenka, discussed at a book-club event for *The Journey Home* in early 2013 how he became an ardent follower of Radhanath Swami through reading his autobiography. Accordingly, his paper organized a gala event for the book launch in Ranchi, in December 2013, as well as a series of speaking events for Radhanath Swami in Patna. The newspaper publicized the events on its front page for four consecutive days, with a note of apology on the final day for having exhausted all entry passes to the events. Pictures of Radhanath Swami accompanied excerpts from his teachings on how to experience "genuine divine love" (*aslī prem*) and quotes from what audience members took away from *swāmī-jī*'s words, cementing him in the role of a respected Hindu guru from whom the public can glean knowledge about *bhakti*.

Through the orchestration of broad media coverage, the publication of *The Journey Home* propelled ISKCON into a new sphere of public visibility, miles away from the sensational news reports of the 1970s and 1980s in the city's news sources.[47] Radhanath Swami's broadcasted devoutness served at once as a call to tradition and cosmopolitan novelty—an American *sannyasi* who links Mumbai's successful businesspeople and actors to Vaiṣṇava pilgrimage towns and *bhakta*s throughout the centuries. While many regional-language news stories in Hindi, Kannada, and Marathi emphasized the timeless (*sanātana*) character of Radhanath Swami's teachings and promoted the importance of Hindu *dharma* to Indians today, Mumbai's English publications focused on his celebrity following. Many prominent public figures who publicized the book's release had taken religious guidance from

Radhanath Swami for years prior to these events, and the advertisement of these connections led to an increasingly normalization of the Swami—and ISKCON by extension—as an available location of religious piety among Mumbai's business elite. And this period cemented the ISKCON Chowpatty temple's visibility in local news media as a celebrity destination for marking important life events, such as a joint family visit to the temple after the engagement of Isha Ambani and Anand Piramal (children of two of Mumbai's most eminent business families) in 2018 and the place of honor accorded to Radhanath Swami at the Ambani-Piramal wedding.[48]

New speaking venues, developed in parallel to the professional networks of close followers, have reinforced the corporate business and engineering profile reflected in many Chowpatty members' professional circles. One example of this is the Artha Forum, an invite-only event that advertised the promotion of ethical business practices internationally under the motto of "Ancient Wisdom, Modern Business." When I attended its second annual summit meeting at the Govardhan Ecovillage in 2012, organized by Chowpatty's prominent business families, Radhanath Swami presented a keynote speech about applying ethics from the Bhagavad Gītā to business practices. Neat rows of followers sat as through any conference presentation, wearing nametags including their company affiliations and holding workshop folders along with the legal pads and pens provided to each attendee on their laps. The forum sought to develop transnational business networks for its corporate attendees, drawing a majority Indian-origin audience from Mumbai and Delhi and as far afield as London and Philadelphia. This was followed by conferences in the United Arab Emirates, Singapore, London, and Silicon Valley throughout 2015 and 2017. At the latter, the first Indian *sannyasi* discipline of Radhanath Swami, Bhakti Rasamrita Swami—who worked at a multinational bank before joining the ashram—spoke alongside transnational Indian business leaders in a series of talks entitled "Dharma in Business."

This popularization of ISKCON among certain circles in Mumbai's business elite has occurred prominently through corporate events organized by followers in business and international technology sectors. Far from ISKCON's temple venues, these events occur at venues such as the All-India Management Association (AIMA) World Marketing Congress in Delhi, the Association of Medical Consultants in Mumbai, and a Confederation of Indian Industry meeting held the prestigious Trident Hotel at Nariman Point, Mumbai.[49] The latter, held in a hotel conference room, began with

Radhanath Swami offering a formal Sanskrit prayer intoning his Gauḍīya guru lineage, with hands folded in a prayerful pose. He looked conspicuous in saffron robes amid corporate managers in suits and ties. Though as he spoke about the importance of maintaining selflessness and humility in one's corporate dealings, the two CEOs flanking him at the conference table (both initiated ISKCON devotees) looked down in polite deference to his words. Radhanath Swami has been foregrounded as a Hindu *sādhu* at similar events organized by followers in India and abroad, including at the corporate headquarters of HSBC, Google, Apple, Starbucks, and Ford Motor Company; and in political spaces, such as before members of Parliament at the UK House of Commons at an interfaith event on "Spirituality and Big Society," responding to the political catchphrase of then–Prime Minister David Cameron.

Beyond this coupling of religious and corporate agendas, Radhanath Swami's appearance in the dress and cultural role of a Hindu *sādhu*, situated within a specific lineage (*paramparā*), represents a shift in popular global religious culture—from the well-known, sometimes caricatured Indian guru in the West to an American guru in India. The cultural space occupied by this Occidental Monk in some ways echoes tropes attendant in Iwamura's discussion of the "Oriental Monk" that pervaded popular culture in the United States throughout the twentieth century.[50] Yet as a "figure of translation" for urban Indians, Radhanath Swami signifies a very different engagement with Hindu traditions. While the Swami is not the first or only individual embodying this cultural combination, his appeal seems to reside not only in the cultural cachet of being American but in the spectacle of a Westerner adopting Indian religious traditions *in place of* his cultural upbringing. This normalization of a Vaiṣṇava guru from Chicago within Mumbai's elite circles speaks to changing discourses of the nature of Hindu tradition and who has the implicit authority to speak for it.

In a meeting in Radhanath Swami's quarters one quiet sunny afternoon, I sat at the foot of the bookshelves lined with *The Journey Home* in Hindi, Tamil, Telugu, and Odia, arrayed facing outward on display. He seemed both delighted and a bit amused at the display of these translations—set up by several of his *brahmacari* assistants—that celebrated his achievements and theirs, as the translators of this volume into ever-more regional scripts. As he gazed at the shelves, he acknowledged the directional reversal in ISKCON's global missionizing. Quoting Bhaktivedanta Swami, he extended his arms fully on each side to illustrate that "people in the West are starting out far from Krishna but are coming closer now," whereas "people from India are starting out very close to Krishna . . . and if we just get them to respect that we really are representing something deep and pure . . . and that's actually what is happening." In other words, it is a matter of conveying to their Indian audiences that they are representing a deep and pure form of Hindu traditions—an inheritance of India rather than something innovative—or in other words, "bringing Krishna back to India."

## Becoming a Local Orthodoxy

Although Radhanath Swami occupies an unparalleled place as guru to most of Chowpatty's congregants, he often travels abroad and has delegated increasing powers to a broad range of senior Indian disciples, some of whom (like Gaur Gopal and Shubha Vilas) are now prominent public figures well outside of ISKCON circles. And institutionally, the community has fully reversed its previously excommunicated status and is now lauded in ISKCON internationally, held up as a model for temple communities from London to Omsk.[51] The incorporation of Chowpatty into ISKCON's global network developed in tandem with the temple's own growth. By the early 2000s, the temple board developed the financial capital to expand and renovate the temple compound. As longtime devotees relate, rusty iron stairwells were replaced with carved sandstone balconies, a central air-conditioning system was installed to keep the temple room temperature-controlled during crowded weekly programs, and previously informal, patchworked structures were renovated and incorporated into a new posh temple complex.

Today, alongside the temple community's visible transnational markers, the temple architecture and its traditionalist atmosphere ground it in the language of a local orthodoxy, depicting links to early-modern and twentieth-century Indian histories. The main temple building is lined with sandstone-carved exteriors and lattice screens, imported from Jaipur and fashioned by Rajasthani craftsmen in an early modern architectural style. The elaborately carved doors, balcony windows, and altar echo this architectural heritage in rich shades of teak wood, evoking the style of early Gauḍīya temples in Vrindavan and around the princely states in Rajasthan, which were constructed under Rajput and Mughal patronage. The inclusion of *bangla* domes also signal both the Bengali heritage of the Gauḍīya tradition and the time period during which the Gauḍīyas developed their presence in North India, under the reigns of Akbar and later Shahjahan, who popularized the *bangla* style in seventeenth-century North Indian architecture.[52] Aside from signaling the Gauḍīya tradition's important development under the patronage of Rajput kings in a Mughal milieu, these architectural elements reinforce ISKCON's indigeneity in an Indian landscape through the material culture they display.

And the material landscape of the temple compound is premised on evoking that heritage, as an alternative to the secular, chaotic city outside. In keeping with that, Western clothing is discouraged and specific food items that are considered impure and polluting—including meat, fish, eggs, garlic, onions, alcohol, and cigarettes—are prohibited on site. But the temple complex aims at facilitating an alternative modern lifestyle as well, by providing food, entertainment, and an active social schedule for visitors of all ages. To this end, newer additions to the temple compound include Govinda's Vegetarian Restaurant, opened in 2006 and operated by the Shetty family, members of the congregation originally from Udupi, Karnataka, and proprietors of the popular Śrīnāthjī restaurant chain of vegetarian restaurants throughout the city. Famous for its twelve varieties of *dosa*s named after the twelve forests of Vrindavan, the restaurant also serves up popular Asian and "continental fare" including an Indo-Chinese menu; a range of sandwiches, salads, and soups; and a selection of pizzas cooked in an oven imported from Florence, Italy—where Radhanath Swami enjoys a small but ardent following. Govinda's caters to vegetarian Gujarati Vaiṣṇava and Jain communities of nearby Malabar Hill and aligns with changing food cultures in the area, as the vegetarian restaurants opened by Udupi migrants to the city over the past fifty years have gradually replaced the ubiquity of South Bombay's historic Parsi cafes, fitting within a civic context that Fernandes describes as increasingly vegetarian and centered in classicized dharmic religious culture.[53]

The transformation of this secular city block into a modern religious oasis is reflected in the gradual expansion of the temple premises into a multifunctioning complex for worship, social events, entertainment, education, and financial services. Guest accommodations, which cater to the constant stream of visitors that swells during festival seasons, have been carved out of adjacent tenant-occupied apartment buildings, as the temple gradually acquires flats from neighbors ready to sell. The reception office in the central courtyard welcomes visitors and serves as a resource point for temple activities. A nearby office block houses the Bhaktivedanta Academy for Culture and Education (BACE), which offers adult scriptural education courses on the Gītā and early Gauḍīya literature. This complex also houses Gopal's Fun

School, a volunteer-run educational center for children that has expanded to provide more generic religious education courses to working adults on weekends and weekday afternoons, including "Tips for Good Parenting" and "Stress Management." As Radhika, one of the volunteer teachers, tells me, they provide a great alternative to the "kitty parties" of wealthy South Bombay housewives. Many courses are developed and taught by a handful of young women—from comfortable middle-class Hindu and Jain religious backgrounds, spanning Punjabi, Marwari, and Kannadiga families. They aim to attract women who might not otherwise think of spending time in a temple context, easing them and their children into regular visits to the temple.

In addition to education, various divisions of the temple administration provide financial services for temple members. On the lower level of the main temple building, the PARTH Seva Department organizes hospitality and develops formal strategies of recognition for new members and the temple's donors. On the first floor, financial offices include a large accounting

**Fig. 2.5** Devotees fill the rooftop of ISKCON Juhu's Heaven on Earth building, listening to a lecture by Radhanath Swami to honor India's Republic Day, 2015. Photo by the author.

division staffed by around ten devotees, as well as a travel office that arranges annual community *yātrās* and the many smaller *yātrās* throughout the year. These staff members share office space with the Yamuna Kinara ("bank of the Yamuna," a name that plays on the riverbank location of Krishna's pastoral *līlās*), a financial center founded to assist devotees in hardship and to provide a safe investment opportunity for their retirement funds and savings accounts.[54] The temple itself has non-profit status as a religious institution, so these services are conducted within that overarching legal identity. The financial office also had to scale back their investment and savings services due to the 2009 financial crisis. However, the intent to provide core financial services for devotees accords with many of the impulses of the temple infrastructure—the cultivation of a devout Vaiṣṇava community parallel to but demarcated from the city outside.

For community members who travel throughout the city to reach it, the temple space functions as a structured and bounded religious utopia—or "eutopia," a good place—to draw from Smriti Srinivas, in conversation with other aspirational urban spaces that seek to construct garden oases amid increasingly polluted and over-crowded metropolitan sprawl (Figure 2.5).[55] Unlike many traditional Hindu temples, it is a place with a solid and defined congregation, a range of community services offered through on-site offices staffed with degree-holding professionals, and an official system of trained volunteers who welcome guests and politely guide them through the process of joining the congregation. Weekly Sunday meetings are the liturgical highlight of the community's regular calendar—stemming, intriguingly, from ISKCON's development in the context of a Christian-centered liturgical context in the United States. In between weekly programs community members are kept informed of upcoming events and *sevā* opportunities through emails, texts, and neighborhood devotee networks, while organized groups within the community offer regular programs for various gender and age groups from their homes throughout the week.

Chowpatty's devotee community thus situates ISKCON's transnational institutional norms within a modern Indian context. As the next four chapters will show, this remakes the categories of family, culture, nation, and religion for Indian devotees through a network of new relationships. For any potential member, all these elements highlight a specific process of joining, as a journey of crossing into new identities as devotees, often through acts that demarcate them from their personal past and family traditions, be they religious or secular, even while inculcating a sense of reviving a lost religious heritage. Indeed, everyone I spoke with had their own narrative of joining—specific moments and interactions that brought them into the community and encouraged them to commit, take on a religious counsellor, and eventually vow to uphold ISKCON's strict lifestyle and *sādhana* prescriptions. It is in these narratives of crossing into the identity of a devotee that the work of revising religion becomes palpable. As I shall show in the following chapters, this recommitment to a religious heritage refigures that heritage as something gained through a systematic process of education and training, premised on replacing the doubt and uncertainty of a modern urban life with the conviction of representing a lineage that can—in a phrase common among devotees—"answer all one's questions."

# 3

# Crossing Over

## Entering the Devotional Family

> At first, I just added going to the temple on to my Jain identity. But after about five years, he gave me an ultimatum: "you cannot keep your feet in two boats. Either you're here or you're there. If you're convinced of Krishna consciousness, then please leave your Jainism." That night, I just thought and thought and thought, and I said I'm definitely convinced about Krishna consciousness.
>
> Meghna, volunteer teacher at the Chowpatty temple's adult-education classes

In contemporary Mumbai, ISKCON's global mission of promoting Vaiṣṇava religious traditions takes on new implications. Unlike its development in North America and Europe, ISKCON in India can claim to represent the historic religion of the majority and employ a rhetoric of reviving traditional Hindu culture. But there is a circularity in religious revivalism—this form of becoming religious is not often a return to practitioners' ancestral pasts but an agentive, interpretative idea of religious traditions. Revivalists imagine a different future for themselves through adopting a lifestyle inscribed with a past ideal. Accordingly, to become religious in ISKCON terms involves the adoption of conservative Vaiṣṇava traditionalism, which differentiates most devotees from their family traditions and the predominant cultures of the city. As many young Indians decide how they want to position themselves in relation to family and heritage—which aspects they want to preserve and which they feel are outmoded—ISKCON's courses and media products guide them toward an ideal of Hindu traditionalism as a lifestyle set apart from Mumbai's secular mainstream. ISKCON's representation of religious traditionalism can be appealing not only among Hindus but also other young people in the city—notably Jains, but also occasionally Sikhs and Catholics

*Bringing Krishna Back to India.* Claire C. Robison, Oxford University Press. © Oxford University Press 2024.
DOI: 10.1093/9780197656488.003.0004

who became acquainted with ISKCON courses on the Bhagavad Gītā or meditation techniques through college friends or their workplace. This chapter centers on the process of "crossing over" into ISKCON, focusing on the stories of several young devotees in the Chowpatty temple community. To convey the significance of their journeys in context, I will begin with a few instances of family and friends' reactions, to illustrate the shifting bonds of kinship that joining ISKCON may entail.

## Outside the Looking Glass

To be religious in Mumbai is nothing new. While the "city of dreams" is known for its permissive film industry and generally liberal social ethos compared to its northern Indian counterparts, religious presence is palpable throughout Mumbai's streets and manifest in many forms. Religion thrives from the wayside shrines that adorn trees, the sides of buildings, and storefronts, to the many established temples, churches, and mosques that serve as neighborhood landmarks and visible testaments to the communities who have lived there over the centuries of the city's development.[1]

Yet many in the city—across class, caste, and age lines—view religious piety pejoratively. Among diverse friend groups I met in the city, a mix of curiosity and concern about religion was tied to anxieties about the hegemonic potential of piety. In contrast to my sustained interest in talking about *pandits*, priests, and scriptures, they barely entered many people's everyday lives, outside of occasional family celebrations or in passing jest. The decision to adopt conservative religious norms seemed both unusual and also like a potential judgment of their own lifestyles—one that could be accentuated through instruments of the state. This sentiment has increased as Hindu nationalist groups affiliated with the Sangh Parivar publicly promote themselves as arbiters of a conservative and chauvinistic religiosity in the public sphere, harassing Muslim college students who wear *hijab* to school in Karnataka, for instance, or young women who go to bars or dare to loiter at night.[2] And aside from discussions of Hindu nationalism, national debates about the phenomenon of mega gurus and opaque temple donation structures elicit suspicion in popular media, such as the films *OMG* (2012) and *PK* (2014). This can imbue religious piety with a sharp edge for those who do not see themselves reflected in public spaces centered on Hindu traditionalism.

Accordingly, Indian friends who came to know of my research joked about how different the daily lives of devout Hindus were from their own. Friends or relatives who joined ISKCON were often viewed as a strange curiosity, spoken about with eyebrows raised at their strict religious norms. This was something a friend and local journalist, Mario, reminded me of regularly. Mario's Goan Catholic family has lived in the historic seaside neighborhood of Bandra for generations. As a historically Catholic locale, where families considered low caste or Dalit have long enjoyed a comfortable middle-class life, Bandra has become a naturally welcoming place for many who do not pass the rigors of conservative *savarna* Hindu communities, wherein securing housing is often dependent on one's perceived religion and caste. The eclectic residents of Bandra range from long-established East Indian Catholic families, to foreigners in the city like myself, to well-known Bollywood stars and aspiring actors who prefer the area's open ethos and seaside location, to Muslim families displaced from their South Bombay homes during the 1992–1993 riots who found safety amid this predominantly religious minority area.

As we strolled amid this diverse and welcoming neighborhood, Mario gestured to one of the many stone cross shrines that pay homage to those who died from the bubonic plague, which devastated the population from 1896 into the first decades of the twentieth century. Inscribed at their base with records of those lost, these crosses serve as wayside shrines for offerings of flowers and votive candles. On a steep winding road leading up Pali Hill, the shrine stood next to an alcove housing an image of the Madonna. It marked the site of Mario's great-grandfather's former farmland, noting that he took a leading role in helping families of plague victims before his own life was claimed. Among his many descendants, some dutifully attend weekly services at St. Mary's or St. Anne's, but many simply congregate in family homes for a shared Sunday meal of *sorpotel*, Goan pork curry, fish curry, or prawns *balchão*.

One of Mario's uncles joined ISKCON decades ago, he relates: "He's a nice guy and all, he still comes to family gatherings. But he just keeps himself a little apart, tells us we shouldn't be eating meat or this and that. He's fully into it, goes to temple, wears his *lungi* and everything, very strict and married a wife there who is just as strict." I envision Mario's uncle Fernando, with his strict Hindu wife, wearing a *lungi* (a traditional men's lower garment, or more likely a *dhoti*) amid a raucous Sunday family gathering. There, the very choice of dress draws clear lines between his uncle's adopted lifestyle and the seaside cool of what has been called the Bandra uniform: a Hawaiian shirt, cotton shorts, and flip flops. Although an outlier in the temple's predominantly Hindu and Jain demographics, Fernando—now called Amala Das, the servant of the pure or stainless one—also signals the reach of ISKCON's appeal to draw Mumbaikars across different backgrounds into their tight-knit community. While he has maintained family ties, others feel hurt by how family or friends who joined the community seemed to end relationships with those who were not practicing devotees.

When Sheela and I met through a mutual journalist friend over lunch at a breezy café near Marine Drive, the main topic of conversation was Modi's recent election for his first term as prime minister. But as soon as she heard about my research topic, conversation immediately shifted to Sheela's closest girlfriend from college, Ruchi, who not only joined ISKCON but married into a prominent temple donor family. Sheela reflected on her own lack of comprehension about her friend's choice. Reminiscing about their college days, she reiterated her surprise: "It seems that she just adopted a new identity. Is that what you have to do to gain *bhakti*?" There was muffled laughter and eye rolls all around from the other local journalists at the table, who were used to encountering that term in its political repurposing for Modi *bhakts*, ardent supporters of the BJP government. Aware of the dual connotations, Sheela balanced her frustration about Ruchi's choice with an empathetic questioning: "Why would she change her life and even her personality so dramatically? I don't know. Does she feel like she had to become fully pious to be the perfect daughter-in-law? Was that the deal for her to marry into that family? Or does she really believe all of it?" In her new, high-profile family, Ruchi has become a public face for ISKCON, often presenting awards and introducing speakers on stage at upscale events. In her graceful saris and a measured public-speaking voice, one would never know that she had been the snarky, irreverent teenager the Sheela remembered fondly, skipping classes and always primed with the perfect excuses to avoid censure.

These expressions of dissonance speak to the gap between ISKCON's devotional piety and everyday life for many Mumbaikars. In such a milieu, joining ISKCON is viewed as a transformative process, of crossing over into a new identity altogether. And on a pragmatic level, for those not "marrying in," devout religiosity carries social baggage. As Gopika, a lifelong South Bombay resident and Chowpatty's most sought-after counsellors, put it: "In Mumbai, parents complain that young people have become Westernized and irreligious. Yet when the young men and women want to take up Krishna consciousness, their parents often worry. 'Who will want to marry such a religious person?' "

And yet, Chowpatty's religious mission exhorts followers to transform their lives through adopting strict, brahmanically inflected Hindu religious and social norms. This promotion of conservative religiosity is articulated as a "return," to an idea of a purer premodern, preindustrial religious heritage, overlaying natal structures of kinship and religious authority with new notions of community and authority through ISKCON's discipleship and counselling systems. These institutional structures offer members an ability to lock into a traditionalist framework that can guide everything from day-to-day decisions to major life choices, from what to eat for dinner to whom to marry. While skeptics may find that restrictive, others welcome the structure and support a tight-knit religious community can provide.

## Becoming Religious in the City

In cosmopolitan, liberal Mumbai, ISKCON's devotees inhabit a visible countercultural status, noticeably more devout in traditional cotton *dhoti*s and *tilak*, clay forehead markings, than most others they may pass on the streets. Infusing one's identity with an ardent devotionalism contrasts with many mainstays of urban Indian life—from the fast fashion clothing trends on display at the malls in Lower Parel and the latest Bollywood films in the cinemas to trendy restaurants in nightlife hubs like Bandra and Kala Ghoda. For many devotees, becoming religious also marks a commitment to try to remake their urban surroundings through their religious aspirations, to change themselves as well as their city—a series of crossings into a new religious modernity.

In these accounts, I will employ Thomas Tweed's language of religion as a series of crossings—translocative and transtemporal but also symbolic—to describe the process of joining a religious community. Tweed emphasizes the fundamental importance of movement, relation, and position in relation to the transnational migration of communities and the malleability of their religious traditions in ways that reflect different stages in the journeys of communities or individuals. But, as he indicates in expanding this language to a theory of religion broadly, the formations of crossing over and crossing into are not unique to the religion of migrants. Rather, religious traditions are never static or unchanging. In applying this approach to describe religious conversion or the adoption of a new religious lifestyle, I want to emphasize how profoundly a person's "location" within a city and relation to family members and friends within it can change through the transformation of religious identity. In this case too, migration even within a country as vast as India can entail a similar sense of self-re-creation, in moving from a tight-knit family in a small town to attend college in a megacity where different languages are spoken and different gods are worshipped. Through examining the two sides of the coin of Tweed's theory of religion—crossing and dwelling—I will examine both the significance of choosing a life of strict Vaiṣṇava devotionalism in a predominantly secular Indian city and also the new spaces for dwelling, or homemaking, that entail the formation of new kinship-like bonds (Figure 3.1). Beyond any one organization, these accounts of crossings or personal transformations are central to living religious revivalism.

Aaditya, who was finishing a PhD in chemical engineering, spoke of antagonism toward religiosity at the local engineering and technology colleges that have been prime missionizing sites for ISKCON. He was largely raised within the Chowpatty community by two South Indian parents who joined when he was a child. Although he was not thoroughly committed to any religious practices when he enrolled as an undergraduate at the Indian Institute of Technology (IIT), Mumbai, he now characterizes college as being particularly challenge for maintaining a devout identity. From drinking and parties on weekends to casual dining-hall conversations, "religious students feel pressured not to show their piety" and to adopt "generally atheistic views." He said he felt this as a first year and then saw it clearly every time a new batch of students would arrive. This, he proposes, is a problem linked to urbanization in India and the journeys people are taking to attend college. Many students at Mumbai's engineering and technology institutes arrive from diverse parts of the country, many raised in small towns or regional cities. For Aaditya, their "simplicity" when they first arrive is a product of that upbringing, and their experiences in the city change them fundamentally by the time of their graduation. He attributes this to a secularizing force woven into the structure of Mumbai's educational and professional institutions. This perceived nonreligious atmosphere led him to want to transform the college experience for others, like himself, who sought a space for religion in its institutions. Today, a decade on from his graduation, he goes regularly to his local alma mater to speak with younger students at ISKCON Chowpatty's college outreach programs and to encourage them, as he sees it, to retain their simplicity

Fig. 3.1 View from a temple balcony of devotional dancing and chanting at a weekly service, 2013. Photo by the author.

without "being corrupted" by the influences of the city. Aaditya's depictions situate ISKCON as a protector and reviver of traditional lifeways that he depicts as under threat from the modern environment of an urban engineering college.

These are views shared by many devotees at the temple. Manu, a medical professional in her thirties, lives up the road in the seaside neighborhood of Breech Candy and owns her own clinic in the neighborhood. Unlike Aaditya, Manu joined ISKCON on her own volition as a young mother in her twenties, after coming across the temple's afternoon classes for children. Although she did not grow up with much religious practice, she was looking for an opportunity to teach them Sanskrit and introduce them to Hindu scriptures. Today, she teaches classes on those same scriptures at the temple for aspiring adult members. Manu describes the challenge of appealing to many locals, however, as particular to the temple's demographic positioning in Mumbai. She emphasizes the "more Westernized culture" that is normative in the city and the affluence on display in South Bombay in particular. And indeed, a stroll through the temple's neighborhood in a sari and the Vaiṣṇava *tilak* forehead marking—the most preferred outfit for women at the temple—would ensure some subtly raised eyebrows from local jean-clad and business-casual residents on their way home from work or school. Yet, while special missionizing efforts are made to appeal to the city's posh, "Westernized" residents—who do represent the demographic of the temple's main financial donors—many of the temple's ardent members commute from middle-class neighborhoods where religious devotion is a more visible part of public spaces. Yet throughout Mumbai's varied social classes, the enactment of ISKCON's visible piety signals a distinct traditionalism.

One afternoon while sitting in the shaded temple courtyard, Aaditya offered his analysis of which people in India are drawn to join ISKCON based on "the traditional character" of their upbringing. Imparting a popularly held view among devout Vaiṣṇavas, he mentioned that South Indians are known to be more religiously devout and are therefore more attracted to join a community like Chowpatty. Hailing himself from Tamil Smarta brahmin heritage, he reasoned that attraction to the community can be correlated to family background, specifically: "how pious that person's upbringing was . . . Generally, those who are simpler in their upbringing are easier to take up Krishna consciousness than people who have a very complicated upbringing and people who are from cities." His view also expresses a larger orientation among many modern religious Hindus, to see devoutness as a characteristic of small-town and traditional upbringings as contrasted with the unclear moral bearings of modern, urban lifestyles.

However, many devotees described their decision to join ISKCON to be precisely because of disaffection with *their* modern, urban life and what they perceive as a lack of mooring in religious traditions. In fact, many of the "coming to Krishna consciousness" narratives that I heard involved a deep discomfort with elite socio-economic status and the urban aspirations for affluence that in intriguing ways mirror a similar rejection made by the also mainly middle-class and upper-class young people who joined ISKCON in 1960s and 1970s America—a comparison curiously made in ISKCON Chowpatty's promotional literature. However, despite their shared institutional link, Chowpatty's Indian followers bear little resemblance to the hippie aesthetic or lifestyle choices associated with ISKCON's early American devotees. In contemporary India, devotees are encouraged to pair their piety with cultivating a successful career, and affluence and professional prestige remain characteristics of congregants' lives, alongside the prominence of humanitarian work and the ethics of *sevā* in the temple's activities.

## "You Cannot Keep Your Feet in Two Boats"

New members and those interested in joining the Chowpatty community described their process of joining in the language of crossing from one way of life to another. This often involved a stage of reflection, sometimes lasting several years, on whether they felt comfortable parting with aspects of their regional and family cultures to adopt ISKCON's cultural norms and religious orthodoxy. This is often an easier transition for those who grew up in brahmanical Vaiṣṇava homes where many of ISKCON's practices were already legible, than it is for those from Jain or Catholic families, who undergo more of a conversion process. However, even members who hailed from Gujarati or Tamil Vaiṣṇava traditions described growing up in urban contexts and leading lifestyles that were far more liberal than the strict regulations that good ISKCON standing demands. This leads to a continuing negotiation of what ISKCON membership means for them and how it can relate to their own upbringings and social identities—an ongoing process of crossing out of the norms of the secular city or even other religious practices and into a Vaiṣṇava devotional identity.

Meghna was brought up in Mumbai's tightknit Marwari Jain community and had already married into another Jain family at the time of her interest in Krishna devotion. When I came to know her, she worked alongside Manu as one of a team of young women who were volunteer instructors and administrators at the temple's weekday adult-education courses on the

Bhagavad Gītā and lifestyle management. Meghna's entrance into the community was gradual, largely through the influence of Anil, her cousin by marriage, who in turn had been brought into the community by another Jain friend who had converted and taken the vows of a renounced monk, *brahmacari*. This loose association of Jain aspirants would meet occasionally at various family apartments in South Bombay to discuss connections between the ethos of austerity and devotion in both Jainism and Vaiṣṇavism. They began to cook meals for their gatherings and offer them to images of Krishna in their kitchens, subtly shifting from the food rituals common in their family homes.

But first, Meghna reflected, she "just added going to the temple" onto her Jain identity, continuing to attend all family functions and frequent her local Jain temple with her mother, particularly large festival gatherings. This, of course, would be a standard approach for generations of South Asians who have occupied liminal religious identities or visited multiple religious sites for healing or divine blessings. ISKCON, however, designates a more exclusive stance on membership—one that requires members to refrain from worshipping at sites other than ISKCON or related Vaisnava temples that share its ritual and lifestyle norms. This exclusivity, consequently, prompts members' commitment to ISKCON to take the form of a more substantial crossing over from one identity to another. Such a demarcation would not take shape in the less institutionalized forms of religious identity that characterize Mumbai's many neighborhood shrines. This crossing over particularly impacts those ISKCON members who are asked to refrain from family and community rituals. Meghna described her own process of crossing to be gradual, beginning from 2001 onward. Five years later, she was still participating in the public Jain rituals associated with the annual festival of Paryushana, including the performance of *pratikraman*. Then, one day she said that Anil, who by that time had become a local ISKCON leader in his own right, sat her down and depicted a crossroads in her religious practice: "you cannot keep your feet in two boats. Either you're here or you're there. If you're convinced of Krishna consciousness, then please leave your Jainism." That night, Meghna relayed, "I just thought and thought and thought and I said, 'I'm definitely convinced about Krishna consciousness.' From that time on, I refused to come for the Paryushana," a major annual Jain festival. There were social consequences.

> After that, every day when all 1,500 families of Marwari Jains in Mumbai would see that I'm not coming, they would call and say, 'what are you

> doing?' They all know each other and are related to each other. And once I took that step, people were shocked that I was not doing *pratikraman* on Paryushana. . . It was a huge hype.

The public spectacle of Meghna's decision to cross into ISKCON—marked as much by her adoption of ISKCON's *sādhana* as by her absence from her family's participation in Jain festivals—was intimately tied to a shift in religious rituals. While ISKCON Vaiṣṇava and Jains share many of the same vegetarian food practices, orthodox Jains are stricter on certain issues, such as the traditional prescription not to eat after dark. The transition to attending ISKCON's many evening gatherings did not always come easily, as she relayed: "Once I started eating at night, I thought, 'God, what am I doing?' So, it was a very difficult transition from Jainism to this. But now I'm totally convinced that what I did is right."

Although breaks with family practices are prominent in how many devotees relay their journey of crossing into ISKCON, their commitment to its religiously grounded life was frequently asserted as a *fuller* practice of their ancestral religious tradition. Therein family traditions were rewritten in the image of ISKCON practices. Ruby, a dental clinician who also grew up Jain in the nearby South Bombay neighborhood of Tardeo, volunteers as a temple administrator, organizing the enrollment and scheduling for the temple's adult-education courses. Like Meghna, Ruby was in her mid-twenties when she decided to join ISKCON and, consequently, to give up her family's Jain practices. She, too, became the subject of criticism from family and friends over her relinquishment of Jain rituals and her sudden refusal to attend community services. But she argued back, first to her mother and then to the aunties in her neighborhood, asserting that *through* ISKCON she was practicing Jain ethics more fully. She centered on their shared adherence to vegetarianism and avoidance of onions and garlic, pointing out to her mother that she was now following those Jain dietary regulations more strictly than many of her devout relatives. That point, she says with pride, even her mother has to concede! With a satisfied smile, Ruby relayed the turning point in her mother's acceptance of her decision to join ISKCON despite a difference in religious beliefs:

> We Jains, there is no concept of God, they just believe in a *tīrthaṅkara* and guru, and they say you have to follow whatever the *tīrthaṅkara* said. . . They're just totally into rituals, mostly fasting and they should not eat onion

> and garlic—anything that grows underground. So my parents are Jains and one day [my mother] told me: "What are you doing? You were born in a Jain family and you've ruined our name and all. You can't just do something else."

We were in Mumbai for dinner and I'm asking for Jain food because I don't eat onion-garlic and they're Jain but they were eating onion-garlic, and I was thinking: "who's following better now, me or you?" And now, after these years, she appreciates it. It just took time, and now she's also like "Oh [my daughter] doesn't have tea-coffee also, oh . . ." So, for her, God is not there, but the fact that I'm not having tea-coffee—the austerity—that she's appreciated because that's what she relates Jainism to. So she'll also tell other people "Oh she is not having onion-garlic, or tea-coffee."

After that turning point, Ruby's mother softened her approach to her daughter's religious transformation and even began bragging to neighboring Jain families about her piety and strict practice of vegetarianism. In large part, Ruby's narrative of leaving the Jain community became transformed into a narrative of more fully practicing the principles of her family's religion—a break with tradition became a return to tradition.

## It's Always Easier for Brahmins

As for Ruby, some devotees even from non-Hindu families have exulted in their victories of convincing family that their adopted religious practices are in fact fulfillments of their family's religious traditions. But those from brahmanical Vaiṣṇava backgrounds can most directly assert that joining ISKCON is a revival of their own heritage. Gopal is a soft-spoken but watchful temple *brahmacari*. He was born and brought up in Mumbai by a family with roots in western Uttar Pradesh, where Kṛṣṇa worship flourished from the sixteenth century onward. In describing the story of his decision to leave a lucrative career in IT to join Chowpatty's *brahmacari* ashram, he painted his monastic life now to be a revival of family traditions dying out in this generation:

> Right from childhood I have seen my grandfather, we had a culture of offering the food, we had the practice of not eating any onion or garlic, nothing which is not offered to the Lord, of worshipping the deities to the extent of even making the garlands every day fresh. Because we grew up

> seeing all these things, so those impressions were there. And we are actually grateful to our parents and grandparents that they gave that culture. That culture is not about speaking, culture is about behaving. Through their behavior, they showed.

For him, crossing into ISKCON enabled him to carry on the culture he saw in his family elders during childhood, connecting with the past in a transtemporal crossing through his religious practices. But in becoming a devout *brahmacari* he also forges a translocative crossing, to channel his family's rural North Indian religious practices into the megacity of Mumbai. For those who joined ISKCON after migrating from small towns and conservative backgrounds to Mumbai for college and career opportunities, ISKCON's regulated religious lifestyle sustains symbolic links to family back home and overlays the disjuncture of their new life in the city with a sense of continuity of religious heritage. In many cases, these crossings are deeply connected to individual family cultures. This is the case for Anjali, a longtime Chowpatty member who grew up in Mumbai's suburbs in a Gujarati Vaiṣṇava family. She insisted: "I didn't have to put any extra effort to come to Krishna consciousness. Because whatever the four regulative principles [vows taken at ISKCON's initiation ceremony], we were already following since childhood. It's not so difficult." For her, ISKCON simply encouraged a next level of dietary strictness—prohibiting caffeine in addition to vegetarianism and abstinence from alcohol. These resonances reaffirm ISKCON's brahmanical orientations, but unlike in brahmanical homes, they are adopted by choice rather than birth-based caste identity.

The emphasis on equivalences between a brahmanical upbringing and ISKCON's lifestyle norms can be a consistent source of affirmation for devotees, especially when ISKCON's strict lifestyle restrictions seem out of step with the outside world in Mumbai. Those similarities serve to write ISKCON into a broader narrative of Hindu orthodoxy for devotees both in India and abroad. Visakha was raised in a devout Gujarati Hindu family in Vancouver but tailors her work schedule so she can spend several months each winter visiting Chowpatty, to reside in a guest house down the street and walk each morning to the temple's pre-dawn *āratī*. Like many ISKCON devotees in North America, she became familiar with the temple community as her parents explored different options for Hindu community and cultural exposure for their children. She became more devout during her college years, when she formally committed to the daily *sādhana* routine of chanting sixteen rounds on a *japa mala*, a practice of mantra-based meditation for approximately two hours every morning. Over several meals together, we talked about what it was like to lead a devout life in a cultural context (Canada) in which many people were unaware of its religious significance. But Visakha emphasized that it is equally challenging during her visits to India itself:

> Modern India is quite different, you see people in tights and t-shirts and stuff, but from the background my parents come from, the culture we have really helps us with Krishna consciousness. The four principles for me—I didn't understand when devotees say it's difficult and you have to give up things, I couldn't understand where the austerity was. So I think that's very helpful.[3]

ISKCON's lifestyle regulations underscore a vision of traditional Indian culture that places the practitioner against the grain in North America and in many urban Indian public spheres, but it also enables them to make a transtemporal crossing, maintaining religious norms generally ascribed to the past. For many devotees, the adoption of external markers of tradition parallels an interest in learning "how to properly respect one's elders," which Sona counts as one of the central things she has learned from being part of the Chowpatty community. She contrasted this with what she sees as a lack of proper respect for elders in modern India in general. And this traditionalist view of Indian culture often elides regional differences. Akash, a *brahmacari* from small town Tamil Nadu who studied engineering at an IIT before joining Chowpatty, brightly reflected that it was not at all difficult for him to take up the practices and lifestyle norms of ISKCON. For, even considering regional differences between North and South India, "basically Indian culture was based on this *sanātana dharma*." In this iteration, ISKCON's religious culture reflects traditionalist religious cultures and unifies them in many Indian devotees' viewpoints.[4]

While undergirded by abstract ideas about traditional Indian culture or *sanātana dharma*, it is often the visible social markers of dress and diet that become central sites for devotees' identity formation and debate. Strict adherence to vegetarian and teetotaler norms elicits a constant negotiation with the more permissive and mixed dietary habits of Mumbai's larger cosmopolitan milieu. For many devotees, food-based boundaries are central to establishing their distinct religious identity and the frontline of conflict with family and broader regional communities. Lalita was raised in a

Sindhi Vaiṣṇava family who migrated to Bombay at Partition. She described growing up with very few religious norms, aside from the occasional *pūjā* her grandmother would perform on her home altar. For Lalita, the most challenging aspect of joining ISKCON has been its impact on her ability to attend family and neighborhood gatherings. She and her husband steer away from their relatives' Christmas and New Year's parties because of the "non-veg food and drinking" there. But, like many in urban India, her apartment building is also composed of her regional religious and caste group. In her predominantly Sindhi Hindu apartment complex, she creates alternate ways of keeping up appearances while not attending building parties, due to the presence of alcohol and dancing there. Instead, she hosts her own gatherings in the shared courtyard a few times a year, aligning Gauḍīya festival times with more mainstream, recognizable Hindu holidays. She said her neighbors warmed to the candle-lighting Kartik rituals she learned to follow through the Chowpatty temple when she synced them with Diwali festivities. And she cooks and serves blessed food, *prasādam*, to neighbors regularly, in a bid to avoid accusations of not being sufficiently involved in their community life.

While neighbors may be pacified with dessert deliveries to their doorstep, crossing over into ISKCON can create divisions within families, the most fundamental social network for many Indians. Members of the temple's Marriage Board tell me that at least half of the marital conflicts they are called upon to mediate concern tension between in-laws and young couples over their newly acquired dietary prohibitions. These can be particularly volatile issues in Indian families in which food and family gatherings are at the heart of social life. When young devotees begin refusing to eat food cooked by relatives, this marks a separation that echoes caste lines. Evoking higher caste refusals to dine with or accept food from lower castes, insistence on the traditionally upper-caste diet of vegetarian food cooked without garlic or onions casts home-cooked fish and meat dishes as polluted and impure. This is thin ice in a society in which religion, caste, and class are frequently bound to those with whom one dines and what one consumes. Foodways practiced by Mumbai's ISKCON members can thus both signal a renewed fidelity to a religious heritage and also erect barriers between their new identity and their extended families.

These foodways serve as a common demarcating line that both devotees and onlookers use to emphasize the difference between ISKCON's lifestyle norms and the secular and more variegated India that surrounds its members. Many conceptualized the stringent food prohibitions required for full ISKCON membership as the hardest hurdle in "joining," and the maintenance of those food standards is seen as a rare feat worthy of praise. During my first winter of fieldwork, I joined forty members of the Chowpatty congregation for a pilgrimage to Kerala. During a long yet eventful twenty-four-hour train ride, my co-travelers—one Tamil Iyer couple and one Gujarati Vaiṣṇava couple who were longtime Chowpatty members—occupied two berths alongside young tech professionals and newlyweds in jeans and flats trying to catch up on sleep on their way back to Kerala to visit family. Along the way, the Iyer couple struck up a discussion with two thirty-something men who were otherwise glued to their laptops preparing for a business presentation in Kochi. It turned out both men were also from Tamil brahmin families and, like the Iyers, had moved north to Mumbai for college. Noticing Mrs. Iyer's sari and *japa mālā*, the men asked whether she was an ISKCON member. On hearing her affirmation, they immediately turned to the pressing issue of food: "So you don't eat garlic and onions?" "No, we don't eat garlic and onions at all." "And no coffee or tea?" "No coffee and tea. And no cigarettes." Both young men expressed respect and awe at these choices, marvelling at the Iyers' sincerity in their religious commitment. What began as a bond over shared regional and caste identity gave way to a distinction of honor based on their dietary choices. Beyond just food, conversation turned to how these commitments distinguished them from the career ambitions and wealth accumulation goals of many in their social and economic bracket, signaling their adoption of a religious life as a higher choice.

For many, abiding by strict dietary regulations imbued one with a power of ethical conduct. This came out frequently in casual conversations, such as at the family home of Narayan, a retired electrical engineer who now works as a volunteer in the temple's offices. Reflecting on how he sees his religious practices as modeling ideal behavior for others around him in the city, he reasoned, "Why we are going [to temple programs] and why we're not drinking, why we're not using onion and garlic . . . . We have to explain very clearly . . . when we change ourselves and they see our behavior, our attitude, then they think 'Oh there's something in this!'" The centrality of ISKCON's food prohibitions here signals another way of living in modern India. This resurfaced weeks later, in a more formal interview with Mr. Iyer, who acts as one of the temple's financial advisors. While sitting in his office, I posed a question about which obstacles ISKCON faces most in India today. I expected to hear a reiteration of the familiar trope about the Westernization of Mumbai's youth or people forgetting the religious practices of the past. But his immediate and confident answer was the danger of ISKCON members "behaving like ordinary people," which he defined as "going out to restaurants and eating ordinary food" as well as "going on vacations"—in other words, partaking in India's post-liberalization middle class. For him, minimizing the activities of "ordinary people" detaches devotees from participation in Mumbai's mainstream consumer economy, producing a parallel community. Through its popular vegetarian restaurants in Mumbai and organic-farm produce and personal-care product line produced by the Govardhan Eco Village, ISKCON also participates in a consumerist economy, but seeks to guide the contours of that centered on community projects, distinguishing religious entertainment and consumption from secular forms.[5]

Through the dramatic step of separating oneself from the bustling culture of restaurants, cafes, clubs, and cinemas—for which Mumbai has long been known—members are encouraged to devote themselves explicitly to creating an alternative religious lifestyle: devout, ascetic, and vegetarian in all the places where the city is secular, consumerist, and carnivorous. As one can imagine, these high standards for living a life "unlike ordinary people" are difficult for many—even devout members—to practice at all times. These expectations can lead to rifts between generations and among friends about how to live their lives, as lines demarcating the pure religious life do not map easily onto a modern urban context—a subject I will delve into later. But they also depict the palpable crossing into the community that one is compelled to take through everyday lifestyle choices, demarcating oneself from the city outside and even one's own family networks. Although many everyday crossings are navigated by individual devotees, Chowpatty's system of joining is structured around the Counselling System, and its counsellors serve as important guides in the ongoing process of crossing into ISKCON. It is to this system in action that we now turn.

## But Can You Become Brahmin?

As the reader may have noticed, even in this modern organization that formally eschews caste markers, many (though not all) of the teachers, *brahmacaris*, and administrators who lead the temple happen to be not only brahmin but South Indian brahmin. This reproduces a predominantly higher-caste leadership structure and reflects embedded ideas about who embodies religious authority, even in this novel, socially mixed community.

However, the temple community also includes many devotees from mercantile *jati*s and OBC backgrounds, some of whom are active members of the managerial and counselling teams. And for devotees not raised in a high-caste family, membership in ISKCON provides access into the world of orthoprax Vaiṣṇava Hindu culture. Joining ISKCON is in many ways a Sanskritizing process as members of the community become deeply conversant in the Sanskrit *śāstra*s, Puranic literature, and brahmanically oriented norms at the basis of the community's often-cited scriptural corpus. Due to the ritual innovations of Bhaktisiddhanta, adopted by Bhaktivedanta in forming the society, one can even *become* a brahmin. Two levels of initiation are theoretically open for all ISKCON members: *hari nāma*, in which one formally receives a *japa mala* and commits to the lifestyle regulations of the group, and *dīkṣa*, known widely as "brahmin initiation" within ISKCON, in which one commits to a higher level of dedication and regulated behavior and obtains the ability to perform the priestly activities traditionally accorded to brahmin males.

All ISKCON temples globally partake in this initiation structure, meaning that one can become a brahmin according to ISKCON's initiation rituals even if born Nigerian, Russian, or Japanese. Birth-based jati or ethnicity is immaterial. And one can also become a brahmin whether male or female, although women receive the mantras but not the *upanayana* thread at their initiation. Accordingly, at formal temple rituals, such as the installation of *mūrtis* at the opening of a new temple, all "brahmin" members of the community will be called up to perform *abhishek* (ritual bathing of the *mūrtis*), regardless of their birth-based identities. However, I was also told in confidence that *dīkṣa*, or "brahmin initiation" is not a stage reached by most devotees in Mumbai but a religious confirmation for a select few who have specific reasons to receive it, such as embarking on temple *mūrti sevā*, or the daily worship rituals of performing *āratī* or cooking for the temple *mūrtis*.

Aside from specialized priestly roles and the formal initiation process that provides access to them for some, ISKCON's reading of the Vaiṣṇava Hindu tradition places strong emphasis for all devotees to develop "brahmanical" conduct or character, *sadācāra*. This refers to a set of ethical orientations and the observance of the lifestyle norms advocated by the community's reading of Vaiṣṇava tradition, encompassing models for the values of humility and selflessness as well as practices such as vegetarianism and the avoidance of alcohol and caffeine. And here is where the Counselling System comes in. For devotees at Chowpatty, forming a relationship with a counsellor is the linchpin to develop the brahmanically inflected ideals of *sadācāra*, commonly discussed as Vaiṣṇava ettiquette. Accordingly, counselling relationships are a central site for lived religious authority.

In the remainder of this chapter, I will examine counselling relationships in depth as the sites in which the most substantive everyday crossings into ISKCON occur. The goal to develop ideal Vaiṣṇava conduct is an ethical standard that incorporates narrative models from Gauḍīya scriptures and hagiographies as well as prescriptions drawn from core Vaiṣṇava scriptures, particularly the Bhagavad Gītā. This is a ground on which notions of class and kinship can be refigured, operating through individual relationships and institutions like Chowpatty's *brahmacari* ashram and Marriage Board, which conduct aspiring members into different stages of life according to Sanskritic Hindu sources on the *varṇāśrama* system. In this regard, crossing into ISKCON is not merely a personal affair but is guided by the mentorship and judgments of temple authorities in an idealized brahmanical social structure.

Although the Counselling System is a bureaucratized structure run by senior temple members, new aspirants can choose counsellors based on existing relationships or the social networks that brought them into the temple community. They are encouraged to find a "good fit" for them both geographically and culturally in this spiritual family, which in practice means groups are often formed through shared language and class lines, reinforced through the social similarities of those who share certain postcodes. Yet, the Counselling System also potentially channels a Sanskritizing class mobility through its interpretation of its core brahmanical structure. Although discussed informally through the language of spiritual mentorship, internal temple manuals connect the system to the notion of *daivī* (or grammatically, *daiva*, i.e., "divine") *varṇāśrama-dharma*, defined in the temple manual "Model of a Spiritual Community" as a "Vedic system" of "social organization with a spiritual perspective."[6] Therein, the system is tied to a sense of naturalized social duties: "For a society to be strong, all members must know their duties."[7] This distinctly Gauḍīya spin on the concept of *varṇāśrama* describes classical *varṇa* categories through personal qualities and actions rather than birth, although a naturalized link can be reinforced, especially for those born brahmin. But ISKCON's interpretation of *varṇāśrama* locates its class-based categories in relation to the core religious goal of Krishna *bhakti*.[8] Indian temple networks connected to Radhanath Swami's leadership have developed an ethical gloss to the socio-occupational system. This is underscored in a foundational set of lectures entitled "The

Spiritual Counselling System," where Radhanath Swami detailed: "we tried to implement this spirit of *varṇāśrama* in our social development programs . . . In essence, *daivī varṇāśrama-dharma* is to educate people—according to their nature and propensity—to utilize their talents in the service of God, to develop pure love of God."[9] This approach fuses an abiding value of the categories of *varṇāśrama* with a focus on personal character development.

Accordingly, counsellors are tasked with identifying and guiding each individual under their care toward an occupation and family situation that fits their "constitution," or assessments of their individual character and proclivities. The creative license in focusing on the "essence" of *varṇāśrama* enables a shift in the language of the discourse from social stratification to emotional care. This system thus opens the door for aspiring members to embody brahmanical markers through their conduct and relationships with counsellors, refiguring the category of the brahmanical from a birth-cased caste designation to a personal trait that can be cultivated in relationship.

Due to its pervasiveness throughout devotees' weekly lives, the Counselling System can also overlay and even supplant the authority held by parents and family elders in prior generations. As mentioned above, each "counsellor" is generally a husband-wife unit. Younger couples and single women are counselled by elder householder couples, assigned based on geographical proximity, linguistic and socio-economic similarities, or prior personal relationships (except for *brahmacaris*, who are counselled by elder *brahmacaris* based on similar criteria). As with the gendered division of temple-based courses and programs, the centrality of the heterosexual couple to the Counselling System reinforces a heteronormative family basis to the community. This celebrates and incorporates the lived authority of women, providing a counterweight to strictly male-based ISKCON authority structures. However, it also locates legitimate authority in the context of community-sanctioned heterosexual marriage. For many counsellees, their counsellor couple provides an analogue to parental guidance, as counsellees seek advice they may have previously sought from parents—from everyday problems to major life decisions such as finding the right spouse. Through shifting authority from natal to institutional structures, an elder's authority is evaluated not through family seniority but resonance with ISKCON teachings.

Counselling groups average generally no more than twenty families as counsellees, to ensure adequate personal attention to each counsellee.[10] Sundari, one counsellor I interviewed, estimated that she and her husband had around fifteen families, a total of fifty people, in their counselling group.

Like the *nāma-haṭṭa* groups described by Bhaktivinoda or Bhakti Vṛkṣa groups, another contemporary version of this congregational formula that is practiced in other parts of India, counselling groups must remain small but are meant to be replicated throughout the larger congregation.[11] While Chowpatty's system began with three counsellors (i.e., husband-wife teams) and about fifteen families, it comprised roughly fifty counsellors and about 1,250 families when I conducted my research in the mid-2010s. These groups were divided geographically in the Mumbai area into four regions: South Bombay (from Sion and Dadar down to Colaba), Central Mumbai (from Sion to Thane), the Western suburbs (from Bandra to Borivali and Andheri), and Northern (from Mira Road to Virar).[12]

Despite its institutional underpinnings, the system is often likened to a family structure. Jahnava, an elder counselor in the community, mentions in a 2002 documentary on Chowpatty called *The Simple Temple:* "Here it's just like you go to your house and your mother and your father are there to welcome you. So, the moment that you see your counsellor, you feel that you have the shelter of some senior Vaiṣṇava."[13] This description even held true for Juhi, a third-generation devotee who was otherwise not a regular temple attendee. Underscoring that she was not an active member of the congregation, she said she still found affirming, family-like support from the *brahmacari* who acts as an informal counselor for students who attended the temple's grade school. She noted: "For us, he is actually a father. We can tell him anything. And he doesn't discriminate between boys and girls. Like he'll give equal importance to us and equal importance to them . . . I think for me he's the main reason I'm stuck, you know, I'm still in contact."[14] While Juhi is busier preparing for college and spending time with friends and does not frequent the temple these days, informal contact with her counsellor provides a tangible link to ISKCON as an institution; it keeps her in the system, literally and figuratively.

Counsellors are enjoined to hold a gathering with their counsellees once every fortnight at the homes of members of the group or at the counsellors' residence.[15] Counselling meetings are billed to offer both "training" and opportunities for *saṅgha*, in an organized and replicable format. "A Report on the Social Development Programme at Radha Gopinath Temple" details the desired format for counselling meetings:

> Vaiṣṇava bhajans; discussion based on Gauḍīya scripture; sharing of realizations, discussion on *sevā*, *sādhana*, and Vaiṣṇava etiquette; optional

> discussion of non-personal problems (personal problems are discussed privately between counsellor-counsellee); exam (based on the scriptural passages being discussed) and memorization of *śloka*s (scriptural verses), *kīrtana*, and *prasādam*.[16]

This structure was followed loosely in the meetings I attended, adapted to be flexible to an individual group's interests and including two or three of the activities listed above. Nonetheless, as a model for the religious guidance of individual devotees, the liturgical format folds even an informal gathering into ordered participation in ISKCON's Gauḍīya tradition.

A focus on training is underscored in an in-house description of the "Purposes of the Counsellor System": "to educate and train married devotees to live according to the Krishna Conscious principles of the *gṛhastha* ashram" and "to provide systematic training to devotees in matters of philosophy, *sādhana*, and Vaiṣṇava behaviour, etiquette, lifestyle, and attitudes." These agendas draw from classical *varṇāśrama* ideals of the duties and social position of householders, but in ISKCON's iteration these ideals are communicated through modern wellness terminology and with the aim of creating novel familial bonds among their communities, as in the following two aims: "to provide a formal framework within which personal care and attention can be extended to all devotees so as to make them feel loved and wanted and part of a wonderful spiritual family" and "to foster warm personal relationships and a spirit of love and trust among devotees based on Krishna Conscious principles."[17] Chowpatty's manual on the Counselling System, "Model of a Spiritual Community," thus links training to religious well-being. Proper training can enable congregations to avoid "social disasters" or even basic disaffection.[18] But most of all, such training inculcates one into a new community, enabling one to cross over into a deepening devotional identity.

The encompassing orientation toward continual self-work and discipline echoes Gauḍīya *sādhana* precedents that have shaped ISKCON's religious ritual structure and lifestyle orientations.[19] Within this, members are encouraged to develop an ever-greater Krishna consciousness in their lives and thoughts, inducting a type of Bourdieusian *habitus* of ISKCON's lifestyle prescriptions into their daily lives. Yet, unlike the inherent quality of Bourdieu's notion of *habitus*—perceivable only when ruptured by a conflicting norm or orientation—devotees are actively encouraged to "program" their own *habitus* through a training process under a counsellor and education in the community. This approach to self-formation resonates with the philosophy of *sādhana-bhakti* put forward in the texts of the formative Gauḍīya authorities[20] but also recasts this focus on the perfection of one's embodied practice of Krishna *bhakti* in idioms of modern institutionalized group practices. The cultivation of careful self-discipline and the embodiment of the institution's core values are discussed as prerequisites for the attainment of the perfection of Krishna *bhakti*. In this context, the display of humility and an orientation toward constant *sevā* is highly rewarded, while lifeways that celebrate a secular enjoyment of life or any form of sensuality are viewed as dangerous and misleading on one's devotional path.

The centrality of performing or modeling perfect Vaiṣṇava etiquette has been shaped by ISKCON's checkered history in India. As Brooks notes in his 1989 study of non-Indian ISKCON members in the Gauḍīya pilgrimage center of Vrindaban, these devotees focused on what he terms positive impression management or giving "a good impression of ISKCON in public," to assure Indian audiences of their piety.[21] Even today, many Indian ISKCON members with whom I spoke seemed quite conscious about a perceived necessity for them to model their community for the purpose of convincing others of its validity as a "bona fide" Hindu tradition and of its preeminence among religious paths. Attention to positive impression management also operates on an internal level, as character and actions are monitored through the Counselling System structure, channeling the maintenance of strict community behavioral guidelines. In this sense, training reinforces the values of the group and is emblematic of an ongoing process of crossing into ISKCON's ideals. As one second-generation American devotee who regularly attended Chowpatty's annual pilgrimages remarked, everyone seemed to imbibe the oft-discussed virtues of humility and *sevā* in their interactions with her, even if "they were not really on that level naturally"; they still acted out the mannerisms of always serving guests first, never criticizing others, and frequently speaking about Krishna, because, as she concluded, "they knew that is where they should be."

## Choosing a Path: The *Brahmacari* Ashram or the Marriage Board

As mentioned above, those who join the Counselling System are channeled toward two potential life tracks in this brahmanically inflected social system: the *brahmacari*, temple-based renunciant, path for young men interested in pursuing monasticism, or the *gṛhastha*, householder, path for young men interested in family life and all young women. Whichever track is determined to be most suitable for each young aspirant through extensive consultation with one's counselor, an ordered system is ready to ensure that one develops a lifestyle within the ideal perimeters of the community.

In the *brahmacari* ashram, the Counselling System aligns with what is perhaps the most visible cornerstone of brahmanical social roles in ISKCON temples and the most vivid form of crossing over into a new life that the temple community offers. This lifestyle of temple-based asceticism and service to a guru was classically available to members from upper *varnas* in premodern contexts, undertaken for a prescribed period of young adulthood. As reproduced in Chowpatty today, it is available to urban aspirants who meet a set of criteria that underscore the temple's desired social demographic, including the attainment of a bachelor's degree and at least several years of professional work experience. This promotes a responsible clientele, while also tethering to class if not caste preferences.

Today almost two hundred *brahmacari* monks reside in the monastic facilities at both Chowpatty and the community's nearby Ecovillage in rural Maharashtra. This central cohort of renounced men practice a temple-based monastic lifestyle rooted in norms and practices spelled out in Sanskritic literature. The *brahmacari* ashram occupies the right-hand side of the temple building. At its entrance sits Radhanath Swami's minimalist quarters, and on its lower level resides the Vaiṣṇava Training Academy (VTA), a trial living space for working male professionals to experience life in an ashram setting. Prospective *brahmacari*s enroll in the Vaiṣṇava Training Academy (VTA) and, after a series of interviews and an application process, live in the temple for one year while still maintaining professions outside. At the end of that year, they may decide to join the Brahmacari Training (BT) program, and if a candidate proves his fidelity and aptitude for the ascetic lifestyle, he is awarded his official saffron clothing in a private ceremony conducted by Radhanath Swami and elder *brahmacari*s in the ashram.

While many *brahmacari*s are long-term residents at the temple and are involved in regular services at the temple and throughout the city, others keep more itinerant schedules, giving talks at festivals or on college campuses and helping to develop affiliated ISKCON centers throughout Maharashtra. They account for only 2 percent of the overall congregation but provide a center weight to the community's religious life, delivering most of the daily scriptural classes and lectures and organizing many of the community's outreach activities, festivals, and daily temple services, from food production to *pūjā*. Earnestness in the *brahmacari* ashram is gauged through a rigorous schedule of *sādhana*, *sevā* determined by one's professional skill sets, and manual labor in the temple's kitchen, cleaning facilities, and other maintenance departments. Mandatory rising time is around four o'clock in the morning, and taking personal time for rest or relaxation throughout the day is discouraged. This atmosphere creates not only strong personal bonds within the ashram but also the potential for extreme exhaustion. An attitude of fortitude and *sevā* over one's physical health was a persistent topic of discussion whenever I would chance upon a chat with one of the more talkative members of the ashram, and it seemed in tension with the temple community's voiced ethos of wellness and holistic care. Purush, a thoughtful thirty-something who left a career in engineering four years back to join the ashram, was a *brahmacari*-in-training when I resided at the temple, and he seemed to inhabit the role of resident observer of its daily norms. The worst situation, the affable Purush told me, was when someone contracted malaria—a common enough occurrence in balmy Mumbai with often insufficient mosquito nets to tie above one's floormat at night. Then, the rigor of the daily schedule would become agony. In severe cases, he noted, *brahmacari*s are allowed time off to recover. However, periods of sickness are also seen as dangerous times for another reason by some in the ashram. When a *brahmacari* falls ill and feels there is no one to care for him, that is when he may decide it is time to go home to his parents or to get married, to know that there is someone to care for him in times of need. To evade this, *brahmacari* counsellors provide regular check-ins for ashram residents and the head of the *brahmacari* ashram, Gauranga, is known to organize personal care for those who are sick or otherwise impaired. This attention to well-being consciously adopts a familial approach in a monastic context in which aspirants have explicitly distanced themselves from natal family bonds. As Gauranga also underscored in multiple conversations, the ashram needs to take the role of a family for young aspirants if they wish to be successful in their renunciation.

In crossing into these brahmanically inflected lifestyle models, caste may be malleable to an extent, but the gender binary is fixed. Women are seen throughout Indic worldviews to be dangerous and destabilizing to male monasticism. Accordingly, Chowpatty's *brahmacari* ashram grounds itself in a thorough distancing from women as a marker of authenticity. Aside from occasional brief professional interactions, such as an intermittent lunch at a sister's family home, *brahmacari*s are expected to scrupulously avoid interacting with women both within and outside of the congregation. Due to this gendering of renunciation, several young women conveyed to me that the congregational system conducts them into a world of marriage and families whether they like it or not, conveying them toward different regulatory standards at home and at the temple. While the ideal promulgated for *brahmacaris* is renunciation, the ideal promulgated for young women is heterosexual marriage within the community and *sevā* in a household context. A few young women who have tried to strike out and explore a more renunciatory role said they found themselves without the support of the temple's counselling administration, which in these contexts ensures the status quo of the temple's congregation emphatically more than it heeds individual desires.

While the Counselling System channels all young women toward marriage with a male devotee, men are also guided toward a limited set of options identified by counsellors and elder temple mentors. Accordingly, if at the close of a young man's year of training at the VTA, the candidate decides celibate life is not for him—or if he is initially more inclined toward marriage anyway—he is encouraged to work with the community's Marriage Board to find a suitable spouse in the *gṛhastha* model desired for members of the congregation.[22] The Marriage Board—a small group of elder counsellors—engage in the specialized role of maintaining a database of an estimated 2,000 congregational members seeking spouses. They cater to all young members of the congregation, confirming their eligibility through consultation of the temple database and their counsellor.[23] And, although functioning only as one analogue alongside the Counselling System, the Marriage Board is perhaps the most profound symbol of the temple community's shift in networks of authority and belonging, replacing natal networks with institutional kinship models by taking on the core familial task of matching spouses.

Members of the Marriage Board spend long hours on the phone, asking questions, counseling, advising, and suggesting. As I spoke to them after their weekly meeting one afternoon in the temple's offices, they described their duties with frequent, jovial laughter and a playfully conspiratorial affect. But they conveyed deep investment in getting to know younger devotees and guiding them through processes that are usually considered to be the most intimate Indian family affair. They often work with both the young people seeing spouses and their parents to assess the details of a match that will satisfy all parties. From the Marriage Board's perspective, this means first and foremost finding a spouse who is also an ISKCON devotee and secondarily matching preferences for caste, class, education level, and personal disposition. After getting to know the prospective husbands and wives through formal and informal talks, including a lengthy intake sheet on which applicants indicate their personal information and marital preferences, board members input the data into a shared spreadsheet and venture appropriate match suggestions.

This system transfers what is often the most intimate and consequential parental duty in a conservative Indian context to the institutionalized service of the Marriage Board. Such a shift away from natal family structures has potential implications for how caste, class, and regional identity figure into marriage choices, if shared religious membership in ISKCON is seen as the prime factor of commonality. In most cases, the Marriage Board members acknowledge, regional or caste background is also specified in applicants' intake forms and emphasized in conversations with their parents—though the couples in the Marriage Board are keen to tell me that they do not support a caste-based value system. In this affirmation, they can lean on the cosmopolitan nature of Mumbai and the heterogeneity of temple members' regional backgrounds, and inter-regional marriages frequently do occur under their auspices. Intermarriages between Gujarati and Punjabi business class families, for instance, were frequently held up as examples of inter-caste marriages, though inter-regional might be a more precise term to describe that pairing. Having said that, inter-caste marriages—inasmuch as caste is a shorthand for *jati*—do frequently occur in the temple community, and members of the Marriage Board described to me with obvious exasperation how they continually take steps to encourage their younger devotees to consider a match from a different regional or even class background, provided the individual is a committed ISKCON devotee. Several such matches are evident within the community's congregational core, though their exceptional status is still noted.

Despite ongoing tensions over how much intermarriage is acceptable—and desirable—the couples who run the Marriage Board clearly enjoy doing this service and take it as an opportunity to connect with younger congregational members. They also view their role as complementary to, rather than a replacement of, natal family approval of a match. As Shamini, a Marriage Board member and senior counsellor, mentioned, that was at the basis of Radhanath Swami's guidance to them on this system: "He understood the Indian mentality . . . the parent's blessing is very important, especially for the girl." In this regard, the Marriage Board provides an organized service that reproduces the structure of a family, in which young devotees can pursue relationships toward marriage within the sanction of temple authorities, delimiting "frivolous interactions" with the opposite sex and preserving the code against unsupervised "gender mixing" that informs the temple's social structures. Thus, whether one moves toward renunciation or marriage, temple elders guide one toward a clearly defined path.

Influences from changing cultural norms in India have begun to nuance this institutionalization of age-old Indian social patterns. For instance, several Marriage Board members related to me that they find an increasing number of their applicants are men and women in their thirties who have already been married. Mainly from a generation in which divorce was highly unusual, the board members are unsure of how to handle these applications. However, they mentioned that they have had some success in pairing divorcees together, creating a new opportunity to fold them back into an idyllic *varṇāśrama* system as envisioned in the community's literature and counselling systems. For two such remarried thirty-somethings, their new social position enabled them to (re-)enter a stratum of religiously conservative society from which they had previously been excluded and to regain good social standing in their families on the grounds of shared religious membership in ISKCON. However, divorce remains a taboo for most of the temple population, even as it is becoming more normative in their wider social circles.

Despite the interweaving of modern urban Indian realities into the fabric of Chowpatty's community, the discipline required of Chowpatty's *brahmacari*s and congregation, including the devout submissiveness encouraged in young women, strikes many Mumbaikars as a thing of the past—a throwback or revival of ancient religious and social conventions.[24] Several community members described that when they told friends and family that they were choosing to leave their careers and enter the *brahmacari* ashram at Chowpatty, they were shocked that the institution even existed in this day and age. To some, it evoked a Puranic past, populated by *rishi*s and sages, not a feature of a modern urban landscape. Comparatively, many of the temple's guidelines for female behavior are more characteristic of an orthodox Hindu family in prior generations than families in often-liberal South Bombay. However, it is the aspiration for such a revival—in the center of South Bombay's posh urban landscape no less—that constitutes ISKCON's place there. This bristles against the social norms that many devotees are asked to give up when they join and becomes a source of tension that has kept both converts and children of temple families at the periphery of formal temple membership. However, for those who do jump into this system fully, it offers what amount to new familial bonds, reproducing the structures and duties of a traditional natal family through the strikingly modern means of intake forms and spreadsheets.

## "She Tells Us What to Do and We Listen": Everyday Religious Kinship

While the community literature on the counselling system lists counsellors' duties and ideal meeting formats, it cannot depict the variety of formats that counselling takes in day-to-day interactions. In this, training is viewed as a central and continuous activity for both counsellors and their counsellees—an ongoing crossing into new kinship-style relationships based on shared religious choice rather than birth or shared upbringing. The counselling system's overlaid kinship model, reinforcing brahmanically inflected Vaiṣṇava social ethics in the lives of new adherents, is often mediated through an institutional format. Yet the most personal counselling interactions take place outside the official meetings, often in day-to-day interactions and in spaces where women occupy a tangible role of familial authority alongside their male counterparts that is not seen explicitly in public temple forums. I will illustrate this here with three examples that depict a range of counselling relationships and the kinship-style power dynamics they encode. These vignettes also communicate how the devotees of Chowpatty style the "family-like atmosphere" that is valued in the way members describe the community itself.

The Patels' counselling group is a most coveted destination. Held in their elegant South Bombay mansion, the handful of young families and middle-aged women who visit every fortnight are treated to a satisfying buffet laid out in their sprawling dining room by a team of discrete and efficient domestic staff. Many in their group also hail from Gujarati families who migrated to Mumbai in the twentieth century, continuing old commerce and trade links that connected the textile mills and manufacturing of Ahmedabad to the Indian Ocean port cities of Surat and Mumbai. Although the living-room setting is formal, guests largely eschew the cream-colored jacquard sofas and armchairs and sit in a circle on the white-and-blue Persian rug that provides a wide space at the room's center. Although Arjun Patel maintains a fevered schedule overseeing the family's businesses, he sets aside his two cellphones for the duration of the counselling meeting and leads the group in an opening bhajan. After the song is complete, he settles cross-legged at the foot of his living room's main couch and introduces the theme of the evening. Humility. It is a simple theme, perhaps the most basic in the temple's repertoire of Vaiṣṇava virtues, and in our collective circle heads nod in affirmation of the need to revisit and refine our own practice of this virtue. Arjun could easily deliver a lecture on how one cultivates humility according to the Gauḍīya scriptures, as one hears routinely from the temple dais or broadcast from radios and smartphones in congregational members' homes in the afternoons. But he prefers to take a more discussion-based approach. Although it is well known that his financial backing supports many of the temple's core programs, he regularly describes himself as a novice in spiritual life, or *kaniṣṭhā*, invoking a Sanskrit term popular in ISKCON in an act of self-described humility itself.

The session's theme is explored in a roundtable, informal workshop format that begins with time for reflection and writing in a notebook what one associates most with humility and then talking to one's partner to discuss each other's perspectives. Finally, we come back together as a group—devotees more relaxed in each other's company after having discussed with their partners. Each pair shares a particularly memorable point from their own conversation. Jayadev, a friendly father of two, is not afraid to voice his own struggles with enacting humility in daily life. How can one practice humility with colleagues if one works in a corporate firm in which competitive ambition is the driving force of any new project? As he speaks, he balances a content but drowsy toddler on one leg as his kindergartener quietly colors in an image of Sītā and Rām from an *Amar Chitra Katha* coloring book edition. The other members of our circle consider Jayadev's point, and Arjun offers a few reflections from his own corporate experience. "Just as Krishna told Arjun in the Bhagavad Gītā, you have to do your duty but do it without attachment. You can act the part and get the job done, but you can also cultivate that inner sense of 'this is not mine; I am doing this for Krishna.'" The questions and answers discussed in the session are at once immediate to the concerns of the devotees present but also fall within a scripted exchange format that characterizes lectures and formal discussions at ISKCON temples.

Our discussion session concludes quickly though, and after another closing bhajan we make our way into the dining room to fill our plates with *prasādam* and return to chat in small groups on the living-room floor. It is here that the more vivid guidance and dynamics of religious authority reveal themselves. For the person in the room who seems to hold the most tangible day-to-day religious authority is Arjun's wife, Shamini. Although she quietly sits through the main discussion, looking on from an armchair near the dining room alcove, women and young men flock to her as the dinner is being laid out on the dining table and make appointments to discuss career concerns and family issues. Shamini checks in with her counsellees throughout the week by phone and spends a sizeable part of her day dispensing advice and checking up on any of the younger women or peers who seek out her support. At the dinner itself, she consults with one female peer in age about issues with her adult children and advises another younger couple about an upcoming work decision, as they ask her whether to stay in Mumbai or move to a nearby city for a job opportunity.

The informal, spontaneous support offered by Shamini seems anything but institutional. Although she and Arjun take on their counsellees officially—registering their relationships with the temple bureaucracy—their group includes nearby neighbors, the grown children of colleagues, and a distant niece who moved to the area for college. Their counselling relationships must be made formal through the temple's counselling board, but after that they take on the character of informal parental guidance, trusting that their counsellees will abide by the rules of the temple community rather than seeking to enforce them. And yet they also keep in close personal contact with each, ensuring that they are adhering to the community's *sādhana* and dietary regulations and acting as ongoing sounding boards for marital and family issues of concern.

This relationship-centered approach to the counselling structure also characterizes Vrinda Shetty's counselling group. Like most Chowpatty counsellors, the Shettys take on counsellees as a husband-wife pair. And like in many spousal pairs, Vrinda takes the most direct day-to-day responsibility for the group. Vinod maintains a respected but muted presence, focused mostly on his twin passions of IT work and weekly service in the temple's media department. One day, as I wound my way through the dark wood-paneled hallways of the media department toward the small reception desk, he emerged from the sound room and joked that they all get used to the dim lighting in the department since they never see the sun. Vrinda, by contrast, is a regular presence at any temple program. As the daughter of a respected early member of the community, she spent her childhood playing alongside the daughters of Arjun and Shamini, who also remain closely involved as adults. Flanked by her own two teenage daughters today, she is often to be found during Sunday kirtanas dancing and laughing amid a group of girls and young women toward the back of the temple.

But Sunday programs are also an important time for her to meet with her own counsellees. Unlike the formal, elite hospitality of the Patels, the five or so young couples who call the Shettys their counsellors are often too busy working late nights and taking care of their in-laws to make a fortnightly commute across Mumbai's northern suburbs on weekday evenings. Recent South Indian migrants to the city, they are no strangers to the hustle of establishing oneself in new occupations and new neighborhoods in this expanding metropolis, like the Shettys, whose parents migrated from Karnataka and Andhra Pradesh during their childhood. Informally, they find as secluded a space as they can on the ground outside the guesthouse in the bustling Sunday afternoon temple courtyard and huddle together around Vrinda. As passersby carefully stepped around the group one breezy spring Sunday, they were deep in conversation, unaware of any onlookers or commotion around them. One couple leaned in particularly close, describing to Vrinda with knitted brows their concerns about a son who has just started junior college and seemed to be getting into party culture. Another couple on the other side of the circle leaned in with rounded backs, mirroring the posture of the others to hear Vrinda's response. They were particularly interested as they anticipated that—with two young teenage sons—they might be asking for similar advice soon. Vrinda commanded attention with the effortless affection and care of an elder sister, circling her eyes around the group as she talked to make sure everyone understood her advice and was able to hear her in the crowded courtyard.

At the end of their condensed half-hour huddle, the group rose in unison and each couple talked with Vrinda individually for a moment before returning to the temple program. For Vrinda's group, the substance of the counselling session is in these tightknit exchanges, which provide a space for young couples who have joined the temple as a unit to navigate what their ISKCON identity means in terms of maintaining family relationships. Arun and Jayshri, a Tamil couple who recently moved to Mumbai and quickly joined Vrinda's group, said their sessions with her were what enabled them to stay loyal to the principles of Vaisnava etiquette that they were just now learning from temple lectures and seminars. They faced blowback from Arun's family for moving out of the extended family home to better practice their new vegetarian devotional lifestyle—a rift that reverberated when

Arun's father had become ill and needed closer at-home care. They were weighing whether they could return to the family home and maintain their new lifestyle "standards" or whether close association with their meat-eating, television-watching family would compromise their devotional identity. Vrinda counselled them to return but to carve out "pure spaces" for their devotional practice, including a separate kitchen space for cooking their own food. Brows now relaxed as they became aware again about the crowd around them, and they exclaimed with laughter: "She tells us what to do and we listen." Vrinda gave them a look of mock disapproval as Arun added affirmatively, "She always gives the best advice. Then we can go back to our families and know how to behave properly."

A number of women in the community command this relationship-based religious authority through their roles as counsellors. Even if their authority lies in closely huddled groups surrounding them during the Sunday program or at private homes during dinner parties and not the platforms and stages of the temple's public-facing programs, they hold the authority of interpretation, explaining to their counsellees how best to implement Vaisnava teachings in their daily lives, practically not just theoretically. This often takes the form of relationship advice and makes manifest in counsellees' lives the moral weight of both a kinship-style network and a religious chain of authority to sanction and guide their day-to-day decisions. It is also what gives shape to the process of crossing into the devotional community on a day-to-day basis, as aspirants navigate not only the decision to join but also how to live that identity authentically in relation to their natal family responsibilities and career paths.

This form of personal mentorship also shifts more easily with the changing culture of the city. For instance, Priya Singh enacts most of her role as a counsellor over the phone. Her status differs from most of Chowpatty's counsellors in that, although she is married, her husband has never expressed great enthusiasm to join ISKCON. They were married right after college, their families both from Rajasthan and brought together by a guild for Rajasthani businessmen in Mumbai. One afternoon, over a mixed fruit-and-vegetable salad that she creatively conjured up in her seaside apartment in Mumbai's seaside Worli district, Priya and I planned an upcoming trip to discount designer boutique run out of an apartment in an adjacent building. As we chatted over lunch, glimpsing seaside views out of the breezy open window in the main room of her tidy 1BHK, she mentioned that her husband is often away on business to Europe and the Middle East.

Because of that—and, implicitly, his lack of interest in taking on the role of co-counsellor—she cannot lead regular counselling meetings at home. Although that colors her public standing as a counsellor, her spirit of commitment to ISKCON is straightforward and undeniable, and she dives into her role as a counsellor with the energy of a natural manager. In place of large home meetings, Priya spends a lot of time one-on-one over the phone and in cafes with her young women counsellees. "You need to meet with them regularly or to stay in contact, because that's how they will keep inspired to stay on track with their Krsna consciousness. The best way is just informally, like meeting a friend," she tells me. "I try to meet with each one once a week, or at least once every two weeks. Otherwise, who has time to go and sit in a big group, and there you can't even ask your real question? This way is much more effective. Then you can really talk about things." Unlike Vrinda's group of mainly South Indian couples who were recent migrants to the city and still establishing themselves among its urban middle classes, Priya's counsellees were primarily young women who had largely grown up in South Bombay's elite seaside neighborhoods. Matched with her because they were single women (since she was unable to take on male counsellees without a husband involved), they were also more candid with her about problems they were facing and more straightforward about their challenges in living up to all of ISKCON's lifestyle prescriptions, including prohibitions on dating, drinking, and spending weekend evenings out with non-devotee friends—the hallmarks of most young people's lives in the city.

As we wound our way through the crowded lanes of Chor Bazaar at dusk on another evening soon afterward, Priya sized up a few vegetable stands, thinking about what to prepare for dinner, and looked through a pile of knockoff handbags from a stall set up in the middle of road. Other women milled buying produce for the evening meal, and men with dried goods and paper products wove in and out of the stands on bicycles, headed for nearby lanes. All the while, Priya picked up calls here and there from her counsellees, checking in on one young woman's search to find a husband through the temple Marriage Board and asking another about an ongoing issue with her new mother-in-law. Although Priya does not work outside the home, she approaches her role as counsellor with the focus of a full-time occupation. As we made our way from shop to shop, she took calls and issued instructions to her series of counsellees on the other line like a businesswoman preparing her staff for an upcoming client meeting. Her direct, to-the-point manner centered largely on helping young women adjust to the challenges of living in their husband's extended family homes and dealing with spouses who, like her own, do not display the same interest in cultivating a religious life. In this, she was the first line of command these young women sought out. Before they would consult their parents, they would come to her, to figure out how to approach them. And she expressed dogged concern that they hold themselves to the highest standards. Even if their in-laws want to cook and serve meat in the house, they should refuse to take part. And most importantly, they must maintain their daily *sādhana* vow of chanting sixteen rounds on their *japa mālas*, even if it means stealing out from the living room while everyone else watches television at night. "You have to establish the pattern and stick with it. Even if your surroundings are not favorable, you can make them favorable." During a particularly extended call, she insisted softly but firmly that one young woman try harder to convince her in-laws to let her keep her own part of the kitchen separate for preparing only vegetarian meals.

As with other discussions about family and foodways, this step held deeply symbolic undertones for a young bride trying to establish a place in her new home. But Priya was unyielding. After she hung up, she turned to me while shaking her head. "It's hard, I know it. They go through so much, especially at this stage. But someone has to tell them what to do. Otherwise, they'll be pushed this way and that." Priya's intensive one-on-one counselling technique seemed to fulfill a need for her twenty-something counsellees who were eager for both guidance and a confidante as they navigated their early adult lives. In the counselling system's structure, her guidance stood in for a religious sanction, giving a weight to her words beyond just that of an elder woman with experience. Her advice affirmed the need for her young counsellees to respectfully abide by the norms of being a young bride in an extended family household. But she also subtly redefined those lines of obedience to hold most closely to a fidelity to ISKCON's brahmanically inflected rules, placing those directives above individual family cultures and norms. In doing so, the young women under her wing also carve out a distinct space for themselves, one that often distinguishes them from their natal and extended families through their continued dedication to ISKCON's lifestyle norms. Here, the bonds to the devotional community are held as more essential than family bonds maintained through shared meals or living spaces.

Throughout my research in Mumbai, devotees often identified their counselling groups as prominent sources of how they became deeply involved in the ISKCON community and as central to their continued involvement with that community. Indeed, the emphasis on personal emotional fulfilment in individual congregational members is still closely paired with a missionizing imperative. Although the "people over projects" motto is a central orienting phrase for many devout Chowpatty followers, community success is still linked to an ever-increasing bevy of initiated and "staunch" ISKCON practitioners. Missionizing is still at the center of the community ethos, but the Counselling System centers the value of personal training, as ongoing self-improvement, or a continual crossing into one's identity as a devotee, incorporating wellness discourse alongside advocacy for ISKCON's *sādhana* and lifestyle injunctions. In that sense, the prerogative to missionize is turned both outward and inward, as the Counselling System trains its members to "be in the world as devotees," responding to one's lived, daily environments with reference to one's identity as an ISKCON devotee over and above other aspects of identity.

In these interactions, both between counsellors and counsellees and within families, the religious authority to interpret ISKCON's strict religious regulations in everyday situations is often negotiated by both men and women, although the latter are absent from the visual culture of religious authority invoked by the statues and paintings on the temple grounds and the figures on the lecture platforms each day. While many of the closest interactions in the counselling system take place within homosocial networks, women with children can take on a role of informal religious authority for both men and women in their counselling networks. In this sense, if one reads the counselling system through its intentions as laid out in the community's literature, they mediate the religious guidance of their guru, Radhanath Swami, in the most pragmatic day-to-day interactions. Through guidance dispensed in informal phone calls or chats in the temple courtyard, they connect their counsellees to the lineage of the Gaudiya *paramparā* of gurus that is so central to ISKCON's identity. Although many Indian ISKCON centers have recently opposed the inauguration of female *dīkṣā* gurus in the society, over cell phones and in café meetings many women and men provide everyday religious guidance. Through their guidance, counsellees find themselves both recommitting to and redefining their place in relation to Hindu traditions and their extended families. This way of becoming religious is not a return to their families' traditions but rather an adoption of new relationships that overlay and mimic kinship relations, guiding devotees in how to become religious against the grain in Mumbai's urban spaces.

# 4

# Ancient Answers to Modern Questions

## Revising Religion

> Now [my parents] have realized that devotees are following our tradition more than we are following. They're not doing something different, they're not Westerners or something, they're not following some philosophy from outside. In fact, they are teaching our own philosophy with more values.
>
> Priti, long-term temple devotee

As the last chapter showed, ISKCON's networks introduce young Hindus and Jains in Mumbai to a traditionalist religious community, centered on the relationships they fortify in the temple's Counselling System. For devotees, these relationships mirror and can even achieve primacy over natal family networks. And indeed, becoming a devotee in India necessitates changes in diet and lifestyle that demarcate most people as more conservatively religious in a brahmanical register than their own families, leading sometimes to tensions over practice and daily life. At the same time, ISKCON's teachings are articulated as a return to a premodern orthodoxy that members assert has waned due to India's colonial past and its industrialized urban present. In this sense, ISKCON's education- and training-centered approach to recruiting new members emphasizes what I call revising religion, a revisioning of how one understands the religious traditions of India to align with ISKCON's modern orthodoxy. By the term revision, I intend to invoke both its valences of presenting a new understanding and of studying as a process toward systematic educational attainment, such as in preparation for an exam. In this form of becoming religious, aspiring devotees and seekers at large are inducted into a framework of Gauḍīya Vaiṣṇavism not only as a premodern orthodoxy but also as a comprehensive system bearing the desired traits of modernity: rationality, scientific rigor, and functionality. This presentation

*Bringing Krishna Back to India.* Claire C. Robison, Oxford University Press. © Oxford University Press 2024.
DOI: 10.1093/9780197656488.003.0005

of Hindu traditions asserts that they are most authentically monotheistic, scientific, and rationalist—and not polytheistic, "superstitious," or "ritualistic." Conveying an internalization of global systems of power that have naturalized preferences for monotheism and rational systems in religious discourse, these depictions do not fit the lived diversity of Hindu practice, and yet, these assertions are now indigenized as a cornerstone of many modern Hindu groups. Nonetheless, given that they differ from common, non-institutionalized forms of Hinduism, they must be learned, and that is precisely what modern revivalist organizations such as ISKCON set about to teach.

ISKCON's articulation of Hindu traditionalism shares much with revivalist traditions globally that have formed in the crucible of the European colonial period and its attendant cultural imperialism, marked as the arrival of "modernity" in conventional accounts of history. Like many modern revivalists, Indian devotees ground their revivalism over against both perceived Western cultural influence and the secular globalism of elite urban India. In this sense, carrying on my argument from previous chapters, members of ISKCON Chowpatty do not imagine themselves part of a New Religious Movement institutionalized in the West but rather as important actors in the re-establishment of Hindu *dharma* in Mumbai's secularized cityscape, forging new religious ways of dwelling in the city that are conveyed as more authentic to the land itself. Communicated through idioms of individual educational attainment and personal choice, consumer logics of the religious marketplace are also at play in this rationalization of Hindu formations. Here, attributes of scientific and systematic cogency are the basis for consumer choice, reflecting a global missionizing ideology that has guided the development of many modern religious organizations. ISKCON Chowpatty's ordered community structure is premised on a systematic educational presentation of Hindu tradition that aims to eradicate doubt—existential and religious—from the lives of adherents. At the forefront of this discourse is the conviction that ISKCON and the Gauḍīya tradition from which it stems can "answer all one's questions," allaying doubt born from modern, urban anomie and presenting the "correct understanding" of Hindu traditions to young Hindus. In other words, this Hindu traditionalism claims to excel both in premodern pedigree and in modern measurements of value.

This chapter outlines how this ordered communication of Vaiṣṇava traditionalism centers on a structure of staged questions and answers which mediate to audiences, through the temple's public courses and exam competitions, an orthodoxy that is grounded in idioms of scientism and educational attainment. My analysis also examines how individual doubt is discussed, managed, and elided amid an education into certainty. Through the temple's cohesive structure of education and training, Indian devotees actively revise notions of their religious heritage.

## Finding Answers in ISKCON

Many devotees told me that they were drawn to ISKCON because of the prominent place given to scriptural instruction over a "ritualistic mindset." They characterized their upbringing in Hindu homes as one in which ritual worship was frequent but explanations few. In response to this, the central place given to Gauḍīya scriptural instruction, which provides "explanations" of ritual practices and mythic narratives, distinguished ISKCON from other Hindu traditions for many followers. Although some devotees described their decision to join ISKCON as the result of shopping around the spiritual marketplace, positioning the community alongside other popular Hindu organizations, others were not particularly interested in religious practice before joining the community. Across the board, however, Indian devotees interpreted their past uninterest or search as stemming from not knowing the "real meanings behind" Hindu rituals and beliefs. And their practice of Gauḍīya *sādhana* was presented as distinct from common Hindu religious practice, as inherited and profoundly specific to one's region and family. Here, this revised Hindu traditionalism is systematic and adopted by personal choice.

Accordingly, a consistent trope about the nature of religious knowledge and the motivations of many devotees to seek religious truth involves the language of "questions" and "answers." Devotees pointed to how listening to an ISKCON guru or senior devotee give a lecture or a chance encounter with ISKCON literature had "answered all their questions," providing a type of existential contentment.[1] Deven was a cordial computer engineer in his fifties who had left a North American career to take a lower-paid managerial position on the temple's payroll. He described his narrative of religious transformation as the journey of an individual who had little interest in religion to someone deeply committed to preserving Hindu traditions—all because of the "answers" he found while visiting an ISKCON temple in Australia. Conversely, Radha Raman, a soft-spoken Assamese computer programmer in his thirties who came to Mumbai to attend an engineering college, discussed with a knowing grin how he had visited practically every modern Hindu organization in his search. He had been interested in spirituality and in finding a path that worked for him, experimenting with Ravi Shankar's The Art of Living and the Chinmaya Mission before starting to attend an ISKCON temple. But those other organizations, he reflected, "could not answer my questions . . . about life, about why we are here, what we are supposed to do during this life." He joined Chowpatty's ashram three years after college, quitting his office job to take up the robes of a *brahmacari*. These narratives reflected that, to Chowpatty's members, religion is a matter of individual choice, unrelated to family heritage.

Moreover, the focus on individual transformative experience at the heart of joining narratives changes the relationship of individuals to their own families and social groups. When Meghna—born into the tight-knit Marwari Jain community of Mumbai—started to attend Chowpatty's programs with a cousin, she also "began to ask what Jainism is really about." She reasoned: "Usually people just follow religion for the sake of following, because their parents do it. They don't enquire, they don't introspect, just because they were born Jains." This interrogation of her religion in general led her to develop a greater attachment to the Gauḍīya tradition as presented by ISKCON and to shift her religious allegiance and join ISKCON—a move that carried a lot of controversy within her Marwari Jain community. As in many joining narratives I heard, Meghna's concern with finding a deeper religious meaning than the one present in existing family and community structures was linked to finding "answers," or finding a sense of intellectual and emotional certainty that seemed lacking in other religious communities—both Hindu and non-Hindu. ISKCON in urban Indian centers like Mumbai prides itself on the sophisticated scriptural literacy of its members, on being able to answer *all* questions.

Probing deeper, a need for these answers also connotes the presence of new questions—questions for which many ancestral religious communities did not seem prepared. The ability of ISKCON to answer all these questions is dependent—according to some accounts—on one's ability to ask the right questions, inscribing a set of power relations in the mediation of religious knowledge that privileges Gauḍīya scholasticism over other forms of intellectual inquiry and religious practice.

This standardization of Hindu identity often expunges more fluid or variegated religious backgrounds. Narayan's family were Hindus who immigrated to Bombay from Sindh during Partition. Their religious practices centered on the reverence of a Sufi saint, like many Sindhis in the region's pre-Partition eclectic religious communities, and they continued following him even after migrating to India. Every year, he described in reference to the teacher's annual *urs*, or death anniversary of a revered figure, "we would go over to his shrine near Breach Candy and dance, sing songs to him. And there was a lot of drinking going on over there, especially on that night of the festival." However, today he reasons that his relatives and friends are not "following" the "correct understanding of Hindu religion" because of ignorance. He notes, in relation to him and his wife: "Of course, we were like that earlier. But when we come to know that the basic goal of life is to love God, *dukḥālayam aśāśvatam*. Everything in this material world is temporary—your name, your fame, your beauty. That at least you should understand. This body is impermanent, but the soul is eternal." Referencing a Bhagavad Gītā verse that is often quoted in the temple's introductory courses, he relates that his shifting understanding of Hindu traditions came through his participation in the Chowpatty-led Journey of Self Discovery course. And indeed, an exposition of this verse—Bhagavad Gītā 8.15—occupies the full second day of the Journey of Self Discovery course. Now, Narayan tells me, he is trying to *educate* his brothers to give up those old Sufi-oriented rituals and adopt this new, "correct understanding" of Hindu practices.

The centrality of education in changing views on Hindu traditions reveals ISKCON's understandings as tailored to appeal to those seeking a greater understanding of the immensely varied body of practices under the umbrella term Hinduism. One young Gujarati follower described, laughing with a matter-of-fact shrug, that he grew up in "the typical Hindu type of family. Nobody had a clear idea of whom to worship. It was more just whomever you had some chemistry with I would say." He and others agreed that ISKCON has a "responsibility to teach Indians about the proper meaning of Hindu rituals." Another devotee, raised in a Puṣṭimārga family in Ujjain, echoed the common view that children tend to follow the religious practices of their parents: "While everyone in India is following some religious path, they should know in depth what they are following, the fundamentals . . . Because here in India, whatever the parents are doing, the child used to do that only." But, like many ISKCON devotees, even those raised in devout families doubted their abilities to *explain* or *rationalize* the traditions they practiced. As Deven elaborated:

> I'm from a Hindu background from Karnataka, the sort of Hindus who eat meat. I always grew up seeing my parents worshipping everyday, that they would take bath and my father would do *pūjā*, but I never understood why they were doing it or why there were so many different photos on my father's altar. So, I grew up in the sort of background where they do believe in God and worship but their understanding is limited.

For Deven, ISKCON provides that missing understanding, conveying to Hindus the history and ideal meaning of their rituals. In this sense, ISKCON in India seeks not (just) to convert but to revise people's understanding about the "real meaning" of their traditional rituals and beliefs. And these meanings often shift practice, such as through the introduction of vegetarianism. Therein, explication of rituals and lifestyle norms that are already embedded in the lives of brahmanical and Sanskritized Hindus attracts brahmin communities to ISKCON and serves to legitimize ISKCON beyond its membership. It also holds open a Sanskritizing potential, since diet is often linked to higher-caste status in India. The continuing self-development agendas inherent in joining narratives and the Counselling System infrastructure parallel a broader focus on training and religious education that underlies many of the temple community's events. Nowhere is this educational revision of religion more evident than in the ongoing religious instruction offered both on the temple grounds and in rented halls, which seeks to instruct Mumbaikars about the "essence" of Hindu traditions, grounded in ideas about Vedic heritage. Diverse modes of training and education for various segments of Chowpatty's extended congregation—the infrastructure for this revision of religion—takes place on the temple grounds from quite literally dawn to dusk.

## From Vedic Texts to PowerPoints

ISKCON's form of revivalism is grounded in close engagement with the Gauḍīya scriptural canon. The temple offers an extensive array of religious courses and lectures, primarily in English and Hindi and with a growing emphasis on Marathi. Daily philosophical lectures serve as formal oral commentaries on core Sanskrit and Bengali texts, centering on the Bhāgavata Purāṇa every morning and the Bhagavad Gītā every evening. Each day, a verse of scripture is repeated several times ritually in Sanskrit by both the speaker and the assembled audience, then commented on at length by the speaker. This daily form of oral scriptural commentary—meticulously delivered in the style inaugurated by Bhaktivedanta in his early ISKCON gatherings—instantiates an orientation toward scriptural literacy in ISKCON's select Gauḍīya canon among those who regularly attend ISKCON's temple programs. This Sanskritic engagement also ties those who partake in temple programs to an ideal of Vedic knowledge, as these texts claim status as explications of the foundational brahmanical Sanskrit texts, the Vedas. While largely a symbolic affiliation, Vedic as a term carries legitimating weight for practices and ideas affiliated with Hindu traditionalism.

Aside from the hour-long morning lecture held in the temple room from eight to nine o'clock in the morning, in the afternoons a group of volunteers—mainly young women—teach and organize the Gopal's Fun School weekday courses. Named after one of Krishna's childhood epithets, these courses are tailored for school kids and their mothers, on topics ranging from the study of the Bhagavad Gītā to courses on parenthood skills. A holistic training of character is also developed for the community's children enrolled at the Gopal's Garden school in the northern middle-class suburb of Borivali. In addition to their academic classes, all children at Gopal's Garden take the VAC: Vedic Art and Culture course series, taught by prominent *brahmacari*s and lay faculty. Arundhati, who teaches the VAC series to first and second graders, described the course as imparting "basic values or the morals that we need to have in our dealings in day-to-day life." In this sense, the range of courses offered on the temple grounds and its educational institutions spans from direct scriptural lessons to encompass also general "value-based training," providing a comprehensive, centralized educational system.

Alongside this, *brahmacari*s lead evening Gītā classes at the temple tailored for young men in the Brahmacari Training and Vaiṣṇava Training Academy programs. Chowpatty shares an exam-centered approach to religious education with other ISKCON centers internationally, which offer course series on major Gauḍīya scriptures—known as Bhakti Śāstrī and Bhakti Vaibhāva courses—with a curriculum based on Bhaktivedanta's specifications, standardized by the Vrindavan Institute for Higher Education (VIHE). As in other ISKCON centers, devotees who seek a greater understanding of core devotional texts are encouraged to complete the Bhakti Śāstrī and Bhakti Vaibhāva courses, held both in person and online. These courses culminate in a formal essay-based examination and the bestowal of a title, or educational qualification, on the successful course participant.

But Chowpatty-based *brahmacaris* have extended this religious education ethos to tailor to the aspirations for educational attainment among their local audiences. In addition to temple-based courses, they offer courses on Gauḍīya philosophy throughout the city, particularly aimed at university students and young professionals, in affiliation with the Bhaktivedanta Academy for Culture and Education (BACE). BACE also offers seasonal courses on the Bhagavad Gītā and other Gauḍīya scriptural topics, conducted in several classrooms on the temple compound. While some courses are explicitly named for core Gauḍīya scriptures, popular courses on relationship and life skills are also delivered with similar rubrics of systematic education. During a typical week, the native Marathi-speaking Govinda—who came to Mumbai from a small-town background in the early 1980s—offered a two-day seminar on "The Heart of Relationships." That weekend, Shubha Vilas, a popular devotee speaker from Kanchipuram, Tamil Nadu, offered a "Secrets of Lasting Relationships" workshop in the temple's Bhaktivedanta Hall. Both teachers have expanded their speaking repertoire in recent years to meet the increased demand for self-help-style seminars, and Shubha Vilas has particularly seized on this trend. Described on his website and in promotional materials as a "motivational speaker and spiritual lifestyle coach" with a professional background in engineering and patent law, he is the author of a series books on management principles gleaned from stories in the classical Indian epics. His articles on spirituality and wellness have appeared in a range of "lifestyle magazines," including *Viva Goa*, distributed in luxury hotels in Western India.

The centrality of Mumbai's corporate and technology sectors in Chowpatty's congregation manifests within this idiom of individualized religious education and training. A small group of congregation members and *brahmacaris* have developed a program of "corporate preaching," recasting Gauḍīya theology and sacred texts—particularly the widely revered Bhagavad Gītā—into the terminology of contemporary self-help and wellness seminars to be delivered at private companies throughout the city. Radhanath Swami's image has also been recast into this parallel terminology, and since the growth of his public image in Mumbai from 2009 onward, he is now often described as a "life coach" as well as a "spiritual teacher." Unlike the overtly religious and perhaps old-fashioned feel of a straightforward presentation of Gauḍīya religious identity, these presentations foreground "tools of spirituality" that can help one "overcome workplace stress" and lead to "better career performance and lifestyle contentment." A digital analogue to this trend of pairing religious practices with professionalization is a focus on "Leadership & Spirituality" in public events, including seminars on Radhanath Swami's leadership lessons distributed by the temple's media department.

Mumbai's ISKCON devotees can stream many of these lectures from home and revisit them through an online media archive called ISKCON Desire Tree. This expansive website is run from the temple's administrative offices by a small team of lay members and *brahmacaris* who upload audio and audiovisual material from ISKCON Chowpatty and neighboring temples.[2] Radha Gopinath Media Services also presents downloadable audio and video content, uploaded daily to its website and YouTube page. Meanwhile, public-relations offices at both the Juhu and Chowpatty ISKCON temples employ on-site teams to inform local press outlets about upcoming temple festivals or public events, serve as spokespeople for reporters, and issue official statements on behalf of the organization. They also seek to reach new publics through the development of social media and the shifting of Mumbai's urban spaces. From an airy second-floor office on the Juhu temple property, the ISKCON communications director for Western India and her office of *brahmacari* volunteers share, with particular excitement, how they set up Facebook and Twitter accounts for ISKCON Mumbai and what they have learned about how to increase social-media followers. As a counter to the inflow of secular social media, they publicize daily pictures of the temple's Radha Krishna *mūrtis* as a form of online *darśan* and track the number of their daily "likes" and followers as part of their office routine.

The religious and linguistic diversity of Mumbai's diverse publics is reflected in Chowpatty's media productions, most of which are available in multiple languages. In accord with Mumbai's multilingual *lingua franca*, Chowpatty's publications and lectures are in one of three languages—English, Hindi, and Marathi, depending on the context of the audience.[3] While Hindi is more common at large festival settings, English has been the predominant language used at temple programs and in public lectures. This preference for English is partially grounded in their religious source material. ISKCON founder Bhaktivedanta Swami (1896–1977) produced English translations of Gauḍīya texts, such as the Sanskrit Bhāgavata Purāṇa, which became canonical texts for ISKCON devotees who consider them to be direct and binding elucidations of scriptural verses. Bhaktivedanta wrote in English from the 1940s onward, while still based in India for several decades, to appeal to a global, English-medium audience as well as to Indian elites. While

Hindi and other regional language versions of Bhaktivedanta Swami's work do exist, the English version—composed for his missionizing in America and Europe—holds a central place in ISKCON globally because it is the version he translated and wrote himself. Aside from this, however, English is a shared language inclusive toward the temple community's North and South Indian members, as many of the latter possess a complicated relationship to the dominance of Hindi as India's national language.[4] This is notable in Mumbai in particular, due to the city's prominent South Indian population.

But crucially, English carries a cultural cachet in Mumbai's posh neighborhoods. Several women I interviewed specified that many residents of the historically elite South Bombay prefer English even in religious settings, as it is carries connotations of cosmopolitanism and higher educational status. In fact, according to them, when the temple administration tried introducing more Hindi into the regular temple functions, attendance rates dropped and English was reintroduced. Dipesh Chakrabarty has argued that Anglophilia in India is, culturally, "as legitimate as any form of orthopraxy. Being Westernized is one way of being Indian."[5] To push beyond this, I would argue that the use of English among Chowpatty's elite and middle-class members does not necessarily accompany any commitment to Westernization but rather a repurposing of the language to reflect Indian societal hierarchies. But alongside this, Chowpatty's community participates in the polylinguistic fluency that is a marker of life in the city. At weekly temple programs, dramas and skits are performed in Hindi and occasionally in Marathi—and most members are conversationally fluent in multiple languages spoken by smaller groups in the temple courtyard, including also Gujarati, Tamil, and Konkani.

Chowpatty's plethora of media production provides for ISKCON's devout members a parallel media industry, aimed at drawing them away from Mumbai's expansive secular-media consumption and into a focused world of devotionally oriented media usage. This "ethical soundscape," to echo Charles Hirschkind's study of recorded Sunni Muslim sermons in Egypt, includes Vaiṣṇava *kathā*, music, and ethical discussions. Audio and audiovisual recordings of temple lecture routinely garner several hundred live views, as community members who cannot make the trip down to South Bombay stream the programs from home. This soundscape can be further enhanced in members' homes by devices available for purchase at the temple store that play recordings of Bhaktivedanta's mantra and *bhajan* singing as continual background sound, to infuse one's home with a focus on Krishna *bhakti*. This expands the educational revising of religion with a palpable sensory component, meant to invoke a process of personal transformation in the devotional aspirant.

In addition to an internally oriented production of devotional media, a range of publicly oriented courses form a sizeable portion of the temple's events. Temple *brahmacaris* organize a range of public courses on a weekly basis in rented halls and college auditoriums, and many spend the greater part of their days planning and orchestrating these events. Chowpatty's routinized public courses attempt to mediate to audiences of college students and young professionals a personalist Gauḍīya interpretation of the Bhāgavata Purāṇa and the Bhagavad Gītā. Alongside a presentation of the Gauḍīya tradition as systematic and scientific, these courses emphasize the professional expertise of their degree-holding teachers, bolstering the assertion not only that Vaiṣṇava—and by extension Vedic—traditions writ large can stand up to the presumed critiques of modern secularism and rationalism but also that a lifestyle of dedication to Krishna *bhakti* is a desirable choice for India's young professionals.

This agenda of reframing Hindus' understandings of their families' religious traditions through formal, enrollment-based courses fashions a systematized approach to "learning the correct understanding" of religion that parallels a number of youth-centered religious revivalist movements internationally.[6] I will focus my examination of this discourse on two regularly offered education-oriented programs in the temple's repertoire: the Journey of Self Discovery, a course that serves as a standard introduction to the ISKCON community for newcomers, and the Gita Champions League competition, an annual examination proctored by ISKCON teachers to test students on their understanding of that core Hindu scripture.[7] Aside from participant observation at courses throughout the city, I also consulted course material distributed through Chowpatty-run websites for both teachers and students of the temple's courses and examinations.

During my research, the six-night Journey of Self Discovery (known in shorthand as JSD) was Chowpatty's most popular "entry-level" course, aimed at introducing students and young professionals to the philosophy and practices of ISKCON. The course is delivered in the format of a corporate workshop presentation and described by one JSD teacher as "a crash course in the Bhagavad Gītā." Taking its title from a BBT-published book compilation of Bhaktivedanta's recorded conversations, JSD began to be offered on a monthly basis in English and Hindi—translated as *Ātmā kā Prayās*, or "endeavor to understand the self"—around 2007.[8] The course is offered in rented public auditoriums and at the community's Bhaktivedanta Hospital, in both English and Hindi, throughout the year. Held in the evenings to accommodate the work and class schedules of its target audiences, the course regularly attracts around one hundred participants to its six evenings of lectures and catered vegetarian meals. JSD teachers work from a shared template, lecturing on basic Vaiṣṇava philosophical themes revamped through PowerPoint presentations and structured audience interaction. The PowerPoint slides intersperse generic stock-art backgrounds with major points listed on the screen in the informally didactic style of mass-marketed self-help seminars one might encounter in the United States.[9] While each speaker brings an individual approach to the course, all follow the same basic six-day structure and explain each day's lessons drawing from a common stock of analogies and narrative didactic devices.

The Journey of Self Discovery aims to convince young urban Hindus of ISKCON's religious tenets. The verb "convince" here holds an important place, as a cornerstone of Chowpatty's self-image as a rational, scientifically grounded Vaiṣṇava community that holds the *correct* beliefs and practices. It is through the act of convincing—by philosophical argument, scriptural reference, and personal example—that many members are brought into the community. This was emphasized in a recent interview for the promotion of a YouTube series released by ISKCON Chowpatty on "How I Came to Krishna Consciousness." Therein, Bhaktirasamrita Swami—a senior *sannyasi* in the Chowpatty community—emphasized the centrality of "becoming convinced," on philosophical grounds, in his own joining narrative. A prominent *sannyasi* in the Chowpatty community who joined the *brahmacari* ashram after receiving his MBA at the University of Mumbai, Bhaktirasamrita became the first *sannyas*-initiated follower in the Chowpatty community in 2010 and is one of the community's most popular speakers. His lectures in Hindi, Marathi, and English are popular for both their linguistic elegance and their simple clarity. Speaking in his characteristically measured tone, he tells his interviewer that through reading Bhaktivedanta's books, he developed "a clear understanding of the philosophy, and I became convinced—that this was the path of truth, that this was the path I wanted to follow in my life." Those books, he says, were important to his "evolution in Krishna consciousness," giving him "the conviction to surrender his life to this process and the mission." Here, Bhaktirasamrita models the education-oriented goal of transformation that JSD teachers strive to achieve through their courses.

At the time, a group of four *brahmacari*s took turns leading the largest courses throughout the city. Going by their initiated names, their online profiles on the course's website were smartly designed, including video clips that showcase their individual teaching styles. Several of them now have prominent followings outside ISKCON as popular public speakers on the circuit of religious lectures throughout Western India. Gaur Gopal, for instance, has showed up multiple times on my Instagram feed in the posts of Hindu friends' parents who attended one of his lectures in Ahmedabad or Surat. As with the introductions given to speakers before temple lectures, the JSD teachers are described in course introductions primarily through their professional qualifications. Full speaker resumés are repeated before the first session of a course begins and are available online for potential students to consult. For instance, on the first evening of Gaur Gopal's JSD course that I attended in 2015, a formal presenter informed the packed audience of his background in electrical engineering; he studied at the Pune Electrical Engineering Institute and worked at Hewlett Packard before dedicating his life to be a monk and preacher. However, personal candor and charisma are also valued. Gaur Gopal has soared to social media popularity also due to his affable speaking style. Radha Gopinath, the JSD founder and main curriculum developer, mentions in his JSD introduction that prior to joining ISKCON he worked as a speech therapist focused on individuals with hearing challenges. He strives to bring these skills of observation and attentiveness to bear in his teaching, a different kind of professionalization of the religious lecture format that emphasizes learned expertise rather than hereditary or regional authority.

The JSD format, like other Chowpatty courses, is premised on providing answers to religious seekers in what is seen as a city of skeptics. In the polished delivery of the course leaders, a confidence in the ability to respond to any existential questions from their audience is conveyed throughout the six evening sessions. This confidence is buoyed by the corporatized delivery of ideas drawn from scriptures already known as authoritative among Hindu traditions. This course is premised not on introducing new ideas but "explaining" old ones. With slight fluctuations, the titles of each day's JSD sessions are: "Search for Happiness"; "Does God Exist?"; "One God or Many Gods?"; "Who Am I?"; "Why do Bad Things Happen to Good People?"; and "Is Spirituality Practical?" As each title suggests, a broad question is posed at the outset of each evening, and the speaker works through a preset structure of scriptural quotations, personal anecdotes, and guided reasoning to answer that question. Kishore, a self-assured teacher with conventional good looks, starts each session by reminding his audience: "The quality of answers that you get in your life will depend on the quality of the questions you ask." As in the joining narratives of many members, an updated version of the formalized *guru-śiṣya* process, of asking questions from a religious authority to obtain all the answers one desires, is central to ISKCON's idiom of education and training. And, through this discursive basis, religious identification is tied to personal choice, grounded in an intellectual examination of the religious traditions nominally shared by most participants. In packaging Hindu traditions into a defined and systematic pedagogical format, JSD introduces a framework for participants to weigh Hindu practices, including their own family's rituals, in relation to its ideal standard.

A focus on answering audience questions is woven in as an interactive part of the classes. In January 2015, Parthi Shah, an anesthesiologist at the Bhaktivedanta Hospital and a counsellor in the hospital's Spiritual Care Department, led her JSD audience in Hindi through a series of PowerPoint slides with stock art and inspirational sayings to convey her points about *karma* and reincarnation. In the "Why Do Bad Things Happen to Good People?" course segment, she related her experiences dealing with patients who ask why an illness or an accident has befallen them. She informally responded to audience members, many of whom were in the room as hospital patients or their relatives, imbuing the discussion with a level of medical empathy as she moved through the slides. Augmenting a conventional lecture format, she involved them in the presentation, asking her audience whether they would like to talk about any recent experiences of suffering or loss. However, in neat several-minute segments, she also worked her way back to her main lecture points in a style characteristic of corporate marketing seminars. JSD speakers display the politeness and well-honed speaking skills emblematic of Chowpatty's public events. Indeed, the course lectures seem as much about modelling ideal Vaiṣṇava etiquette—of concern for the well-being of others but also deference to authority—as they are about their stated educational agenda of providing the right answers to the right questions.

## The Science of God

Confidence in the answers provided by the JSD course is rooted in common assertions that these answers—and the Gauḍīya philosophical tradition from which they spring—comprise a scientific tradition. That is, each element of its worldview, from the presence and nature of God to the nature of the individual self, are asserted to be grounded in systematic and rational principles. Through the frequent invocation of these descriptors, ISKCON's Gauḍīya orthodoxy is connected to the legitimizing symbols of modernity, foregrounding a style of rationalizing exegesis that is implicitly put forward as the core of the religious tradition. They partake in a larger Indian cultural trend of proclaiming that Indic religious traditions are inherently scientific—or at the least compatible with modern science.[10] Many groups in contemporary India have invoked science as a marker of value in affirming their religious traditions, although the appeal to science is often used more symbolically than literally in relation to fields such as physics or chemistry. Accordingly, Peter Gottschalk proposes scientism as a more accurate description of the legitimating power of the term science in religious communities.[11] Further, Subramaniam reads the relationship between science and religion in contemporary India as one valorizing a "scientized religion" premised on an "archaic modernity," which proclaims the presence of the values of Western modernity in an ancient Vedic past.[12]

The ideals of a rational and systematic philosophy are rooted in Hindu, Jain, and Buddhist scholastic traditions, which are rich in categorization schemas to depict different levels of existence and the natural world. ISKCON's scientistic or scientized discourse builds on these textual resources to offer a network of cerebral explanations and down-to-earth analogies employed to explain Gauḍīya beliefs and practices. This channels new members into a focus on philosophical literacy and orthopraxy, through which they can assess other religious phenomena around them with new criteria, while depicting this religious education as an exercise of scientific thinking.

The Journey of Self Discovery course is oriented on what are designated as the "five systematic topics" covered in the Gītā. These are defined, in the words of course leader Radha Gopinath, as: *īśvara* (lord), described in English throughout the course as the "science of God" and in Hindi as "*bhagavān kā vijñāna*"; *jīva* (living being), similarly described as the "science of the soul" or "*ātmā vijñāna*"; *prakṛti* (primordial matter) translated as the "nature of this world"; *kāla* (time), the "time factor"; and *karma* (binding action), the "law that governs the activities that you perform."[13] These topics are indeed discussed systematically throughout the course, beginning with *īśvara* and *jīva* on the second and third evenings, and moving onto *prakṛti*, *kāla*, and *karma* on the fourth, fifth, and sixth evenings, with some necessary categorical overlap. Radha Gopinath's arguments for the existence of God and discussion of the "science of the soul" draw on a range of strategies, from Gauḍīya exegesis of the Bhāgavata Purāṇa; to a discussion of the Gītā's notion of spheres of influence grounded in the attributes (*guṇas*) of *sattva, rajas, and tamas*; to the employment of analogies linked to the rhythms of the natural world.

The JSD course is also built around the assertion that Gauḍīya lineage, or *paramparā*, is an authoritative source of knowledge because of its grounding in a taxonomy of *pramāṇas* ("means of acquiring knowledge"). Influenced by the classical *nyāya* philosophical school's categorization of *pramāṇas*, Radha Gopinath leads his JSD audience through arguments drawn from the early Gauḍīya works of Jīva Gosvāmin and others. In this categorization, the four modes of perception identified in *nyāya* philosophy are ranked according to their asserted accuracy in a theistic Gauḍīya interpretation. *Pratyakṣa pramāṇa*, sense perception, is the most basic mode of perception and is subordinate to *anumāna*, logical inference, which in turn is superseded by *upamāna*, analogy or comparison. However, due to their potential for fallibility, these modes of perception are collectively subordinate to *śabda*, the "verbal authority" based on the scriptural testimony of past authorities. Radha Gopinath describes the Vedas as "infallible, perfect knowledge," the way to understand the "causes of all causes, the source of everything." Here, a tendency toward typologies parallels a concern for categorization in the modern sciences, but according to this typology an acceptance of scriptural testimony ultimately supersedes an introductory methodological focus on scientific reasoning.

Scientistic resonances of Vaiṣṇava religious knowledge are particularly employed to discuss conceptions of *karma* and reincarnation. In one Hindi JSD session, an energetic, thirty-something *brahmacari* named Deen Dayal drew from the Bhagavad Gītā's philosophy of *guṇas* and *saṁskāras* (impressions formed in the mind from previous acts) to elaborate on a standard interpretation of the effects of *karma* on one's birth: "Whatever *saṁskāras* we develop, we will be born from a corresponding womb accordingly. Whoever has the quality of goodness will be born as a *deva* [divine being]; whoever has the quality of passion will be born as a human, and whoever has the quality of darkness or ignorance will be born as an animal." In another session, Radha Gopinath elaborated this with an apt analogy for Mumbai's cut-throat housing market: "So what kind of a body we'll take depends on our *karma*—just like whatever kind of money you give, that kind of a flat you'll get. It depends on how much you can afford." While the JSD approach to *karma* and rebirth is grounded in brahmanical Vaiṣṇava scriptures, teachers also describe *karma* as "Newton's third law: for every action there is an equal and opposite reaction," presenting it in a system grounded in a precise science.[14] As above, this allusion to scientific reasoning is more grounded in *śabda* than the other evidence-based *pramāṇas*, but it communicates rigor through its assertion of a system linked to classical philosophical modes of reasoning.

Beyond systematic scriptural categorizations, the correlation of Hindu traditions with scientific and technological achievement forms a central tenet of many groups that seek to promote the value of India's Hindu heritage in modern contexts, often tied to an unmarked upper-caste identity.[15] This discourse of scientized religion serves as a primary framing of ISKCON Mumbai's public image. Informally, a visitor to the temple on a quiet afternoon may encounter one of the several volunteer greeters on duty and receive an introductory booklet entitled "The Scientific Basis of Krishna Consciousness," along with a brochure offering answers to "Frequently Asked Questions" and a leaflet listing the temple's daily *pūjā* schedule. The legitimacy that scientistic language—itself a modern description of value—conveys in Chowpatty's public courses is often centered on assertions of premodern orthodoxy, such as that ISKCON is the descendent in an unbroken chain of gurus in a "bona fide" *paramparā*, the Madhva-Gauḍīya religious lineage, within the *catur-sampradāya* model. In linking ISKCON's credentials as a "bona fide" religious tradition to assertions that it possesses a scientific grounding, an argument for revivalism is advanced: that the premodern system is valuable in contemporary contexts as well.

Although the emphasis on a scientific and systematic basis for ISKCON Chowpatty's articulation of Hindu traditions was often presented to me more as a missionizing strategy, to attract the secularized youth in Mumbai, this description of Gauḍīya tradition appeals to many who have already joined the community, compelling them to affiliate with a religious organization in ways they might not have otherwise. Devotees routinely told me it was ISKCON's "scientific" presentation of Hindu traditions that attracted them to join the community, enabling them to overcome what were often expressed as aversions to Hindu traditions from their youth. Arushi, a fifty-something human-resources manager, joined ISKCON two decades prior and related this narrative in her own memories about that time:

> I'm born in a South Indian Hindu brahmin family, so we already have a lot of religious culture at home from childhood. Always there were a lot of *pūjās* and ceremonies, but more of a ritualistic kind. And that put me off—I was not very much into it. I was not understanding the real meaning of all of this. And I was always searching for the real meaning. Because nobody was explaining to me in a scientific way, why we are actually doing all these rituals.

This is a representative framework; many community members were from religious Hindu (and often Vaiṣṇava) households from across North and South India but were disinclined toward what they described as the "ritualistic" and "empty tradition" of the Hindu traditions they encountered as young adults. Reshmi, a secondary-school administrator who had been raised in ISKCON and now had children of her own, echoed this in her assertion that ISKCON's "scientific, systematic presentation of Krishna consciousness" was central to the organization's success in Mumbai. For these devotees, ISKCON provided a streamlined, modern Hindu traditionalism, something they could *rationalize* following, in which they could take pride. This iteration of Hindu traditions as systematic and scientific closely relates to expressions of pride in Indian national heritage read into premodern South Asia. By magnifying intellectual achievements of medieval Hindu philosophers, an inherently "scientific," "correct" Hindu tradition is contrasted with "ritualistic" religion.

Premodern religious systems are also bolstered in the language of modern systems of value through the prominence given to educational achievements and career accomplishments among Chowpatty's *brahmacaris*, pairing religious and secular educational authority for greater effect. Baladev, a computer-science graduate who worked in technology for several years before joining the *brahmacari* ashram, glossed the adjective "scientific," in relation to ISKCON's lectures and courses, as signaling that the speaker is well read and well educated. While leaning over his laptop in the temple's reception-area sofas and preparing PowerPoint slides for a college presentation the following day, he casually remarked: "people have never seen a *sādhu* presenting spirituality in a very scientific way. [They think] the monk is also a well-read and well-educated person like me. The students are very impressed that this is a person who is a very educated engineer and a graduate and he's using a laptop!" When I pressed him to further describe this "scientific" orientation, he responded, referring to his own spiritual search, that an "authentic spiritual tradition" is free from "any sort of ritualistic inklings." This "scientific" focus of ISKCON's courses betrays the assimilation of a Protestant-inflected critique of ritual and the tropes of priests as ritual mediators that accompany it.[16] In relation to its Hindu context, however, scientistic language is also tied to the aim of resuscitation of a Vedic religious heritage, as the teacher Rasikacharya reflected: "Previously the Vedic wisdom was not properly presented. So ISKCON is doing that—that is what we are trying to do here and in many of the programs, so people are getting attracted." Some suggested that this formulation of Vaiṣṇava teachings, tying together both the "traditional" and "modern," is why the temple community continues to draw a largely young population. Yet suspicion toward Western modes of knowledge acquisition, including the development of secular scientific inquiry, is also commonplace. After praising the scientific character of the JSD, Baladev changed course and described the "scientific bent of mind" in Mumbai as a result of "modern, Western scientific study" and as a "barrier between them [Indian youth] and their pious backgrounds." The utilization of a scientistic discourse, then, clearly has its limits, even if it bolsters the authority of JSD teachers at the outset.

Nonetheless, the term "science" is also woven into the Gauḍīya taxonomization of Hindu deities in perhaps the most challenging segment of JSD for many Hindus: "One God or Many Gods?" On an immediate level, the JSD course affirms a universality of the Hindu traditions. Yet embedded in this universalism is a determined hierarchical taxonomy, argued in the language of scientific veracity. As Radha Gopinath tells his audience, there is a big difference between *bhagavān* and *devatā*, "God with a capital G and demigods."[17] He began his introductory lecture to an English-medium JSD course held at the Bhaktivedanta Hospital in June 2014 with an explanation of the course's content:

> The Journey of Self Discovery is truly the essence of all the scriptures, which talk about understanding oneself, understanding the world around us, and understanding our roots, so that our lives can become more meaningful, more purposeful, and more fulfilling ultimately. This is actually extracting the essence of the conclusion of the Vedic literatures, the Bhagavad Gītā.[18]

After defining the broad category of Vedic scripture as "infallible knowledge," however, Radha Gopinath then questions his audience: "if God is one, the creation is one, why are there different scriptures?" In answer to this, JSD teachers lay out a hierarchical analysis of both Hindu scripture and scriptures from other major "world religions," with an entire evening out of the six dedicated to *educating* the audience about the hierarchy of the Hindu pantheon according to Gauḍīya Vaiṣṇava tradition.

While speaking to his forty or so mainly middle-aged male hospital attendees one January evening, Radha Gopinath asserted this systematic hierarchy is also universal: "different scriptures are meant for different audiences, and are revealed according to time, place, and circumstance."[19] It is the "product," or the "essence," that is the same—the difference concerns "details" or, in other words, "different people's levels of understanding."[20] The details of varying religious traditions differ, he says, because of "different levels of scriptures," revealed according to "different levels of audience." Teachers of the JSD course rank different Hindu traditions according to their "attribute" or *guṇa*, drawing on the Bhagavad Gītā's sixteenth-chapter discussion of the three attributes of *sattva* (purity), *rajas* (passion), and *tamas* (darkness). This places Durgā and Kālī worship, for instance, in the realms of *rajo-guṇa* and *tamo-guṇa*, translated by Bhaktivedanta and later ISKCON sources as the "modes of passion and ignorance."[21]

This categorization of deities—and by extension, religious systems—along the lines of *sattva*, *rajas*, and *tamas* derives from strong assertions in Bhaktivedanta's scriptural commentaries against the worship of "demigods," a category to which he assigned non-Vaiṣṇava Hindu divinities, following such categorization in Vaiṣṇava texts like the Bhāgavata Purāṇa and Viṣṇu Purāṇa.[22] Prohibitions against worshipping Lakṣmī, Gaṇeśa, or Śiva as the supreme divinity met little resistance from Bhaktivedanta's Western followers, but with the influx of Indian diaspora families into Western ISKCON centers, taboos about worshipping other Hindu gods and goddesses have become more contested.[23]

Radhika and Meghna, two newly married volunteer teachers who spent many weekday afternoons preparing their adult education classes in the temple's classrooms, told me that the discussion on the fourth evening of the seminar, entitled "One God, Many Gods," is "a big blow to attendees." The JSD teachers readily acknowledge the difficulty in asking a Hindu audience to consider giving up their own family's religious traditions in the name of regaining touch with Hindu scripture. To counteract this blow, as he calls it, Radha Gopinath seeks to convince his audience that his association of Vedic tradition with science is not merely a missionizing strategy. Rather, it is what drew him to a life of serious religious engagement as a *brahmacari* monk.

He frames this in relation to a discussion of the categories of polytheism and monotheism.[24] ISKCON presents itself as a monotheistic tradition, and a significant part of the Journey of Self Discovery course involves striving to convince its Hindu audiences that the divine, according to Vedic tradition, is both singular and singularly embodied as Krishna. In developing this argument, Radha Gopinath draws on his own prior religious search:

> This is a very troubling question, because we start questioning our own tradition, our own faith. We have become so alienated from our own culture and tradition because it has not been systematically, logically, and scientifically presented. Therefore, we cannot defend it even though it is so scientific and so advanced. I'm not being biased because I'm coming from the same tradition, but a very objective, scientific look at it proves that it has been very scientific.[25]

Radha Gopinath employs an interpretive framework that casts this seeming break from familial Hindu traditions as a revival of a common lost Hindu tradition in an emphatic singular. He acknowledges religious diversity is "what makes this culture so rich and so divine" and affirms the efficacy of worshiping other popular Hindu divinities, telling the audience of how his father taught him prayers to worship Gaṇeśa, and how he continues to turn to these prayers at times. He also allays his audience's fears of displeasing a hereditary deity through an analogy frequently used by Bhaktivedanta in his commentaries: "By watering the root of the tree, every part of the tree is nourished. If you please the Supreme Lord, you please all the thirty-four crore *devatās*."[26] Throughout all of this, he leads his audiences to a revised understanding of Hindu traditions that celebrates Vaiṣṇava traditions while curtailing Śaiva, Śakta, or other regional Hindu traditions that cannot be fitted into a Gauḍīya framework.

This recalibration of diverse Hindu traditions under a unifying sectarian structure is characteristic of modern transnational revivalist movements across religious boundaries.[27] Through constructing a unified presentation of Hindu religious history determined by Vaiṣṇava brahmanical mores, the sectarian diversity of Hindu traditions is cast as a result of historic loss—a temporal fracturing and forfeiture of an earlier systematic perfection, corruptions of a Vedic ideal. And the road back to perfection is through religious education, conveyed to be simply systematic and common-sense reasoning. Radha Gopinath, for instance, drives this home in one anecdote he includes in the "One God or Many Gods" segment, imparting Vaiṣṇava *avatāra* theology through a vivid Hinglish conversation with a *rickshaw-wala* about the iconic Hindi film star Amitabh Bachchan. One evening en route to a *satsaṅg* program, he describes being stuck in Mumbai's debilitating rush-hour traffic in the busy Kurla neighborhood. While navigating an intersection, his driver took note of his saffron robes and began to ask him theological questions:

> I was just trying to prepare my evening lecture when the *rickshaw-wala* suddenly turned around and asked "*Mahārāja, ek praśna pūchūṅgā?*" ("can I ask a question?") I said "*Hāṅ, pūcho pūcho bhāī*, but *sāmne dekho!*" ("I said, yes, go ahead and ask brother, but look at the road too!"). He said, "*Mahārāja, Rām baṛā yā Kiśan baṛā?*" He asked me, "Who is greater? Rām or Krishna?"
>
> I said: "Sometimes I take seven days to do this Gītā course, now while driving in the middle of traffic, in the peak of traffic time, I have to answer this question!" So, I was praying for the answer, and suddenly I saw in his auto *rickshaw* so many stickers—it was full of stickers practically—and all the stickers were of Amitabh Bachchan.
>
> So I said "*Maiṅ āp se praśna pūchūṅ?* ("Can I ask *you* a question?") "*Hāṅ, pūcho pūcho.*" ("Yes, ask, ask!") I said: "Amar Akbar Anthony *kā Anthony baṛā? yā* Baḍemiyā *baṛā? yā* Śarābī *baṛā? yā* Don *baṛā?*" [Giving a succession of Amitabh Bachchan's characters from his most classic film titles: In *Amar Akbar Anthony*, is Anthony greater?" and so on]. And I went on, you know, Amitabh *sahasra-nāma*![28] Because all these different movies were available there.
>
> And for ten seconds this fellow was driving, and suddenly he turned the vehicle to a corner and stopped it. And he turned around and said: "*Mahārāja, samajh gayā! Donoṁ ek hī hain, na?*" ("Mahārāja, I understand! Both are simply the same, right?"). I said: "*Hāṅ! To donoṁ ek hī haiṅ. To yahī Rām hai vahī Śyām hai. Daśāvatār pūrā nām* I just told him." ("Yes! Both are the same. In one place, it's Rām, in another, Shyām [Krishna]. The *Daśāvatāṛa* [ten classical *avatāras* of Viṣṇu] gives all these names.") So it's the same Lord who is reciprocating with different devotees in different ways.[29]

This anecdote, which translates Gauḍīya *avatāra* theology into popular culture, is now repeated in shorthand by a number of Chowpatty's *brahmacaris* in their public talks. And underlying the playful analogy is a commitment to a systematic presentation—a revision of varied Hindu traditions in the taxonomy of Krishna-centered Vaiṣṇava orthodoxy.

In JSD courses, ISKCON's brahmanically inflected Vaiṣṇava tradition is imbued with the qualities of being rational, monotheistic, and systematic, correlating Vaiṣṇava deities such as Rāma and Krishna and ascribing the worship of non-Vaiṣṇava deities to a lower level in a taxonomy of religious gradualism. Such strategies echo the mapping of Hindu traditions onto techniques of Vedāntin philosophical discourse in the identity formation of *bhadralok* in nineteenth- and early twentieth-century Calcutta.[30] In laying out the history of scientism as a discourse developing in and through the processes of nineteenth-century British colonialism, Gottschalk notes that the nineteenth century provided a critical junction during which "the trajectories of meaning for *religion* and *science* crossed," with the latter acquiring hegemonic status as the representation of a unified form of knowledge rather than merely a set of disciplines. When the practice of institutionalizing Gauḍīya Vaiṣṇava doctrine and practice in the nineteenth century began in the Bhaktivinoda-Bhaktisiddhanta line of Gauḍīya reformers in late colonial Bengal, the audiences for their English-language publications were both India's bureaucratic elite, including other Hindu intellectuals, and the colonial authorities. Consequently, an aspect of this reformulation of identity in relation to frameworks of Western modernity included assessing it alongside developing hegemonic notions of science. It was important to impress upon both groups the inherently systematic and rational—and by contrast, not superstitious or ritualistic—nature of what they articulated to be authentic Hindu traditions, precisely because those latter qualities were the grounds for colonial denigrations of any religion aside from Protestant Christianity.

Stemming from this connection, assertions of a "scientific basis" to Hindu Vaiṣṇava tradition have been central to the public representation of ISKCON in India since the organization's inception in 1965.[31] ISKCON founder Bhaktivedanta employed the term "science" in relation to a wide breadth of terms, from "spiritual science" and "science of *bhakti*" to "the science of Vedic culture" to "the science of Krishna," terms Bhaktivedanta used as early as 1944.[32] Indeed, Bhaktivedanta's widely distributed *Science of Self-Realization* lays out the basic philosophical orientations of his global Gauḍīya mission as a "science." Science has been a particularly integral theme in ISKCON's engagement with Mumbai's Hindu public spheres from the 1970s onward. A group of Indian and American ISKCON followers founded the Bhaktivedanta Institute in Mumbai in 1974, with the aim of "studying modern science in the light of Vedic knowledge and presenting Vedic knowledge from a scientific point of view."[33] Gottschalk contrasts the colonial-era development of scientism as both the "cultural currency held by the notion of science" and an oppositional term to (a unified notion of) religion.[34] The employment of scientistic discourses in ISKCON Chowpatty's educational courses seeks to harmonize these realms while also subsuming the legitimizing power of science under a hegemonic notion of Vedic knowledge. In Mumbai today, the primary audiences for this message are urban, middle-class and upper-class Hindus, many of whom are employed in the science-and-technology sector. In using the language of science and rationalism to style their religious messages, Chowpatty's *brahmacaris* assert not just that their religion's epistemological basis fits a framework of scientific inquiry but further, as Baladev proclaimed, that "our religion *is* the highest repository of scientific knowledge." It is this understanding to which another popular *brahmacari* preacher appealed when speaking to a group of several hundred college-aged young men at the temple's December 2014 Prerna gathering. There, Krishna Chaitanya painted a picture of ancient India in which technical knowledge and religious knowledge were not seen as separate epistemological spheres. He noted: "there was a culture of perfection which actually brought them the science. It was not science that brought them the perfection. And we think that science will bring us perfection—it is actually culture which brings us to the perfection of science."[35] ISKCON's religious discourses thus seek to adopt the legitimizing power of science and to subsume it symbolically under a notion of Vedic knowledge as a higher form of cognition—to revise both religion and the meanings of science itself.[36] This reflects an enchantment with science pervasive among not only middle-class Indian audiences but also modern societies generally.[37] And, strategically, through appropriating and domesticating a discourse of scientific knowledge on one's own terms, the superior status of Hindu religiosity is advanced.

The sense of religion as a tested and reproducible system is also conveyed through shorthand taxonomic formulas popular among Mumbai's devotees. The fashioning of religious knowledge as taxonomic has strong roots in Gauḍīya theological identity,[38] but Indian ISKCON centers today have excelled in further distilling religious practices into formulas that are taught and repeated in the form of mnemonic devices. Some of the most popular—quoted to me on several occasions as a shorthand for the practice of ISKCON lifestyle norms—are MATCH (Mercy, Austerity, Thoughtfulness, Cleanliness, and the Holy Name), ABCD (Association, Books, Character building, Diet and proper lifestyle), and CCD (Character, Competence, and Devotion). The ABCD formula, for instance, forms the basis for the Bhaktivedanta Hospital Youth Foundation seminars Arushi gives to high school and junior college students throughout North Mumbai. A recent "topper" in a highly competitive exam for engineering graduate programs attributed his success in attaining entrance to the Indian Institute of Technology to his practice of the CCD formula.[39] Through the memorization of these acronyms, Hindu—and specifically ISKCON's Vedic-Vaiṣṇava—traditions are rendered as a discrete and systematic body of knowledge. In *sūtra*-like form, mnemonic devices also encode aspects of contemporary ISKCON practice into a series of test-based assessment procedures given to aspirants throughout their process of religious education. This approach culminates, fittingly, in the public spectacle of formal examinations, the ultimate revision of religion.

## The Systematic Gītā: A Quiz and Its Champions

As we saw in the Journey of Self Discovery courses, the representation of the Gauḍīya tradition as a scientific system draws from Bhaktivedanta's mid-twentieth-century writings but is foregrounded within contemporary Indian idioms of education and professional achievement. In this sense, revising religion (as studying, relearning) is imbued with professional rigor. A prominent aspect of Chowpatty's Gauḍīya religious education is communicated in the rigorous style of India's examination-centered educational ethos. Resonant with broader ISKCON trends toward the systemization of Gauḍīya religious knowledge, the pattern of philosophical presentation given in the Journey of Self Discovery course is also followed in the Gita Champions League competition, which engages teenagers and young adults in an annual examination on the Bhagavad Gītā. After procuring the Gita Champions League textbook, designed to prepare students for the exam, one can register and enter the competition, study with online help, and attend classes at the temple on the quiz subjects in the months leading up to a springtime exam date.

The quiz attracts a range of contestants from secondary schools and colleges throughout the metropolitan area. Available in English, Marathi, Hindi, or Gujarati, the exam was developed for students from the fifth to tenth standards (equivalent to grades in the American educational system).

Due to interest from adults, the contest was expanded to include a second category for participants over the age of fifteen. One exam coordinator relayed to me that the most interest for the exam came from Mumbai's northern and western suburbs of Kandivli, Borivli, Nalasopara, Vasai, and Ulhasnagar (known within the city as middle-class and developing metropolitan areas) rather than in South Bombay, although the exam has been held on the Chowpatty temple grounds. It received international attention in April 2015, when Maryam Siddiqui, a twelve-year-old Muslim girl from the Mira Road neighborhood, won the championship out of over 3,000 contestants.[40] Maryam enrolled in the exam's preparation course along with other students in her local high school class, and her success became widely publicized. Local and national news sources interviewed Maryam and her father and dwelt on her father's assertions that he sought to instill in his daughter respect and knowledge of religious traditions other than her own. News media also showcased meetings of the father and daughter with Prime Minister Narendra Modi and then–Uttar Pradesh Chief Minister Akhilesh Yadav, who flew the pair to Delhi and arranged public events to congratulate Maryam. This spectacle of Muslim participation in an event to promote knowledge of a central Hindu scripture segued with political aims to showcase "communal harmony" during the fraught period after the BJP's parliamentary victory. Additionally, it underscored the extent to which ISKCON's exams have been accepted as a neutral purveyor of Hindu religious education.

Aside from facilitating a chance for all of Mumbai's young residents to become familiar with the teachings of the Bhagavad Gītā, the quiz also partakes in a wider cultural obsession with testing and ranking that pervades contemporary middle-class Indian educational and child-rearing culture.[41] Though the full exam study guide is available only to registered participants, practice exams are available on the Gita Champions website under the title "Vedic Quiz." Therein one can test one's knowledge of the Gītā in categories that parallel the themes of the Journey of Self Discovery course: namely, the "Search for Happiness"; "Does God Exist?"; "One God or Many Gods?"; "Who Am I?"; "Why do Bad Things Happen to Good People?"; and "Practical Application." Based on earlier ISKCON systematizations of Gauḍīya theology, particularly the Bhakti Śāstrī course,[42] the quiz format engages each contestant in mastering ISKCON's systematic presentation of Vaiṣṇava Hindu philosophy, advertised as a generic body of knowledge about Hindu traditions for the general public. The quiz is given in a series of multiple-choice questions, compiled by a group of initiated ISKCON members based throughout India and in Singapore, and the exams themselves are distributed by volunteers of Chowpatty's media-distribution service.

The series of exam questions follows popular theological tenets of Vaiṣṇava Hindu traditions, centering on the Bhagavad Gītā and articulations of Krishna *bhakti* drawn from Bhaktivedanta's scriptural commentaries. A number of questions are based closely on Gītā verses, asking contestants about the words and actions of key characters and the definition of philosophical terms in Krishna's discourse. However, other questions in the quiz demand a standardized knowledge of ISKCON's philosophy as put forward in Chowpatty's print and audio media. This requires the contestants to become familiar with a range of figures in Gauḍīya Vaiṣṇava history, including Rūpa Gosvāmin and Haridāsa Ṭhākura, who would not be known to Hindus outside of the tradition. It also requires them to assimilate an understanding of Hindu traditions that is based on ISKCON's Gauḍīya interpretation of the Gītā—a point that is particularly meaningful in the "One God or Many Gods?" section. Therein, contestants must know that all gods and goddesses in the Hindu pantheon, aside from Krishna, are considered "demigods" and that, according to question 106 in Section Three, Level Two, demigods are not (a) controllers of this universe but in fact (b) empowered administrators.[43] This language, which draws directly from the wording in Bhaktivedanta's commentary of Bhagavad Gītā 3.11, intriguingly parallels the bureaucratic organizational structure of ISKCON, normalizing a model of power that is reflected in material and spiritual hierarchies. Furthermore, a Gītā quiz topper will also know the answer to question #203—Who is the only worshipable object according to the scriptures? (a) Śiva, (b) Supreme Lord, (c) Brahmā, (d) any demigod—and that answer would be (b) Supreme Lord, namely, Krishna. Or, as another question in the examination asks: "What is the essence of Vedic culture?" The options given are (a) serving the relatives, (b) planting trees, (c) worshipping *devatās*, or (d) chanting the holy names of the Lord. Any contestant who answers the question correctly will know that it is (d) chanting the holy names of the Lord, a popular ISKCON English translation of *japa* and *harināma saṃkīrtana*. Through numerous questions such as these, specific aspects of Gauḍīya *siddhānta* and *sādhana* are worked into a didactic format for the several thousand students in the competition annually, most of whom enroll through public schools and may only have a tangential understanding of ISKCON as an organization.

The Gita Champions League exam does not set itself up in rhetorical opposition to modern educational systems in the same manner that some JSD teachers do in relation to modern science. Rather, even more explicitly than the JSD format, the GCL examination employs modern educational rubrics to communicate that the information gained therein is to be considered on par in intellectual rigor with subjects taught in a secular educational format. In this sense, the GCL exam taps into the aura of a verifiable, systematized rationality underlying the modern educational process in a display of ISKCON as a streamlined Hinduism for the modern, urban, and well-educated citizens of Mumbai. This traditionalist identity, marketed in the secular vocabularies that are seen as its epistemological competition, reflects a number of focal points across urban Indian middle and upper classes. It embraces a globally integrated professionalism conveyed through elite networks and media forums, while also asserting the preeminence of a Hindu (Vaiṣṇava) religious heritage. That Vaiṣṇava heritage is preeminent because of its ancient roots *and* its asserted rational composition, and it offers its audiences the chance to "understand" their Hindu heritage more fully through education in its systematic nature.

## Managing Doubts, Practicing Certainty

Although the answers communicated through the JSD courses and GCL exams tend to be packaged as neat and reproducible knowledge systems, the lived experience of this systematized religious knowledge is much messier. Many devotees used the English term "questions" when discussing their choice to join ISKCON, but the Hindi equivalents used in Chowpatty's lectures range from *praśna* to *śaṅkā*, the latter of which is also translated as doubt or uncertainty. Doubt in the semantic range of Indian English does not carry the same meaning of a lack of faith as in the United States but rather an incomplete understanding of a topic, an issue on which the thinker is still uncertain. Yet, in many students' voicings of "doubts," or questions about the veracity of ISKCON's worldview or benefits of its *sādhana* prescriptions, doubt did also convey skepticism. In other cases, the airing of questions or doubts conveyed an interface in people's lives between aspirations toward markers of urban success—career security, wealth accumulation—and a feeling of disconnect from the religious practices and cultural traditions of past generations.[44] To be clear, many young Mumbaikars I met outside temple networks lived their lives quite happily without any overt relation to religious traditions or heritage. However, for those attracted to Chowpatty's

ISKCON community, the interface between secular urban modernity and familial traditions produced a decisive re-centering of religious practice in their lives, in forms that could even sometimes seem excessive to their family members and peers. For them, there was little room to explore doubt in relation to skepticism about their chosen religious path. Rather, the realm of doubt was expressed as a feeling of being unmoored within their lives in Mumbai, of doubting in the safety of one's present state in the world. This uncertainty, many devotees insisted, could be remedied only through accepting the answers of Krishna consciousness.

While the conviction of finding answers is at the heart of many devotees' narratives of their religious awakening, not all JSD attendees respond with unbridled acceptance of ISKCON's interpretation of Hindu traditions. When I attended several JSD courses in the fall and winter of 2012 and 2013, I was introduced to deferential male college students who had already "become convinced," as they told me, through hearing the lectures and receiving personal guidance from the *brahmacaris* they now deferred to as "authorities in the meaning of life." They voiced a disquiet with the secularizing context of their elite colleges that mirrored ISKCON teachers' descriptions, such as those used by Aditya at the outset of the last chapter. Some aspired to join the *brahmacari* ashram after their graduation and a few years of work experience, as preferred by the ashram. Others responded with a shy giggle at the notion of abandoning their careers and families for that lofty renounced state; yet they did hope to one day qualify, through increasing their *sādhana* practice, to receive formal initiation into the ISKCON community.

However, alongside these enthusiastic participants—many of whom were repeat attendees of the JSD course—slightly older young professionals and their friends viewed the course with a range of responses. For Shilpa, a well-dressed administrator in finance who attended the nightly courses in pencil skirts and sensible heels, JSD provided a re-centering experience. She had paid the few-hundred-rupee charge for the second time, after being so impressed with the course she had attended last summer that she wanted to return and gain a "deeper understanding of the Bhagavad Gītā" through these "informational sessions." Shilpa confessed that she had never thoroughly read the Bhagavad Gītā growing up, and even now she was always a bit too busy between work and her social life to spend time reading. "Actually, I am not really a big reader. And if I do it's just novels or some magazine or something. So, coming to these courses gives me the same benefit," she cheekily reasoned. This time, she had brought a college friend,

Mahesh, who works in a nearby office building. The two had reached the course venue by sharing a taxi from the rapidly expanding financial district of Lower Parel. Mahesh, also dressed in the business-professional attire of Mumbai's finance sector, politely agreed that he found the course sessions informative. "Actually they have answered some questions I have always had about the Gītā. Particularly the nature of the soul, its relation to the supreme." Although he had already adopted the questions-and-answers-based conceptual framework emphasized in the JSD course, Mahesh retained more skepticism about whether the content of the course provided all the answers for him. While he dutifully came back to another two remaining sessions that week, he seemed more interested in checking email on his smartphone than in the PowerPoint slides. Indeed, a five- to six-night intensive course is a tall order for any working professional.

But Deen Dayal, the *brahmacari* who led that course, readily acknowledged that it would not appeal to everyone. In a room of one hundred, he reasoned, one may only reach a handful of people: "maybe five or ten will be ready to inquire about the real meaning of the Gītā. Then you get those people who just come to challenge, but that is a different thing. So each session, maybe five-ten percent will be ready to receive the knowledge of the Gita. But ten percent is actually a great success rate! And then they go on to learn more." Framing his perspective in the marketing terminology common to many discussions of ISKCON's missionizing, he shrugged and responded—undaunted—that 10 percent was a laudable response rate for any company. And indeed, this role of authority in dispensing religious knowledge about the Gītā and Hindu traditions to Mumbai's publics at large, irrespective of their future connection with ISKCON, underscores the implicit authority now enjoyed by the JSD teachers in Mumbai.

The confidence Chowpatty's teachers carry in the implicit authority of their Gauḍīya system shines in the seminar-style logic outlined above. On an existential level, it is also premised on the ability of Gauḍīya practice to lead the practitioner to a state of *preman* (in Hindi: *prem*), divine love for Krishna—the goal of this *bhakti* tradition. The educational focus at the heart of Chowpatty's process of "systematic training" is meant to bring about a fundamental change in an individual's mind and habits. Through "personality development"—a term intriguingly drawn from contemporary Indian coaching classes and used increasingly to advertise ISKCON's courses in Mumbai—one awakens the *habitus* of a devotee, centered on the performance of Krishna *bhakti* and *sevā* to other Vaiṣṇavas.[45] This desired state should arise not only when one is engaged in religious rituals at demarcated times. Rather, "twenty-four hours a day one should remember Krishna," constantly working toward the inculcation of the performance of Vaiṣṇava etiquette as a display of *bhakti* in one's personal conduct. This goal echoes the Counselling System's pairing of a focus on emotional fulfillment with a highly systematized formula for religious participation.

The ability for a practitioner's lifestyle and even thought processes to move from doubt to certainty is attested to be a result of the workings of *bhagavat prem*, divine love for God or Bhagavān, once the practitioner progresses in the prescribed practices of *bhakti*. This desired transformation comes alive in relation to the temple's frequent Vaiṣṇava *kathā*, or stories told about Krishna and other *avatāras* and saintly figures in the tradition. As the Chowpatty-affiliated *sannyasi* Bhaktirasamrita Swami mentions in his description of several prominent Āḻvārs, Tamil *bhakti* saints:

> The devotees (*bhakt*) of Bhagavān, they two are not independent, they too are *g͟hulam* (servants)—like those who pursue an irreligious life. But not to the forces of illusion in this world—rather, they become the servants of divine love (*bhagavat prem*). And such a wave of divine love keeps flowing in their hearts, according to their sentiments, their thought processes and their lifestyle habits keep changing. Divine love remains, flowing, in such hearts.[46]

This desired state comprises an ultimate revision of oneself in a religious register. Yet, as Chowpatty's teachers tell their audiences, this love must be cultivated through training. Ultimately, *bhakti* is affiliated with grace (*dayā*), but the practices that lead toward it are communicated as rational, scientific processes—a path that can be reproduced systematically in a conducive environment.

In this devotional *habitus*, a rootedness in the methodical reproduction of Rupa Gosvāmin's principles of *vaidhī-bhakti* lays at the heart of Chowpatty's institutionalized lifeways. That cultivation is tied to the production and sensory consumption of media in many forms. This is related to oft-quoted verses from a central Gauḍīya scripture, Bhāgavata Purāṇa 9.4.18–20, that describe the multisensory nature of *bhakti* in the devotional practice of a legendary monarch, Ambarīśa.[47] Revisiting this well-known example in a Sunday program lecture, Radhanath Swami paraphrased the exegetical import for his followers:

> Mahārāja Ambarīśa lived in such a way that everything he had was immersed in remembering Krishna's love. With his tongue, he would speak the glories of the Lord, with his ears, he would hear the glories of the Lord, with his eyes, he would see the beautiful form of the Lord in the temples and holy places . . . with all of his desires, his power, his wealth. . . . According the *bhakti* tradition, this is the perfection of meditation.[48]

This focus on an embodied, aestheticized devotion draws on early Gauḍīya understandings of the nature of devotional practices and in particular the systematization of the sixty-four practices of *vaidhī-bhakti*.[49] An important aspect of such training is to center one's life on the reception and engagement with Krishna-centered media. Hearing about Krishna's *līlās* and the philosophy of the Bhagavad Gītā and Bhāgavata Purāṇa is seen as mentally and spiritually purifying, helping Chowpatty's practitioners along the road to developing devotion to Krishna. This also explains the impressive length of a typical philosophical lecture at the temple or in its public programs—between one to three hours—with expected attendance by community members on a regular basis.

In addition to the lectures and classes above, this can also take the form of a simple oral reception of the trademark mantra, or sacred chant of the Gauḍīya tradition: the Hare Krishna *mahā-mantra*. Akshayi, an administrator at the Bhaktivedanta Hospital, described her efforts to bring this sensory devotional media into her family's daily life. She acquired from her counsellor a "chanting box"—an electronic device that, when turned on, plays the voice of Bhaktivedanta Swami softly chanting the Hare Krishna mantra and singing *kīrtans* continuously. Hoping to draw her husband into the devotee community as well, she took to keeping it on continuously at low volume in her kitchen and told her husband that it was "for her benefit only." However, as she kept it on throughout the days and nights, she began imperceptibly raising the volume. Although her husband initially balked at the constant noise, after a certain time, she related with pride, he told her that he could no longer sleep unless he heard the mantras on in the background. The presence of this Krishna-centered audio media had become an integrated part of their daily lives, in both waking and sleeping, and Akshayi could then rest assured that her husband was on the right path.

Not everyone is equally enthused about the repetition involved in this systematic process of attaining *bhakti*. At the Annual Republic Day Program at Juhu in January 2015, Radhanath Swami addressed the discomfort some congregation members had expressed to their counsellors about the length and frequency of ISKCON's *kathās*, particularly focusing on the repetitiveness of religious narratives (*līlās*). He exhorted his audience: "Even with the same pastime, it's never 'Oh, I've heard that already,' because every time you hear it, you go deeper into love for Krishna."[50] Rather, the frequency of these repetitions should bring one into a new mindset or way of dwelling, steeped in the emotional orientations that are beneficial to developing Krishna *prema*. David Haberman has discussed the Gauḍīya construction of a spiritual self through the "acting" and visualization practices involved in Gauḍīya *sādhana* practices. In this context too members are encouraged to enact and embrace ritual repetition as a means of their systematic religion, to impress the values and sensibilities of Gauḍīya perfection more deeply into their minds with the aim of awakening a dormant religious selfhood. And the performance of attainment itself becomes a tool for preaching to others, spreading the certainty of this religious path.[51]

For many Mumbaikars who joined ISKCON, their prior lives are rendered in retrospect as a state of existential anomie. The realm of doubt is shifted outward, as uncertainties of one's career, relationships, and place in the world are contrasted to the attractiveness of a system that *works*, that can be seen and proven. The *proof* discussed in courses such as JSD is contrasted with frustrations about a "culture of corruption" and all that does not *work* in modern political and social systems. It is also a proof mediated by a community of engineers and doctors, a religious tradition certified by trained professionals. In this iteration of religious traditionalism, doubt is managed through a system—a tried-and-tested system of premodern pedigree *and* one communicated through the symbols of elite modern India.

## ISKCON Has Arrived

Lalita, a dutiful second-generation Chowpatty member who has mastered the *mṛdaṅga* drum in the temple's *kīrtans*, relaxed with a girlfriend one afternoon at the foot of her platform bed. Posters of Rādhā and Krishna, the sacred path around Govardhan Hill, and Shahrukh Khan in a vintage *Kuch Kuch Hota Hai* poster were taped to the pastel-colored walls. Both friends had some time off in between college exams and could enjoy a rare relaxed afternoon at home. Laughing together about some their parents' stories from the time they joined ISKCON, Lalita reflected that "times have changed."

Whereas her parents' college friends in the 1990s felt that they were joining a foreign movement, now her college friends do not have that impression. Rather, they just see her involvement in the community as being "too much into spiritualism and tradition."[52]

Today, ISKCON has arrived as a player in India's Hindu public spheres. Although many devotees still emphasize the challenges of crossing into their devout religious community, ISKCON increasingly dwells as a representative of Hindu traditionalism in Mumbai through the efforts of its Indian *brahmacari*s and lay practitioners, bolstered by the prominence of its JSD courses and GCL competitions. They have revised the place of ISKCON in Hindu public spheres, which reflects in contemporary news-media representations. Many of the major English-language news articles about ISKCON in Mumbai's newspapers draw heavily on the well-worded press releases issued by various ISKCON communications teams concerning upcoming events or developing projects. Other independently contracted articles contact ISKCON's Chowpatty and Juhu centers as go-to places for news on Mumbai's annual Janmashtami celebrations, marking Krishna's birth. But most frequently this good press revolves around humanitarian engagement in Mumbai and the surrounding rural areas of Maharashtra. Members from ISKCON Chowpatty run several humanitarian initiatives—most notably the charitable Bhaktivedānta Hospital in the North Mumbai Mira Road neighborhood, and the Annamrita Midday Meal program, which operates in connection with ISKCON's Food for Life Midday Meal programs in Delhi, Rajasthan, Haryana, Madhya Pradesh, Jharkhand, and Andhra Pradesh.[53] These projects are marked visually by standing billboards and information booths at the temple's public events. Even in the midst of a series of Midday Meal food adulteration scandals throughout India over the past several years, ISKCON's Midday Meal kitchen at Tardeo received praise in the local papers, detailing the high hygiene standards at the facility that cater to 64,000 students in 431 government-aided schools daily.[54] This positive reputation has more recently earned ISKCON (and an ISKCON-adjacent charity Akshay Patra) a greater stake in the Midday Meal programs, and in 2013 the BMC chose them to replace local organizations as their main institutional partner.[55]

Mumbai's news media is also driven by the star power associated with local ISKCON centers, as we have seen above. Both the ISKCON Juhu and Chowpatty temples have become sites for Mumbai's film celebrities and the city's business elite to host rite-of-passage events, including weddings and memorials.[56] They also regularly serve as a destination for Hindi film celebrities who want to display religiosity in public.[57] This extends to liaisons with Mumbai's fashion world. Beginning in 2008, local papers reported that Manish Malhotra, one of India's premier fashion designers, was designing special outfits for the ISKCON Juhu *mūrti*s of Rādhā and Krishna. Malhotra was invited to perform the *kalaśa abhiṣeka* ceremony to the *mūrti*s on Janmashtami, along with local Hindi film celebrities Rani Mukherjee, Sonam Kapoor, and Raveena Tandon.[58] As with ISKCON's ties to Indian politicians, membership in the group offers both a connection with Vaiṣṇava religious heritage and a way to root aspirational narratives of urban Indian success, including the display of high-society wealth and glamour, in an attractive contemporary religiosity. As Hema Malini, a regular attendee at ISKCON Juhu, told the *Times of India* in 2014: "I am a die hard devotee of lord Krishna and ISKCON. . . . The basic teaching of ISKCON is the cleanliness of the soul. If your soul is clean, then you will be beautiful."[59]

On a transregional Indian scale, this indigenization into elite Hindu public spheres has also brought governmental support for ISKCON projects across India, including in relation to ISKCON's proposed "Vrindavan Chandrodaya Mandir," a massive multiuse complex in its initial stages of construction in the North Indian pilgrimage city of Vrindavan, and the ambitious "Vedic Planetarium" complex at ISKCON's Mayapur, Bengal center—a projected seventy-five-million-dollar undertaking funded partially by Alfred Ford, an American ISKCON member and heir to Henry Ford. In this context, transnationalism is by no means a liability for ISKCON in the present day; however, today it increasingly radiates out from India instead of in from ISKCON's Western base. One example of this trend is Anil Agarwal, a Bihari-born, self-made billionaire mining magnate associated with ISKCON in Mumbai and London.[60] His mining conglomerate is aptly named Vedanta Resources. In 2012, Agarwal chaired the Gita Champions League competition and addressed the exam takers over a microphone in the Chowpatty temple room. He reflected that his success has been grounded in his religious commitments. For the past thirty years, he noted, Radhanath Swami "has been guiding me, telling me how to balance the life, how to study properly, how to do business, how to respect your parents. And whatever I got, what we are today . . . is because of his guidance."[61] Radhanath Swami, and the Chowpatty community that surrounds him, are thus rendered as forces to maintain Indic traditions both theological and cultural, including how to respect one's parents, that can enable a wildly successful businessman to bolster—and sanctify—success in the multinational corporate world.

Not everyone is on board, of course, with promoting the Bhagavad Gītā and the principles of Hindu *dharma* in Mumbai's public spheres. Many Mumbaikars worry about the rise of Hindu majoritarian religiosity, sensing an abandonment of India's post-Independence Nehruvian secular ideals and the growing marginalization of India's religious minorities alongside the country's turn toward economic privatization. For them, ISKCON is troubling not on account of its transnational development but because of its participation in conservative Hindu networks in the city and its messaging on the need to instantiate a particular tradition of Hindu religiosity (Vaiṣṇava, brahmanically inflected, Sanskritic) in Mumbai's cosmopolitan public spheres. Other reservations pervaded my interactions outside the temple community, particularly when I asked friends and acquaintances about their own perceptions of ISKCON. While many lauded their humanitarian work, which is today perhaps the most forward-facing aspect of the community, "doubts" about "what actually goes on in those temples" still exist. One girlfriend in her early thirties, who was employed as a mid-level manager at one of India's growing chain department stores, cautioned me in a firm tone: "To this day, no respectable girl would be seen at an ISKCON temple." Although she simultaneously expressed an interest in joining me one day during my research, she also made it clear that her mother and grandmother, devout Gujarati Hindus in Ahmedabad, would not approve given the ongoing suspicions that ISKCON is a Western organization (and therefore not sufficiently orthodox). Yet by far the most popular reservations toward ISKCON that I encountered were among Mumbai's more socially liberal circles, who cast the organization's members as the equivalent of Hindu evangelicals, strictly devout and adamantly insular. As residents of what is perhaps the least socially conservative major urban center in India, such evangelism seemed an encroachment, not from abroad but from *within* India's social fabric. ISKCON's promotion of vegetarianism, cow protection, and a strict brahmanical lifestyle, and its denunciation of dating, drinking, and many forms of popular entertainment in the city (in parallel to many Hindu right groups across India), sounded alarm bells for more secular-minded Mumbaikars. However, that secular India stands in opposition to ISKCON's imaginary of the nation's cultural heritage. In this sense, the growth of ISKCON's Juhu and Chowpatty centers signifies the long-term success of the earliest ISKCON campaign: to protect Hindu *dharma* in Mumbai's secularizing cityscape.

On a pleasant evening in late January 2015, I sat on the rooftop of one of ISKCON Juhu's many sprawling buildings, awaiting the beginning of the annual evening program, usually held on India's Republic Day. According to tradition, on that day every year Radhanath Swami comes to Juhu to speak about ISKCON, relating the significance of Indian independence on the site where early devotees had struggled and succeeded to establish their first Mumbai temple. I arrived early to the large compound, which was abuzz with relatives and friends coming from work for the evening *darśan*. The open-air temple and its adjoining white marble courtyard seemed formidably packed, so I wandered around the back of the property to seek out a familiar face who might be heading to Radhanath Swami's talk. In an adjacent parking lot, a wedding reception was just about to begin in a separate hall.[62] Guests arrived in luxury cars and approached the jasmine-lined reception hall entrance in gorgeous silks. I felt significantly underdressed in my cotton *kurtī* and leggings, so quickened my pace toward the other side of the compound.

Finally, I came to the entrance of the right building, named "Heaven on Earth," in which the evening program was to be held. Five flights up, the elevator opened out onto the roof where seating mats had been spread out for the anticipated several hundred guests. The sun was just setting, and the twilight framed the temple's Odishan-style towers. The leafy lanes of the posh Juhu suburb stretched out in every direction as a breeze from the nearby ocean contributed to the relaxed evening atmosphere. As guests began to arrive and the program began, I looked around at the several hundred people present: men and women who came straight from work, some dressed in business professional attire, others dressed in saris, *dhoti*s, and with fresh *tilak* marks on their foreheads, interspersed with young women in jeans and pashminas slung over their plaid button-down shirts. Guests sat in rows of chairs and on the padded floor. The overall mood spoke refinement and comfort—a well-placed societal gathering, running smoothly due to the characteristically flawless organization of the *brahmacari*s behind the scenes. These Mumbaikars were clearly here because they resonated with the religious message and the atmosphere created in this space. This was not an inherited religiosity but the community they had chosen, and built, for themselves. ISKCON has arrived in India.

# 5

# *Bhakti* and Its Boundaries

## Enacting a Religious Nation

> [We will] glorify all the arts of India which the British killed—it is time to give them a life again . . . Artisans all over the villages will be invited to bring their arts back to the standard . . . And here is the Festival of India, the most vibrant and grand festival of India, which the British wanted to stop but couldn't stop.
>
> Krishna Chaitanya Das, Chowpatty *brahmacari*

> India was the guru of the world. But, *was* . . . Because our education is wrong-headed. There is no spiritual education . . . All we can do is try to teach the next generation *pūjā, dharm, arth, nīti* . . . Then a generation will arise who says "*mera Bhārat hoga*," my India will come to be.
>
> Subhash Ghai, film director, speaking at ISKCON's "India Rising" festival, Mumbai, 2015 (from Hindi)

Now that ISKCON has arrived in India, what kind of India has it reached? In revising religion, Indian devotees reframe their relationships to family, regional origin, and religious background. ISKCON does not center on a particular ethno-linguistic community, as in the case of Gujarati Hindus in the Swaminarayan community. But joining ISKCON affects one's own relationship to diverse Hindu traditions—be they Gujarati Vaiṣṇava, Tamil Smarta brahmin, or Maharashtrian Vārkarī—through its proclamations to represent India's manifold *bhakti* traditions. The idiom of a systematic Hindu traditionalism adopted through personal choice distinguishes one from family, *jati*, and regional groups. But Chowpatty's media products also fashion visions of the Indian nation and its precolonial past. What does this India look like? Who does it represent, and how are its borders and contents constructed

*Bringing Krishna Back to India*. Claire C. Robison, Oxford University Press. © Oxford University Press 2024.
DOI: 10.1093/9780197656488.003.0006

in retelling its histories? In this, how might revised religious identities in ISKCON correlate to political identities?

This chapter considers depictions of the nation and its regions in the temple's pilgrimage routes, lectures, and dramatic productions. These forums map out a religious vision of the Indian nation, linking the length and breadth of its modern states through regional Vaiṣṇava *bhakti* traditions. I will trace, through visual culture analysis, how religion and politics intertwine in the articulation of a religio-national imaginary in Chowpatty's pilgrimages (*yātrās*) and public festivals, centering on a detailed analysis of the "India Rising" Rath Yatra and the annual Drama Festival. Through these examples, I assess the implications of this vision of India, which inscribes a specific type of religious nationalism onto India's past and celebrates the Gauḍīya tradition as the summation of India's devotional legacy while also projecting that heritage outward, toward cultural missionizing on a global scale.

This pan-Indic *bhakti* imaginary engages with multiple nationalisms. Strands of Nehruvian nation-building meld with a Gandhian romanticization of Indian village life and post-liberalization aspirational narratives of India's global rise. But foremostly, through a framework of religious revivalism, India's success as a nation is linked to the fidelity to Vaiṣṇava devotion. The development of such a religio-national imaginary demonstrates that ISKCON's public discourse has shifted from an expression of anxieties about their place in India to anxieties about India's place in the global economy. This marks its transformation within Mumbai to an Indian-led organization echoing popular views among conservative middle classes that India's economic and political success rests on a Hindu-centered national culture. Here, religious conservatism is twinned with an embrace of neoliberal capitalism in a pairing that impacts both, revising the forums through which traditionalist ideas are mediated and reshaping urban capitalist aspirations through devotional Hindu formations.

## Charting a National Heritage of Hindu Devotion

While sitting in the Chowpatty temple accounting office one afternoon, waiting for an appointment with the head of financial services, a desk calendar beckoned me to: "Experience the Culture and the Blessings of Gods from across India at ISKCON Pune." The calendar presented an array of Vaiṣṇava deities in select pilgrimage locations throughout India, tracing the visuality of Vaiṣṇava devotion in its many regional variants. Issued by the Pune temple, a close affiliate of Chowpatty in history and leadership,[1] the calendar speaks to one of ISKCON's central messages about the heritage it seeks to represent.

Debates about the relation between India's diverse cultural and linguistic regions have occupied the nation since its Independence in 1947. The concern to establish connectivity among diverse religions and cultures within the national borders manifests from the most formal level, in the floats of the nation's annual Republic Day parade, down to the most domestic, in the colorfully illustrated "National Integration Party Tissues," a major brand of table napkins found in corner stores and supermarkets during my research. Its stylized portrayals sported smiling couples representing each of India's prominent religious communities by attire: Hindu couples in saris and white *kurtas*, a Christian couple in a sleeveless cocktail dress and suit with bow tie, and a Muslim couple inexplicably wearing an red Ottoman style fez and burqa.[2] Celebrations of religious harmony among India's diverse regions formed the foundation of early postcolonial India's state policy, as imagined under India's first prime minister, Jawaharlal Nehru. Yet the ideal of a shared Indian identity that embraces religious and linguistic plurality has contended with the rise of a majoritarian notion that upper-caste, Hindi-speaking Hindus most fully embody the Indian nation.[3] A national imaginary centered on Hindu identity is a particularly fraught proposition in liberal circles but has been decisively centered in Modi's BJP government over the past decade. It is amidst this contentious climate that Chowpatty's lectures, festivals, and dramas fuse nation and religion in the articulation of *bhāratīya saṁskṛti*, or brahmanically inflected Indian culture. Yet they also revise what is essential therein. As discussed in Chapter 3, joining ISKCON often means parting ways with family worship practices and adopting a new understanding of one's own Hindu traditions, even if they are articulated as a return to one's heritage. At the same time, ISKCON's revivalism is deeply invested in representing Hindu religious heritage, mapped along the lines of the Indian nation-state. It is in these forms that, I would argue, the transnational organization has most palpably come to dwell in India. It is no longer a "foreigner's Hinduism," as the local concerns of Indian devotees are visible through the depictions they perform and produce at ISKCON's events.

As Talal Asad and others have noted, the religious is never, in fact, neatly separate from the political. Straightforward nationalist idioms are embedded into some courses in ISKCON's repertoire, a central example of which is the

"Mera Bhārat Mahān" ("My India Is Great") course. Therein, depictions of a grand, ancient Indian past obscured by intrusions of foreign political actors evoke the tripartite model of rise, golden age, and decline characteristic of many British colonial histories of the Middle East and South Asia. Information from these courses is also employed in the monthly Prerna programs held for young men on the Chowpatty temple grounds. Yet beyond just assertions to develop national pride, the *greatness* that audiences are exhorted to uncover is linked to a transregional Vaiṣṇava *bhakti* heritage. On the temple site, lecture series over the past few years have included those on "Rāmāyaṇa Līlā," focusing on the North and South Indian locations that Ram traversed in his exile from Ayodhya; "Rāmanujācārya Kathā," celebrating the life and theology of the South Indian preceptor of Śrīvaiṣṇavism; "Narasiṃha Līlā," celebrating regional religious narratives of the Vaiṣṇava *avatāra* Narasimha (Nṛsiṃha) from Karnataka and Tamil Nadu; and "Alwaron kī kathā," a twelve-part series on the Āḻvārs, a group of Tamil *bhakti* saints whose poetry is seen as some of the earliest extant examples of the vernacular poetic styles that were to become a central feature of popular Hindu *bhakti*. Therein, a Gauḍīya superordination framework communicates a connected but ordered network culminating in Krishna devotional traditions.

To introduce his series on the Tamil Vaiṣṇava Āḻvārs, Bhakti Rasamrita drew out an extended analogy about the sacred verses of the *sants* as carrying forward the *bhagavān kī nadī*, or river of God. He likened their words to a storm (*tufān*) that released these *sundar stotras* ("beautiful verses"), through the force of *bhakti*, or *bhagavat prem*, like the origin of the *gaṅgā* (Ganges) at Gurumukh releases the river to flow through North India.[4] He then went through the popular narratives of each Āḻvār, celebrating their devotion to Viṣṇu and particularly remarking on analogies in their poetry to what one might recognize as Gauḍīya, Krishna-oriented devotion. Āṇṭāḷ, who is known for her verses in praise of child Krishna, was given special emphasis. In the process of telling these stories, speakers like Bhakti Rasamrita also wove in the subtle sectarian taxonomies encoded in stories of other regional Vaiṣṇava traditions, for instance casting Śiva as a divine figure subordinate to Viṣṇu in the story of Āṇṭāḷ's life, underscoring a Vaiṣṇava orientation in the depiction of India's devotional heritage. Concomitantly, South Indian Śaiva *bhakti* traditions, such as those stemming from the Nāyaṉār poet-saints who composed hymns to Śiva contemporaneously to the Āḻvārs, are not visible in this devotional topography.

As these regional Vaiṣṇava *bhakti* saint narratives are incorporated, they are also placed in a hierarchy that points to Gauḍīya Vaiṣṇavism as the consummation of all regional *bhakti* traditions. This point is made through narrative and performance, in the retelling of hagiographies of the Maharashtrian poet-saint Tukārām or the Tamil Śrīvaiṣṇava *ācārya* Rāmānuja in Indian ISKCON centers, particularly by speakers who reframe their own regional religious traditions through a Gauḍīya lens. For instance, ISKCON narratives about Tukārām link his *abhaṅgas*, devotional verses, to ISKCON's signature Hare Krishna mantra and to the Gauḍīya founder himself, through the shared appellation of Caitanya in the names of two gurus in Tukārām's lineage, Raghava Caitanya and Keshava Caitanya.[5] Thus, a local Maharashtrian story is described in relation to a pan-Indic, Gauḍīya-centered *bhakti* lineage. A parallel narrative of Tukārām's life is performed at Chowpatty on a regular basis, as will be discussed below. For ISKCON teachers from Maharashtra, connecting Tukārām's religious development with Caitanya of Bengal enables ISKCON to affirm both historic regional traditions—sanctioning them within ISKCON's orthodox framework—and their own regional traditions revised in a Gauḍīya *bhakti* taxonomy.

A shared devotional culture can be traced across India, according to Jahnavi, a retired biochemist from Kerala who moved up the coast to Mumbai as a young girl. Although from an affluent family and at the end of an eminent career, she decided after her husband's passing to adopt a *vānaprastha* lifestyle and has lived on the temple grounds since 2002. What gave her conviction, she said, to join ISKCON—although it meant she had to stop worshipping at her family's altar and abstain from their fish potlucks on weekends—was the notion that this tradition shared in a transregional worship of Krishna. It was not just something from one part of India:

> Suppose you go to Gujarat. Most of them are very staunch Krishna *bhaktas*. In the South also, same thing. This Rāmānuja, he has spread this worship of Krishna. So it was there—Madhvācarya, Tirupati, Udupi. All these things were there, but then after, because of the British rule, Muslim rule, those things were entering into it, so certain things stopped. . . But in every house, if you go to see, there will be some deity photograph or something in their house. In some villages this is there, people are practicing this everywhere.

These narratives emphasizing a devotional connection among India's regional *bhakti* traditions are given further tangible form for Chowpatty's members in the frequent *yātrās* the community takes to diverse regions of India and the lectures that accompany them. Pilgrimages have become central events in the temple's festival year and impart the community's values to members and newcomers. Chowpatty is one of many ISKCON communities who organize *yātrās* to Vrindavan—a major symbolic center for Gauḍīya pilgrimage circuits—during the autumnal Kartik season. Beyond Vrindavan, Indian-led ISKCON pilgrimages to Vaiṣṇava *tīrthas* and *pādayātrās*, pilgrimages on foot, have increasingly developed to guide devotees to diverse regions of India.[6] By the early 2000s, Chowpatty's pilgrimages were well known within global ISKCON circles for two aspects: their size (growing from around forty pilgrims in the initial 1986 trip to around 4,000 by the early 2000s) and their finely tuned organization in food distribution, accommodations, travel arrangements, and crowd control—hallmarks of Chowpatty's approach to festivals. Throughout the past two decades, *yātrās* for smaller groups within the community have ballooned into continuous events throughout the year.

The community's *yātrās* developed their distinctive character from 1992 onward, shortly before Radhanath Swami officially assumed spiritual leadership of the Chowpatty temple in 1993. He encouraged a professionalization of the *yātrā* management, and the sites of annual pilgrimage also expanded to include first Puri in 1993; Rameshwaram, Srirangam, and Tirupati in 1994; Jaipur in 1995; and Ahovalam, Mangalgiri, and Simhacalam in Tamil Nadu—as well as Ayodhya and Naimisaranya in Uttar Pradesh in 1999. Thus, from essentially the earliest days of Chowpatty's *yātrā* itineraries, pilgrimages were planned not only to the crowning Gauḍīya pilgrimage sites, as per ISKCON convention, but also to a range of Vaiṣṇava *tīrthas* in a sacred mapping of the nation to encompass the historic centers of diverse regional communities. Led at first by Radhanath Swami and now increasingly by other elder male members of the community, the large annual *yātrās* draw upward of 5,000 participants, while smaller groups within the congregation, tied together by age, occupation, or service interests, organize their own *yātrās* in groups of between fifty and several hundred. These smaller *yātrās* include trips by ISKCON Youth Services, for teenage boys and young men, and the annual temple staff *yātrā*, mainly for married couples, which has expanded pilgrimage routes to Pandharpur, Guruvayor, Ujjain, Chitrakoot, Dwaraka, Badrinath, and Haridwar, establishing destinations that were not previously on the map of sacred geography for ISKCON communities. These diverse places are approached in the *yātrā* format through daily *kathā* related to their connections with Vaiṣṇava *avatāras*; from Pandharpur, the Maharashtrian pilgrimage town centered on the *mūrti* of Viṭṭhala, to Chitrakoot in Madhya Pradesh, the site of Rāma and Sītā's sojourn during their forest exile from Ayodhya.

The rise of Chowpatty's pilgrimage tours from the late 1990s onward parallels the rise of pilgrimage as a mode of leisure during that period among India's middle classes broadly.[7] In that sense, *yātrā*s, like Chowpatty's Prerna and Chetana events, provide a structured social life to community members, channeling the growing middle-class norm of taking vacations into an expression of ISKCON's transregional *bhakti* identity. ISKCON Gauḍīyas have a historical precedent to draw on as well: the central place of pilgrimage in the life of Caitanya and his early hagiographic texts.[8] The memory of these formative pilgrimages continues in the narratives of Chowpatty's contemporary *yātrā*s. Pilgrimages are premised on uprooting devotees from their ordinary lives and engaging them in a concentrated and rigorous schedule of visiting holy Vaiṣṇava sites, hearing Krishna *kathā*, and performing exemplary *sādhana* and *sevā*. On pilgrimages, devotees can both attain a deeper connection to their Vaiṣṇava tradition, through experiencing the physical sites marked by divine *līlā*s, and also have the chance to model Vaiṣṇava etiquette, as idealized religious community, in a sanctified space. However, I would argue, in addition to further inculcating individuals into the ISKCON community, *yātrā*s also provide a delimited space for Indian devotees of diverse regional and religious backgrounds to revere their families' own traditions through the lens of their acquired Gauḍīya identity. In this, they present opportunities to both celebrate and contain regional religious identities.

In the *yātrā* for temple administrative staff, annual itineraries are set by volunteer organizers, led by the enthusiastic, recently retired banker, Vasudeva. He seamlessly keeps morale high during the inevitable long bus rides that puncture each day's travels, leading the group in storytelling, singing songs with exaggerated bravado, and personally checking in with each passenger throughout the day. Recent itineraries have included the iconic Vaiṣṇava temples in Kerala at Guruvayor and Thiruvananthapuram and Haridwar along the Ganges in North India. I was able to join the administrative staff *yātrā* to Kerala in January 2013. The leader of our *yātrā* described the trip as part pilgrimage and part vacation, to give something back to the temple employees for their service but also to maintain focus on a religious goal. "This is how vacations should be—in addition to relaxation, you connect with the Lord," he reasoned. Our group of roughly forty that year traveled by train from Mumbai Central station to Thiruvananthapuram, a trip that took just under twenty-four hours. Along the way, the significance of the trip for these particular pilgrims came to the fore. Many on the *yātrā* were from South India and had settled in Mumbai only as adults. As we passed through Udupi just after sunrise, our group of Tamils, Goans, Keralans, and Kannadigas became visibly happy to be "home." Our facilities organizer, who came to Mumbai from the Tulu-speaking region of Karnataka as a student, jumped onto the train platform at Udupi station and returned with freshly cooked *iḍlī* and *sāmbar* for us all. While it was decided that the *sāmbar* should not be consumed because it most likely contained onions, the *iḍlī* was successfully paired with homemade chutneys brought by a fellow pilgrim. This experience of buying but not fully consuming the *iḍlī* and *sāmbar* conveyed something of the dialogue between regional backgrounds and institutional identities in ISKCON Chowpatty. *Yātrās* provide opportunities for Indian devotees to celebrate pilgrimage traditions in their regions of origin, as the spiritual topography of ISKCON expands to include the Vaiṣṇava temples of Guruvayur and Padmanabhaswamy in Kerala, where we went on that trip, and the forested region of Chitrakoot, near the natal home of a *brahmacari* staff member, where the *yātrā* went the following year. On our South Indian *yātrā*, we visited a range of Vaiṣṇava temples in coastal Kerala but avoided sacred spots linked to non-Vaiṣṇava traditions. Regional *bhakti* histories were accentuated in relation to ISKCON's Gauḍīya theology. Thus, the *iḍlī* was all right, but the *sāmbar* avoided.

As in Bhakti Rasamrita's *kathā* on the Āḻvārs, the *kathā* told during these *yātrās*—generally for hours each day—emphasizes the transregional roots of early Gauḍīya Vaiṣṇavism, particularly Caitanya's travels, and the pan-Indic network of Vaiṣṇava *bhakti* heritage. One of our destinations in 2013 was the rural Ādi Keśava temple in Western Tamil Nadu. The well-preserved historic temple sat just past a remote hamlet near a pristine river, an hour east of the Keralan border. Although it took most of the day to reach in our chartered bus, the rush was palpable as we left our shoes on the bus and walked barefoot (according to the *yātrā* leaders' instructions) through the village and into the lofty Chola-era hallways of the large temple compound. As we sat in a sunlit corner of the inner courtyard beneath the elaborately carved stone pillars, the *brahmacari* teacher accompanying the group retraced narratives of Caitanya's visit to South India as recorded in the *Caitanya Caritāmṛta* through a series of Hindi lectures. Later, while taking a meal of *prasādam* from banana-leaf plates alongside other temple guests, we marveled at how centuries earlier Caitanya's travels had included this very spot.

That pilgrimage's organizational committee, many of whom were native to Tamil Nadu and Kerala, brimmed with nostalgia to take our group to some of the sacred sites affiliated with their family's religious backgrounds, including Kerala's Guruvayor temple, at which one couple in our group had been married twenty years prior. At night we would return to a modest hotel or one of the ISKCON guesthouses dotting the Keralan coast. Devotees could stroll around familiar neighborhoods and practice their rusty Malayalam with the fruit vendors. However, the extent to which devotees could pay homage to the religious roots of one's family entailed a constant negotiation with the strict guidelines of ISKCON's Vaiṣṇava *siddhānta*. This became visible in informal interactions, such as the afternoons I spent wandering around Keralan towns with two spirited women on the trip, Akansha and Mallika. Throughout the trip, we had formed a joyful connection, as Mallika would banter with me in my fledgling Hindi and jokingly make me repeat back the Hindi devotional stories to her to check my comprehension and Akansha distributed Gujarati treats from her well-packed snacks bag throughout the trip. They ardently tried to include me in every aspect of the pilgrimage, even when I tried to defer to avoid being a burden amidst the strict entry rules of many local temples. One morning, they had single-handedly wrangled with a group of brahmin priests and guards to enable me entrance to otherwise "Hindu only" temples. Another afternoon, they hatched a plan. Insisting that I cover my head and arms completely with my sari to obscure my white skin, they formed a human chain around me as we stealthily slid past the guards at another temple, laughing the whole time. I tried to insist that I had not expected to see the interior of these strictly guarded temples—I had joined the pilgrimage just to travel with them—but they would not be deterred: "You have come this far. You must see the Lord."

That afternoon, near a small beachside resort, we waded into the waves with saris hiked up to our knees and looked out onto the horizon. In a welcome moment of calm amid a busy pilgrimage schedule, Akansha reflected on how she has felt connected to this ocean throughout her life. When she was young, her parents moved from a coastal area in the Saurasthra region of Gujarat to Mumbai, both hugging the same coastline though hundreds of kilometers apart. Their family's *kula-devatā*, Jhūlelāl, is a regional deity associated with rivers and bodies of water, and her ancestors, part of the Gujarati business class who traded across the Arabian Sea, had prayed to Jhūlelāl for generations. Although now thousands of kilometers farther south, she marveled that we were still connected by the same sea along the Keralan coast. Mallika, whose family left the coastal province of Sindh during Partition, said with surprised laughter that her family's deity had also been Jhūlelāl, who was worshipped throughout the coastal regions that connect present-day Pakistan and India.[9] In response, Akansha began to recite what she could from memory of one hymn to Jhūlelāl, splashing offerings of water with cupped hands back into the sea in a playful nod to her childhood rituals of worship. Though Mallika smiled at the memory, she was quick to respond that of course worship of local deities like Jhūlelāl was merely worship of lower-level divinities, the demigods—not a valid Vaiṣṇava *avatāra*. Reiterating ISKCON's strict rejection of the pluralist worship embedded in many Hindu traditions, she decisively affirmed that the link to her ancestral worship of Jhūlelāl had been cut now that she "knew the scriptures better." This doctrinaire approach seemed a bit disappointing for Akansha. With a slight roll of her eyes, she stopped singing and offered one final palm of water with a faint, conspiratorial smile directed at the ocean. Although the borders of orthodoxy were clearly drawn, they seemed to not always map the full extent of an individual's life story and emotions.

In other contexts, however, the incorporation of diverse regional identities is precisely what attracted devotees to Chowpatty. Shivan, a chartered accountant who works in the temple's financial services, joined the community in the early 1990s after his wife, already a member, encouraged him to attend a *yātrā*. For several months, he said he felt out of place at temple gatherings. But they both told me, with broad smiles on separate occasions, what had allayed his skepticism was "seeing other South Indians already there," particularly devotees from their Iyer background. After he met a fellow Iyer while washing his stainless-steel plate after the Sunday feast meal, he introduced him to a whole group of Tamil devotees. Suddenly, ISKCON seemed more approachable and the prospect of joining more feasible.

While *yātrās* can be a site for members from similar backgrounds to connect with one another, they also provide an opportunity to build a cohesion of the community across regional and class lines. Several of my *yātrā* companions told me that they felt pilgrimages enabled them to get to know members of the community outside their regular circles in Mumbai. On occasions when business executives and retired civil servants serve food to the rest of the community, through the practice of *sevā*, or when women from the community help prepare a meal alongside local village women, *yātrās* enable links that would otherwise not occur. These suspensions of ordinary class placement are encouraged by the focus on *sevā* that is emphasized throughout *yātrā* lectures. In this sense, pilgrimages connect devotees to new people as well as new places.

However, the annual *yātrā* is tightly controlled, admitting only devotees who fulfill their daily *sādhana* vows. Eligibility is determined by an individual's counsellor, who must confirm that the individual follows the prescribed chanting on their *japa mala* and lifestyle, including strict vegetarianism and abstinence from caffeine. As "A Report on the Social Development Programme at Radha Gopinath Temple" manual describes, a *yātrā* is "also an occasion for practical training in Vaiṣṇava etiquette and behaviour. It is meant only for those who follow the principles and are willing to perform austerity."[10] Participation in a *yātrā* with the community, then, provides a ground to further develop one's performance of idyllic Vaiṣṇava *saṅgha*. This reinforces the lines of the community's institutionalized framework, making clear that community membership is acquired through practice and training, not religious or familial background. In this sense, the experience of touring *tīrtha*s with the community is only possible through continued affirmations of Gauḍīya identity.

However, by extending annual pilgrimages to Vaiṣṇava locations throughout India, the Chowpatty community physically traces the relatedness of the *līlā*s, *avatāra*s, and saints associated with these diverse *tīrtha*s, affirming a type of inclusivism-in-orthodoxy. Through their pan-Indian *yātrā*s, the community has also forged relationships with Vaiṣṇava groups outside of ISKCON circles that have expanded their network among Hindu publics.[11] For instance, priests of the Jagannātha temple at Puri, in the eastern state of Odisha, are annual attendees of Chowpatty's winter festivals. And, although ISKCON has been held at arm's length by many orthodox South Indian Vaiṣṇava communities, devotees frequently recalled the Srirangam *yātrā* of 2010, during which Radhanath Swami was honored with ceremonial garlands usually reserved for Śrīvaiṣṇava *ācārya*s—an unprecedented event, particularly considering his Western origin.

This larger network of Vaiṣṇava religiosity forged through Chowpatty's *yātrā* networks is also central to how many members see their overall religious heritage. For Shivan and others I spoke to while on pilgrimage, sites such as Srirangam and Puri are connected through a shared religiosity, as *tīrtha*s within the sacred body of India as a whole. In that sense, their identity as Gauḍīyas frames but also enhances their participation in regional pilgrimages, enabling a space to honor the traditions from which many of Chowpatty's community members came—be it South Indian Vaiṣṇava, Gujarati Vallabh, North Indian Rām *bhakti*, or Marathi Vārkarī—and engaging in a distinctive transregionalism that breaks from the regional centralization of many *bhakti* communities.

## Performing Pan-Indic *Bhakti* on Stage

The theological taxonomy in Chowpatty's pan-Indic *bhakti* imaginary is made vivid in the community's frequent dramatic productions. The performance of dramas—ranging from depictions of Krishna's *līlāṣ* to the lives of *bhakti* saints and Puranic stories—are a central part of the temple's repertoire. Productions of scriptural and hagiographic narratives are frequently adaptations of written and orally transmitted stories, mixed with undertones of contemporary social relevance.[12] These productions are performed alongside creative pieces that seek to communicate morals and religious orientations to their audiences. Dramas are ubiquitous in the community's calendar, from the annual Drama Festival, which draws evening crowds to a rented hall for hour-long professional productions on a proscenium stage, to informal ten-minute productions acted in costume in front of the Sunday program congregation (Figure 5.1).[13]

In a nod to their cinematic influences, Chowpatty's formal dramatic productions include a full musical score that parallels conventions developed in Hindi films and serials. I detected several instrumental scores that had been lifted directly from popular Hindi film soundtracks. At the annual Drama Festival, elaborate cinematic cues punctuate each scene, with urgent crescendos demarcating danger from a villain. Through incorporating styles and story arcs from both "mythologicals" (cinematic reproductions of Hindu religious stories) and mainstream Hindi cinema, the dramas convey a type of mythological 2.0. A crowd who grew up on mainstream Indian media genres can now repurpose those popular cultural styles for their own religious productions. [14]

These dramas often depict a universalist *bhakti* community, mapped historically along the national lines of India's borders and extending globally through ISKCON's missionizing activities. As Chowpatty's discourse of a pan-Indic *bhakti* movement asserts a commonality between Vaiṣṇava communities throughout the Indian nation, the performance of this history

Fig. 5.1 A group of actors perform at the annual Drama Festival, a ticketed ISKCON event organized at a public hall in South Bombay, 2015. Photo by the author.

also enacts the community's place within that heritage. The global extension of this *bhakti* tradition is also key to ISKCON's history, as a Gauḍīya tradition institutionalized by Bhaktivedanta Swami in New York. However, ISKCON's Indian roots are just as important; since, as in many ISKCON temples in India, Chowpatty members have had to contend with suspicions of being part of a Westernized, and thus inauthentic, version of Hindu tradition.

In a 2013 Drama Festival play on the popular Maharashtrian saint Tukārām (ca. 1577–1650), the saint's life is described in a blend of Hindi, Marathi, and English. This narrative was framed as an explanation to two Western travelers in India, satirizing the common sight of Western spiritual seekers in India but also implying *bhakti*'s global relevance through their eager reception of the narrative. Alongside dramatizations of the standard hagiographic narratives from Tukārām's life, parallel to those above, the drama included a vignette in which Tukārām envisions Caitanya and accepts him as his guru in a dream. This vignette draws support from Vārkarī textual traditions that recognize two guru figures named Rāghava Caitanya and Keśava Caitanya in the lineage of Jñānadeva, as well as oral traditions that detail Tukārām's reception of a mantra from a certain Bābājī Caitanya. For temple productions, it was an easy equation to highlight the similarity of name and timeframe between the Bābājī Caitanya of Maharashtra and Caitanya of Bengal. This envisaged disciplic connection creates a link between the devotional compositions of the Tukārām tradition, the *abhaṅgas*, and Gauḍīya Vaiṣṇavism. It also superordinates Maharashtrian *bhakti* tradition under a Gauḍīya theological taxonomy, according the role of Caitanya as guru to one of the most prominent local *bhakti* saints. While the link between Tukārām and Caitanya is not found in Vārkarī and broader Maharashtrian historical traditions, writing Caitanya into Tukārām's hagiography locates the Gauḍīya tradition within Mumbai's Maharashtrian context. The drama conveys that this is not a foreign tradition—it is linked to local *bhakti* saints in a pan-Indic history of *bhakti*, and in fact it is at the very root of these traditions.[15]

*My Sweet Lord*, another 2013 production, carries this pan-Indic narrative of *bhakti* heritage forward. The drama begins by recounting a hagiographic folk account of the life of a seventeenth-century Odishan Muslim-born devotee of Jagannātha named Sal Beg, who according to tradition was the son of a Mughal *subedar*, or army captain, named Lal Beg.[16] At the end of Sal Beg's dramatized life story, as the curtains close, the narrator segues into extended praise for many regional saints throughout India. Tukārām appears from stage right and crosses in front of the audience, absorbed in song. Then Mīrābāī, the celebrated Rajasthani saint, enters from stage left playing her *vīṇa* and reciting the name of Krishna—Giridhārī—that her poetic tradition most frequently employs. As these and other regional *bhakti* poet-saints dance across the stage, the narrator's voice links them together, stating that they will all be remembered through their devotional songs. The incorporation of diverse *bhakti* saints representing a range of Indian states is grafted onto a unitary national tradition, drawing a collective history along post-Independence nation-state lines.[17]

But ISKCON's own story carries this assertion of national *bhakti* heritage outward. Bhaktivedanta Swami appears and stands center stage. The narrator links him to these previous figures by introducing him as "a modern saint who spread devotion through emphasizing the power of song, in *kīrtan*."[18] This eulogy leads into another, unexpected twist, as this now-established pan-Indic tradition of devotional song is mapped globally through the spread of ISKCON. The narrator emphasizes *kīrtan* practiced in ISKCON temples worldwide but also the influence that Gauḍīya *bhakti* has had even on Western musical traditions, namely through Bhaktivedanta's friendship with the Beatles and religious mentorship of George Harrison. The finale emphasizes Harrison's close relationship with Bhaktivedanta and ambitiously posits that his Gauḍīya-inspired music had "a great impact on the history of the Western music industry since."[19] These depictions underscore the movement of Indian *bhakti* outward; pan-Indic *bhakti* conquers even modern Western culture through devotional song, to encompass a now-global community grounded in its Indian roots.

Large public festivals also provide opportunities to curate religious heritage through visual culture and performance. ISKCON's largest annual festival centers on several Rath Yatra (*Rath Mahotsav*) processions that traverse neighborhoods throughout Mumbai in January. At variance with the July timing for the Jagannātha Rath Yatra in Puri, these Rath Yatras capitalize on the mild January weather to provide their blend of entertainment and education through the festival framework. Chowpatty's Rath Yatras partake in features of a "standardized" ISKCON festival, derived from Bhaktivedanta's threefold model for ISKCON festivals (*kīrtan*, *pravacan*, and *prasādam*), but they also partake in the visuality established by post-Independence Festival of India programs. In Mumbai, neighborhood Rath Yatras are organized in the northern and central suburbs of the city, from Borivali and Mira Road to Chembur and Ghatkopar, where growing numbers of community members live. The largest, city-wide Rath Yatra has generally been held at Shivaji Park in Dadar, a central, upper-class urban neighborhood and longstanding seat of the Shiv Sena. Beginning as a procession through the neighborhoods of Worli and Dadar, the Rath Yatra ends with a grand evening celebration in Shivaji Park, in which thousands of attendees can sit on rows of folding chairs or the sprawling lawn to hear a philosophical lecture broadcast from the central stage, participate in devotional singing, and, of course, receive a vegetarian meal.

Annual permission to hold the event must be procured from the local establishment, in what often becomes an arduous and lengthy process of amassing authorizations. This also becomes an occasion to see how the representation of a pan-Indic *bhakti* heritage is strategic in multiple capacities, including through developing alliances with local cultural nationalist groups. The Marathi-nationalist Shiv Sena is a dominant political force in Dadar, the neighborhood in which the Rath Yatra culminates. In 2012, the festival leaned into the theme of Maharashtrian *bhakti* history. The floats and stage décor foregrounded the deity of Viṭṭhaldev, the pilgrimage site of Pandharpur, and the Maharashtrian saint Tukārām. This focus on Maharashtrian Vārkarī heritage enabled ISKCON Chowpatty both to emphasize alignment with Maharashtrian Hindu religious traditions and to underscore a discourse of Vaiṣṇava universalism that sees diverse *avatāras* and *tīrthas* as connected to a greater pan-Indic religious unity. This orientation was reflected in Radhanath Swami's address to the crowd, the culmination of the stage program following the parade, and highlighted by the approximately eighty-foot-tall plaster statue of Viṭṭhaldev towering above the stage. On left and right stage, statues of Bhaktivedanta Swami and Tukārām flanked Viṭṭhaldev, visually suggesting their analogous position in relation to the Vaiṣṇava deity. This threefold representation—of Viṭṭhaldev, Tukārām, and Bhaktivedanta—had been displayed prominently in billboards throughout the city for weeks leading up to the event. On large posters also present at the event, a montage of the *mūrti* of Viṭṭhala in Pandharpur occupied center focus, as a dancing Tukārām stood out in a bright white jacket and *topī*, and Bhaktivedanta appeared in the lower right corner, gazing reverentially at both. These visual and spatial depictions presented Viṭṭhaldev in a position analogous to Krishna—a position that is indeed resonant with Gauḍīya *avatāra* theology.[20] Such visuality asserted commonality between these two traditions—one from Bengal, one from Maharashtra—as being in a fundamental sense the same larger *bhakti* tradition, indigenizing ISKCON into Mumbai's local Hindu landscape.

Political maneuvering aside, the equivalence of regional Vaiṣṇava traditions is underscored at Rath Yatras throughout the ISKCON world, in which the shared identity of Jagannātha, Krishna, and Caitanya—seen as forms of the same supreme Vaiṣṇava divinity—are emphasized in lectures, songs, and the visual culture of the events.[21] Gauḍīya *bhajans* assert that Caitanya is none other than Jagannātha, the Odishan deity whose major temple is at Puri, where Caitanya spent the second half of his life. They are both viewed as synonymous with Krishna, as well as his established Puranic *avatāras*, such as the lion deity Narasimha and Rāma. This polymorphic notion of the divine forms the cornerstone of Vaiṣṇava universalism and provides an in-built transregional orientation. Assertions of the underlying linkage among various regional Vaiṣṇava traditions is also embedded in Radhanath Swami's *līlā kathās*, or retellings of the scriptural stories of Vaiṣṇava *avatāras*. Yet as ISKCON becomes a more public face of Hindu traditionalism in India, visual and performative links to regional traditions seek to persuade viewers that their modern transnational organization represents local traditions as well.

## India Rising: Representing the Indian Nation

In addition to fashioning religious links across a span of regional *bhakti* traditions, Rath Yatras provide a space to publicly display ISKCON's lifestyle and religious precepts, enshrined in exhibitions in tents throughout the festival, a series of "cultural programs" on a main stage, and staffed festival booths that promote discussion on vegetarianism and reincarnation. A number of people I spoke to throughout the city knew ISKCON primarily through the Rath Yatra, along with annual Janmashtami festivals held at the temple. However, the ability to maintain a visible public identity requires constant negotiation with the city's bureaucratic forces, which are themselves embroiled in a contestation over the proper uses of public space in the city. Every year, a team of dedicated Chowpatty members led by a fiery and determined Gujarati grandmother, Mrs. Gandhi, undertake the process to procure permission to hold the Rath Yatra from the Brihanmumbai Municipal Corporation and on occasion the Bombay High Court.[22] Although the 2012 event theme seemed poised to please Maharashtrian nationalists, they are not the only local voice. A legal challenge brought to the Bombay High Court in 2010 argued that Shivaji Park is public, civic space and should not be used for religious festivals at all. This prompted a shift in location for the Rath Yatra after a high-court decision in 2014.[23] That year, the leadership of Somaiya College opened their college grounds for a three-day Rath Yatra celebration, and, in 2015, an industrious team arranged for a five-day gala event named "India Rising" at a large park in the adjacent Ghatkopar neighborhood. This Rath Yatra, while echoing the conventional Festival of India model, was also the first major Chowpatty event after the historic resurgence of Hindu nationalism in India's 2014 prime ministerial election, and it provided a particularly explicit representation of the political connotations of the Vaiṣṇava *bhakti* nation.

Though born from a setback in the usual venue at Shivaji Park—which was restored by 2017 but again paused in the pandemic—the "India Rising" festival held in January 2015 was the grandest yet. The middle-class, Gujarati, Hindi, and Marathi-speaking Ghatkopar and Tilak Nagar neighborhoods saw guest appearances by Hindi film celebrities and local Bharatiya Janata Party (BJP) leaders still aglow from their sweeping 2014 general election victory. The event combined star-studded entertainment and political support with five nights of professional stage performances, educational workshops, and opportunities to contribute toward Chowpatty's humanitarian outreach programs. There were also opportunities to take *darśan* and make ghee lamp offerings to the presiding *mūrti*s, Jagannātha, Baladeva, and Subhadrā. The festival culminated in a cart procession of this divine trio throughout the surrounding neighborhoods, held on the fourth day of the event. Echoing the 2003 "India Shining" campaign by a previous BJP government, the festival shared in the agendas of promoting an unmarked Hindu vision of India's cultural heritage, as well as its business and technology potential, packaging these advertisements of "brand India" that conveyed urban middle-class nationalist aspirations.[24] The festival logo conveyed its purpose with the motto "Empowering India the Indian Way," which was further described in the promotional material as: "propagating Spiritual Knowledge, Unity, Peace and Teachings of Dharma among the masses." Ahead of the festival, promotional flyers distributed throughout the city appealed to guests to "Rediscover Your Heritage."

Held in a large circular park that had been cordoned off for the event, the festival tents were surrounded by apartment buildings and families strolling around the park's walkways. Amid the calm bustle of the residential neighborhood, nightly programs showcased a series of regional Indian dance and musical performances. Elaborate curtained walls, carpeted walkways, fairground booths, seminar spaces, and a large central stage with neatly arranged rows of chairs transformed the park into an elite event venue. Rows of shops sponsored by the Indian national government showcased regional crafts and artwork from across India's many states. Side areas were set up for smaller displays on the history of India, regional *bhakti* traditions and Vaiṣṇavism, and the promotion of vegetarianism and Āyurveda, while booths sold ISKCON literature and advertised the community's humanitarian projects. The central stage was illuminated by a white lotus–themed backdrop, with ISKCON Chowpatty's logo marked subtly in the corner, as two cinema-sized screens projected high-definition views of the performances and showcased the entrance of the VIP guests who were seated in a row of white sofas directly opposite the stage. Celebrity guests included actors known for playing Vaiṣṇava-related roles on Hindi television and popular Hindi film stars, with paparazzi coverage and bodyguard entourages befitting Mumbai's storied elite. Juhi Chawla, a Hindi film actress and regular speaker at ISKCON Chowpatty's events, arrived one evening, smiling and nodding appreciatively toward the audience's applause as she was ushered to sit on the central white sofa up front. Punchy electronic music—the type one would hear at one of Mumbai's film awards ceremonies—punctuated her entrance as cameras projected her onto the two large screens flanking the stage. On another evening, as the arrival of popular Hindi film actor Ayushmann Khurrana drew near, crowds of college-aged students, in skinny jeans and ballet flats, flanked the entrance gate, more concerned with catching a glimpse of the dapper Ayushmann than the Rath Yatra's "cultural program." Khurrana finally arrived and was quickly surrounded by bodyguards in matching red turbans, who encircled him with linked arms to usher him the stage.

As I strolled around on the fourth night, after the Rath Yatra had paraded through the streets of Ghatkopar and Tilak Nagar for four hours that afternoon, the festival grounds were packed. Perhaps a thousand people sat, filling all the chairs around the stage, while many more streamed in and out through the rows of craft stalls. With an estimated attendance of 100,000 over the five days according to publicized internal sources, the main stage event—in contrast to Chowpatty's temple programs—was conducted entirely in Hindi. The only English-language components were Radhanath Swami's short talks on two nights that were accompanied by a Hindi translation. My presence as an American observer—while already remarkable in ISKCON Chowpatty's temple events—was markedly more out of place here. The feel of the event was as a space created by and for local Mumbaikars. In fact, it was precisely "the Marathi people in this neighborhood—very pious, hardworking middle-class people," who, as one devotee told me, were the target demographic—a shift from the South Bombay denizens drawn to ISKCON because they did not want "some Hindi-speaking guru seated on a dais," as discussed in Chapter 2.

However, the audience was also suitably diverse for a Mumbai festival occasion. ISKCON devotees were visible in their Vaiṣṇava *tilak* and *tulāsi* neck beads. Several Swaminarayan men, wearing their *tilak-chandlo* with emblematic red *bindi*s, filed through the crowds with their families. Several women in black niqabs even strolled through the exhibitions along with husbands and relatives. Many others, unmarked by any religious affiliation, meandered through with spouses or multi-generational families (Figure 5.2). Mothers and daughters shopped for saris, and families claimed whole rows of chairs, keeping an eye on their children running through the aisles as they

Fig. 5.2 Dancers perform on stage at the India Rising Festival as visitors stroll behind the seated audience, 2015. Photo by the author.

tried to enjoy the stage entertainment. As guests strolled through the crafts stalls at the start of the evening, the master of ceremonies, smartly dressed in a cream-colored silk *dhoti-kurta* and festive red turban (*paghri*), exhorted the audience to contribute to the launch of a new social welfare initiative, Hunger Free Mumbai.[25] The stage program fluctuated between a variety of dance performances, short speeches, and the elaborate welcoming of important guests on stage with garlands and handcrafted gifts. In between one series of dance performances, as a *tabla* and flute duet broadcast under the cool, open sky, cameras panned across the audience. Screens projected live footage of three *brahmacari*s circling ornate, multi-tiered *ghee* lamps in worship of the festival *mūrtis* and a diorama of the Ganges River, as a group of children intoned melodic Sanskrit *ślokas*. The effect was an ecumenical exhibition of Hindu religiosity—carefully orchestrated to be of resonance to a wide range of Hindus in attendance while also displaying Gauḍīya religious identity.

As Thomas Blom Hansen has argued, public performances are the "site where historical imaginaries, the state and notions of community and 'society' become visible and effective."[26] In this sense, in the visual and performative media of Chowpatty's festivals, the depiction of a national imaginary is not separate from the performance of an idyllic Vaiṣṇava community. Each evening's events at the "India Rising" festival interwove themes of national importance with the celebration of regional Hindu and implicitly Vaiṣṇava heritage, explicitly tying together connections between regional cultures, national identity, and Gauḍīya Vaiṣṇava traditions. The opening night of the festival was timed to coincide with the Makar Sankranti spring holiday (also known as Udaan), popular in the Western Indian states of Gujarat and Maharashtra. Generally celebrated by flying kites at dusk, this festival was rendered nationalist through its description in promotional materials: "Udaan stands to create an opportune time for reunion and bonding of people of this nation and extend solidarity to one another." The interweaving of national unity and collective Hindu heritage was inaugurated by a stage appearance by the actor Mukesh Khanna—known for his role as Bhīṣma in B. R. Chopra's *Mahābhārata* television serial—and speeches from two prominent *brahmacari*s, Govinda and Gauranga, on the "four sacred 'G's of Indian culture: *gau* (cow), *gāyatrī*, *gaṅgā*, and Gītā." The second and third festival days promoted "*dharohar*" (heritage) through arts and performance, including an "India Heritage Exhibition," which promised to "unravel the marvels of Bhāratīya Civilization . . . translating Indian heritage into an Atlas journey consisting of glorious past, happening present and potent future" and a *kalaa haat*, handcraft bazaar, promoting regional craft forms from across India's states.[27]

Alongside this, a group of stalls lining the elaborate, winding entrance bore uniform signs advertising their region and specialty and stating their promotion by the development commissioner of handicrafts in India's Ministry of Textiles and sponsorship by the Mumbai-based fashion and design institute, Le Mark Institute of Art and ISKCON Chowpatty. Stalls included saris from western Gujarat, *bandhini* scarves from Kutch, embroidered vests from Punjab, Madhubani and Mithila paintings from Bihar, pashminas and embroidered jackets from Kashmir, carved wooden flower arrangements from Haryana, and iron craft and basket work from Chhattisgarh. Through these funding bodies, ISKCON Chowpatty's Rath Yatra festival extended a national governmental aim of promoting traditional handicrafts across Indian states and also allied with Mumbai's contemporary textile and design industry, placing the festival alongside broader national trends toward cultural preservation and industry.[28]

Stylized curations of artistic traditions from each state were also reflected in the performance schedule. Dances on the main stage, billed as a collection of Indian folk performances, included region-specific dances such as Manipuri performances of Krishna's *rasa līlā*, Punjabi *bhangra*, Maharashtrian *lezim*, Assamese *bihu*, and Keralan *theyyam* and *kalarippayattu*. These celebrations of regional tradition are often mediated through a vector of modern media in cultural consumption at large, and here too an Odissi classical dance was performed by the "Prince Dance Group," veterans of the India's Got Talent competition. On one night, Rajasthani folk dancers filed into their choreographed positions in full mirror-clad skirts. As the young dancers begin to twirl, their skirts ballooned to reveal skinny jeans and capri leggings underneath—a reminder of the present culture that underlies these urban performers' lives beyond the homage to regional cultural traditions. On the evening of the Rath Yatra proper, Ram Kumar Panda, from a family of Jagannātha *pūjārin*s, was welcomed to the stage and garlanded as a special guest celebrating the festival's Odissi roots in the seaside city of Puri. Odissi dancers then performed the *Daśāvatāra* sequence from Jayadeva's *Gītā Govinda*. As this performance was introduced, the master of ceremonies remarked that "all of India" has been brought together in this program, and in between performances he reminded the audience of the importance of the festival's theme:

> Our culture (*saṁskṛti*) is so great that it's older than all other cultures and yet we still don't ask questions about our culture. Therefore, in this "India Rising,, we are asking questions about our ancient culture with its artists. Then we can all together tell everyone that Indian culture is so great.[29]

Echoing Vasudha Dalmia's observation that the 1980s Festivals of India propagated "the image of an India immortal . . . to draw upon the arts in a way that once again sought to bring the classical and the folk as timeless categories,"[30] Chowpatty's Rath Yatra festivals also harness a presentation of Indian culture that inscribes the nation as intrinsic to the land and renders the nation's diverse artisan, craft, and performance heritage as evidence of continuity and interconnectedness.

An urban elite desire for cultural preservation of India's artisanal heritage parallels discourses of heritage in the development of India's craft-related institutions since Independence. The juxtaposition of state-represented craft stalls in ordered rows—each professing to represent distinct yet related forms of traditional Indian artisanship—created an effect similar to that of Delhi's Dilli Haat craft bazaar, another government-sponsored initiative that showcases arts and crafts stalls affiliated with modern Indian states and joins together wide-ranging artisan histories into India's nation-state as a whole.[31] As Paul Greenough notes: "craft museum exhibits are intended not to illustrate changing artistic themes, genres, styles, and media throughout time, but to demonstrate the static equivalence in form and function between the present and the past."[32] As Greenough's work draws attention to the crafts museum's ability to naturalize the nation by smoothing out India's vast regional and local artisanal variations,[33] the "India Rising" display of artisanal crafts and performance arts also reinforced the premise that India's regions are an organic representation of regional cultural essences within a preordained national whole.

The musical performances that attend every large ISKCON Rath Yatra in Mumbai and the brahmanically inflected character of these depictions of Indian cultural history also pay an implicit allegiance to post-Independence productions from the Bharatiya Vidya Bhavan and the organization's similar patronage of classical Indian arts.[34] Coincidentally, the Chowpatty temple sits within a block of Mumbai's Bharatiya Vidya Bhavan, on a street named after K. M. Munshi, who founded the Bhavan in 1938 and was also an active founding member of the Vishva Hindu Parishad (VHP). Although ISKCON has no formal connection with the Bhavan—and their links to the VHP are tenuous and uneven—their attempts to revision Indian art, culture, and education from the perspective of a religio-national Vaiṣṇava discourse echoes Munshi's own equation of an Indian past with an idyllic Vedic Hindu past.[35] Indeed, both institutions not only center a Vedic-Vaiṣṇava rendering of Indian heritage but, in their productions, also echo a modern effort to represent "All India," a fundamental nation-building exercise that flourished in the mid-twentieth century, as the very character of the nation was debated through attempts at conceptualize the nature of citizenship and Indian identity through the representation of groups (women, Muslims, Dalits) and articulations of heritage (Sanskritic, Hindu, secular).[36]

The educational products of ISKCON's temple communities in Mumbai and Pune parallel the Bhavan's productions within an explicitly Vaiṣṇava framework, asserting a Vedic and Sanskritic heritage to India's contemporary cultural traditions. In distinction to an early postcolonial vision of India as a conglomeration of linked states generally coterminous with major linguistic regions,[37] Chowpatty's performative displays reinforce a religious vision of the Indian nation in which each region is heir to a variant of Vaiṣṇava *bhakti—this* is the ultimate link that speaks to their unified roots. In this sense, dance performances were linked through their shared expression of regional forms of depicting Krishna's *līlā*s, and craft stalls tended toward the portrayal of Vaiṣṇava themes in their products, such as in the vivid Bihari Madhubani–style paintings of Rādhā and Krishna and the peacock-themed decorations sold by an Uttar Pradesh–based jeweler and silversmith. These displays served in the project of naturalizing the nation, echoing a range of Festival of India programs before them. And by claiming the authority to represent the entire nation, even if on the level of crafts and performance arts, ISKCON Chowpatty's Rath Yatra also naturalizes its place as representative for the culture of the nation.

These productions of cultural heritage also reflect a particular urban Indian view of a rural ideal. Echoing the early post-Independence agenda of refiguring rural India through a lens of national productivity and progress, the executive director of Maharashtra's Model Village Program was invited to launch two ISKCON humanitarian initiatives centered on sustainable farming and cow protection. The Chowpatty-led Govardhan Ecovillage—an organic farming community in the rural Thane district two hours north of Mumbai—also had its own vendor, Bio Bliss, that displayed hygiene, cleaning, and beauty products containing cow-related ingredients produced "according to Āyurvedic prescriptions" but packaged for commercial distribution. Their overarching banner declared: "Cleans Well and Smells Wow! Bio Bliss Products of Cow!™"—a trademarked motto for product advertisements. Farmers from eight farming collectives were also present and made their produce available, advertising their products as "healthy consumer choices." The importance of resuscitating a healthy rural environment here paired with concern over the preservation of artisanal traditions, both depicted as central to traditional Indian culture. Echoing Rashmi Varma's assessment of the postcolonial city, rural spectacles within the urban landscape enabled the urban attendees of the festival "to claim roots in tradition while enjoying the benefits of progress and modernity."[38] Through contributing to ISKCON Chowpatty's projects—including donating to the Hunger Free Mumbai campaign or buying the Āyurvedic products of the Govardhan

Ecovillage—Mumbaikars were invited to reverse the tide of urbanization and globalization through the very forms of capitalist engagement that define modern urban life. In the festival proceedings, the juxtaposition of artisanal traditions and humanitarian initiatives were paired with corporate sponsorship and an orientation toward India's impact in transnational business, finance, and technology markets. Displaying Gandhian, Nehruvian, and post-liberalization idioms about Indian nationhood, as idyllic past and precious present, artisanal traditions were portrayed as a compliment to India's economic and corporate development and future global economic impact.

And for ISKCON as a transnational organization, this naturalization of the nation also carries global valences. The master of ceremonies introduced ISKCON's "Kalaa Raksha Scheme" ("venture for the protection of the arts") to "enable a global platform for promoting rural handicrafts," suggesting custodianship in their preservation and promotion abroad. And this outward-facing orientation is also framed as postcolonial resistance. A month prior to the festival, Krishna Chaitanya Das promoted it to an audience of several hundred young men at the monthly Prerna program through this lens:

> [we] will glorify all the arts of India which the British killed. It is time to give them a life again. . . . Artisans all over the villages will be invited to bring their arts back to the standard. . . . And here is the Festival of India, the most vibrant and grand festival of India, which the British wanted to stop but couldn't stop.

Although India had been an independent nation for almost seventy years, the silhouette of British presence loomed large, particularly during assertions of national pride. For Krishna Chaitanya, national pride was still in need of revival several generations after official independence. This focus on redressing a perceived lack of national pride was buttressed during the festival itself by the validation of high-profile guests from Mumbai's entertainment industry, members of the Indian armed forces, and politicians from Maharashtra's Bharatiya Janata Party (BJP), who were honored in succession throughout each evening's stage programs.

The assertions of a muscular, postcolonial national pride were explicitly linked to political affiliations in the festival itself. Each of the five evenings showcased the support of a local BJP politician, with local representatives of the new Modi government reinforcing a public allegiance to both the governing body and their political causes. This presence often came in contrast to the curated recreational tone of the gathering. During one evening's stage events, around thirty young men suddenly came tearing down the center aisle in a whirl of testosterone, flanked by two policemen running to keep pace. Sporting saffron BJP scarves wrapped uniformly around their necks, they walked in with an air of urgency and importance, escorting Poonam Mahajan, a BJP Member of Parliament from Mumbai, to the front of the assembly. On another evening, Maharashtra's Chief Minister Devendra Padnavis sent a recorded message of appreciation for ISKCON's activities in Mumbai that was broadcast from the high-definition screens flanking the main stage. Recent initiatives undertaken by the Modi government's cabinet were also lauded by the master of ceremonies, including support for recent comments made by Prime Minister Modi on the proclaimed ancient Indian origins of genetic engineering and plastic surgery through examples such as Ganesh's head transplant.[39] Affirming the decision of Smriti Irani's Education Ministry to replace the study of German with Sanskrit as the third language in central government schools throughout India (then making waves in Indian news media), he remarked how people all over the world—naming Germany, England, and the United States—are learning Sanskrit, so Indians too should take pride (*garv*) in their Indian culture (*bhāratīya saṁskṛti*). In this context, as in the examples given above, the legitimizing power of the West lurked amidst these assertions of resurgent cultural identity. But through a vocal public show of allegiance with the BJP, the organizers of "India Rising" advanced a display of pan-Indic Hindu solidarity resonant of that which galvanized Modi's election.

The focus on the defense of India's Sanskritic heritage paralleled a celebration of India's armed forces. The second day of the festival commemorated India's defense personnel, known as *javān*s, coinciding with Indian Army Day. The "Namaste Jawaan" logo accompanied all promotional material for the event, and a keynote speech was arranged for Major General G. D. Bakshi, who was introduced as an eminent Kargil war veteran and counterterrorism commander. Mumbai's police force was honored for their personal sacrifices to protect the city from the "26/11" terrorist attacks of 2008, with accompanying advertisements on flyers and online describing the occasion as a "forum for [the] expression of India's superpower status and supremacy in the world's global order," furthering the imbrication of the global with the national in the unexpected pairing of the Indian armed forces and ISKCON in the assertion of a global Indian identity.

However, throughout the remaining four nights of the festival, defense was spoken of more as a cultural battleground, as the need to defend—and revive—Indian religious culture in its many facets. Govinda, a senior *brahmacari* at Chowpatty, addressed the crowd in a mixture of Hindi and English on the importance of Indian culture (*bhāratīya saṁskṛti*), which he lamented was destroyed for eight hundred years, referencing a length of time that encompasses the British colonial period and the earlier presence of Muslim-led kingdoms throughout various regions of modern-day India. Referencing colonial-era archival studies, he described an ideal educational system in the region's past: "In the British archives, we can see how much education there was, that not only brahmins but everyone studied living skills, loving skills, and leading skills. From the Mahābhārata and other scriptures, *bhagavat prem* was studied." Now, he asserted, it is the role of Indians to reclaim that heritage, to restructure their educational systems to reflect India's spiritual inheritance, to promote "Vedic education and appreciation of Vedic heritage" with the goal of "introducing these knowledge systems into schools and colleges, as well as setting up mobile museums and exhibitions" in rural and urban areas.

The call to restructure Indian educational systems was intimately linked to a revisioning of India's past, to replace colonial narratives that rendered India inferior to a technologically superior West by asserting their own narratives of success—even superiority over the West—revising the story of technological modernity. In the early December Prerna program, Krishna Chaitanya put his listeners on the spot, arguing that the educational system they have gone through—English-medium, rooted in British educational models—does not include Indian stories about Indian history. Challenging them about how much pride they have in their own history, with the affect of a strict but charismatic schoolmaster, he continued: "The easiest way to erode a person's identity is to erode a person's history, the nation's history, the culture's remnants . . . [so that] they have no ideology, no history, they are simply followers of a dictate of created identities." To counteract this, he foregrounded the importance of Vaiṣṇava traditions:

> Please try to understand the Bhagavad Gītā that you're reading is actually a book to safeguard our legacy. So that not "we will become great" but that we have a great opportunity to help everyone. The world needs India more than India needs itself. . . . And therefore Krishna appeared, Rāma

appeared, all the *avatāras* came in this land of Bhārat. Why do you think this land is so pious?. . . . Bhārat is wanted even by the gods.

Krishna Chaitanya concluded the talk with an exhortation for the audience members to write their contact details on a form distributed by temple volunteers, "so whatever way you can contribute to the nation, to the heritage, to the legacy and wisdom, is available here . . . And you can join the force, become a rising Indian." Such exhortations for pride were coupled with assertions that India not only *equaled* Western powers but *exceeded* those powers in technology and culture. Back at the "India Rising" festival, exhibition posters on the festival grounds described "the golden era of pre-occupation of India" that consisted of "sustainable ecosystems of countryside" and a "harmonious social atmosphere." Historical individuals, from medieval South Indian brahmin mathematicians to Shivkar Bapuji Talpade, a nineteenth-century Maharashtrian physicist, were connected across space and time as exemplars of an inherent scientific and technological genius in Indian cultural heritage.[40] These sentiments were also reflected in a common base of knowledge from which many Chowpatty members drew in our discussions during my research period, reiterating the power of these narratives beyond public proclamations.

This postcolonial revisionist approach to history was also displayed on stage during a film launch held for the local actor and heartthrob Ayushman Khurana's 2015 film, *Hawaiizada*, directed by Vibhu Puri. After Khurana was welcomed on stage and garlanded by one of the financial backers of the festival, he told the audience about his exciting discovery, through reading the film script, that Talpade had indeed made the world's first aircraft. Continuing in a mix of Hindi and English, he elaborated that people may think this story about an Indian aircraft invention in 1895 is just a conspiracy theory: "that after 1857, we were totally subordinate to Britishers, that 'now we are under the British Raj, we cannot do anything.'" In that era, he continued, "when there was no social networking, no social media . . . and the press was controlled by Britishers. . . . Shivkar Bapuji Talpade didn't announce this event to anyone. But I think it's high time now." That overdue recognition of India's historic precedence is indeed the aim Chowpatty's "India Rising" festival hopes to achieve. The success of that aim was exhibited again in the words of Juhi Chawla, who told the audience that after coming to this event, she was filled with pride (*garv*) for her country and for its diverse performance arts and inventions. Speaking in the same familiar mix of Hindi and

English that characterizes many elite Mumbaikars' speech, she elaborated on how much knowledge, wealth, and depth there is in this soil from which all of us have been born. Yet she lamented that the film industry today is influenced so much by Western culture. In such a context, she concluded, this festival is necessary.

Because Chawla and Khurana are not members of ISKCON, their public support for the organization showcases that ISKCON now operates in tandem with elite urban Indian trends, embedded into networks of celebrity culture and popular nationalist discourses. And ISKCON's revisionist historical discourses are not simply purveyed by the organization; rather they have become central because of the organization's devotees in India. In public displays of pride in the Indian nation and the achievements of Indians historically, the India Rising festival sketched out a devotional imaginary of the nation that is widely resonant with the view of history that many conservative Hindus hold. And, through visual and performative topographies, a consonance was traced between precolonial religious culture and the Indian nation-state's aspirations in global business and technology networks, a coupling that has defined many Hindu public spheres in post-liberalization India. The centering of these religio-political discourses reflects ISKCON's localization in Mumbai's Hindu communities, as the organization takes on and subtly reshapes popular ideas through its aim to revive and revise Hindu practice. This devotional mapping has political valences, reflected most palpably in the elected political leaders included in its public promotion. However, it equally stakes out political territory in its depictions of those deemed threatening to the *bhakti* nation. It is to this latter category that the remainder of this chapter will now turn.

## The Others of the *Bhakti* Body Politic

Within ISKCON's discourse of pan-Indic Hindu revival, the Indian landscape and its diverse cultures are painted in a Vaiṣṇava *bhakti* idiom, a concept that has a long history in medieval and modern Indian discourse. The presentation of a pan-Indic devotional heritage through popular culture participates in a prominent discourse of *bhakti* as movement, *bhakti ka āṅdolan*. In charting the genealogy of this concept, John Stratton Hawley notes that a conceptual weaving together of poet-saints from across diverse regional and linguistic identities crystallized in Hindi and

English publications in the early twentieth century.[41] This notion, which Hawley calls the *bhakti* movement paradigm, has been grounded in school textbooks and in visual media in nationalist and independent India.[42] Indeed, as he notes, the seventeenth-century Gauḍīyas were central players in constructing the narrative of a pan-Indic, implicitly Vaiṣṇava *bhakti* tradition that has become embedded in modern national narratives. Thus, in performing a pan-Indic *bhakti* unity, Chowpatty's members participate in a lineage of Gauḍīya religio-political formulations of *bhakti* while also positioning themselves in relation to political discourses within the postcolonial Indian state.

In tracing the nation through the concept of a *bhakti* movement, the historically complex, interreligious landscape of the Indian subcontinent is rendered as implicitly devotional and Hindu. One may ask, where are Muslims, Sikhs, and Christians—for instance—in this narrative of national heritage?[43] Similarly, in ISKCON's conceptualization of Indian *bhakti* heritage as Vaiṣṇava, where are the Śaivas, Śāktas, and Adivasis? One does not have to look far for answers, for while Chowpatty's productions present an encompassing picture of what the community *is*, many of the community's day-to-day negotiations of identity take place through asserting what the community is *not*. During my research period, the temple's media products often constructed identity in contrast to three Others: non-Vaiṣṇava Hindus, specifically embodied by Śaivas and Śāktas, portrayed as corrupting or at best misdirected; Indian Muslim rulers, portrayed as a historic and abiding threat to Hindu well-being; and the West, as a historical colonial force and agent of contemporary globalization (more on this last point in the following chapter). Through these constructions of alterity—in oral discourse, dramatic performance, and casual conversations—devotees reinforce their understanding of Gauḍīya *siddhānta* by way of juxtaposition. Such performative tensions imbue a sense of the preciousness of their tradition and the miraculous nature of its survival and spread, despite all external threats. But they also present potentially troubling implications for people deemed outside the lines of correct practice. In plays and dramatic retellings, performative confrontations are resolved through the conversion of Others or the perseverant devotion of Gauḍīya saints in the face of adversity. Therein, religious identity is defined as much through mapping out the pan-Indic *bhakti* nation as through marking the boundaries around it, in context staking a claim for the moral preeminence of devout Vaiṣṇavas amid an interreligious, cosmopolitan city.

Echoing early twentieth-century Hindi theatre, Chowpatty's Hindi- and English-language productions often take the form of morality plays, discussing a moral issue through their scripts and coming to a strong religio-ethical conclusion as a model of right religious behavior, Vaiṣṇava etiquette—or, conversely, the tragedy of not behaving according to proper Vaiṣṇava etiquette. The themes depicted foreground positive moral values by presenting ideal figures in Vaiṣṇava tradition—great *ācārya*s, gurus, and saints well known in Gauḍīya history. In the 2014 *Jewel of Faith*, the female ascetic Śabarī (a minor Rāmāyaṇa character popularized through Ramanand Sagar's 1987 Doordarshan television serial on the Rāmāyaṇa) embodies the important virtue of faith (*viśvās*), described as "infinite faith in the words of guru." In the 2007 *Spiritual Renaissance*, the Gauḍīya theologian Viśvanātha Cakravartin (1626–ca. 1708) advocates the notion that "the highest principle of *dharma* is compassion and not self-preservation." Rādhā and the *gopī*s are also frequent sources of ethical inspiration for the community, and one finds the exemplary virtues of selflessness and willingness to give up everything for Krishna frequently repeated through allusions to their *līlā*s.[44] The Gauḍīya ideal moral universe here consists of a *saṅgha*, community of selfless, humble *bhakta*s helping one another and orienting their activities around the worship and praise of Krishna and Vaiṣṇava *avatāra*s. When one encounters scenes of these devotees, placid flute and *tabla* music sets the tone for their agreeable social dealings. They never display anger toward others, even when severely provoked, but rather embody the values of compassion and humility that are particularly emphasized by Radhanath Swami in his interpretation of the Gauḍīya Vaiṣṇava tradition.

However, a significant portion of Chowpatty's dramas focus on disruptions of this ideal moral universe and the struggle for reconciliation that ensues. This generally takes the form of a politically powerful elite threatening the well-being of the Gauḍīya *saṅgha*. These antagonists are marked by qualities opposite to the Gauḍīya community: anger, lust, greed, hunger for wealth and power, and the desire for vengeance. Frequently these vices are discussed within their didactic moral framework by a narrator at the beginning and end of the play. For instance, in *Devastating Sacrifice*, a depiction of a *līlā* involving Śiva and Pārvatī from the fourth *skandha* of the Bhāgavata Purāṇa, Act One begins with negative foreshadowing in a warning from the narrator: "The Bhagavad Gītā mentions anger to be one of the doors to hell."[45] Disruptions of the ideal moral universe are acted out colorfully—in the above, through elaborate depictions of the anger of the Puranic character Daksa.

Alongside retelling Puranic tales, many dramas depict the Gauḍīya tradition's early formation and its triumph over historic religious rivals. Dramas highlight rivalries over patronage circuits between Hindus, including parallel devotional groups such as the Rāmānandīs and the Puṣṭimārgis, as well as sometimes violent confrontations with Śaivas and Śāktas over divergent *sādhana* practices. However, as the dramas developed over the past two decades, the most frequently represented role of religious alterity was reserved for early modern Muslim rulers, a representation of a Muslim Other that seemed to accentuate an affective commitment to uphold Vaiṣṇava devotion in contemporary India.

While the plays' antagonists generally redeem themselves under the influence of enlightened Gauḍīya protagonists, much time is devoted to vivid depictions of their vices beforehand. The character of Chand Rai in *Jewel of Faith* begins as a cruel Śākta *zamīndār*, or landowner, whom the narrator tells us is given over to "hateful violence and uncontrolled sense enjoyment." After he changes his ways and adopts the Gauḍīya Vaiṣṇava path under the guru Narottāma dāsa Ṭhākura (a historic Vaiṣṇava figure, born ca. 1466), he is arrested by his political rival, a local Muslim ruler, who scoffs at such newly developed virtues, responding thus: "Well I'm not a changed man; I love my money! And I love to give pain to my enemy." The Muslim ruler then puts Chand Rai in jail and laughs cynically as he goads his guards to beat him, though later he too is redeemed by observing Chand Rai's equanimity even in the face of oppression. The narrator proclaims in conclusion: "Power, money, jewels: all things of this world are perishable. The real jewel is faith."[46] Still, the enactment of virtue is tied to vivid depictions of vice and redemption.

Many of these binary depictions follow characterizations in the scriptures from which the playwrights draw their stories. In sixteenth- and seventeenth-century hagiographies of the early Gauḍīya community, religious groups that opposed the young community were often described in polemical terms.[47] Expanding on these polemics, depictions of corrupt Śaiva brahmins, cruel Śākta landowners, and *yavana* Muslim rulers—from Mughal emperors to local nawabs—punctuate countless dramatic plots. However, Chowpatty's dramas also owe much to the melodramatic genre of Hindi cinema in their straightforward dichotomization of an aggressive villain and a protagonist whose equanimity and poise eventually overpower the villain's vice.[48] In dramatic productions that illustrate the power of Vaiṣṇava *bhakti* along lines of religious alterity, differences in behavior between sectarian religious actors affirm the superordination of other deities under a Vaiṣṇava taxonomy.

Even more overtly, in the case of followers of Śiva and Devī, their deities themselves are cast in the dramas, revealing to their followers in dreams or conversations their true identity as subordinate to Viṣṇu or Krishna. In the 2013 *Devastating Sacrifice*, Śiva tells his consort, Pārvatī, that although "all around him people are chanting his names," he is "meditating upon the name of Rāma." In the 2014 *Jewel of Faith*, Durgā appears to a follower in a dream, insisting that he "take shelter of the Supreme Lord Krishna, the all-powerful, all-merciful being." In these relatively innocuous forms, a religious hierarchy is formed, placing Vaiṣṇava worship at the top of India's diverse Hindu traditions. A similar strategy is employed with Muslim characters.[49] In the 2013 *My Sweet Lord*, Sal Beg and his father Lal Beg pray fervently to Allah to heal the former from a severe illness. However, they find that the illness is cured only when they begin to pray to Jagannātha, underscoring that Vaiṣṇava deities display the greatest power among their various religious competitors.

Alongside this, the frequent representation of Hindus under Muslim-led governments in early modern North India depicts formative stages in the development of the Gauḍīya Vaiṣṇava tradition from which ISKCON derives. This context presented historic challenges to Hindu groups, including high-profile temple demolitions during times in which competing religious power was seen as threatening to a local ruler. But it also brought economic opportunities, such as the historical role of several Muslim-led courts in patronage and institutional support for early Gauḍīya communities.[50] In many community dramas during my field research, however, Muslim rulers were depicted as typecasts of tyranny, threatening to Hindu life and religious identity.[51] These depictions are commonplace in numerous Hindu communities' retellings of medieval and early modern Indian history, and indeed a foregrounding of tension between Hindu citizens and Muslim rulers has been seen as a central aspect of contemporary Hindu identity fashioning.[52] In Chowpatty as elsewhere, these figures of Muslim alterity are constructed as ideal types. Even when notable characteristics reveal them to be historical figures (for instance, Aurangzeb, a well-known Mughal ruler) their specificity is flattened through the reiteration of typologies surrounding the character of the "Muslim king," with a corresponding costume and set of mannerisms accentuated for dramatic effect. This characterization is part of the revelry for those organizing the dramas. While sitting in the Bhaktivedanta Hospital one day, Dinesh, a gracious and affable coordinator of the Spiritual Care Department, regaled me with pictures of his annual performances as the

Muslim king. He relished donning his beard and turbaned headdress and readying his boisterous, angry persona for the event.

Several productions open with a dark screen and the echoing sound of the *azān*, the Muslim call to prayer. The lights then reveal images of wealthy and belligerent monarchs, luxuriating in their *darbār*s and planning violent attacks on Hindus.[53] The following narrative, taken from the opening scene of the 2005 *Escape of Rūpa and Sanātana*, encapsulates many of the themes present in these depictions. This drama presents hagiographic sketches of two sixteenth-century Gauḍīya theologians, Rūpa and Sanātana Gosvāmins, born in the Jessore district of present-day Bangladesh. As recorded in hagiographical tradition, Rūpa and Sanātana were high officials in the court of the Muslim Naẉāb of Bengal, Husain Shah (r. 1493–1518 CE).[54] This was a prestigious employment opportunity but also a challenge to their perceived religious purity among fellow high-caste Hindus. Early Gauḍīya literature depicts the brothers' decisions to quit their jobs after meeting Caitanya, to pursue a life of asceticism and dedication to developing his nascent community of Krishna *bhaktas*. The play, however, foregrounds their choice to renounce their careers as an *escape*, not only from the non-spiritual pursuit of a career in government but also from a clearly threatening environment.

Against a dark stage, the narrator opens the play with the statement: "They [Rūpa and Sanātana] had love for every being. At that time, Bengal was under the Mughal regime of the *yavana* king, Nawab Hussain Shah." The call to prayer begins, starting with an "*Allahu akbar*" drawn out vocally against the dark stage. The scene then opens on a *qazi*'s court, with an eclectic mixture of South Asian Islamic visual representations. A tomb stands shrouded in a green prayer shawl on one side, and a turbaned and bearded government official sits on a *divan*, fanned by two attendants in white skullcaps. Enter stage right: a Hindu man in a *dhotī* is thrown on the ground by a turbaned man wearing a *kurtā pajāma* and whipping him. The call to prayer continues as the man shakes from fear and is pulled up by the man with the whip. He begs to be released.

As the man cries, the *qazi*, unimpressed, addresses his guard: "What's the matter, Rahman? Who is this wretch?"[55] The guard replies: "This pauper claims that he has no money. He has not paid his taxes for the last two years." The man pleads: "But *qazi sahib*, you know there have been no rains these last two years. And I had to get my daughter married." Dramatic *filmī* music escalates as the *qazi* taunts the man, "I've heard in your Ṛg Vedas, there are mantras to appease the rain god. So why don't all you Hindus come together and perform some *yajña* [ritual sacrifice]?" All the *qazi*'s men laugh in ridicule, but the Hindu man begs: "Please, as soon as I get some money, I will pay everything. I can hardly provide for my family. And you have already killed my cows!" The guard whips him: "Shut up, you fool! We want your money, not your empty promises." And the *qazi* responds: "In case you have forgotten, let me remind you of the nawab's order. If a Hindu doesn't pay taxes in six months, I take his cows. They are made *halal*! If he doesn't pay his taxes in one year, he will lose his land . . . and then he shall lose his life! Unless . . . unless he becomes a Muslim." "No, No!" the man recoils in disgust, "I can't do that . . . I have faithfully served Lord Krishna throughout my life!" But to this the *qazi* retorts: "And now you shall serve Allah!" He then drinks from a glass of water and moves toward the man, who is recoiling on the ground in horror. "The mercy of Allah is contained in this glass of water," he laughs maniacally while splashing water on him. The audience understands, in line with traditional brahmanical purity laws, that the man has now lost his caste from such "contamination" and will be forced out of brahmanical Hindu society and into an "untouchable" or Muslim social identity—a potent theme in Hindu nationalist retellings of Indian history. The stage then goes dark and the audience claps. A narrator concludes: "In this way, the Nawab Hussain Shah made policies heavily favoring the Muslims and consistently depriving the Hindus of even the basic rights of freedom."[56]

In this one sequence, numerous contested narratives of the history of Hindu and Muslim communities in India are contained: forced conversion, the danger of losing one's caste and forced exodus from the Hindu community, a depiction of early modern Muslim rulership in India that emphasizes violence and religious intolerance, a conflation of religious and political identity, and of course the cow-protection issue.[57] In a 2007 production, *Spiritual Renaissance*, these issues are reiterated in a vivid and lengthy sequence of monologues delivered by an actor playing the Mughal Emperor Aurangzeb. In other productions, such as the 2002 *Life and Pastimes of Srila Haridas Thakur* and the 2014 *Jewel of Faith*, similar depictions are joined by scenes of imprisoned Gauḍīyas, held in dungeons in which the *shahādah* is written on a banner in Urdu and strung up for decorative background. Beatings, taunts, and torture are extensively depicted in long dramatic sequences, and the aggression depicted is always unidirectional.

This religious alterity is always reconciled in the dramas through the long-suffering compassion of a Gauḍīya protagonist, sometimes in ways that blur lines between religious groups. The 2002 production "The Life and Pastimes of Haridas Thakur" was particularly notable for its performance shortly after the Gujarat anti-Muslim pogrom and subsequent Hindu-Muslim violence that swept many Indian cities that February.[58] Drawing on accounts of the *Caitanya Caritāmṛta*, the play depicts a hagiography of the saint Haridāsa, who converted from Islam to adopt Gauḍīya *sādhana* and is celebrated in Gauḍīya sources as the *nāma-ācārya*, "teacher of the holy names [of Krishna]" and a dear associate of Caitanya. The play both celebrates him and portrays the challenges that he encountered because of his commitment to Gauḍīya practices. As described in the hagiographical accounts, irate Muslim villages encourage the local *qazi* to arrest him for his act of apostasy and perceived attempts to convert others. After a series of attempts to torture and kill him, they acknowledge his fortitude in the face of harm and proclaim: "Haridāsa now we can understand you are a truly great saint, beyond any religious distinctions." Haridāsa replies: "My dear brothers, we are all sons of the same Supreme Father." A repentant Muslim man, represented with a skull cap, beard, and Kashmiri-style *kurtā pajāma*, then embraces a Hindu villager as Haridāsa looks on with a radiant smile.[59] In all these instances, threats to individual and community well-being are neutralized through the longsuffering piety of Gauḍīya saints.

Although these dramatic narratives draw from scriptural narrations, their elaborated depictions reproduce familiar postcolonial Hindu rhetorics of Muslim political rulers as religious Others in India's history, often centering on tropes of bellicose Muslims threatening the sanctity of Hindu lifestyles.[60] Similar visual and dramatic representations of Muslims through a lens of religious alterity can be traced in Hindi films and Doordarshan serials from the 1980s forward.[61] But such representations are a transnational media form as well. In the Chowpatty dramas' depictions, scenes draw from familiar tropes of both classic Hindi cinematic depictions of nawabi courts and depictions of Muslim religious symbols mixed with displays of violence that are most evocative of post-9/11 American film and television productions.

The enactment of these contested historical moments, however, is often implicitly tied to contemporary political debates. This was evident in a casual production performed in January 2014 at the temple's Sunday program that elaborated on a Gauḍīya depiction of Caitanya's religious debates with a local *qazi* (*Caitanya Caritāmṛta* 1.17.115–215).[62] The drama foregrounded one topic in that debate—the inviolability of cows—and included a refrain that Muslims "kill and eat cows every day." As the tension builds, the man-lion *avatāra* Narasimha warns the *qazi* in a dream: "if you continue to try to stop the *saṃkīrtan*, I will kill all of your family and all the meat-eaters."[63] Thankfully, the *qazi* relents and comes to support the public *kīrtan* processions. This performance took place against the backdrop of a state-wide discussion occurring during this time, as Maharashtra moved toward enacting a long dormant bill banning the slaughter, sale, and consumption of beef—a political move that was widely understood to affect the livelihoods of many lower-class Muslim butchers and leather-workers in the state.

These scenes certainly build dramatic tension, but they are disquieting in a climate of bellicose anti-Muslim rhetoric throughout many regions of India. Most recently, the considerably different historical rulers Tipu Sultan and Aurangzeb have both become flashpoints in public debates over India's Muslim heritage, leading to acts of public violence and the arrest of Indian Muslim men who shared messages related to them on social media.[64] This frenzied debate about how past Muslim rulers can or should be depicted sits parallel to threats levied toward many living Muslims in India, often justified through depictions of early modern rulers as violent and intolerant. Drawing from traditional Hindu stage performance genres and popular Indian cinematic tropes, such performances encode a religious history that echoes anxieties among India's Hindu majority. To be clear, ISKCON productions do not advocate violence. By contrast, they celebrate longsuffering compassion toward others, highlighting the dedication of humble devotees without worldly might. But they do reproduce widespread local stereotypes of tyrannical Muslims that can shape how audiences view India's past.

However, these dramatic representations are layered. Reflecting the complexity of interreligious relationships throughout Gauḍīya history and the explicit commitment of many Chowpatty devotees to religious ecumenicism, they center on attempts to transcend difference in pursuit of religious harmony. In the 2002 production, the protagonist Haridāsa communicates a strong ecumenical moral resonant with Indic religious pluralism:

> Your honor, please listen. There is only one God for everyone. We may call ourselves as Hindus or Muslims, but the fact is the Vedas and the Qur'an both speak of the same supreme Lord who resides equally in every living being's heart. God knows everyone's nature. I follow the orders that God gives me in my heart, and it is he who has inspired me to chant the holy names![65]

This offers a view of religious alterity balanced toward individual flexibility rather than religious supremacy. Though this message is, significantly, communicated through the Gauḍīya tradition's prime representative of domesticated religious alterity, nonetheless in the dramas generally characters do cross over, to change their status in Gauḍīya legend from foe to friend—as indeed Husain Shah does in the *Caitanya Caritāmṛta*'s depiction. The visual and dramatic depictions of alterity, however, serve as a proving ground, constructing ideas of idyllic Vaiṣṇava conduct maintained *despite* threats from rival religious communities, and ultimately a unifying devotion, recognized by all, prevails.

The performance of communal harmony through joint celebration of a Vaiṣṇava ethos expands beyond the proscenium stage. For instance, the victory of Maryam Siddiqui in the 2015 Gita Champions League examination, as discussed above, received ample Indian media coverage in the midst of a series of violent attacks of Muslims and Dalits throughout North and Western India.[66] There is a salience of Siddiqui's image in ISKCON-based and national news media, including coverage of her official meeting with India's Prime Minister Narendra Modi and the chief minister of Uttar Pradesh, during the time and in the state in which many of these attacks occurred. Through Siddiqui's successful participation in the knowledge-production systems mediated by Chowpatty's Gita Champions League exam, she and her supportive father affirmed a seemingly neutral and conciliatory message: the benefit of Vaiṣṇava religious teachings for all Indians, or the promotion of the *bhakti* nation.

## The Blurred Boundaries of Religious Nationalisms

While the Vaiṣṇava *bhakti* imaginary in Chowpatty's festivals and dramas at times echoes discourses of Hindu nationalism, a conflation of the two would be inaccurate to represent the community's ideological breadth and the complexity of their relationship to political groups. Some devotees do explicitly ally with political parties and many support India's current Prime Minister Narendra Modi (like many middle-class and upper-class Hindus). Others eschew political affiliations altogether in keeping with Bhaktivedanta's affirmation of an age-old current of Indian religiosity—exemplified from Kabir to Chisthi Sufis to the Gauḍīya Gosvāmins—that views political power with suspicion. Even from his early writings, Bhaktivedanta affiliated nationalism and, broadly, identifying one's self with a particular body or land of birth, as a material disease.[67]

Additionally, Chowpatty's community has been the victim of religious and regional nationalisms in Mumbai. Their charitable hospital, Bhaktivedanta Hospital, was targeted by a violent "direct action" by the Bharatiya Kamgar Sena, a labor union affiliated with the Shiv Sena, which led to property damage and the hospital's closure for almost a year in 2003. Several hospital administrators with whom I spoke attributed the attack to the prominent presence of South Indian employees—frequent targets of the Sena's regional nationalism.[68] With large numbers of South Indian and Gujarati devotees, who have been prime targets of the Sena's Marathi nationalist politics, the temple community embodies a marked cosmopolitan in contrast to the Sena's ethnolinguistic politics. In that sense, they do not reflect a nativism but rather resistance against it through their own demographics. But grounded in local political necessity, ISKCON continues efforts to maintain a peaceable relationship with the Shiv Sena, as their public festivals in Sena-influenced neighborhoods are secured by these relations.

ISKCON balances affiliations with Mumbai's cosmopolitan and nativist sectors, and Chowpatty's media producers consequently engage in these overlapping discourses, seeking to ally with traditionalist Hindu publics but also translating their religious messages into popular frameworks of corporate marketing and wellness, to appeal to "secular" audiences. Through the public figure of Radhanath Swami, they articulate a discourse of modern, urban, and globalized Vaiṣṇavism. Nonetheless, the devotees active in events such as the "India Rising" festival represent a new stage of ISKCON's localization in Mumbai, as pan-Indic *bhakti* discourses are tied together with contemporary aspirations for an increased Hindu religiosity in Indian politics and public life.[69]

In broad scope, the synergy between Hindu traditionalism and Hindu nationalism is complex. As John Zavos and others have noted, one does well to caution against making easy or uncomplicated correspondences among the symbols, religious orientations, and practices of modern Hindu religious organizations and modern Hindu nationalist political organizations. Even amid many devotees forging explicit public alliances with Hindu nationalist and regional nationalist parties, as above, the waters still are muddied by the co-optation of Hindu symbols by political parties like the BJP. This is perhaps seen most dramatically in the very symbol of the Rath Yatra. An annual temple-based cart procession revered since the time of Caitanya and codified in historic Gauḍīya participation through early followers' participation in the annual event at Puri, Prabhupada instated the Rath Yatra as a prominent annual event for ISKCON communities globally in the 1970s. Yet in India today, the term Rath Yatra most popularly invokes the political pilgrimage led by the BJP's *kar sevak* campaign to destroy the sixteenth-century Babri Masjid in the early 1990s. Support for Rath Yatras and their purposes thus reflects a multilayered intertwining between religious and political symbols of Hindu identity. These dual valences have been emblematic of the development of Indian nationalism in its prominent elite Hindu form since the late nineteenth and early twentieth centuries.[70] As Christophe Jaffrelot notes, nationalist ideologies of this formative period promoted a conception of space in part inherited from premodern elite textual portrayals of ancient India, as mentioned in the epics and *dharma śāstras*, wherein "Bhārat is described as the land of *dharma* and as such, she has a unique ritual, religious, and magical status, whose territory, as Arya-varta, is defined along the lines of the range of the caste system."[71] Therein, ritual places are imbued with a national value, as the presence of Vaiṣṇava *tīrtha*s or Śiva *liṅga*s throughout the country also signify a religious and territorial unity. Implicit political claims can be merged with religious practices in a Hindu reading of the Indian nation, supported by appeal to descriptions of the region in premodern religious texts, such as the Mahabharata.

But of note for a community deeply invested in the writings of Bhaktivedanta is his own distaste for nationalism generally, labelling it another symptom of "false, bodily identification" in place of what he saw as the more genuine, permanent identification with the soul. In a 1956 publication, Bhaktivedānta responded to the proposals in newly independent India for dividing states along linguistic and regional identities, by bemoaning the "frenzy of national or provincial hatred for men speaking in another language" and "the frenzy of national love for the land of birth." [72] This thread of suspicion toward political affiliations has led some devotees to question those who have become more enamored with the BJP and related Hindu nationalist thinkers, to the extent of asking, "Is your guru Radhanath Swami or Rajiv Malhotra?" Instead, for them, the proper role for a devotee is to cultivate *bhakti*, not political power.

Yet, as prominent Hindu nationalist parties hold popularity across many Indian states, they both reflect and stoke discourses that Hindu interests have long been neglected in postcolonial India's ideals of socialist economics and religious diversity. Concomitantly, India's economic and political success is linked to its fidelity to an assertive Hindu *dharma*, conveying the inextricability between these religious and political goals. In the case of ISKCON Chowpatty, during the run-up to the 2014 Lok Sabha elections and after Narendra Modi's victory, many members expressed elation at the BJP's stated agenda to support Hindu interests—including state-mandated vegetarianism and cow protection, two issues for which Bhaktivedanta himself lobbied in political venues. A decade on, celebratory remarks released ahead of the January 2024 inauguration of a temple to Rām on the site of the Babri Masjid in Ayodhya, for instance, test the limits of how far devotion can be separated from politics.[73] While explicit support for Hindu nationalist politicians and political agendas has been clearly displayed in public events, including Rath Yatra festivals, Radhanath Swami insisted in one of our personal conversations that support for political parties was negotiated in Chowpatty on an individual basis. He acknowledged the partiality of some devotees, particularly the business elite who comprise the temple's donor base, toward the party's "pro-business" (and anti-regulation) policies, but he emphasized that he has never given instructions to his followers regarding political support. He qualified this: "If people ask, I may feel that one party may be more helpful to us and more coming forward . . . But we don't publicly promote any political parties." This provides a clear space for pursuing an alliance between the shared agendas of this Hindu traditionalist community and the Hindu nationalist parties in power, and these shared national agendas were often praised in both private discussions and public venues. But it also points to a pragmatic approach to politics in ISKCON. For this community that once almost saw its first Bombay temple demolished because of a lack of local political connections, making solid political ties to the powers-that-be also secures the temple mission of spreading Krishna *bhakti*. And if those powers-that-be also align with the community's own vision for a dharmic India, political affiliation could be construed by some devotees as a new instance of *yukta vairagya*, harnessing the resources around one to achieve a religious goal.[74]

In any case, ISKCON festivals could not be further from the bellicose rhetoric of RSS *sevaks* at a public protest. Rather, this public identity—conveyed through measured speeches, a celebrity guest list, and elite Indian visual cultures—conveys an urban milieu that is interested in increasing the role of Hindu *dharma* in public life through corporate investments, well-placed promotions, and the shaping of popular media. Indeed, the twin agendas of India's transnational capitalist growth and assertion of an irreducibly Hindu character of the Indian nation have guided many public-culture products of elite urban Hindu communities.[75] In this sense, nods to nationalist ideas are channeled in ISKCON festivals through overt class signaling as well as a core religious messaging. In contrast to the decentralized atmosphere at Gaṇapati *utsavs*—perhaps Mumbai's largest annual public religious festival—Chowpatty's public festivals, even during the Rath Yatra processions, are characterized by careful organization. The festival grounds themselves resemble an elite wedding venue, cordoned off from the city outside with decorated entrance gates, featuring organized lines at food and drink stalls and a central stage with seating arrangements for the audience. While nationalist messages are present in both events, Raminder Kaur has noted the prevalence of an overtly nationalist "*rāṣṭrīya* tableaux" at Gaṇapati *utsav* events, depicted through their diorama exhibits and *maṇḍap* (pavilion) displays.[76] By contrast, Chowpatty's nationalist imaginary is subordinated to the precedence of what Kaur deems the "*dharmic* tableaux," or the higher calling of *dharma* within a Vaiṣṇava idiom, that is seen as the unique gift of India on the *global* stage. Therein, ISKCON's Mumbai communities remain fundamentally oriented around a transnational, multiethnic identity that emphasizes the importance of engagement in *bhakti* and *daiva varṇāśrama-dharma* over birth in a Hindu family—a refiguring of what it means to promote religious identity in India's public spaces. And in their cosmopolitan institutional identity and central goal of "bringing Krishna back" to India, many devotees hold an earnest belief that they are subverting ethnic and national identities in their core valuation of ideal devotional character.

Given that ISKCON devotees hold a range of political views, what can be said with certainty about what ISKCON in urban India represents today? In contrast to early ISKCON festivals in 1970s Bombay, portrayed in news media as exotic Western imports, Chowpatty's festivals can be read as a form of local public culture, as according to Breckenridge and Appadurai's definition they participate in what they deem "the tensions and contradictions between national sites and transnational cultural processes."[77] In other words, the organization has indigenized, but being local today is intertwined with ideas about both the Indian nation and its relation to the world at large. Engaging with an intertextuality between several realms—including Gauḍīya scripture, vernacular Vaiṣṇava *bhakti* histories, Hindi cinematic imagery, and competing Indian nationalist ideas—Chowpatty's conceptual mapping of the Indian nation-state through the lens of Vaiṣṇava *bhakti* heritage renders the nation profoundly personal, guiding individual religious subjectivities through its public displays. As Sumathi Ramaswamy notes in relation to the cartographic and artistic representations of Bhārata Mātā that represented the territorial landscape of the nation-state in the early twentieth-century popular imagination, such conceptualizations transform geographic space into an intensely human place—in some sense even a somatic being.[78] While not employing the visual representation of Bhārata Mātā through performance, Chowpatty's representation of *līlās* and poet-saint narratives from India's diverse states trace a vision of India as an interconnected devotional space. This reflects the producers of such content: Indian devotees who bring their own interests and concerns to the organization of festivals and dramatic productions. And through depicting the Indian nation through a network of regional Vaiṣṇava *bhakti* traditions, devout audiences are guided toward behavior and practices deemed central to devotional heritage, just as they are inducted into a notion of devotional history that paints members of different religious groups to be in the dangerous borderlands of that polity.

ISKCON's revision of religion is premised on infusing *bhakti* into India's public culture and national history. In that sense, the crossings devotees make in entering the devotional community are then directed outward, to seek transformation of the nation itself, and even the world, in a revivalist religious mode. Abundant performative depictions of *bhakti* poet-saints and regional Vaiṣṇava deities do the work of nation building precisely because of their transregional focus. Diverse linguistic and regional histories are united in a notion of a shared devotion, mirroring a desired unity in diversity among the varied demographics of the Chowpatty temple community itself. Extending devotional heritage on an international scale, they reflect ISKCON's own transnational development. This reflects tensions inherent in many Mumbaikars' globally integrated elitism, as they balance a suspicion of Western colonial power dynamics with Indian aspirations to become a global superpower. Here, as ISKCON has localized in Indian cities, its productions both reflect and seek to shape urban Indian concerns. Amidst high-stakes discussions of how India's past should be represented, Chowpatty's productions promote the message that *bhakti* heritage is for the benefit of all modern Indians; and indeed for the benefit of the world. In this approach, Indian devotees in Mumbai continue the early missionizing agenda of "bringing Krishna back to India." But can this Krishna truly embrace the city in which he now dwells?

# 6

# A New Traditionalism in the City

## Transforming Local Culture

> I remember once I went to him . . . because it was the Westernized culture to be very proud and think that you don't know how to cook, I'm not like a backward woman. And he reacted by saying: 'You don't know how to cook? Only lazy people don't know how to cook!' So, then I realized that he was trying to teach me Indian culture, to be more in line with our culture, which is like every woman should know how to cook . . . Even with the sari. He's the one who encouraged me to wear sari.
>
> - Arushi, long-time devotee

> If I wear anything, it would be a *kurta* [the handspun shirt worn by men], not a sari. I'll feel much more comfortable in that. These feminine things are not for me.
>
> - Shaya, regular temple attendee

At a 2012 gathering of thousands of college students at the MTV-sponsored INSPIRO Youth Fiesta in Mumbai, a local indie rock band named the Madhavas played a loud set powered by competing sounds from their electric guitar and rhythmic electronica beats. While their lead singer shouted deep-throated choruses into the microphone, stage smoke rose, framing their figures against a color-fade screen. Dressed in black skinny jeans and infinity scarves, the group of four young men and women later posed for local news and entertainment channels alongside the event's celebrity guest host, the actress Sonam Kapoor, in the red-carpet media zone. Although twenty-somethings who grew up going to ISKCON's Mumbai and Chandigarh temples and tailor their music to combine Vaiṣṇava spirituality with pop music trends, the Madhavas appeared no different from

*Bringing Krishna Back to India*. Claire C. Robison, Oxford University Press. © Oxford University Press 2024.
DOI: 10.1093/9780197656488.003.0007

other bands at the event, including the recent *India's Got Talent* winners who headlined the show.

After their set, a pumping baseline signaled a segue between entertainers as the teeming crowd shouted and raised their hands in the air, hoping to be captured by the panning camera's live video feed. But the music quickly changed to a recording of a traditional Indian *raga* played on *tabla* and *santoor*, as two event guards escorted Radhanath Swami up the under-lit stairs to the stage. Although appearing small under the bright stage lights, the Swami seemed puzzlingly at ease in his saffron *sannyasi* robes and plastic *chappals* at the concert venue. A tentative round of applause and a sea of quizzical stares greeted him as he folded his hands in a *namaste* gesture to the audience and began a half-hour address on the importance of maintaining Indian culture and carrying it forward into the next generation. "This culture is the nation's greatest treasure," he said in confident, earnest tones, because "the foundation of Indian culture is its compassion and spirituality." To instill the mission of carrying on this culture into the young Indian audience is what the ISKCON-affiliated INSPIRO fest aimed to achieve.

Culture was a frequent topic of conversation during my time at Chowpatty. Classifications of what is appropriate Vaiṣṇava culture or what fits within the purview of "Vedic culture" guide devotees' decisions on what to eat, with whom to be friends, where to work, and how to spend their free time. In this sense, this culture—whether one calls it Indian, Vedic, Vaiṣṇava, or *bhāratīya saṁskṛti*—is the semantic ground on which ISKCON's identity is constructed and negotiated by devotees. At in-house events, Radhanath Swami maintains an emphasis on ethical principles in his description of Vaiṣṇava culture, repeating pronouncements in both lectures and *darśan* with disciples that "the spirit of Vaiṣṇava culture is exemplary character, compassion, loving relationships, and deep absorption in *bhakti*." While expressed amorphously, visions of this culture often exist in dichotomy with depictions of what it is not. ISKCON's notions of Vaiṣṇava culture are used in parallel with Indian culture, glossed as inherently Sanskritic and Hindu. This is often contrasted with Western culture, which is marked as secular modernity in India as well as the Global North. Although brahmanically inflected, ISKCON's Vaiṣṇava culture is asserted to be "universal" and can be adopted by anyone regardless of their ethnic and national background. Indeed, it can be promoted on stage at MTV-sponsored music festivals. It is centered on Krishna *bhakti*, but an American-born guru embodies this culture and teaches it to his Indian disciples. Therein, a disdain for Western cultural influence in India is negotiated alongside reverence for a swami who symbolically transcends his identity as a Westerner through the practice of this culture. Many Indian followers, raised in modernized urban settings, tell me that they began to learn about and adopt this culture only after joining ISKCON. Accordingly, it symbolically revives their ancestral heritage but is a novelty in their own lives. It is in this regard that although traditionalist, ISKCON's construction of an ideal Indian culture is not nativist but rather a significant reformulation of Hindu traditionalism.

While Radhanath Swami's pronouncements situate Indian culture in affirmations of an ethical core, Vaiṣṇava etiquette manuals and regular classes within the Chowpatty community also detail a specific, bounded system: what I will call a Vedic-Vaiṣṇava cultural worldview. The terms Vedic and Vaiṣṇava are used somewhat interchangeably in ISKCON circles, with the connotation that medieval and early modern Vaiṣṇava traditions mediated an earlier Vedic heritage, an assertion made explicit in the early Gauḍīya theology of Jīva Gosvāmin and others. Beyond the centrality of Krishna devotion, discussions about culture play out most frequently in tensions over modern, urban lifestyles—in relation to dietary restrictions, modes of dress, gender relations, and social interactions, as well as in conflicts between members' familial obligations and membership in ISKCON. As vanguards of a Vedic-Vaiṣṇava cultural revival in an urban setting, devotees see themselves in tension with the city around them. Debates about how to embody this culture are often hashed out in counselling relationships—a training-centered approach that underscores this culture must be actively *adopted*, rather than passively embodied due to being from a place.

As ethnographers now know, there are no homogenous, "pure" locations of culture. Aisha Khan has shown how religion and culture are discursively constructed in relation to other identity categories, including race and nation.[1] Notions of an inherent purity or essential quality invested in these categories—such as the notion of a singular Hindu or Indian identity—ignore the inherent heterogeneity of cultural forms that defines communities everywhere in practice. To express the multifaceted nature of local cultures, Arjun Appadurai adopted the language of "scapes," including "ethnoscapes" and "mediaspaces," highlighting the varied landscape of people across borders that renders local cultures heterogeneous.[2] Therein, Indian ethnoscapes are present not only in Mumbai but also in Kuala Lumpur and London, at a bodega in Jackson Heights as much as a Keralan house-church in Abu Dhabi. Yet, although scholars of religion view such identities as inherently heterogeneous and in continued states of flux, religious communities may celebrate essentialized notions of pure or authentic culture as grounds for shifting behavior and positioning oneself in relation to the surrounding society. Amid the growth of the nation-state and neoliberal policies, national cultures have also become reified alongside assertions of religious, linguistic, and ethnic primacy in a region, an ideology that erases historic fluidity and diversity. These forms of ethno-religious nationalism are tied to global capitalist networks, as Aihwa Ong has argued in analyzing new cultural representations of "Chineseness" in relation to transnational Asian capitalism.[3] ISKCON's religious programs, in parallel, depict a cultural model of "Indianness" that is intended to appeal to Mumbai's publics and—as "brand India," a catchphrase used at the India Rising festival. This discursively constructed notion of culture produces ideas of ethnicity and place that are also intended as a commodifiable global export. But how do these notions of culture actually fit "at home"?

This chapter draws on a range of archival materials and ethnographic encounters to tease out how Hindu traditions and Mumbai's urban landscape are negotiated through this elastic understanding of culture, which has roots in Bhaktivedanta's writings but has also developed in new ways by contemporary Indian devotees. Claims that Vedic or Vaiṣṇava culture is universal affect how members understand their own Indian cultural backgrounds and lived experiences in Mumbai today. This produces paradoxes when a local community centers the teachings of an American guru and decenters life in India outside of the organization. Shaped as much by a rejection of mainstream urban Indian cultural trends as it is by the behaviors it prescribes, this ideal culture is thus attained through a type of deterritorialization.[4]

Deterritorialization can be described as a restructuring of what is local or native to a place, an eradication of social or cultural practices and reterritorialization of new norms in their place. Appadurai deemed it a product of globalization—a disjuncture wherein tensions between homogenous and heterogeneous cultural forms become a central problem in a society.[5] ISKCON's centering of a dichotomy between Indian and Western culture speaks to one form of deterritorialization that devotees experience: feeling cut off from traditional Indian culture amidst the homogenizing influence of Western modernity. But I argue there is also another form of deterritorialization at work here, as the essentialization of traditional Indian culture as Vedic and Vaiṣṇava devalues local cultural forms that do not fit its notion of purity. Therein, the "West" is as much a threat in Mumbai as in

America, not geographically bound, just as Indian culture may be adopted irrespective of location and ethnic identity. Drawing on the interpretation of José Casanova, I see deterritorialization here as "the disembeddedness of cultural phenomena" from what is perceived as their "natural" territories, illustrating that territories themselves are "imagined spaces, mental mappings."[6] What is "natural" to a territory is a matter of how we map it mentally, including how we interpret local diversity in relation to cultural ideals. In Mumbai, are brahmanical traditions more natural than the Koli fishing villages that pre-dated the city? Is a Hindu temple more natural than a mosque, a local cinema, or a Parsi café? All are part of the tapestry of the city and their presence resists homogenization. But culture discourses have the power to reshape local landscapes. Vaiṣṇava traditionalism makes strange—indeed glosses as foreign—local norms in clothing, behavior, and lifestyle that were commonplace to many Indian devotees in their youth. Coding these cultural forms as "Westernized," devotees are encouraged to maintain a separation from their surroundings in pursuit of a higher ideal. This chapter will examine the two aspects of this culture discourse: the assertion that Indian followers can learn about Indian culture from a non-Indian guru and the struggles of some devotees to reconcile their lives in India with adhering to ISKCON's ideals. To start, I examine the roots of this culture discourse in ISKCON's formation.

## Claiming Culture, Revising Culture

The word "culture" has become ubiquitous in modern Hindu organizations to describe their public activities and engagement with society, from the RSS's self-description as a "cultural organization" to the "cultural programs" organized by religious organizations in India and in diaspora. While often downplaying class, caste, and regional differences, these ideas about what is culturally Indian possess a referential power through repeated public assertions.[7] Modern cultural-heritage discourses have not formed around brahmanical Hindu symbols alone.[8] Through their genealogy in colonial-era formulations, however, a common denominator is an articulation that this culture is under threat and in need of defense. As we saw above, notions that devotional culture must be protected amid changing times and religious Others are interwoven into devotees' articulation of their mission in contemporary India.

Both the English word "culture" and the Hindi word "*saṁskṛti*"—a neologism that preferences the Sanskritic heritage of South Asia—occur pervasively in Chowpatty's lectures, dramas, and print media.[9] The title "cultural presentations" is given to public presentations of lifestyle norms, including vegetarianism and cow-protection initiatives, as well as performance arts affiliated with Indian *bhakti* heritage at events like the "India Rising" festival or programs held on the temple property. During my research, events advertised as cultural presentations included dance, drama, or music, and ranged from Bharatnatyam dance performances by teenage girls, to Vārkarī devotional singers hired for Rath Yatras, to choreographed children's dramas at private homes. These explicitly "cultural" events, distinguished from the ritual core of ISKCON religious programs, speak to the abiding importance of representing Indianness—as both celebration and preservation—among contemporary communities.

For many modern Hindu groups, notions of an authentic cultural past are tied to a universalizing narrative of India and Hindu traditions through the terms "Vedic" and *sanātana dharma.*[10] These umbrella terms can encompass specific lifestyle injunctions, worship styles, and ideas about society and politics. The "Vedic" has been often conjoined with the philosophical orientation of Advaita Vedānta.[11] For ISKCON, however, "Vedic" is synonymous with a personalistic Vaiṣṇava devotional orientation toward Krishna. ISKCON's ritual repertoire is linked to a Vedic lineage in their media products. For instance, under the "Festivals" bar of the Chowpatty's temple website, one is informed that: "festivals were an integral part of Vedic culture," a statement that situates participation in the festivals, held at the center of the temple's annual ritual schedule, as a continuation of that Vedic heritage. Vedic civilization and its stated elements can also be pragmatic products in a contemporary marketplace, as in the "Vedic maths" booths that promise superior school quiz preparation at Rath Yatra festivals.

In informal conversations, some devotees glossed all aspects of brahmanical culture *as* Vedic culture, while others juxtaposed Indian culture—rendered corrupt in the present day—with premodern Vaiṣṇava or Vedic culture. While appeals to Vedic culture are widespread, the exact referent for the appellation "Vedic" remains ambiguous, and some devotees eschew the term "Vedic culture" altogether as a hollow referent to whatever values one hopes to link to the Gauḍīya tradition. Giridhari, an affable friend who started attending ISKCON temples as a British teenager of Indian descent in

London, laid out his own method of reconciling the seemingly irreconcilable nature of this culture:

> You have the more conservative people who say that ISKCON should be promoting Vedic culture across the world. Women shouldn't be allowed to do this and that, and men shouldn't be allowed to do this and that . . . And then you've got the other people who say you've got to be accommodating to time, place, and circumstance. I don't like to see myself in either of those perspectives, because I don't think they're real. I think for me Vedic culture is seeing what's practical rather than sticking to something rigid . . . I mean, Vedic culture is what you make it. Vedic culture is wearing rollerblades and eating ice cream if you want it to be!

Giridhari's quick take, offered during a brisk evening walk along Marine Drive while catching up about friends back in England, betrays a fatigue with the longstanding ISKCON debates over the character of this ideal culture.[12] Yet its parameters acquire new contours within an Indian context. In most cases, ISKCON devotees' definition of the Vedic is informed by Bhaktivedanta's statements, and Giridhari's approach reflects the fluidity in Bhaktivedanta's usage of the term. Bhaktivedanta did at times point to specific social aspects in what he meant by "Vedic" culture or civilization; for instance, respect for elders, a patriarchal society that regulates women's "independence,"[13] and *varṇāśrama*-based occupational divisions.[14] However, many ISKCON followers appeal to the overarching interpretative tool of *yukta vairagya* to provide the same context-specific flexibility as Bhaktisiddhanta harnessed in the early twentieth century, when he bypassed monastic taboos against *sannyasis* driving in vehicles to employ cars and other forms of technology to spread religious teachings.

While Bhaktivedanta's own presentation of what is comprised in the term Vedic was fluid, he consistently asserted that Vedic heritage is expressed in Krishna *bhakti*, and he promoted his mission as the inculcation of that as a culture, described interchangeably as Vaiṣṇava and Indian. During his 1971 *pandal* program in South Bombay, Bhaktivedanta asserted to his Indian audience: "It is our mission. It is India's culture. People are hankering after this culture, Krishna culture. So, you should prepare yourself to present Bhagavad Gītā as it is. Then India will conquer all over the world by this Krishna culture."[15] By contrast, Bhaktivedanta often pitted "Krishna culture" against the predominant cultural modes of the West. Drawing from H. Richard

Niebuhr's foundational 1951 *Christ and Culture*, Tamal Krishna Goswami and Ravi Gupta have noted that in regard to culture in a North American context, the approach by Bhaktivedanta and his early followers oscillated from a "Krishna *against* culture" model toward a "Krishna *of* culture."[16] Throughout North American and European ISKCON centers, an initial deep suspicion toward "Western culture" (encapsulated in the binaries "devotee" and "*karmi*") gradually gave way to a more accommodative approach based on Bhaktisiddhānta's notion of *yukta vairāgya*, which encourages one to imbue or import a type of "Krishna culture" into one's own local setting.

In both iterations, "Krishna culture" is cast in the language of import and export. It is not assured through birth nor exclusive to an ethnic group or region, but rather something that can be taught and consequently learned. As we have seen, ISKCON positions itself as bringing this culture *back* to India. To do that, Indian devotees must fight against cultural norms already present in India.

## Contesting Western Modernity

Although once stigmatized in Mumbai's news media in the 1970s and 1980s as a Westernized Hindu community, ISKCON's own media products juxtapose their messages over against "Western modernity," marked as irreligious and synonymous with social vices. One recent advertisement for a monthly Chetana program, the "girls-only" space for young women in the community, announced an emblematic theme of "Femininity vs. Feminism." The flyer juxtaposed a picture of Bollywood actress Aishwarya Rai in a sari and elaborate traditional ornamentation with a stock image of two white women smoking cigarettes—a visual contrast that reproduced ideas about Western modernity in contrast to Indian traditionalism (Figure 6.1). Many individual devotees expressed their wish to promote "traditional Indian culture" over against what many see as an encroachment of Western culture and media into Indian life. During my time in India, widespread social ills (including alarming cases of violence, such as the 2012 Delhi Rape Case) were linked by politicians and devotees to the encroachment of Western values on an Indian social landscape.

This reflects much broader discourses about the West in Indian public culture.[17] But in Mumbai, the threat of the West is mediated differently than in diaspora contexts. Rather than an ethno-cultural threat close at hand in the

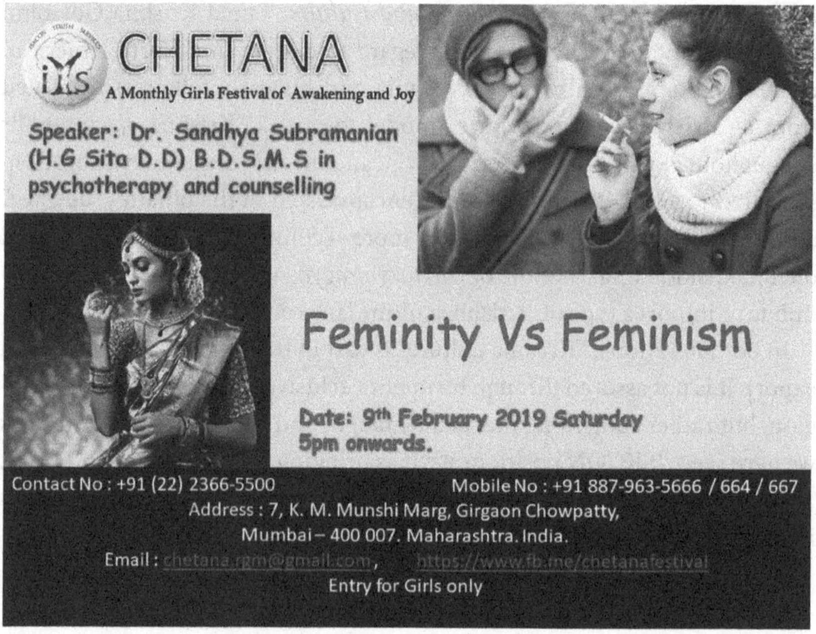


Fig. 6.1 Promotional flyer for the Chetana program, 2019. Used with permission.

geographic West, Chowpatty's media critiques the Westernization of fellow Indians. As mentioned above, many Mumbaikars are not overtly religious or interested in their parents' and grandparents' religious rituals. In middle-class and upper-class secondary schools and colleges, outward marks of religiosity are often seen as parochial or old fashioned. Devotees relayed to me that it was hard for them to maintain relationships with college friends after becoming more devout, because either their friends found their religious focus excessive and conversely they no longer felt comfortable with their friends' lifestyles. Several teenagers I met who were raised in ISKCON and remained devout found themselves befriending students from other communities with strict lifestyle norms, such as devout Jains or Gujarati Puṣṭimārgis, finding allies amid a majority who could not relate. Accordingly, the discourses against Western culture and secular modernity that pepper Chowpatty's productions are oriented not toward Westerners per se, but toward Mumbaikars.

For many devotees, the struggle against Western cultural influence in India is not merely theoretical. Gopal *brahmacari*, who in Chapter 3 discussed how

ISKCON enabled him to continue his North Indian brahmanical heritage, explained that he sees the culture in India changing:

> I have seen personally in my family, that there is such a culture of respect, especially even the gender respect, that the men of our family would not speak to the women directly, speak in a very cultured way, and they [the women] would also be not coming in an assembly of men. If they want to call someone, they will send some child—*acchā*, call your father, I want to speak something.

He juxtaposed that generation to the next generation, "who are wearing some Westernized clothes" and in which "people have totally unbridled behavior." In his thirty-four years, he said with the air of an elderly man, he has seen this cultural shift, and he attributes the main cause to be the Western influence brought by television. He clarified: "It also came in a very subtle way—it started with *Rāmāyaṇa* and *Mahābhārata* serials. In India, the TV culture started with these two serials. And then after that all the other things started coming. It was like cheating them in one sense."

Nandalal also drew attention to the influence of Westernized media on Indian society. He grew up in Darjeeling, where his South Indian Iyer family immigrated to work for Tata Industries, and he trained as a chartered accountant before joining the Chowpatty temple as a *brahmacari*. A current member of the temple's public relations department, he specializes in interacting with governmental agencies and crafting the temple's press releases. In India today, he noted: "I feel very few organizations are actually standing up against this fast decline, and ISKCON is actually playing a very important role in upholding the Vedic traditions, the four basic principles," referring to the four lifestyle vows of: "no meat-eating, no intoxication, no illicit sex, and no gambling." As many devotees are themselves from non-devout households, this traditionalism is a self-critique of Indian elites and middle classes, often linked to a rejection of the values they previously strove toward. As Rasik, a forty-something administrator at the temple school told me, he joined ISKCON after realizing that the films of his childhood hero Sylvester Stallone—the muscular, All-American Rocky—were not "real" films but "reel" films, illusory representations of a lifestyle that could not be attained.

When I began fieldwork, I was surprised to find how often "the West" entered into devotees' conversations as a category of cultural influence and general antagonist. The West looms large in Chowpatty—as in most of India—not just in personal discussions but also in public lectures, official literature, and in a variety of subtler forms in the performance of religious identity.[18] Western and Indian culture are categories that routinely undergird discussions, from debates about women's dress, to an increase in divorces, to debates about popular forms of entertainment, such as going to movies and restaurants. The dichotomy between Indian and Western cultures pervades media products tailored for Indian publics and informal conversations among friends. Unexamined statements about "typical" American or Western lifestyles (decadent, drug-fueled) sat unevenly with the time spent living abroad and transnational social networks of many upper-class devotees. Moreover, Chowpatty remains a member of a transnational organization still tied to a prominently Western managerial system. However, as was clear from my interviews with several gurus, ISKCON leaders of Western origin routinely disassociate themselves from Western culture—sometimes more strongly than Indian gurus—in order to embody their religious mission of reviving Indian culture in its homeland. In all of this, the Western-Indian dichotomy forms a central axis on which the Chowpatty community's identity is negotiated.

This orientation is grounded in Bhaktivedanta's reinforcement of an East-West cultural dichotomy in his lectures and writings, exhorting Indians to take note of the importance of their spiritual heritage over against what he described as Western materialism—here defined along the lines of the Global North broadly. On his return to India in 1970 after three years developing ISKCON's early centers abroad, Bhaktivedanta addressed a crowd of Indian followers in Calcutta: "I have been around the world and have found that happiness and peace cannot be established in this world by materialistic advancement. I have seen Japan, which is highly advanced in machines and technology. Yet there is no real happiness there."[19] Satsvarūpa, Bhaktivedanta's most prolific biographer, describes his motivation: "Prabhupāda's idea was that when Indians saw young Western people adopting the principles of Krishna consciousness the faith of the Indians in their own culture would increase."[20] Through inverting colonial categories of civilizational superiority in a Gandhian mode, Bhaktivedanta located the hope of a revival of that Indian culture through ISKCON's development in India. And the reversal of Indians' "loss" of this culture could then be achieved through domesticating the perceived threat of Westernization by converting Westerners themselves.

In his keynote address to the 2012 Artha Forum, Radhanath Swami drew from Bhaktivedanta's culture discourse to liken "the Western world" to a "powerful ship without a compass." As he looked around the room, seeking to engage the rows of Indian businesspeople who had driven the two hours outside of Mumbai to listen to his lecture, he defined "the people of India" as "people who have values, who have non-judgmental, compassionate attitudes." Quoting his parents, after their first visit to the Chowpatty community in the 1990s, he reiterated their impressions: "We've never met people with such love and goodness as the people of India." Then, retelling the familiar exchange of Bhaktivedanta and a reporter in London, he asserted that even after the two hundred years in which the British exploited the treasures of India, "the greatest treasure of India is its culture, its spiritual wisdom. It is a culture of spiritual values that can change the world. Vedic literature teaches universal, essential principles of *dharma* and contains a wealth of *avatāras*. India can give a foundation of spiritual culture and values to the world."[21] This discourse follows suit with Bhaktivedanta's conceptualization of the West as a cultural antithesis to India, but now this message is communicated by a Westerner who has adopted the markers of a Hindu *sādhu*, speaking to Indian audiences.

But a rejection of modern India's purportedly Westernized culture does not mean a rejection of its cultural forms, just a transformation of them. This is vividly displayed in the temple's dramatic productions, some of which respond to popular Bollywood films through revised screenplays that produce a religious conclusion. I will give one example at length here.[22] In the popular 2012 Hindi film *OMG: Oh My God!*—directed by Umesh Shukla and based on the Gujarati play *Kanji Viruddh Kanji*—a self-proclaimed atheist Hindu, Kanjibhai Mehta, files a lawsuit against God out of frustration with the injustice he sees in his own life. In the film, Kanji wins the verdict, forcing religious organizations to pay compensation to the plaintiff. However, Krishna makes a timely entrance and proves his existence (while also affirming Kanji's skepticism toward contemporary Indian gurus). Even though the film ends by affirming the existence of Krishna in a distinctly modern twist, critiques flooded Chowpatty temple programs in late 2012 and early 2013, appearing in Sunday feast dramas, at monthly Prerna and Chetana programs, and in audio and video content uploaded on the community's Desire Tree website and YouTube page.

Responding to the film's satire of gurus and *mūrti pūjā*, the local *brahmacari* Chaitanya Charan wrote and published an imagined sequel that was later performed on public stages around Mumbai and neighboring cities. The sequel mimics the film's satirical courtroom drama genre skillfully, with plot twists, surprise witnesses, live newscasters, and a score of dramatic music augmenting each new development. Act 1 opens with newsroom-themed headline music and focuses in on a journalist named Sunil Bhatia as he introduces details about the case in front of a live news camera.[23] This scene takes off from the end of the 2012 film, after Kanji has won his legal case against God. In the play, a diverse Mumbai crowd is arrayed around a journalist at the courtroom's entrance, including a woman in a South Indian style sari with jasmine in her hair; a Vārkarī devotee with his distinctive white cap; a South Indian Śaiva brahmin priest, shirtless in a bordered *dhoti*; and an Indian teenager with tussled shoulder-length hair, jeans, and big headphones around his neck (read: Westernized). All of them declare, in a character-appropriate local mixture of Hindi, Marathi, and English, that Kanjibhai has *convinced* them that religion is "no longer of any use and they will give it up." As the Westernized teenager says, in English: "Hey bro, after hearing Kanjibhai, I'm one hundred percent convinced that worship of stone idols is sheer madness. I've told my parents to please excuse me from all these things."[24]

The play then introduces a second lawsuit filed by Kanji to excise "*Bhagavān*" (God) and "*dharm*" (religion, sacred duty) from the Indian constitution. Kanji lays out his logic: "Every day the name of *Bhagavān* ruins the lives of thousands of people. It is growing like a cancer. Therefore, all types of *dharm*, *mazhab*, *rivāz*, and *kathāyoṅ* [terms encompassing religious practices for both Hindus and Muslims] should be stopped." Because, Kanji says, "these things are fine. But in the West for the sake of economic development, such things are left behind because they have no monetary value." Of course, no one in the Chowpatty audience was worried that the defendant would lose the case. But Kanji's pro-development, anti-religion arguments reflect anxieties that India's economic development will marginalize its religious traditions. The example posited in the drama's dialogue—that "the West" has given up religious traditions for the sake of economic prosperity—prompts the audience to affirm that India's religious and cultural riches should never be left behind, as so callously done in other countries. Here, the play's performative stereotyping of "the West" is directed toward its urban Indian audience, including workers in Mumbai's business and technology sectors, many of whom are actively involved in India's urban industrial development. Thus, as much as the play performs a rejection of secularism, it also displays an appropriation of mainstream Indian cultural forms to communicate its form of religious revivalism, creating a parallel mediascape for devotees to consume in place of mainstream Hindi cinema.

## Making "Universal Religion" Local

Just as Western cultural encroachment is seen to be globally pervasive, devotees liken ISKCON's cultural forms as beneficial for all. Traditionalist Vedic-Vaiṣṇava cultural forms are linked to a universalist scope, preferable for Indians but promoted for "humanity in general." Bhaktivedanta's missionary agenda encompassed attire regulations (saris and *dhotis*); ritual purity in hygiene, eating, and worship; and forms of social organization that idealized an agrarian-based *varṇāśrama* system and restricted gender interactions, including prohibitions against the "mixing of boys and girls" and the suggestion that women cover their heads with the *saripallu*, or end of their sari, in public.

These embodied cultural practices were often drawn from Bhaktivedanta's childhood in Calcutta and the examples of his relatives, providing templates for non-Indian devotees to emulate. This imbues ISKCON's religious practices with Bengali styles, including for instance the performance of *nāga saṃkīrtanas*, or public musical processions centered on the melodic chanting of Krishna's names, not a traditional practice in Mumbai. Female devotees wear saris in the brahmanical Bengali style rather than the local Marathi or Gujarati styles and, in early decades of the organization, married women often donned the *shakha pola*, characteristically Bengali red-and-white conch-shell bangles. In ISKCON's development, these specific cultural forms were interpreted through a universalist glossing of brahmanical practices, sharing romanticist visions of the premodern Indian village with Gandhian and broad mid-twentieth-century nationalism.[25] William Deadwyler cites an early unpublished letter of Bhaktivedanta to this effect:

> [Gandhian programmes] if systematically carried on will help very much in the spiritualizing process. They can be given a real spiritual shape in accordance with the principles of *Bhagwat Gita* and other authentic scriptures. And by doing so India's original culture will not only be revived and re-established but also will foster India's indigenous culture in other parts of the world. That will be a sort of cultural conquest of all [the] world by India.[26]

In regard to ISKCON's mission in Mumbai, many devotees promote the Vaiṣṇava specificity of this "original culture." For Mohan, a pensive *brahmacari* teacher who speaks with the confidence of someone used to winning arguments, asserted straightforwardly: "Krishna consciousness is the mother of Indian culture." But today's cultural norms in India, he continued, contain only "bits and pieces."

And yet, some devotees strive to transform today's cultural terrain in India on its own grounds. Arushi is a trained dentist who works at the community's charitable hospital, Bhaktivedanta Hospital. After she gets off work in the afternoons and before cooking dinner for her family, she also leads "values education programs" in secondary schools in the suburbs of North Mumbai. One evening I sat in the back of the hospital's auditorium among a room full of about a hundred tenth-standard high school students as they read poems, danced in choreographed covers to Beyoncé and Taylor Swift, and presented PowerPoint presentations on the importance of staying true to oneself. The pre-arranged theme of the evening's presentations was how to resist peer pressure toward drinking, drugs, and premarital sex. Throughout the evening, Arushi beamed as she introduced each high school group and congratulated them for working so diligently on their performances. She was in her element—wholeheartedly applauding at the end of each group's PowerPoint and giggling conspiratorially when some of the hospital's more conservative staff walked by the auditorium with eyebrows raised during one group's choreographed hip-hop dance. For her, spreading values through these youth programs did not need to mean cutting off young people entirely from pop culture. Although—as she later confided with a playful grin—some of Chowpatty's counsellors would have surely been shocked.

But Arushi also views the norms taught in ISKCON as imparting India's original culture. The next morning, we reflected on the success of the program the night before over breakfast, while sitting on floor cushions in her sunny living room. Arushi brought up her own experiences of starting to frequent the temple during her junior college years. The culture she found there, she said, shaped the way she related to her own South Indian brahmin background. She no longer wanted to run away from all the conservative strictures she had rolled her eyes at as a teenager. Rather, she found happiness in ISKCON—and still managed to marry a brahmin boy from the same town who had also joined. That self-confidence in the greatness of her own culture is what she hopes to give Mumbai's high-school students—at least indirectly—when she organizes values-based programs. What is particularly important now, she expressed, is to help young students make the right choices; to show them that they do not have to give up their culture. As she described this with conviction, she interwove her own vision of ISKCON culture that fuses the Vedic and universal:

> I strongly feel that the basis of Krishna consciousness is Vedic culture. It is the root of Krishna consciousness because it's based on Vedic scriptures . . . When we say Vedic culture, it actually encompasses not only Indian, because in ancient times the Vedic culture was all over the world. It was not just restricted to India. In the Vedic times, the whole world was considered as Bhārat-*bhūmi*. The Vedic culture is still very prevalent in India, because the origin was here. India was like the center of the world . . . If you go to the South, Odisha and downwards, the Vedic culture is still maintained. Very much in line.

This mixture of universalism and cultural specificity renders Vedic culture as the inheritance not only of Hindu India but, in a literal sense, of *all* people globally.[27]

Perhaps because of this broad conception, the forms in which this culture can be mediated can also change. Kanhaiya, an outspoken but mild-mannered *brahmacari*, was not afraid to critique what he saw as outmoded forms of ISKCON's proselytization, including the book distribution that has formed such a backbone of the community's public engagement. As a volunteer in the temple's communications department, he finds himself exasperated with temple organizers who seem intent on carrying on the exact missionizing strategies ISKCON established during the 1960s and 1970s. "Those times are gone," he says, letting out a gasp of annoyed but good-humored frustration. "You can't approach people in the same way or do the exact same things that worked back then. People have different priorities now. It is just self-evident." In his straightforward, confident cadence, he expressed what he thinks are better ways of trying to reach people, to open their hearts to Krishna. The point, he insisted, is that there is no one set standard. ISKCON's missionizing approach should change and adopt to contemporary cultural orientations:

> When we talk about Indian culture and Vedic culture, we're talking about something which is universally acceptable. Śrīla Prabhupāda's teachings are universally acceptable. Someone of any caste, creed, or nationality should

> be able to accept it and grow by it. The only hitch between how you present the universally applicable teaching in a present-day context is what we need to differentiate . . . Vedic culture is going to be acceptable at every human point of time, but if you're smart enough to present it in a way that is applicable.

But throughout the many uses of culture among devotees lays the conviction that Hindus have forgotten their "original culture." This assertion is often punctuated by reference to political history, especially antagonistic depictions of medieval and early modern Muslim kingdoms and British colonialism, as mentioned in the last chapter. Beyond—or through—these influences, a greater trend is seen to be at work in the loss of authentic religiosity brought on by the Kali Yuga, the "age of darkness," which began to take effect around five thousand years ago and is due to last many thousands of years more.[28] In written material distributed through the temple's bookstore, the present Kali Yuga is glossed as "a time of rampant faithlessness, sin and materialism." This is a hermeneutic for the modern world for devotees, who see ISKCON as providing a religious answer for Hindus whom they describe as having forgotten the real meanings behind their religious rituals and scriptures. This context accounts for the difference between the ideal imaginary of Vedic culture and the lived reality of Indian cultures. As an elder female devotee noted casually one morning, while we were stringing garlands near the temple room, the degradation of Indian culture in Kali Yuga makes it necessary to come to the temple to remember Krishna. In earlier times, the culture of *bhakti* was all around. Dayal, whose parents—brahmins from Chennai—joined ISKCON before he was born, echoed this point as he was showing me around Gopal's Garden. A successful recent graduate, he is now training to be a chartered accountant, yet also wary of navigating life outside the protected atmosphere of the temple's religious school. He noted with casual resignation: "The definition of religion has deteriorated heavily in India. It has become more of a business now." Whereas ISKCON, in "bringing values back to people's culture, bringing values down to the society," can counter "degradation" today.

This revivalist mission extends to reach Indians in diaspora and highlights the transnational interconnections of devotees lives. Shubhnaam, originally from the South Indian region of Mangalore, was eager to describe his own gradual religious awakening, which occurred when he worked at an information-technology company in Canada in his late twenties. Although he "really did not see the point of Hindu rituals," he began attending an ISKCON temple in Ottawa along with a group of friends—other Indian engineers who went almost every weekend. After a few months, he was surprised to find himself transforming from his "relatively agnostic" past, and he began attending services on his own. In retrospect, he credits this newfound religiosity as what spurred him to return to India, giving up a lucrative corporate career to work in Chowpatty's guest reception department. However, while still in Canada, he began to take *darśan* and later do *sevā* in the temple kitchen with another young Indian engineer. The story of their religious journeys highlights the role that ISKCON seeks to play in India—and for Indians abroad—in engendering a religious revival through transforming aspirations in modern life:

> I have seen it practically. When I was in Canada, I had a Śrīvaiṣṇava friend who was from a priestly class. His father and his family live near a famous Partha Sarathi temple in Chennai, a very old temple where Madhvācārya's parents went to pray when they didn't have children and then Madhva was born. They live maybe five-hundred meters from the temple. So that's the kind of background they are from—people who stay close to the temple, serve the temple—and their son, his name is Sarathi.
>
> He was in Ottawa with us, and when I met him, he was sort of lost, you know. He was not so much grounded in his culture, and he was visiting the Hindu temple there once in a while doing some service there, but he was really sort of lost his connectivity to his culture. Then when he started coming to the ISKCON temple and we started serving together, it was such a pleasure, because he had so much nice background—so much he had but it's just that the environment around him was not suitable to express. But when he got to the ISKCON environment, immediately he could connect, he could serve, his whole natural propensity came out.
>
> And by the association of devotees for a few years, he got so revived that now he's back in Chennai staying right outside the Partha Sarathi temple. He's still working for a Canadian firm, but he works from home! And he's now dedicatedly serving the temple.

Shubhnaam reclined in his office chair, smiling at the serendipity that brought a group of young Indian engineers—uprooted and chilled by the Canadian winter—to appreciate their religious culture in a way they never had back in India.

Revivalist understandings of culture often point to an ideal culture as congruent with a particular population group.[29] However, through ISKCON's transnational development and incorporation of non-Indian practitioners into positions of the highest religious authority, a radical deterritorialization of this culture is advanced within a traditionalist religious framework. Shubhnaam underscored this in his own religious transformation narrative:

> Now if ISKCON was not there in Ottawa, I feel he may not have reconnected to his roots. I've practically seen it work that way. In Ottawa there are a few Indians but also a lot of Western devotees, and they have helped him practically to revive his culture, and he became so convinced that instead of being in the West and trying to earn more money and middle comfort, he decided, "let me go back and serve" . . . He had already bought a house, he had a job, he had everything set there, but because ISKCON was available and he came into the environment where he could practice devotional service, he then could take that decision and say that "this is more important for me, so let me come back." This is what I've practically seen.

Alongside instances of the miraculous revival of Vaiṣṇava devotion in an unexpected transnational setting, devotees' family and local cultures are also revised through their adoption of ISKCON's culture discourse, reframing lived experiences of local Indian cultures as defined by region, language, class, and caste. As we saw above, regional performance and ritual traditions are both incorporated and subsumed within ISKCON under a Vaiṣṇava taxonomy with Gauḍīya Vaiṣṇavism at the pinnacle. In this vein, some devotees proposed "ISKCON culture" as a separate identity, which linked and transcended diverse regional communities within and outside India. In certain cases, this has enabled Chowpatty members to marry across regional lines, bringing together Bihari and Sindhi families or Punjabi and Tamil families based on a shared ISKCON culture. The palpability of a shared international ISKCON culture is also what one British-Indian devotee identified as enabling him to fit into any ISKCON community from Nairobi to Hyderabad. He regularly passes through the Chowpatty temple while on business trips, and he said the cultural similitude of ISKCON guest houses and temples across the several continents he visits makes him feel like he is somehow always close to home.

This new cultural identity can change ideas about class and caste, to an extent, even in the sensitive domestic sphere of marriage and family relationships. While chatting in a temple classroom one afternoon, Priti—a businesswoman in a major telecommunications firm in Mumbai—spoke with pride about how her parents have finally come to accept her husband as an integral part of the family, even though early on in their courtship her parents had expressed strong reservations on account of his regional and caste background. Priti is from a Punjabi mercantile family, predominantly Vaiṣṇava Hindu but with a close Sikh grandmother. Priti's husband Anirvan also grew up in a prosperous and religious Vaiṣṇava family of merchants, but his family belong to the Yadav caste of Bihar, a group that has claimed martial status but is legally considered in the OBC (Other Backwards Caste) category by the Indian government.[30] While this difference in both regional and caste backgrounds caused a potentially serious concern in Priti's family, the couple managed to reframe their inter-caste relationship through their "shared culture" of ISKCON's Vaiṣṇava practices. Priti and Anirvan met at one of the JSD programs while they were both searching for stable jobs in the months after college graduation. They soon found themselves taking all the same introductory courses at the Chowpatty temple, and eventually chatting afterward over chai and samosas. Anirvan, a mild-mannered computer-scientist specialist, diligently worked through ISKCON's training courses and received the highly respected honor of *brāhmaṇa dikṣa*, the formal initiation into a "brahmanical" life standardized in ISKCON by Bhaktivedanta, in which particularly devout adherents receive formal training to conduct temple-based worship procedures, generally reserved for those born into brahmin priestly families.

When Priti and Anirvan were newly married and still navigating family resentments, an uncle unexpectedly passed away and his memorial service had to be hastily arranged by Priti's parents. At that time, Anirvan volunteered to take charge of performing the rituals. Priti's parents—apprehensive at first—became "so impressed by his thoughtfulness" and competence in performing the service that her father exclaimed "he should perform all the family functions from now on—there is no longer a need to hire an outside priest!" Now, Priti relayed with an air of triumph, her family invites him not only to perform brahmanical *yajña*s but also for informal housewarming *pūjā*s. Anirvan's occupation of the brahmanical priestly role in this extended family context has reshaped both form and practice, promoting an increasingly popular focus on explanations in the performance of *yajñas* that includes translating the Sanskrit mantras for the family in attendance: "He tells them the meaning of everything. Now they've realized that they [ISKCON] are following our tradition more than we are following . . . In fact, they are teaching our own philosophy with more values. So, they appreciate that." Priti added, getting to the bottom line, this has also stopped her family from giving money to "all those ritualistic priests they used to hire." This acceptance of an inter-caste marriage and a non-brahmin performing the family's priestly rituals also signifies how fluid lines of religious orthodoxy can be reconstrued in shifting urban contexts. Through Anirvan's membership in ISKCON, his identity was refigured in a notion of religious orthodoxy defined through practice rather than birth. The elasticity in ISKCON's traditionalism enables it to be adopted, shifting who represents Hindu traditionalism.

## Saris in the City

Although Chowpatty's devotees grew up in India, many described their upbringings in Mumbai and other urban contexts to be cut off from traditional Indian culture. Lalita, a working woman in her forties, highlighted this in her description of the first time she came to the Chowpatty temple, to attend her cousin's wedding, in December 1999: "There, for the first time, I saw His Holiness Radhanath Swami Maharaja. I thought that nowadays when Indians are rejecting their culture, here was Maharaja, who although a foreigner, was so nicely teaching our countrymen their own tradition and culture." Gopika, a devotee whose parents joined the Juhu temple before her birth in the 1970s, expanded on this theme, telling me: "There were some things we did not know were part of Indian culture and we learned them because of ISKCON." Her mother, Vaishnavi, agreed with knowing laughter: "a *lot* of things."

Vaishnavi grew up in a brahmin household. She was in her mid-forties when we spoke alongside her twenty-something daughter. Her parents had migrated from Karnataka to Bombay in the early twentieth century. She joined ISKCON in her first year of college and quickly met and married another young devotee from a South Indian brahmin background. While her parents were supportive of her partner choice, they were distressed when she dropped out of college after marriage, became pregnant with Gopika, and—at the age of twenty—moved with her husband to establish an ISKCON center in a remote pilgrimage town in North India. Vaishnavi described that as the most challenging period of her life, not only because of the temporary estrangement from her parents but also due to the lifestyle adjustments involved in moving from a large metropolis to a remote provincial town. There, she washed the family's laundry by hand and struggled to adjust to the domestic life of a woman in a socially conservative region. However, this early decision to orient their lives around the aspiration to spread Krishna *bhakti* as lay missionizers, rather than to develop successful careers in the Mumbai area, seemed to them an arduous but valiant goal.

As we spoke, Gopika went on to elaborate: "Because like we are from a very high class brahmin family, but nowadays people forget their culture." At this, Vaishnavi chimed in: "Yes, like I am from a very high class brahmin family, but we don't follow such rules and regulations which devotees here follow. Even behavior, men-women behavior, and so many things, we didn't know before coming to Krishna consciousness." She referred specifically to brahmanical diet and bathing regulations and elaborated on the norms for gender segregation observed in ISKCON communities, in which devotees are encouraged to limit social interactions with members of the opposite sex and many events are spatially divided into two sides for women and men. Pointing out the gender segregation during *darśan* that has become standard in ISKCON centers transnationally, she attributed this as another thing they "did not previously know" and "learned" after coming to ISKCON. The gender-based segregation of ISKCON temples is at odds with the free-form congregating in less institutionalized Hindu temple settings. And, as Vaishnavi mentioned, gendered social segregation was not the practice of her brahmin family growing up, nor that of her neighbors and friends. In this context, membership in ISKCON reshaped her understanding of her own cultural heritage.

The contours of ISKCON's culture worldview include the adoption of what are seen as traditional gender roles, particularly by the female members of the community. This, too, has been mediated through the figure of Radhanath Swami for many devotees. Given his American origins, it was surprising to hear many of his Indian followers tell me that they not only did *not* see him as a cultural outsider, but rather they felt that he taught *them* more about Indian culture than they had known growing up in India. As Lilavati, one long-time devout follower born and raised in a Gujarati family in Mumbai, explained:

> By birth, he is definitely a Westerner, but he knows Indian culture more than anyone of us. And since he's dedicated his life to Prabhupada, so he's inspired us so much. Because whatever Indian culture is there, *he* has taught us . . . Maharaja is very sensitive in Indian culture. He taught us what the husband-wife relationship should be, what the mother-child

> relationship should be, in reference to Krishna consciousness. The kind of understanding he has, I have never seen it.

Indeed, it was due to Radhanath Swami's instruction that she and her friend Sundari, when they both started coming to the temple in the late 1990s, began wearing a sari and *tilak* daily to their college campus. She reminisced about this as we sat on the local train one morning, the compartment barreling toward her office in the cool breeze of a winter morning before rush hour traffic began. Her silk sari was neatly pressed and her *tilak* still freshly marked on her forehead, as she proudly related their conversations with their guru from those early days. "When we finally showed up one day wearing saris, he would tell us, 'You look so beautiful in a sari, just like a goddess. You should always wear a sari.' And because of this, we started wearing saris and still do." While saris are still commonplace garments for elder Indian women and throughout rural and small-town India, they are increasingly rare as daily attire among urban Indians, especially in elite or upwardly mobile communities. She said it was certainly a shock to her college friends. "They thought we were crazy, or that it was just a phase." Her parents were more amused, but "they were also glad to know they didn't have to worry about us staying out late at parties. It was always so safe at the temple in those days, especially for young girls. Even if we would be out late at night, they would know where we were and that we were all together. We all became a new group."

Back in her sunlit apartment that one morning over breakfast, Arushi also emphasized that she never even thought about Radhanath Swami as a Westerner, "because he knew our culture through and through."

> I remember once I went to him . . . because it was the Westernized culture to be very proud and think that you don't know how to cook, because you want to show off that I don't cook in the kitchen, I'm not like a backward woman. I'm more into studies and I'm more professional. So that was the thinking pattern that I had. So once Maharaja asked me "Do you know how to cook?" And I very proudly said, "No I don't know how to cook!" And he reacted by saying: "You don't know how to cook? Only lazy people don't know how to cook!" And I was like really shocked, and he said: "You must learn how to cook." And it inspired me that immediately I started learning . . . So, then I realized that he was trying to teach me Indian culture, to be more in line with our culture, which is like every woman should know how to cook. So always he was encouraging me to be more Indian

> than what I was in my thinking. Even with the sari. He's the one who encouraged me to wear sari.

In this embrace of gendered domesticity, the women of the community in particular have been inspired to adopt a more conservative model of Indian culture by their American-born guru. When I related some of these statements to Radhanath Swami during one of our conversations in his quarters on the temple grounds, he reflected on the peculiar intercultural position he holds for his followers in Mumbai:

> I came to India in 1970, and I lived as a *sādhu* in the Himalayas, and then I lived in Vrindavan. I traveled around and really adopted the culture quite deeply in many ways. As years went by, most of the people that come [to Chowpatty], I've been living in India before they were even born in India! So, I don't think they see me as an American so much.

His adoption of the vows and cultural styles of a Hindu guru, wearing saffron *sannyasi* robes and presiding over a temple ashram, signals that within ISKCON's dispensation, a Vaiṣṇava model of sanctity is not dependent on birth-based identity. However, while Radhanath Swami has undoubtedly gained some popularity in India due to his American identity, it is through his thorough adoption of a Vaiṣṇava model of religious authority that he has been accepted as an authority on Indian culture.

Of course, this can be interpreted as an authenticating power of whiteness, even amid communities who ardently reject Western cultural influence. The claim that Western gurus can represent Indian traditions seemed unproblematic for the devotees with whom I spoke, who placed them in a category distinctly separate from other Westerners. They instead read their piety as an affirmation of Krishna *bhakti*'s universal potential. By contrast, other devotees asserted that it is much easier for Indians to follow the lifestyle regulations of ISKCON since they were born in Krishna's land—*puṇya-bhūmi*—connoting that the specialness of non-Indian Western devotees is not on account of their place in a hierarchy of racial privilege but because of the difficulty involved in adopting Krishna *bhakti* after an upbringing in a purportedly materialistic culture. Nonetheless, there is a thrill in the spectacle of non-Indian devotees. Cursory social-media scrolling reveals photos of blond Russian families in ironed *dhotis* and saris or white and Black New Yorkers dancing in *kīrtan* in Brooklyn, shared enthusiastically on many devotees' Facebook pages on a regular basis. As one recent caption promoted: "Anyone can take up Krishna consciousness and become a Vaiṣṇava! You do not have to be an Indian!"

The glorification of non-Indian devotees does seem at times to eclipse local devotees in the temple space itself, such as at the annual Flower Festival celebrations where central temple space is accorded to predominantly white American yoga groups visiting the temple after their teacher training at the Govardhan Ecovillage. During my research period, at that festival all local devotees were requested to remain behind the velvet ropes cordoning off the main temple space or view the festival from the balconies. Notably, this practice changed in 2024, when two Flower Festivals were held: one at the temple for local devotees and another at the Govardhan Ecovillage for the visiting yoga groups. But even that centering is more complex than at first glance. In the years I attended, the yoga group was joined in the temple room by international pilgrims, including a Ukrainian devotee group who received widespread sympathy in the aftermath of the Russian seizure of Crimea. At many ISKCON events, space is provided to international devotees in general. At the Pune temple opening in 2013, for instance, I sat in a balcony reserved for international visitors, among Taiwanese devotee pilgrims and British and South African devotees of Indian descent. While condemnation of the West as an ideological adversary often sits alongside the celebration of Western Krishna devotees, these celebrations also extend beyond white Westerners. One Drama Festival production performed in the weeks after the Flower Festival in January 2014 was "Black Lotus: The Spiritual Odyssey of Bhakti Tirtha Swami," a biopic of the life of a Black *sannyasi*, born John E. Favors in Cleveland, Ohio, who became a prominent ISKCON guru and developed a close friendship with Radhanath Swami in his final years. This production, enacted by Indian devotees, showcased Bhakti Tirtha Swami's education at Princeton, years preaching Krishna *bhakti* in Africa, and achievements of speaking at the United Nations. There, blackness was the vector through which a non-Indian *bhakti* was celebrated, while the focus remained on the global potential of Krishna consciousness for all.

## "Phir Bhi Dil Hai Hindustani"

If the global appeal of Krishna *bhakti* is celebrated in Mumbai, what does that mean for local culture itself? As the classic Hindi cinema song proclaims,

"My shoes are Japanese, these trousers are English, the red cap on my head is Russian, but still my heart is Indian."[31] This 1955 composition became an anthem of early independent India; public deliberations over globalized cultural markers and modern Indian identities are nothing new. But, while Radhanath Swami is celebrated as an exemplar of Indian culture within the Chowpatty community, devotees often dubbed their own Indian upbringings too "Westernized" through the lens of ISKCON's worldview. Even though many devotees are drawn to join a traditionalist organization, others find its dictates conflict with aspects of their personal identities. These tensions and the negotiations that ensue can be as pedestrian as a decision about whether to eat at the trendy new neighborhood restaurant that is not purely vegetarian or as fundamental as concerns over whether one can be openly gay and still accepted in the community. But all point to the role of ISKCON's culture discourse in reframing and bracketing out segments of life in an Indian metropolis in pursuit of the ideal.

In quotidian decisions about food, dress, and entertainment, many devotees find ISKCON's strict codes of lifestyle regulation clash with their surrounding family, work, and friends. Adherence to vegetarian and teetotaler standards are enshrined in the community's regulative principles. The pervasive dichotomy between modern Western culture and Indian-Vedic culture is in some ways parallel to another fundamental dichotomy in the ISKCON worldview, between the "material" and "spiritual" worlds. In this context, several devotees who were raised in and have chosen to remain within Chowpatty's congregation related to me that they have "never really gone over to the other side" or "the other world." For them, membership in the ISKCON community is seen as a protection from that outside, material world. Through the association of devotees, going to the temple regularly, and heeding a counselor's advice, this state of protection can be maintained, though one must always be vigilant to the pull of *māyā* that wants to bring you back into the material world outside. But, as Arushi's teenage daughter Malini insisted, "Sometimes you just want to go to the mall! It's how we spend time together—you can't just go to the temple all the time!" Eating with friends and family in restaurants and going to films at the nearby three-story Palladium shopping mall are all parts of a modern lifestyle that almost no one wants to forfeit.

While sitting with two friends one bright, breezy spring morning a few weeks later, drinking herbal tea on an apartment rooftop in the reserved, middle-class neighborhood of Sion, the topic came up again. Radhika and

Kanta were both in their late twenties and dressed in the *salwar kameez* and leggings combination that had become standard attire for slightly "traditional" young women throughout the city. Radhika asked in disbelief: "Did you know that ten years ago we could not have even worn these on the temple property? Every woman had to be in a sari according to the counsellors. I mean, some women just stay home, so they can wear them, it's no problem. But we can't just show up at some company meeting in a sari and a *bindi*." Kanta chimed in, "My manager would think I'm crazy!" But, pausing over her words, she clarified, "Clearly, we respect anyone who can wear saris. It just makes it more difficult. You can't really ride the trains in them. You would need a car and then you would have too much traffic!" Of course, many women wear saris on the Mumbai local daily, as women also wear saris when harvesting vegetables in rural Maharashtra or when lecturing to classrooms as university professors. The sari has many associations, modulated through region, class, and age. But these reservations convey the sense among many Mumbaikars that saris are too formal or limiting for the rhythms of their daily life, which makes their adoption by women who join ISKCON all the more notable, as an assertion or conscious choice of tradition.

Radhika's brother, Jay Gopal, an avid devotee who diligently attended the monthly Prerna programs, happened to be passing by the connecting rooftop hallway just then. He shyly pulled up a white plastic folding chair to join us as the conversation developed. "Did you know," he ventured, "that some counsellors tell their groups not to watch TV or go online unless they're checking email? They want them to be completely cut off. I mean, I love going to the temple—I go all the time, but . . ." Kanta chimed in, "We go too. The deities are beautiful. You know, Radha Gopinath! Who could resist? But it is hard with all the strictness. You have to also live a normal life." Radhika agreed, "the whole counsellor system—they just keep track of you a little too much. It's too oppressive! Even Jay won't take a counsellor!" Jay Gopal looked sheepish but confirmed with a shrug, "I prefer to kind of have my own life. I follow all the rules and I'm around devotees every day, but I have to balance it with other temples. That's why I come to Juhu! They don't ask any questions here! They just leave you alone!" he went on, to laughter in the background.

The strictures laid out in some counselling groups—against watching television and films or taking vacations aside from a missionizing or pilgrimage intent—strike many younger members of the community as extreme. For slightly older married couples with children, the constant pressure to attend programs and counselling meetings across town through Mumbai's busy traffic can also become a logistical challenge. Wary of these expectations, some devotees refrain from formally joining the community and accepting a counsellor, even though they regularly visit the temple. Others stand at arm's length from actively attending counselling meetings and instead check in with their counsellors during the bustle of the Sunday program or over the phone. And, while many devotees support ISKCON's gender norms, the expectations regarding women's dress are complicated for Mumbaikars who grew up attending secular schools and wearing the casual skirts or jeans common in the city's seaside neighborhoods. As Radhika and Kanta attested, many women who hold professional positions do not see saris as feasible work attire. However, in ISKCON-related spaces, saris or *salwar kameez* are often mandatory. At the Gopal's Garden school, the head school administrator—a high-functioning, energetic mother of two with a disarming manner—boasted that a primary criterion during the hiring process for teachers and staff is that women working there will wear either saris or loose-fitting *salwars* with a *dupatta*, or scarf, draped over their shoulders. "Western dress for women," she emphasized, "is explicitly prohibited," a deal breaker for any job applicant, although it is normative for men in most of the same spaces.

Such conservative standards lead to small tensions within congregational settings. During a high-profile wedding between two business families on one November evening, Dina arrived in a designer sari with transparent netting and appliqué stitch work. Her husband, wearing the suit and tie customary for formal weddings, went off to congratulate the father of the groom, leaving several of us women standing in a circle to make small talk. After the requisite complements, the transparent effect of Dina's sari did not go without notice. An elder counsellor, who had shown up in an austere cotton number in the traditional loom-work of rural Bengal, asked whether Dina's counsellor knew that she wore such risqué designs. Taken a bit aback by the pointed comment, Dina took a minute to recover her cordial social occasion smile. With a lighthearted tone, she responded that "one has to keep up with the latest fashions!" Especially, she added, since she regularly attends the weddings and other formal functions of her husband's business partners, it was necessary to have a few designer pieces. When her cotton-draped interlocutor did not show signs of backing down, she tried a different strategy, graceful smile still intact. "You know," she offered, "I didn't even know how to wear a sari when I was growing up! We would only really wear them to weddings and even then my mother or an aunt would help. Day to day you would just wear anything—jeans, tee shirts, you know? So, I'm glad I was even able to tie this one properly!" After encouragements from the rest of us about how elegant she looked, her husband returned with a plate of Indo-Chinese appetizers and the conversation topic could stealthily be changed.

Tensions over how to define and apply an ideal notion of the Vedic-Vaiṣṇava cultural worldview in devotee's lives also extend to more fundamental issues of identity. While most women in the community grew to feel comfortable wearing saris at least for temple-related functions, Shaya was much more comfortable wearing loose collared shirts and trousers. Over a pizza dinner at the temple's Govinda restaurant one evening, an elder member of the Devotee Care Committee persistently questioned her about her tomboyish style and short haircut. As we waited for our entrees, she seemed determined to convince Shaya that she would feel more comfortable if she became accustomed to dressing in a more "feminine," conservative style.

Shaya had grown up in a brahmin family in Chennai and started taking *darśan* at ISKCON temples with her mother as a child. Although she was no longer on good terms with her parents—she said without much further explanation—she still loved coming to the temple regularly. She would often show up for the evening *āratī* and stand toward the back of the temple room, poised in between the female-male divide as devotees swayed to the *bhajans*. On her Facebook profile, she posted picture after picture of Radhanath Swami with hands folded in prayer, ethereally backlit by a window or other source of light. But when it came to the temple's strong preference for women to wear saris, she would not be convinced. "If I wear anything, it would be a *kurta*, not a sari. I'll feel much more comfortable in that." As the conversation dragged on through the course of our dinner with no hope of either side ceding ground, the underlying complexities of Shaya's gender identity seemed unfortunately lost on our older interlocutor, who either did not see or did not want to acknowledge that her resistance to the temple's standard dress code was related to a much broader personal expression of gender identity.

A few days later, I saw Shaya again at the evening *āratī*, this time dressed in a well-ironed white *kurta*. Determined to stand her ground, she seemed comfortable and content with her choice, and merely nodded with a sly smile to the older women who complemented her attire. But sometime after that, over a dinner of wraps and salad at a trendy café, she opened up more about how she found certain pressures in the temple community simply too stifling. She loved listening to *bhajan*s and attending Radhanath Swami's lectures, she said with enthusiasm, but she felt constantly judged. When we next touched base several months later, she had stopped visiting the temple. Between a busy work and travel schedule, she came to find a sense of community elsewhere, in a capoeira dance community that met on the city's beaches to practice. The pictures of the temple *āratīs* on her Facebook page were replaced by images of her friends dancing, singing, and catapulting into well-choreographed sequences. She even started posting pictures of herself, grinning from ear to ear as she perfected a new move in her knee-length shorts and a baggy tee shirt.

Shaya never—to my knowledge—broached topics of gender and sexuality directly with any counsellor in the community. However, others have come to a similar crossroads in relation to their gender identities or sexual orientations. Options for those who want to "come out of the closet" in this traditionalist community are few. Mumbai, however, is home to a dynamic chapter of the Gay and Lesbian Vaishnava Association (GALVA), a group founded in Hawai'i with chapters throughout several countries that operates parallel to and sometimes within their ISKCON communities. Still, when I spoke with several GALVA Mumbai members who identify as gay and sometimes engage in same-sex relationships, they expressed uncertainty about how they would navigate a relationship with a counsellor in Chowpatty's rigorous system given their "unorthodox" identities. This leaves many members of GALVA in a liminal position. They may regularly attend temple services, but they steer clear of conversations over when they will receive initiation or seek out a counsellor.

While ISKCON echoes many discourses of religious and cultural nationalism common among India's upwardly mobile middle classes, their vision of what comprises Vedic culture is radically different due to their global missionary framework. The centrality of training and not birth to their community provides a gateway to a Sanskritizing community but also creates social boundaries that some members find it difficult to inhabit. ISKCON's Vedic-Vaiṣṇava cultural worldview has deterritorialized both "Indian culture" and the "West," linking them not to ethnic or national background but to lifestyle. But alongside making non-Indian gurus familiar, this culture discourse also makes strange the lived experiences and backgrounds of many Indian members. This can partition the lives of devotees into a series of adherences to and breaches from ideal culture practice, as middle-class notions of family, entertainment, and leisure are rendered Western, something to be expunged to revive Indian culture. As one devout friend said, inviting me out to dinner: "I'd love you to join us at Barbeque Nation and meet my sister and her family, but please don't mention it to anyone at the temple." We had a fun night out, enjoying a vegetarian meal with three generations gathered around the table—a family tradition they maintain on Saturday nights and an oddly wholesome secret to keep.

This raises issues for devotees in modern India. Does membership in ISKCON necessitate a breech from mainstream Indian media and cultural forms? Can there be space for devotees who are not invested in brahmanical traditionalism? Or who do not locate themselves within cisgender identities or a heteronormative family structure? Inasmuch as ISKCON's regulations are both adaptable by non-Indians, they are also far removed from the lived culture of many urban Indians. For some devotees, this is not a problem but a badge of honor. Therein, ISKCON's model of religious traditionalism seeks to rewrite local cultures, as the lived realities of devotees are reframed through a set of aspirations that are deeply suspicious of what modern, urban India has become. Here, culture—like *varṇāśrama*—is based on practice, not on birth.

# Conclusion

## Producing a Religious Modernity in Urban India

Revising religion involves remaking oneself and one's surroundings. ISKCON's identity in Mumbai is encoded with processes of geographic and cultural crossing for devotees, reflecting both the local and global networks that formed it. Such crossings reconstitute family, religion, nation, and culture, and recalibrate devotees' relation to the city itself. Their networks in Mumbai exemplify religious place-making, serving as structured "eutopias," or "good places," in parallel to other aspirational religious imaginaries in urban India.[1] Therein, devotees embody a contemporary form of Hindu community that is both cosmopolitan and traditionalist, remaking their relation to the world around them through media products that delineate who is included, how to live well, and aspirations for the public culture of the nation itself.

ISKCON in India should not be pigeonholed as a Western NRM but taken seriously as a form of transnational religious revivalism that represents discourses of postcolonial identity and Hindu traditionalism in India today. While influenced by Bhaktivedanta's late-colonial Bengali context and its early roots in North America, ISKCON's institutional structures and aesthetics have been remade to address contemporary urban Indian sensibilities. This exemplifies the extent to which local, lived religion in urban India is interwoven with transnational actors and ideas and underscores how traditionalism can be grounded in globally informed interpretations. Therein, Chowpatty's dramas, educational courses, and public festivals can be viewed through Appadurai and Breckenridge's analysis of public culture and modernity. As they note, what is distinctive about a particular society is not "the fact or extent of its modernity," but its "distinctive debates *about* modernity, the historical and cultural trajectories that shape its appropriation of the means of modernity, and the cultural sociology (principally of class and state) that determines who gets to play with modernity and what defines the rules of the game."[2] In the process of critiquing Westernizing forms of modernity in India,

*Bringing Krishna Back to India*. Claire C. Robison, Oxford University Press. © Oxford University Press 2024.
DOI: 10.1093/9780197656488.003.0008

Chowpatty's members employ modern media technologies and concerns for a logically verifiable basis for religious traditions, styling Krishna *bhakti* in the aesthetics of an achievement-oriented, tech-centered elite society.[3] This religious revisioning celebrates an "archaic modernity" (Subramaniam 2000, 2019), valorizing Vedic knowledge traditions as valuable antecedents and tools for the present. It also presents Hindu traditions through a methodical organizational model that casts religion as a discrete, reproducible system, reflecting a contemporary urban Indian focus on education and coaching for personal attainment. However, Indian devotees leverage status markers—such as advanced degrees in the sciences and engineering and career experience at highly competitive firms—alongside a celebration of those who have renounced them to adopt an ascetic lifestyle, practiced to varying extents by *brahmacaris* and laypeople. This positions them perhaps even more in a privileged vector of modern Indian society, as it showcases that the temple community cultivates a way of life seen as superior even by those who possess the most desired markers of urban attainment. In that sense, although many Indians see their brahmanically inflected lifestyle norms as something from the "age of Puranas and *rishis*," this is a traditionalist form of religion specifically tailored by and for contemporary urban aspirations.

ISKCON has developed in tandem with Mumbai's own dual character in postcolonial India. Alongside the liberal currents of the city, its devotees are cosmopolitan and globally focused. While, aligned the socially conservative currents, they often assert Hindu religious precedence and contest the Westernized culture that pervades the same elite neighborhoods in which their temples thrive. Their Vedic-Vaisnava cultural worldview is framed in relation to ISKCON's transnational identity; in that sense, East and West become deterritorialized, present not in fixed geographic regions but in everyday lifestyle choices in the city.

Engaging with an intertextuality among multiple genres of Indian public culture, Chowpatty's media productions develop religious responses to trends of globalization and urbanization in Mumbai, fashioning a religious modernity. This construction of a religious Hindu modernity centers India in a global frame and resembles revivalist movements in other postcolonial contexts, as myriad groups seek to de-yoke themselves from the economic and political effects of colonization (internal or external) or the violence incurred in being minorities in settler-colonial societies.[4] These orientations point toward a broad transnational discontent with the power that the "West" exerts in postcolonial nation-states. Projects of asserting cultural independence from hegemonic models of Western secular modernity are a characteristic of groups ranging from the post-Soviet rise of state-allied Russian orthodoxy, to discourses of Islamic revival from Indonesia and Iran. In comparison, ISKCON in India becomes one set of voices amid a larger trend in the Global South, representing old grievances against a colonial past and the determinative power still held by Western countries over the global economy and culture markets. And they share with other transnational communities a critique of both the culturally specific confines of what can be deemed "modernity" as well as the transnational agreements on which this modernity is based. But, as the "West" is deterritorialized, a critique of Westernized paradigms of modernity in the Global South is also a local conversation, serving as a hermeneutic of present experience of government and society, an interpretative tool to make sense of why self-rule (*svarāj* in Hindi) remains far from utopia.

The development of an assertively Indian modernity is not a new intellectual proposition.[5] The discussion can even be traced back to the early twentieth century, when political philosopher Krishna Chandra Bhattacharya called for Indian intellectuals to develop a "*svarāj* in ideas," extending Mahatma Gandhi's popular nationalist movement toward political and economic *svarāj* into cultural and intellectual spheres.[6] Similarly, at the top of an early *Back to Godhead* issue, published in Delhi in 1956, Bhaktivedanta centered the phrase "We have to defeat tyranny on the realm of thought and create a will for world peace," to frame his critique of early Indian nation-building policies.[7] Akeel Bilgrami interprets *svarāj* as not only independence from the West but also a critique of it.[8] Although grounded in a religious tradition rather than in a secular ideology, ISKCON members in Mumbai employ the resources of their Vaiṣṇava *bhakti* imaginary to construct a framework for Indian modernity that includes both independence and critique embedded into their structures of discourse and social engagement.

However, proclamations that premodern Indian culture is unitary, inherently Vaiṣṇava, and brahmanical or Vedic in character traffics in new hegemonies that threaten to erase local religious diversity and devalue notions of Indian identity that do not center historically elite Hindu cultures.[9] As reflected in recent political developments, discourses of Hindu revivalism can be used to elide the postcolonial nation's commitments to religious pluralism and secular democracy. ISKCON today operates in a context not marked by a lack of political or economic power; rather, its development mirrors an increasing shift in Indian political culture toward discourses that the indigenous is most properly Sanskritic and Hindu—expressed in the ongoing renaming of cities and historical buildings, from Bombay to Mumbai, Victoria Station to Chhatrapati Shivaji Terminal, Allahabad to Prayagraj. This is a salient concern for many Mumbaikars—Muslim, Catholic, Dalit, Adivasi, and non-observant *savarna* Hindu—who do not see themselves reflected in a Hindu revivalist rendering of India's modernity. And yet, although ISKCON devotees sometimes align with these political trends, their core identity speaks to a much broader, transnational cosmopolitanism.

As many middle-class Hindus gravitate away from left-leaning secularism and India leans toward muscular Hindu nationalist politics, where does a Vaiṣṇava temple led by an American guru fit? How can that organization claim to represent Hindu traditions and be accepted as such by those born and raised in India? Here, the development of a religious modernity by Mumbai's ISKCON members fuses together the global and local networks that have shaped their own modern traditionalism. While some devotees can certainly embrace conservative Hindu identity politics with open arms, this can never encapsulate their place in India. ISKCON's dislocation of brahmanically inflected social norms from caste-based identity reconfigures Hindu authority structures, including the indigenization of non-Indian practitioners into the highest levels of authority as well as new social mobilities for a range of Indians who join the organization. For Indian devotees, to become religious is to remake oneself as a new sort of modern citizen—one whose primary allegiances are not to a political apparatus but rather to a transnational religious organization that transcends national boundaries in its institutional structure. And through a process of revising religion, urban Indians who join ISKCON are oriented to realign their Hindu identity from shared regional and linguistic-specific traditions to personal choice, separating religious practice from family backgrounds.

ISKCON's faces in urban India continue to change. Since my research formally ended, more second- and third-generation devotees, such as Rupamanjari Dei Dasi and Baldev Maheshwari, have begun to bring devotional practices into trendy local contexts. Kirtan Mumbai organizes *kīrtan*s at stylish cafes in Bandra and Colaba, fashioning new venues for devotional practice tailored to the city's liberal cosmopolitan spaces. Their Instagram account, #kirtanmumbai, showcases beautifully produced video clips of candlelit rooftop performances and testimonials of regular attendees. These events connect to similar transnational efforts, as at New York City's Bhakti Center and Kirtan Dubai, including guest visits and collaborations between these international *kirtan* groups. New religious media now radiates outward from Chowpatty networks, circulating on Instagram and Spotify, where Baldev has released several albums of contemporary *bhajans*, including "Hanuman Chalisa Unplugged." And innovative devotees are gaining popularity in Hindu public spheres far beyond ISKCON temple networks. Gaur Gopal, the popular JSD teacher mentioned in Chapter 4, balances his role as a monk, dressed in the saffron robes and *tilak*, with a public profile as a motivational speaker and lifestyle coach, sharing inspirational quotes on Instagram with his 8.1 million followers and speaking in public venues including TEDx and multinational corporations in India and abroad. He recently began distributing his audio and video content through Monkify, an app created by his publicity team to "share principles that can help you boost your mental, emotional, and spiritual wellness," demonstrating the ever-expansiveness of this brand of religious modernity in new media spaces.[10] This positions a new generation of Indian ISKCON teachers as public gurus alongside other social media icons such as Sri Sri Ravi Shankar and Sadhguru. And global networks of celebrity continue to augment the community's remarkable place as a destination for spiritual solace, including a restorative visit to the Ecovillage by Will Smith after the controversial 2022 Academy Awards.

I have situated ISKCON's growth in India as a new form of being religious, expressed in the language of a return or excavation of a lost orthodoxy but marked by modern processes of mediating religious knowledge and forming community. This highlights how religious modernities have gained popularity in recent decades. The changing role of religion in urban India is not merely due to an increase in secular identities among younger generations or the rise of Hindu nationalism in political spheres. Rather, the institutionalization—indeed, corporatization—of Hindu communities in transnational spheres shifts core notions of authority and tradition. ISKCON's development in Mumbai offers devotees and broader Hindu publics a chance to recalibrate their urban realities, matching their already-existing participation in urban networks of business, finance, and information technology with a parallel engagement in a modern, tech-savvy religious community. This study thus provides a template for understanding how local religious belonging reflects globalized, cosmopolitan networks. In reframing categories at the core of how Hindu traditions are practiced, devotees guide Mumbaikars to "bring Krishna back" to India and into their lives, revisioning religion's space in the city. And, because Chowpatty's devotees have refined their religious messages to appeal to urban India's diverse Hindu publics, the community is evolving to inhabit a solid space within the multifaceted metropolis of Mumbai.

# Notes

## Introduction

1. When speaking of the contemporary city, I use the name "Mumbai" in references after its official 1995 name change but retain "Bombay" to references beforehand and to reflect popular usage among the city's residents, who retain the older name in general and specifically for neighborhoods such as "South Bombay."
2. I recognize that the Christian-inflected term "congregation" can be construed as problematic, but I use the term to refer to ISKCON temple communities, and specifically the Chowpatty Mumbai temple in this study, because devotees themselves use the term. It does reflect the lingering legacy of Christian organizations in India whose civic society structures were adapted by Hindu leaders in the formation of their own modern religious organizations.
3. The term "Hindu" is rhetorically critiqued by many religious groups that took root in nineteenth- and twentieth-century Bengal, and Bhaktivedanta often preferred the terms Gauḍīya Vaiṣṇavism, *sanātana dharma*, or Krishna consciousness instead. Although the Gauḍīya text *Caitanya Caritāmrta* contains some of the earliest uses of Hindu as a self-descriptor, its usage alongside the neologism "Hinduism" in colonial-era, European-authored publications is tinged with support for an imperial project that constructed racial and religious hierarchies through the categorization of world religions to legitimize colonial power (Masuzawa 2005). But recent work has drawn attention to the term's salience and central role in maintaining caste and religious hegemonies in India (Lee 2021). Accordingly, I use the terms Gauḍīya Vaiṣṇava or ISKCON devotee to specify religious affiliation. However, the majority of ISKCON's Indian members classify themselves as Hindu on the Indian census and in social circles, and it remains a core category of identity in society and politics. Moreover, as I will argue, the identity of Hindu traditionalism has been key to ISKCON's local growth in Mumbai. Therefore, I employ the term to discuss social collectivities and identity markers in India's majority religious community.
4. For formative work on the concept of multiple modernities, see Göle 1996 and Eisenstadt 2000.
5. See McGuire 2011; Brosius 2014; Alter 2021; Moodie 2021.
6. Although all ISKCON devotees are free to choose any initiating guru within the organization, and increasingly younger generations of Indian teachers (mentioned below) are becoming more central figures in Chowpatty and elsewhere.
7. Goswami 2012.

8. For details about these dynamics in Bhaktivedanta's early life, see Goswami 2012, 92–102 and Robison 2021, 196–201.
9. Data obtained from ISKCON Centres, a global directory for the organization, at www.centres.iskcon.org (accessed on August 21, 2023).
10. See Satsvarūpa dāsa Goswami 1982–1983, vol. 1, ch. 32.
11. "List of Initiating Gurus in ISKCON," gbc.iskcon.org (accessed on August 21, 2023).
12. van der Veer: 2002a, 102.
13. Washbrook 1993, 239.
14. See Beckerlegge 2000, 52ff. for a succinct discussion of this intellectual history.
15. Sen 2001; Scott 2016; Weiss 2019; Hatcher 2020. The reform and revival frameworks became popular discourses among cosmopolitan intellectuals in colonial-era India. They reflect in part a hegemonic Protestantism that denigrated ritual and priestly authority structures, exalting premodern "golden age" traditions while depicting lived practices as "degraded." But it also developed as a prominent discourse by many Hindu groups and remains salient among Hindu formations today. While aware of the problematic potentials of these terms, following Scott (2016) I examine these discourses as an opportunity to highlight multidirectional agency in the construction of ideas about modernity and contemporary identity.
16. This discourse in ISKCON, stemming from the writings of *bhadralok* Gauḍīya predecessors as will be described below, positions their organization in contrast to the "ritualism" of other Hindu traditions through depictions of corrupt "priests" or gurus in other Hindu traditions, invoking familiar characteristics of a transnational discourse that has its roots in an Indian dialogue with European colonial-era Protestantism. See Scott (2016).
17. See Dodson and Hatcher 2012; Ramberg 2014.
18. Goswami 2012, 30.
19. See Cort 2000 for a comparative discussion of reform in the Jain tradition.
20. See Zavos 2000; Sarkar 2001; and Sardella 2013, 233.
21. See Sardella 2013, 226ff. for a related example.
22. Grewal 2014.
23. Srinivas 2018.
24. Moodie 2019.
25. This is a characteristic of many contemporary Hindu organizations, popular among Hindu organizations since the Arya Samaj and Brahmo Samaj critiqued contemporary Hindu practices in favor of idealized notions of Vedic religion and Upanisadic philosophy.
26. Srivastava 2017; Poonam 2018.
27. Rich 1972, 18.
28. As in Karlekar's 2005 study of photography as a form of self-representation and site for the production of multiple meanings in colonial-era Bengal.
29. See Janson 2014, Lucia 2014, and Napolitano 2016 for examples of this across a range of religious communities.
30. Tweed 2006.
31. See Mayaram 2004, 87.
32. Vertovec 2000; Zavos et al. 2012.

33. McKean 1996; Kent 2000b; Srinivas 2001a; Warrier 2005; Srinivas 2008; Srinivas 2010; Brosius 2012; Zavos et al. 2012; Waghorne 2013; Wuaku 2013; Grewal 2014; Lucia 2014; Saunders 2019.
34. Warrier 2005; Brosius 2004; Novetzke 2008; Zavos et al. 2012.
35. Spivak 1988.
36. Zavos et al. 2012, 16.
37. See Radha Gopinath Mandir's *Manual of Vaiṣṇava Etiquette and Lifestyle* (2000 [1994]) for a discussion of this, aimed at new members of the community.
38. The corporate orientation of the community mirrors other recent urban Hindu formations that fuse aspirations for successful business with religious piety (Warrier 2003, 2005; Fuller and Harriss 2005; Upadhyay 2016).
39. For instance, Bialecki 2017 discusses the role of pedagogy in the North American Charismatic Evangelical movement.
40. The book's popularity guided conferences and workshops held at North American ISKCON centers in the late 1990s and early 2000s. See Nicole Piscopo, "The Hare Krishnas: Coming of Age," *Tampa Bay Times*, June 30, 1996. A leadership seminar entitled "The Swamis' 7 Habits of Highly Effective Devotees," led by Bhakti Tirtha and Sridhar Swamis in January 2002, further popularized the language among devotees in the US and abroad.
41. Gooptu 2017; Moodie 2021.
42. See Thapar 1997 and Nanda 2009.
43. Nanda 2009, 2.
44. Hancock 2008, 82ff. See also Frykenberg 1989 on remarkable precedents in British East India Company rule.
45. See, for instance, Banerjee 2005, Menon 2012, and Fernandes 2020.
46. Privatization and economic changes were grounded in India's acceptance of an IMF loan agreement and World Bank Structural Adjustment Loan in 1991. Different dimensions of this pairing have been explored by Blom Hansen 1996; Varma 2004 and 2012; Sud 2012; and Kaur 2020.
47. See Anderson 2007, 126 for Bhaktivedanta's early policy ideas for "cow protection."
48. See Held et al. 1999; James and Steger 2014.
49. Appadurai 2001, 3–6.
50. Srinivas 2010, 29.
51. Srinivas 2010, 23–26; Sassen 2001, 260, 271ff.
52. Mayaram 2004; Sassen 1998; Appadurai 2001 respectively.
53. Judah 1974; Daner 1976; Poling and Kenney 1986; Shinn 1987; Bromley and Shinn 1989; Das 1997. Burke E. Rochford's early work is also relevant here, though his later work traces what he calls "Hinduization" from rising Indian-American majorities in North American temples. Larry Shinn (1987) also noted the transnational complexity of ISKCON's communities early in the organization's development.
54. Robbins 2001, 176. See also Mehta and Desai 1993; Puttick 1997; Chryssides and Wikins 2006.
55. "The Hare Krishna Movement in Bosnia and Herzegovina." Unpublished essay by Sabrina Grozdanic.

56. Karapanagiotis 2021 delves into ISKCON's branding practices, while Rochford 2018 considers ISKCON's pivots to different audiences as a pattern of frame alignment. Either way, ISKCON's multinational corporate form is not unique to their institution but rather emblematic of contemporary urban Hinduism (Moodie 2021) and, arguably, consonant among religious organizations in general (Watanbe et al. 2020).
57. For the former, Rochford 1985 and 2007; for the latter, Brooks 1989. John Fahy's (2019) work considers the ISKCON community in Mayapur, Bengal—an exception to the predominantly Indian congregations elsewhere in the country—but does not discuss the international, multiethnic composition of the community there.
58. King 2007, 165. See also Bryant and Ekstrand 2004; Dwyer and Cole 2013.
59. Hopkins 2007, 175.
60. Wuaku 2013; Fahy 2019; Karapanagiotis 2021; Shankar 2021.
61. The multiple reasons for this shift include the disaffection of many non-Indian converts due to abuse scandals and leadership controversies, as well as the growth of Indian-origin diasporas with an appreciation for the Vaiṣṇava temple atmosphere facilitated by ISKCON temples. These facets of change have been charted by Rochford 2007, 2013; Valpey 2006; Dwyer and Cole 2007; and Vande Berg and Kniss 2008.
62. See Wuaku 2013 particularly for an excellent study of Krishna and Shiva devotees in Ghana.
63. In this context, ISKCON fits squarely into Manfred Steger's 2009 notion of religious globalism, through its aim to counter perceived forces of secularization within the development of a global religious community.
64. Ong 1999.
65. While *brahmacārin* and *saṃnyāsin* are the correct Sanskrit grammatical forms for these categories of renunciation, ISKCON devotees use the terms *brahmacari* and *sannyasi*. I will adopt this popular usage when referring to renunciant members of the community and will reserve the former for discussions of the vocation in historical context.
66. Such claims have been a central feature of many modern Hindus. See discussion of Karsondas Mulji and Dayānanda's use of the concept of *ved dharm* in Jordens 1978, 128ff.
67. For a discussion of this in relation to the Sathya Sai movement, see Kent 2000a; Srinivas 2010.
68. For a comparative example of this global-local dynamic, in the BAPS Swaminarayan community, see Brosius 2012.
69. The city often leads the way in cosmopolitan trends for the country, such as the appearance of India's first newsprint matrimonial ad for a groom-seeking-groom. This is grounded in historic trends; see Green 2013 and Fernandes 2012.
70. Khilnani 1997, 136.
71. Fernandes 2013, 133.
72. Fernandes 2013, 70. According to Fernandes (2013, 56), the word first appeared in *The Times of India* in relation to the city in 1878, in an article about Afghans visiting Bombay.
73. A "cosmopolitan" apartment building, for instance, means an apartment building in which not only Hindus but also Muslims and Christians are able to live, as mentioned

in the forthcoming work of Zahir Janmohamed, *The Permitted Hours*. This conveys both inclusivity but also reveals an abiding unequal power dynamic that cleaves spaces between *savarna* Hindus and religious minorities in urban India. It is into this conversation that religious revivalism is often viewed with suspicion by Mumbaikars as a threat to cosmopolitanism.

74. See Elison 2018.
75. Prakash 2010, 349.
76. Kaur 2004, 50.
77. Fernandes 2013, 113.
78. Varma 2012, 128ff. This tension has been captured in film (Mani Ratnam's 1995 film *Bombay*) and literature, as poignantly in Jayant Kaikini's short story "Unframed." Such tensions were stoked again around the 2008 terror attacks.
79. Varma 2012; Fernandes 2013.
80. Following Appadurai and Breckenridge 1995; Zavos 2012.
81. See Freitag 2007; Rajagopal 2001.
82. See Elison 2018.
83. Van der Veer 2002a, 2002b.
84. In this formulation, I echo Lucia 2014, who draws a distinction between inheritors and adopters among global Amma devotees. Although my focus is on devotees in India, not in diaspora, I see this distinction as increasingly blurry in relation to ethnicity. In ISKCON, for instance, many Indians could be classified as adopters, due to their decision to join the organization independent of family religious background. Moreover, the multiethnic composition of many devotee families and the presence of second- and third-generation devotees from a variety of ethnic backgrounds complicates the notion that only ethnic Indians are inheritors. Lucia signals the beginning of such complexities among Amma devotees' categorizations as well (Lucia 2014, 56).
85. I was guided by studies including Saunders 2019 that emphasize this inherent composition of many contemporary Hindu communities.
86. Pérez 2016.
87. Flueckiger 2006; DeNapoli 2014.
88. Orsi 1985; Bloomer 2018; Larios 2019.
89. Tweed 2006.
90. I underwent an IRB review prior to the start of my research in 2012, and my project was determined exempt according to federal IRB regulations. I obtained consent from interviewees at the outset of our interactions and recorded and later transcribed all interviews. As mentioned above, I have also sought to minimize any potential risk due to the disclosure of sensitive personal information by anonymizing personal details.

## Chapter 1

1. Ramanujan 1989, 132.
2. See Bryant 2007, 11, 442ff.; Dimock 1989.

3. See De 1986.
4. See Stewart 2010; Sardella 2013; and Gupta 2014 for detailed histories.
5. For extensive discussions of Gauḍīya theological and ritual identity, see Holdrege 2015; Gupta 2014; Stewart 2010; Haberman 2001; Dimock 1999; O'Connell 1993; De 1986; and Chakravarti 1985.
6. See Stewart 2010) for an argument of this work's importance for the crystallizing Gauḍīya orthodoxy.
7. See Dimock 1999; Stewart 2010; Okita 2012 and 2014.
8. See Horstmann 2001 for details.
9. These socio-occupational categories are, respectively, priests and teachers, rulers and administrators, merchants and agriculturalists, and laborers.
10. These stages of life are, respectively, celibate studenthood; married, householder life; partial renunciation within society; and a complete renunciation of one's home, wealth, and family relationships.
11. See Olivelle 2005, 24–25 for a treatment of the *dharma śāstras*.
12. This schema is laid out in Lorenzen 2004. See Holdrege 2015, 184–185, 190.
13. For instance, the prominent early Gauḍīya gurus Narottama Dāsa, a *kāyastha*, and Śyāmānanda, a *sadgopa*, took brahmin disciples (see Dimock 1999, 442, n 100), and Caitanya famously flaunted caste and purity restrictions when dancing with the corpse of Haridāsa, the Muslim-born convert lauded in the *Caitanya Caritāmṛta* (Dimock 1999, 905–907). For additional examples of the complexity of caste practice in Gauḍīya communities, see Sarkar 2000, 2011; Stewart 2010; and Dimock 1999, 273, 373, 489, 592, 621, 948–949.
14. See Holdrege 2015, chapter 1 for a full treatment.
15. For a full discussion of their place within the orthodox Gauḍīya community history, see the introduction to Broo 2003; Haberman 2001; Gupta 2007; and Holdrege 2015. See Holdrege (2015, 95–96) for a comprehensive study of *sādhana-bhakti* as discussed in the works of early Gauḍīya writers, including Rūpa's *Bhaktirasāmṛtasindhu*.
16. Dimock 1989; Nicholas 2001; Fuller 2003.
17. Sarkar 2006, 40.
18. See, respectively, Hawley 1981 and Zarrilli 1999. See also Lutgendorf 1991; Haberman 2001; Hess and Schechner 1977.
19. See Wulff 1985, 183.
20. See Stewart 2010.
21. See Hardy 1983 for a history of the development of Krishna worship and Busch 2011 for a comparative study.
22. As well as his other works, including the dramas *Ujjvāla Nīlāmani* and *Lalitā Mādhava*.
23. See Valpey 2006 for a discussion of South Indian ritual influence. Odishan influence can be seen particularly in the incorporation of Jagannātha into Gauḍīya praxis.
24. See Valpey 2006 and Holdrege 2015.
25. See Okita 2012 and Hawley 2015.
26. Koch 1991; Asher and Talbot 2006.
27. The followers of Vallabhācārya and the Swāmīnārāyaṇa community are additional examples of *bhakti* communities that negotiated transregional identities across North

and West India. However, their communities have not expanded across ethnic lines to the extent of the Gauḍīyas.

28. See Stewart 2010, 23ff., 44.
29. See Stewart (2010) and Dimock (1999, 29ff.) for discussions on the text's dating. The general range of the text's completion is between 1590 and 1615. I would argue the date is on the earlier end of that spectrum.
30. See Haberman 1994; Salomon 1985.
31. See Stewart 2010, 274 for dating this text.
32. See Stewart 2010, 284–291.
33. O'Connell 2018; Fuller 2003; Sardella 2013.
34. Fuller 2003, 181.
35. Nicholas 2001.
36. Sardella 2013; Fuller 2003.
37. Sardella 2013, 1.
38. Sugirtharajah 2003, 38ff.; Dalmia 2003.
39. See Chidester 2013 on the imbrication of many nineteenth- and early twentieth-century studies of comparative religion with colonial structures of knowledge and power.
40. Beckerlegge 2000.
41. For examples of this, see John Murdoch's *Vedic Hinduism and the Arya Samaj: An Appeal to Educated Hindus* (1902), Nicol Macnicol's *Indian Theism* (1915), and J. N. Farquhar's *The Crown of Hinduism* (1920).
42. For instance, a ruling by an income tax tribunal in Nagpur, Maharashtra granted tax-exempt status to a local Śiva temple in a case pertaining to expenses incurred by the trust in 2008 and the tax benefit sought under Section 80G(5)(vi) of the Income Tax Act, 1961. A similar argument was made successfully by the ISKCON Juhu temple in regard to the proceeds of their vegetarian restaurant.
43. For further discussion on the rise of "eternal religion" and *sanātana dharma* movements in the nineteenth-century movements of Vivekānanda, Aurobindo and others, see Vivekananda 1992–1994; Brian Hatcher 1999 and 2007; Peter Heehs 2003; Fuller 2009.
44. Bhatia 2008, 5.
45. See Sardella 2013; Fuller 2004; Bhatia 2008.
46. This was later revamped under Bhaktivinoda's son, Bhaktisiddhanta, as the Harmonist. See Sardella 2013, 65; Das 1999, 10.
47. Sardella 2013, 65, 78.
48. Robison 2014.
49. For elaboration on this concern, see Bhatia 2008, 249ff.
50. See Manring 2011 and Dimock 1989 for examples of these varied communities.
51. While systematic religiosity has a resonance in the Gauḍīya *vaidhī-bhakti* and *rāgānugā-bhakti* paths, the growth of institutionalized community from Bhaktivinoda's era onward institutionalized the systematic nature of Gauḍīya practice. See Bhatia 2008.
52. Sanford 2005.
53. Bhatia 2008.

54. See Beckerlegge 2000, 2006; Vrajaprana 1994.
55. Sardella 2013, 98.
56. Though opposed by Bengali *smarta*-brahmin communities, Bhaktisiddhanta was not the only guru in late nineteenth-century Hindu India to accept non-Indian disciples through formal initiation. For instance, the Radhasoami community also attracted Europeans and Americans. See Juergensmeyer 1991, 52.
57. Sardella 2013, 97.
58. I have included here an abridged form of the charter laid out by Sardella 2013, 97–98.
59. See Sardella 2013, 28ff. for a discussion of the politics of this canon, including its role in delimiting orthodoxy and excluding other Vaiṣṇava-related groups of Bengal.
60. Translated as the latter, according to Sardella, by Bhaktisiddhanta in *Sajjanatoṣaṇī* 1920, 9–13. See Sardella 2013, 204ff. This concept is based on a reading of Rūpa Gosvāmin's *Bhaktirasāmṛtasindhu* 1.2.255–256.
61. Outlined in Valpey 2006; Sardella 2013.
62. From, respectively, *Young India*, November 24, 1927. Republished in Hingorani ed. 1965, 64–66; *Young India*, February 25, 1920. Republished in Hingorani ed. 1965, 1; *Young India*, October 20, 1927. Republished in Hingorani ed. 1965, 43.
63. See Sardella 2013, 82ff.
64. Sardella 2013, 28ff.
65. See Sarkar 2006.
66. See Satsvarūpa dāsa Goswami 1982–1983, vol. 1, chapter 2.
67. See Goswami 2012, 33–36 for further details.
68. See Bhaktivedanta Swami 1995.
69. For an elaborate and detailed history of ISKCON's early years in America and beyond, see Satsvarūpa dāsa Goswami 1982–1983.
70. A choice echoed by Indian contemporaries, as Mira Kamdar mentions in her family's decision to send her father there in 1949: "Why not? America was the land of the future. England was washed up." Kamdar 2000, 158.
71. "What is ISKCON?" ISKCON's GBC website, http://gbc.iskcon.org/what-is-iskcon/ (accessed October 18, 2019).
72. For an early description, see Brooks 1989, 72ff.
73. Brooks 1989, 223.
74. For a discussion of this legacy within ISKCON congregations, see King 2007, 1.
75. See Rosen 2003 for a discussion of these lifestyle regulations.
76. See Juergensmeyer 1991, 129.
77. See Beckerlegge 2000, 113 for a discussion of this visual culture in regard to Ramakrishna, Sharada Devi, and Vivekānanda.
78. See Okita 2012 and Hawley 2015) for background of the development of *catur-sampradāya*. Okita 2012, 2014 provides an analysis of the Gauḍīya affiliation with the Madhva *sampradāya* and Hawley 2015, 99ff. examines the four *sampradāyas* as a legitimating model within Vaiṣṇava *bhakti* traditions. Deadwyler 2007, 108ff. discusses the concept of *paramparā* in Bhaktivedanta's thought and contemporary ISKCON communities.
79. Goswami 2012, 37.

80. See Gold 2005.
81. For an elaboration on this, see Valpey 2006 and Deadwyler 1996.
82. This would become an association that would follow ISKCON to India in unhelpful ways, as we shall see in Chapter 5, and is still ensconced in many public culture representations of the group, as in the AME television series *Madmen*.
83. See Brooks 1989, 78–84; Oliver 2014, 13, 75–76; and Goldberg 2010 for a broader context.
84. See Satsvarūpa dāsa Goswami 1982–1983, vol. 3, chapter 22.
85. Rochford 2018.
86. Other modern Hindu organizations have attempted to implement this model. See Juergensmeyer 1991, 45 for a discussion on the attempted formation of a ten-member Central Administrative Council in the Radhasoami communities.
87. Beyond adherence to the ritual and social norms laid out in the GBC law books—based on a consensus of interpretation of Bhaktivedanta's words, writing, and example—there is a degree of individual variation among individual ISKCON centers.
88. I examine this issue in depth in Robison 2023.
89. Tattvavit Dasa 2015. For an elaboration of ISKCON's early American countercultural context, see Stillson Judah's classic 1974 work, a satirical take by Wallace 1981, and a more recent assessment by Rochford 2013.
90. Bhaktivedanta Swami 1990.
91. This title provided the inspiration for Chowpatty's popular Journey of Self Discovery course, which expounds on some of the same strategies for presenting ISKCON's brand of Gauḍīya Vaiṣṇavism, now directed toward Indian audiences.
92. See Srinivas 2010, 11ff. in relation to Sathya Sai's early American devotees.
93. King 2013.
94. For a discussion of Bhaktivedanta's notion of Vaiṣṇava mission and its sociopolitical context, including the 1965 reform of American immigration laws, see Rosen 2007; Melton 1989; and Knott 1986 and 2000.
95. Bhaktivedanta 1995, 39–40. This prayer was composed in September 1965 in Bengali and later translated into English by Bhaktivedanta under the title "Mārkine Bhāgavata Dharma."
96. Deadwyler 2007, 103.
97. This standardized translation can be found in ISKCON song books and at the start of printed material published by the organization.
98. Gandhi 1997, 71.
99. Satsvarūpa dāsa Goswami 1982–1983, vol. 4, chap. 33.
100. The Wordsworth reference is discussed by Deadwyler 2007, 107, alternately (and in the sonnet original) written as "plain living and high thinking." It is taken from the sonnet "O Friend! I know not which way I must look," written in London in September 1802, according to the 1918 *Index to Poetry and Recitations* by Edith Granger.
101. From a recorded conversation, later entitled the "Real Advancement of Civilization," Surat, India, December 21, 1970. See Bhaktivedanta Swami 1993. In regard to feminism, see King 2007, 156–157; Knott 1993.

102. As Ambedkar noted in his critique of Gandhi's idealism, those who are far enough away, geographically and socially, from lived village settings can ignore the unequal power relations that defined Ambedkar's experience of village life as a *dalit*.
103. See Zeller 2010. This is part of a broader trend toward scientism among Indian religious and political organizations (see Subramaniam 2019), which I will discuss further in Chapter 4.
104. Sardella 2013 and Eck 1979.
105. Particularly the Bhakti Śāstrī and Bhakti Vaibhva programs, which take the student through a study of key Gauḍīya scriptures, culminating in a written and graded exam.
106. Other former members of the Soviet Union, including Hungary, Lithuania, Kazakhstan, have also been home to prominent ISKCON communities. For background, see Tkatcheva 1994; King 2013; and Pranskeviciute and Juras 2014.
107. Entwistle notes with curiosity the "new arrivals"—ISKCON devotees in Vrindavan—as an attraction for local pilgrims but also separate from the brahmanical social network of the region (Entwistle 1987, 224–225).
108. Brooks 1989, 165ff. For an updated vision, see Hawley 2020.
109. See Satsvarūpa dāsa Goswami 1982–1983, vol. 4, chap. 32.
110. Brooks (1989) brings out the complexities and unevenness of this acceptance in 1980s Vrindavan.
111. B. S. R., "Miscellanea." *The Times of India*. October 11, 1970, p. 11. For the former, see Rosen 2012, 39–43. Suspicions that ISKCON was a covert American intelligence operation were developed more seriously in the Soviet Union. See Serge Schmemann, "Hare Krishna sect alarms Kremlin," *The Times of India*, August 4, 1983; William J. Eaton, "Moscow Police Break Up Hare Krishna Gathering," August 30, 1987. For additional background, see Squarcini and Fizzotti 2004.
112. Soma Wadhwa, "Krishna's Errant Disciples," *Outlook India*, November 16, 1998. While suspicions are still occasionally aired in Indian media, the tone changed noticeably by the late 2000s. See, for instance, Rashmi Belur, "ISKCON Never Asks Anyone to Serve It," *DNA India: Bangalore*, June 27, 2009.
113. B. S. R., "Miscellanea," *The Times of India*, October 11, 1970.
114. For above, see Satsvarūpa dāsa Goswami 1982–1983, vol. 4, chap. 33, who reports that 10,000–20,000 people attended each day.
115. Satsvarūpa dāsa Goswami 1982–1983, vol. 4, chap. 33.
116. Bhaktivedanta ordered two sets of *mūrtis* to be made in white marble at Jaipur, funded by a donation by Rameshwar Das Birla. Satsvarūpa dāsa Goswami 1982–1983, vol. 4, chap. 32. This was the beginning of a multi-generational Birla patronage of ISKCON Mumbai that continues to this day.
117. The ISKCON Mumbai Society, for instance, controls copyright of the ISKCON name for other Indian ISKCON centers, and controls distribution and taxation reporting for donations collected by regional ISKCON centers. This centralizes interbranch issues, particularly in the case of ISKCON Bangalore which seceded from ISKCON's parent organization and has been the subject of a protracted leadership struggle in the Karnataka High Court and the Supreme Court. See Hawley 2020, 141–142 for an introduction.

118. A sentiment also echoed by one critic to Brooks 1989, 218. However, reserved defenses were also offered. See, for instance, Murzban P. Zaiwalla, "Hare Krishna," *Times of India* (Letters to the Editor), February 7, 1971, A2.
119. G. N. Nakhate, "Hare Krishna," *Times of India* (Letters to the Editor), December 20, 1970, 20.
120. Narendra K. Aneja, *Times of India* (Letters to the Editor), December 6, 1970, A5.
121. For instance, Giriraj das Braumachary, "Hare Krishna," *Times of India* (Letters to the Editor), New Delhi, January 10, 1971.
122. Giriraja dasa Brahmacari 1971. For another description of their complex cultural role in bringing Indian culture "back" to Indians, see Kalakantha Das 1998.
123. Jayadvaita Swami 1975.
124. "40 Years of 'Harinaam' Chanting," October 1, 2011, *DNA Mumbai* (accessed October 31, 2019).
125. A detailed multi-volume account of Bhaktivedanta's years leading ISKCON describes the early history of the organization in Bombay with reference to a range of archival sources. See Satsvarūpa dāsa Goswami 1982–1983, vol. 5, chap. 38.
126. See Singh 2010 and Brosius 2012, who examines the theme-park aesthetic as a popular mode of contemporary Hindu religious culture. This is a hallmark of the aesthetics of larger ISKCON temples in urban India. Hawley 2020, 118ff. provides a critical analysis of the urban development and theme park aesthetics of Vrindavan, with a focus on ISKCON's influence on contemporary architecture and tourism.
127. Satsvarūpa dāsa Goswami 1982–1983, vol. 5, chap. 44.
128. For an internal account, see Satsvarūpa dāsa Goswami 1982–1983, vol. 5, chap. 41; Satsvarūpa dāsa Goswami 2003, 197–260. See also: "Demolition of temple shed raises civic row," *The Times of India*, May 22, 1973, 6.
129. I analyze these connections in detail in my chapter "A Hindu by Any Other Name?" in Graham Schweig ed., *The Worldwide Krishna Movement*, forthcoming from Oxford University Press.
130. Just six months later, on June 2, 1978, another court case was filed against ISKCON, reported in India's major newspapers. For a more recent instance, see: "Juhu Citizens Spurn ISKCON's Heaven," *DNA Mumbai*, October 12, 2005, http://www.dnaindia.com/mumbai/report-juhu-citizens-spurn-iskcons-heaven-5442 (accessed October 22, 2022).
131. Brosius 2012; Kim 2009; Warrier 2005.
132. ISKCON's media usage has often developed in tandem with public-relations campaigns, particularly in locations where they acquired a negative public image. See Rochford 2007; Barker 2013. ISKCON Communications, developed in the United States, now has offices in each major geographical region whose staff coordinate at annual GBC conferences in India.
133. ISKCON's cultivation of this public identity has analogues in other successful contemporary transnational Hindu movements. McCartney 2011 points to the matrix of "Vedic religion-patriotism-social work" as a formula for numerous contemporary Hindu communities.
134. Satsvarūpa dāsa Goswami 1982–1983, vol. 6, chap. 48.
135. See Waghorne 2013.

136. As Prabha Krishnan points out, the title song for Doordarshan's *Mahābhārata* serial unfolded against a backdrop of an iconic ISKCON-produced painting of Krishna and Arjuna on the battlefield of Kurukṣetra, which also famously graces Bhaktivedanta's *Bhagavad Gītā As It Is* (Krishnan 1990). The *Mahābhārata* serial credits its title photographs to ISKCON-BBT.
137. For instance, reproductions of ISKCON renderings of Krishna and Viṣṇu can be seen in the community hall of the Imam Shah Bava Dargah, a contested shrine whose followers claim Hindu and Muslim heritage, in Pirana, Gujarat.
138. See Zavos et al. 2012.
139. See Brooks 1989, 3–22.
140. Nye 2001; King 2007, 144ff.; Rochford 2007: 183; Warrier 2012; Vertovec 2000, 101; Zavos 2009, 2012, 74ff.
141. Rochford 2007, 2013. See also Vande Berg and Kniss 2008 for the role of Indian immigrants in reviving the ISKCON congregation in Chicago, Illinois and Karapanagiotis 2021, 12–13 for a summary of the causes and effects of this demographic shift.
142. See Sugirtharajah 2003, 114ff.
     Chapter 2: Between East and West: Introducing Chowpatty.
143. Rochford 2007.

## Chapter 2

1. Fernandes 2013, 101.
2. These spatial and aesthetic montages find a partial parallel in the BAPS Swaminarayan temples of urban India. See Brosius 2012, 457.
3. Drawn from interviews by author with N. D. Desai and R. K. Maheswari, Mumbai, 2013. Efforts to corroborate this with documentation in Mumbai's High Court archives did not prove fruitful.
4. Enumerated by R. K. Maheswari as twenty-one cases in all, many settled out of court. Local Indian legal databases and archives did not yield clear records of all of these, perhaps because many were out-of-court settlements.
5. McKean 1996, 4.
6. This focus on training and education fits within larger modern Hindu organizational trends, reflected in the structure of organizations from the Rashtriya Swayamsevak Saṅgh (RSS) to The Art of Living Foundation and pointing back to a late nineteenth-century conceptualization of education and religious reform. See Dimitrova 2008.
7. Found in *Caitanya Caritāmṛta* 1.17, *śloka* 4 (Bhaktivedanta trans. 1.17.31). Also repeated in 3.6, *śloka* 3, and 3.20, *śloka* 5.
8. These statements and future quotes are from interviews conducted between 2012 and 2015. Quotes are transcribed in the original English or translated from Hindi when noted. As mentioned above, most names and some identifying personal details have been obscured to protect privacy.

9. The routinization of security was bolstered by the bombing of an ISKCON temple in Manipur in 2006 and an ongoing concern over attacks in Mumbai, including a hoax bomb threat received by the Chowpatty temple in 2011.
10. Aside from interviews and personal conversations, I was able to consult anonymized data in the temple's database, in which information about devotees is updated annually. I last received data in 2016.
11. In Gujarat, the Vallabhite Vaiṣṇava tradition; in Karnataka, the Śrīvaiṣṇavas and the worship of Viṣṇu at Udupi are a central feature of the Hindu religious landscape, and the Madhva *sampradāya* (from which the Gauḍīyas claim their philosophical lineage) has a historic stronghold. In North India, particularly Uttar Pradesh, the worship of Krishna and Rāma are both prominent aspects of the Hindu religious landscape.
12. See Rochford 1985 and Judah 1974.
13. For further details, see Rochford and Bailey 2006. The original order of expulsion is found in the ISKCON Governing Body Commission Resolutions, March 1987.
14. Particularly noteworthy was Radhanath Swami's 2014 Vyāsa Pūjā—or birth anniversary celebration—in which the Cross Maidan grounds were rented out, and an exclusive crowd of 5,000 people were able to get tickets to attend the *mela*, during which frequent mention was made of Radhanath Swami's original meeting with Bhaktivedanta Swami at the same site in 1971.
15. For an earlier example of this dynamic, see the story of Marathi, the "Westernized pilgrim" (Brooks 1989, 135–139).
16. Rosen chronicled Desai's combination of devotion and international business in his aptly titled *Bhakti Yoga in Business* (2012). Regarding the dual name, all initiated ISKCON members have a "spiritual name" bestowed by their guru at the time of initiation. These Sanskrit names are drawn from a lexicon of Gauḍīya texts and Vaiṣṇava deities, including names of *avatāras*, Kṛṣṇa's epithets, and sacred places and articles involved in Vaiṣṇava worship. Names are followed by *dāsa* for men, *dāsī* for women, recasting what is generally a term of degradation, "servant" or "slave," through an ethos of religious service.
17. Karapanagiotis 2021 examines the phenomenon of branding among ISKCON communities. This parallels my own fieldwork experiences, as devotees highlighted their organized PR work and branding successes with pride.
18. The system has also recently expanded to include an entry-level Mentorship System for those who are not yet able to follow the lifestyle requirements that serve as prerequisites for entering the Counselling System. In addition, Chowpatty's devotees also organize explicit *nāma-haṭṭa* programs, interchangeably called *satsaṅg* programs, extensively in the greater Mumbai area. According to internal temple documents in 2014, there were seventy-two registered *satsaṅg* or *nāma-haṭṭa* programs connected to the Chowpatty temple alone, most consisting of small groups of families organized around a neighborhood residence. These are divided into seven regions throughout greater Mumbai and surrounding regions: South Mumbai, Sion, Bandra-Borivali, Mira Road, Navi Mumbai, Kalyan region, and Thane region.
19. Temple documents fluctuate between the American "counseling" and the British "counselling." However, the standardized pamphlets I received from interviewees indicated a preference for the British spelling, which I will use here.

20. This information is based on interviews with the financial administrators of the temple and consultation of in-house manuals that are unpublished but in regular use by the temple committees.
21. "A Report on the Social Development Programme at Radha Gopinath Temple" (Radha Gopinath Mandir n.d.) is a manual describing the major organizational structures of the temple community that was co-written by Chowpatty's managerial staff (date unknown, estimated as early 2000s) and is kept in the temple's main offices.
22. See Bryant and Ekstrand eds. 2004 for background. This shift of emphasis is reflected in "Model of a Spiritual Community" (Radha Gopinath Mandir 2012, 1), an unpublished document circulated as a community organizational manual among members of ISKCON Chowpatty, which asserts that the first of the seven principles governing the Chowpatty community is "people over projects."
23. This has led to an ISKCON-wide reorientation, foregrounding what is often called "devotee care" in the global institution.
24. Details of the "Emotional Care Action Plan" are available through ISKCON's Devotee Care promotional material.
25. Radha Gopinath Mandir n.d., 34.
26. For a genealogy of the term, see Miller 2005. ISKCON's usage of wellness terminology includes a contemporary casting of both its *sādhana* and community discipline as counseling or therapy. For further details, see Anderson 2007, 128–129.
27. See, for instance, the mention of Radhanath Swami in Dwyer and Cole 2013 and ISKCON Congregational Development Ministry 2006, 9, 15, 84–85, 203.
28. "Welcome to E-Counseling," the ISKCON Desire Tree website, February 1, 2016, http://www.iskcondesiretree.com/profiles/blogs/e-counseling (accessed May 15, 2018).
29. See, for instance, Versluis 2014; Kent 2000b; Lucia 2020.
30. Comparable examples include the American-born Sadhvi Bhagawati Sarasvati of the Parmarth Niketan Ashram, Rishikesh president of Divine Shakti Foundation, and South African–born Sri Rama Ramanuja Achari, appointed as the first Western disciple of Varada Yatiraja Jeeya Swami to establish a Western branch of the Śrīvaiṣṇava Śrī Perumbudur Maṭham.
31. Indeed, some recorded statements by Bhaktivedanta perpetuate deeply hierarchical views on race and caste. His work as a whole spans a complex combination of liberatory messages combatting social discrimination and the perpetuation of brahmanically oriented hierarchies of race, caste, and gender, consonant with the writings of many other twentieth-century upper-caste Indian thinkers such as Gandhi.
32. Grewal 2014, 165–166.
33. ISKCON's institutional policy encourages followers to see themselves primarily as members of the organization and secondarily as followers of a particular guru. The choice of one's guru is seen as an individual affair, within the confines of ISKCON's list of initiating gurus.
34. Chowpatty's *yātrās* are rooted in pilgrimage destinations of the Gauḍīya tradition and broader Vaiṣṇava pilgrimage circuits. They use the word to indicate an annual community pilgrimage, distinct from its use to describe traditional Bengali folk theater.
35. Desai sadly passed away in 2016. I was grateful to have had the chance to meet him.

36. The Chowpatty temple's official website is: "ISKCON: Sri Sri Radha Gopinath," http://www.radhagopinath.com (accessed August 1, 2019). Aside from the temple website and the temple-run ISKCON Desire Tree website, about fifteen websites pertaining to Radhanath Swami and his public profile are run by temple *brahmacari*s.
37. Later published with Mandala Publishers and distributed by Simon and Schuster in the United States and followed by the sequel *The Journey Within* in 2016.
38. Swami 2008, 346.
39. Swami 2008, 345.
40. Swami 2008, 346.
41. Shubha Vilas managed the publicity of *The Journey Home* throughout India. As of my research period, Tulsi Books had released five books of ethical teachings of Radhanath Swami for broad audiences, five books of Radhanath Swami's quotes for ISKCON audiences, and a comic series for devotee children. Shubha Vilas has also authored a six-volume series on personal growth lessons from the Rāmāyaṇa in collaboration with Jaico Publishing.
42. Parijata Devi Dasi, "ISKCON Swami's Book Launched by Mumbai Celebrities," *ISKCON News*, August 29, 2009, http://news.iskcon.com/node/2251 (accessed March 22, 2019).
43. "Celebs at Book Launch," *India Times*, August 21, 2009, http://photogallery.indiatimes.com/events/mumbai/ celebs-at-book-launch/articleshow/4922222.cms (accessed October 22, 2019).
44. "Swami's Tale," *Outlook Magazine*, September 7, 2009, http://www.outlookindia.com/glitterati.aspx?5068 (accessed October 22, 2019).
45. Including the Gujarati-medium December 1, 2011; Ahmedabad-based editions of *Samachar*, *Divya Bhaskar*, and *Vaibhav*; and even the Bhuj-based *Kutch Mitra*. For the Surat book release, media coverage included the December 2 and 3, 2011, editions Gujarati *Sandesh*, *Rakhewal*, *Phulchaab*, and *Nav Nirman*, as well as English media reports in these same cities. In the Delhi area, similar positive pieces appeared in the Hindi *Navbharat Times*, *Amar Ujala*, *Jagran*, *Nayi Duniya*, *Veer Arjun*, and Punjabi *Punjab Kesari*. I am indebted to the *brahmacari*s of Chowpatty's ashram, particularly Shubha Vilas, for assisting me in locating these articles and assisting me in translations.
46. "*Adhyātmakī jairake bhāratanī aurkan*," *Divya Bhaskar*, Ahmedabad edition, December 1, 2011, 1.
47. See, for instance, Anuradha Verma, "Spirituality Is Me!," *The Times of India*, August 21, 2010; Radhanath Swami, "Awakening to Love," interview by Ashish Virmani, *DNA India*, August 24, 2009.
48. "Ambani family arrives at ISKCON temple with Ajay Piramal," *ANI News Official* YouTube video, May 6, 2018, https://www.youtube.com/watch?v=znhMjQHXNfw (accessed June 16, 2023). The event was also documented by DNA, *Outlook India*, and other online news publications.
49. For a recording of the event, see: "Interaction with Radhanath Swami at CII," YouTube video by Radhanath.Swami, December 17, 2014, https://www.youtube.com/watch?v=eY CcumSvm6I (accessed October 22, 2019).

50. Iwamura 2011.
51. In the internationally distributed ISKCON manual *The Nectar of Congregational Preaching*, a profile of an ISKCON temple in Omsk, Russia describes itself as "The Russian Chowpatty" and relates they have adopted their Counselling System. Attempts to export the system have also occurred in the United States and England.
52. Koch 2006; Asher and Talbot 2006.
53. Fernandes 2013, 101.
54. See Vertovec 2000 for an analysis of these factors in relation to diverse regionally based Hindu temples in India, the Caribbean, and the United Kingdom.
55. See Srinivas 2015.

## Chapter 3

1. See William Elison 2018 for a vivid depiction of the city's religious landscapes.
2. See Shilpa Phadke's *Why Loiter? Women and Risk on Mumbai Streets.*
3. The transition seems particularly smooth for the many members of the temple's congregation from Gujarati Vaiṣṇava backgrounds, particularly followers of the Puṣṭimārga. Ironically, Caitanya and the early Gauḍīyas were religious rivals to Vallabhācārya and his followers in early modern North and Western India. However, both groups developed similar religious and aesthetic styles (worship of Radha and Krishna, focus on *rasa* aesthetics, *mūrti pūjā*, central use of the Bhāgavata Purāṇa), as well as shared lifestyle norms (including strict vegetarianism).
4. I will explore the political implications of this in Chapter 5.
5. See Srivastava 2017 for parallel examples in North India.
6. Radha Gopinath Mandir 2012, 2. As noted in Chapter 1, in the early twentieth century, Bhaktivedanta followed the lead of Dayananda Saraswati and Gandhi in arguing for the implementation of a reformed, "spiritual" *varṇāśrama* system, rather than the abolishment of caste categories.
7. Radha Gopinath Mandir 2012, 2.
8. Cited by Bhaktivedanta from Viṣṇu Puraṇa 3.8.8 and also elaborated in *Caitanya Caritāmṛta* 2.8.58.
9. Radhanath Swami, "Caring for Devotees: The Spiritual Counselor System," the Dandavats website, September 15, 2015, http://www.dandavats.com/?p=1378 (accessed July 4, 2018).
10. Radha Gopinath Mandir n.d., 4.
11. This is particularly the case in the Mayapur, Bengal center, where the model is disseminated through the ISKCON Congregational Ministry based there, but it is also a reproducible model that ISKCON communities from Uttar Pradesh to the United Kingdom have instituted on a local scale.
12. In 2014, several temple managers involved with overseeing the Counselling System estimated that there were around fifty-six counselling couples, as well as fifty-five to sixty active mentors in the Mentorship System.

13. Quoted from *The Simple Temple* (Avatar Studios, 2002).
14. Radha Gopinath Mandir n.d., 12.
15. "A Report on the Social Development Programme at Radha Gopinath Temple" goes into detail about counsellors' duties. Within Chowpatty's Counselling System, there are a network of subcommittees that address subsets of the congregation. These include the Business Enterprise Committee, Employment Committee, Marriage Board, Housing Committee, Financial Assistance Committee, and Variṣṭha (Elder) Vaiṣṇava Committee. The central managerial core of these committees tends to overlap and coincides with the central figures in the temple's administration and major donor base.
16. Radha Gopinath Mandir n.d., 8; cf. Radha Gopinath Mandir 2012, 5.
17. Radha Gopinath Mandir n.d., 3.
18. Radha Gopinath Mandir 2012, 4–6.
19. See Haberman 2001.
20. Holdrege 2015, 95 also compares the early Gauḍīya practices of what she calls the "devotionally informed body" to the "socially informed body" implied through Bourdieu's notion of *habitus*.
21. Brooks 1989, 127, 141.
22. This model is notably for men in the congregation. Women, as per local conservative norms, are expected to reside with their families until marriage.
23. There seemed to be an implicit understanding, consonant with a conservative but pervasive ethos in India, that people seeking the services of the Marriage Board would be in their twenty or possibly thirties but not older.
24. See Waghorne 2013 for a discussion of the reception of Vivekananda's similarly demanding social norms in both India and the United States. Preceding ISKCON's transnational development by decades, Vivekananda's followers struggled with similar conflicts.

## Chapter 4

1. The philosophical focus originates in Bhaktivedanta's formulations of the Gauḍīya tradition and parallels his presentation to early American devotees. In Rochford's 1985 study of ISKCON across the United States, he notes that the most common "reason for joining" given (at 39%) was the "philosophy of the movement" (Rochford 1985, 71).
2. ISKCON Desire Tree joined YouTube in April 2009 and is housed under the banner of Radha Gopinath Media Service. It has a following of 84,000 subscribers as of January 2023.
3. See Naregal 2002 for a discussion of the historical roots of this institutionalized multilingualism in Mumbai. Marathi, although the official language of Maharashtra, is not the mother tongue of a prominent percentage of the city and of ISKCON's congregations.
4. For an analysis of these linguistic politics, see Ramaswamy 1997.

5. Chakrabarty 2002, 42.
6. For instance, Janson 2014.
7. The frequency of these courses peaked during my research period in the mid- to late 2010s. They are now in transition as the pandemic suspended large events and brought many courses online.
8. The Chowpatty-developed course format has also been picked up by ISKCON communities as far away as Patna, Birmingham, and Houston.
9. These PowerPoint resources are also available online for individuals to use in their own presentations.
10. For recent work, see Subramaniam 2019 and Heifetz 2021. As Thomas 2020 notes, this often connotes an implicit high-caste perspective in ostensibly secular contexts.
11. Gottschalk 2013.
12. Subramaniam 2019; 2000, 81–82.
13. Radha Gopinath Das, "Journey of Self Discovery Day 1."
14. Radha Gopinath Das, "Journey of Self Discovery Day 5."
15. See Gottschalk 2013; Prakash 1999a, 1999b; Baber 1996; Nanda 2003; Kurien 2012; Thomas 2020.
16. See Scott 2016 for the genealogy of this intercontinental exchange of ideas between colonial-era Indians and Europeans.
17. Radha Gopinath Das, "Journey of Self Discovery Day 4."
18. The full six-part series is distributed through ISKCON Desire Tree, as well as related media services.
19. Radha Gopinath Das, "Journey of Self Discovery Day 1."
20. This also corresponds, we will find later in the course, to different religious responsibilities based on one's level of knowledge.
21. This is mentioned, for instance, in Bhaktivedanta's commentary to *Caitanya Caritāmṛta* 2.24.330.
22. As mentioned above, the Gauḍīya Vaiṣṇava *sampradāya* is grounded in the *acintya-bhedābheda* school of Vaiṣṇava Vedānta philosophy, and interpretations of the core categories that comprise the Journey of Self Discovery course are discussed with reference to this philosophical school alongside the Yoga-Saṁkhya systems of Indian philosophy. The systematic basis for Chowpatty's courses lies in ISKCON's chain of Gauḍīya commentarial traditions filtered through the translations and commentaries of Bhaktivedanta.
23. See Rochford 2007. Information also gleaned from discussions with ISKCON temple management in Washington DC and London, where ISKCON members of diverse ethnic origins have on occasion prohibited Indian diaspora members of their congregations from celebrating events like Durga Puja or Shiv Ratri in the temple space.
24. The assimilation of a certain hierarchical ordering of religious traditions according to the terms "monotheism" and "polytheism" speaks to the profound influence of colonialist and Orientalist taxonomies of religion within some postcolonial communities in the present day. In ISKCON's media productions within India and abroad, the term "monotheism" is often levied as a marker of authenticity, and the Gauḍīya tradition is then explained as the summation of it in universalist terms.

25. Did he say scientific? Radha Gopinath Das, "Journey of Self Discovery Day 2."
26. Radha Gopinath Das, "Journey of Self Discovery Day 3."
27. See Mayaram 2004, 87.
28. A reference to a devotional genre of reciting one thousand Sanskrit names of a Hindu deity.
29. Radha Gopinath Das, "Journey of Self Discovery Day 4."
30. See Raj 2007; Raina and Habib 2004.
31. Scientistic discourses grounded in the writings of Bhaktivedanta have been influential also in ISKCON's missionizing strategies on a transnational level. See Zeller 2010.
32. Mentioned in Bhaktivedanta's *Back to Godhead* periodical, first published in India throughout the 1940s–1960s and later incorporated as an official monthly ISKCON publication. See volumes 1, no. 4 (Bhaktivedanta Swami 1944); 3, no. 1 (Bhaktivedanta Swami 1956); 3, no. 4 (Bhaktivedanta Swami 1956); and 3, no. 18 (Bhaktivedanta Swami 1960).
33. Singh et al. 1987.
34. Gottschalk 2013, 33ff.
35. Krishna Chaitanya Das, "Prerna Festival—Bharat Gatha," temple lecture, December 6, 2014.
36. Such interpretations of religion and science are resonant among many contemporary Indian religious groups, as highlighted in productions such as Shekhar Kapur's "Science of Compassion" about Amritanandamayi Ma, as well as in Aukland 2016; Subramaniam 2019; and Heifetz 2019.
37. Heifetz (2019, 40) compellingly applies the work of Michael Saler to another contemporary Hindu community, the Gayatri Pariwar.
38. For a full treatment of early Gaudiya theological taxonomic structures, see Holdrege 2015.
39. "Gate Topper Spreads the Message of God," *DNA India: Mumbai*, April 11, 2011.
40. See "Muslim girl in Mumbai wins Gita contest," *Times of India*, April 3, 2015, http://timesofindia.indiatimes.com/city/mumbai/Muslim-girl-in-Mumbai-wins-Gita-contest/articleshow/467898 57.cms (accessed November 23, 2018).
41. Highlighted in films including Aamir Khan's 2007 *Taare Zameen Par* and Rajkumar Hirani's 2009 *3 Idiots*, the rigors of India's testing culture and educational competition have received ample news coverage as well.
42. Developed on instructions for scriptural study laid out by Bhaktivedanta, this course is now a standardized module offered throughout ISKCON centers transnationally under the supervision of the Vrindavan Institute of Higher Education (VIHE). The course is offered locally, at Chowpatty, through the Bhaktivedanta Academy for Culture and Education (BACE).
43. "One God or Many Gods?" Section 03, Level 02, the Vedic Quiz website, http://vedicquiz.com/questions/text/gita-champions-league/one-god-or-many-gods/section-03-level-02/ (accessed November 23, 2018).
44. See Bubandt 2014 for a parallel discussion of doubt in relation to modernity.
45. See Srivastava 2017 and Poonam 2018 on coaching and "personality development" courses in urban North India. Haberman 2001 expounded upon the performance aspects of the Gaudiya *sādhana* process.

46. Translated from Bhakti Rasamrita Swami's Hindi "Alwaron ki Katha" lecture series.
47. This draws from Bhaktivedanta's (1972–1977) translation of Bhāgavata Purāṇa 9.4.18–20 (H. G. Shastri ed. 9.4.18–20).
48. "Glories of Ambarish Maharaja," a lecture given by Radhanath Swami at the Chowpatty temple during the Sunday program on January 22, 2012.
49. See Holdrege (2015, 95) for a discussion of this verse from the Bhāgavata Purāṇa in relation to the early theological works of Rūpa and Kṛṣṇadāsa.
50. Radhanath Swami, lecture at the Annual Republic Day Program at ISKCON Juhu, January 2015.
51. See Fletcher 2013 for a comparative example of what he terms performance activism among American evangelicals.
52. Gopika Dasi, interview by author, Mumbai, January 26, 2013.
53. In collaboration with the government of Maharashtra, the program is jointly subsidized with government funds and private corporate backing, including the Piramal Group, the Aditya Birla Group, and the Bank of India. They are also in affiliation with the Rotary Club and the Lion's Club of Mumbai. Information confirmed by annual financial reports viewed on site in Mumbai.
54. See "DNA Hygiene for Kitchens: Hygiene Tops ISKCON's Kitchen," *DNA India*, November 19, 2011; "'Kitchen Religion' Hits 1,000,000 Mark," *DNA India: Mumbai*, September 18, 2011.
55. Hawley (2020, 125–129) considers the Akshay Patra's program's scope.
56. Mumbai's local press focuses more on the celebrity attendants than the site itself, but I would argue this reiterates ISKCON's indigenization into Mumbai's elite landscape, as in the widely published photo documentation of guests arriving at Surinder Kapoor's memorial in September 2011: "Surinder Kapoor's Prayer Meet," *Times of India*, September 26, 2011. See also Parijata Dasi, "Hema Malini's Daughter Seeks the Blessings of Sri Sri Radha Rasabihariji," *ISKCON News*, July 5, 2012.
57. The *Daily Bhaskar*, for instance, tells us that: "Divya Dutta Turns Spiritual, Offers Prayers at ISKCON Temple," *Daily Bhaskar*, March 29, 2015. Meanwhile, Madhuri Dixit is also a regular attendee of ISKCON Juhu's services, while Juhi Chawla, Raveena Tandon, and others regularly grace the public festivals of ISKCON Chowpatty.
58. Nimisha Tiwari, "Manish Malhotra Dresses Lord Kṛṣṇa," *Times of India*, August 27, 2008. See also: Parijata Devi Dasi, "Indian Fashion Icon Designs for Sri Sri Radha Rasabihari," ISKCON News. August 30, 2008. Since then, Malhotra has organized other significant donations to the ISKCON congregations of the greater Mumbai area, including an October 2014 fashion show in Surat, proceedings of which went toward the construction of the new ISKCON temple in Khargar, Navi Mumbai.
59. Hema Malini, "I Wonder Why Directors Don't Cast Married Actresses?," interview by Sumit Jha, *Times of India*, October 10, 2014.
60. Agarwal has held religious events with Radhanath Swami at his homes in London and Mumbai and has donated toward the development of a new ISKCON temple in Patna, Bihar, his hometown.
61. From a short documentary showcasing the event, "Gita Champions League," distributed by Radha Gopinath Temple. Released March 17, 2012.

62. Many ISKCON centers, in India and abroad, rent out their facilities for Hindu weddings, with no mandate for personal connection to the ISKCON community. Such weddings occur on a weekly basis at both ISKCON Juhu and ISKCON Chowpatty.

## Chapter 5

1. Many of whose leading members were also involved in the early temple development here.
2. That montage by Jackson Brand Paper Products evoked Srirupa Roy's analysis of postcolonial documentary films produced by the state-owned Films Division of India and the visuality of India's annual Republic Day parade. See Roy 2007 and Ramaswamy 2007.
3. This selective curation of national identity has roots in colonial and early postcolonial political and literary cultures. See Fernandes 2020, Bose 2014, and Bhagat-Kennedy (forthcoming) for historical counternarratives that make visible non-Hindu populations within constructions of India's national identity.
4. Translated from the original Hindi.
5. Lokanath Swami 2009.
6. See Lokanath Swami 1983 for a description of his *padāyātrā*. The Chowpatty community's annual pilgrimages began in 1986, first to the historic Gauḍīya sites of Vrindavan and later Mayapur, which was proclaimed by Bhaktivinoda as the site of Caitanya's birth and is the other major sacred site for ISKCON Gauḍīyas. For further reading on the history of Vaiṣṇava pilgrimage to Vrindavan, see: Vaudeville 1976; Haberman 1994; Entwistle 1987.
7. Nanda 2009; Brosius 2010; Aukland 2018.
8. Discussed in O'Connell 2018.
9. Jhūlelāl has indeed been an *iṣṭa-devatā*, or tutelary deity, of the people of Sindh altogether, revered in the historically eclectic religiosity of the Hindu and Muslim communities there. See Ramey 2008.
10. Radha Gopinath Mandir n.d., 43.
11. Due to the exclusivist tenor of ISKCON, forging links with other Vaiṣṇava groups has been a controversial move for Chowpatty, which has sometimes put them under fire from ISKCON's less ecumenical wings. However, as shown below, the links they have forged have enabled them to attain a level of integration among Hindu publics not attainable by the more insular approaches.
12. For comparative examples of Vaiṣṇava religious dramas (often called *līlās*) in relation to Indian national imaginaries, see Schechner 1985; Lutgendorf 1991; Dimitrova 2008; and Hawley 2015.
13. See Dimitrova 2008 on the nineteenth-century background of religious Hindi drama productions on the proscenium stage. While not a direct link, certain parallels are striking.

14. For a discussion of mythologicals in Indian discourses of Hindu history, see Hughes 2007; Thomas 1995, 160. For broader discussions of melodrama, see Anker 2014; Zarzosa 2013.
15. The discourse that a new religious system is the fulfillment of local religious traditions, in a teleological or theological sense, is found across South Asian traditions. See Asani 2002 on the missionary framing of the Nizari Ismailis in Western India.
16. For a discussion of the significance of Sal Beg (also spelled Salabeg) in Odia cultural history, see Kanungo 2011. This figure seems to be distinct from the Lal Beg of Eastern Uttar Pradesh and Bihar who is affiliated with the Balmiki caste (Lee 2021).
17. See "Introduction" in Menon 2006 and Hawley 2015 for comparative examples.
18. Transcription from the English-medium *My Sweet Lord* (2013).
19. Harrison's 1970 single, "My Sweet Lord," serves as the title of the 2013 drama, *My Sweet Lord*, highlighting the relationship between Harrison and Bhaktivedanta that culminated in Harrison's donation of the property that became the London Bhaktivedanta Manor temple.
20. This inclusive Vaiṣṇava *avatāra* theology is laid out by Kṛṣṇadāsa Kavirāja in *Caitanya Caritāmṛta* 2.20 yet is developed in a multilayered taxonomy of divine manifestation within a Gauḍīya Vaiṣṇava idiom. See Holdrege 2015 for a full treatment of Kṛṣṇadāsa's taxonomy.
21. For more on the Jagannātha tradition in Puri, see Eschmann et al. 1978.
22. This annual jostling to obtain city permits is not specific to ISKCON's public festivals, but plagues even the Marathi-dominant Ganesh Chaturthi organizers. See Kaur 2007.
23. Rosy Sequiera, "HC Dismisses Plea for Shivaji Park yatra," *Times of India*, February 13, 2015. https://timesofindia.indiatimes.com/city/mumbai/hc-dismisses-plea-for-shivaji-park-yatra/articleshow/46223559.cms (accessed on January 11, 2024).
24. See Srinivas 2010, 2n1 for an elaboration on the India Shining campaign.
25. This program expands ISKCON Chowpatty's work in the Maharashtra's Midday Meal Project, as mentioned above.
26. Hansen 2004, 23.
27. India Rising promotional material, January 2015.
28. While these state-based craft stalls are not a regular feature of most Chowpatty Rath-Yātrās, the stage performances described below, called "cultural programs" by the community, are emblematic of the Festival of India format that accompanies many ISKCON Rath-Yātrās in India and abroad.
29. Speech by the Master of Ceremonies, my translation from Hindi, ISKCON Chowpatty "India Rising" festival, Mumbai, India, January 16, 2015.
30. Dalmia 2001, 177.
31. Paul Greenough explores a similar overlay in relation to the construction of New Delhi's National Handicrafts and Handlooms Museum under the Ministry of Textiles in the 1950s, which linked curatorial work to the commercial market for "traditional" and "ethnic" items in the growing tourist economy. See Greenough 1995, 221.
32. Greenough 1995, 217, 220.
33. In another intriguing parallel, the crafts museum also engages in missions of cultural diplomacy through Festivals of India abroad. Greenough 1995, 220.

34. See Aligarh Historians Group 1979; See Khalidi 2008.
35. See Bhagavan 2013.
36. For a historical study of the All India phenomenon, see Rook-Koepsel 2021.
37. See Khilani 1997 and Oommen 1986, 62.
38. Varma 2012, 122.
39. Those proclamations are reproduced in Subramaniam 2019, 5–6.
40. This discourse implicitly centers brahmins as the natural receptacles of scientific knowledge, a phenomenon common in professional as well as religious contexts (Thomas 2020).
41. Hawley 2015, 3, 19ff. See also Sharma 1987.
42. See Sinha 2007, 69; see also Vaudeville 1996.
43. See Hawley 2015, 3-4 for this line of questioning.
44. See for instance the 2013 *Bhatrol.*
45. The play follows the account in chapters 4.2 to 4.7 of the Bhagavat Purāṇa, which are nearly identical in H. G. Shastri's critical edition (1996–2002) and Bhaktivedanta's translation (1972–1977).
46. *Jewel of Faith* (2014).
47. For the historical context of these scriptural narratives, see Dimock's (1999) introduction to the *Caitanya Caritāmṛta.*
48. See Thomas 1995.
49. For a long view of a historical context to some of these narratives, see Green 2004.
50. For the complexity of this relationship between political power and religious patronage, see Mukherjee and Habib 1987, 1988; Asher 1992, 2020; Ray 2012; Okita 2014; Burchett 2019.
51. I have heard that discussions in response to this trend, in part prompted by senior ISKCON leadership including Radhanath Swami, steered the drama groups away from these representations in the years following.
52. McLain 2009; Ganneri and Sen 2012; Menon 2012.
53. Examples of this motif are found in: *Life and Pastimes of Haridas Thakur* (2002), *Escape of Rupa and Sanatana* (2005), *March 24, 1984: The Journey from Fear to Shelter* (2009), *My Sweet Lord* (2013), and *Jewel of Faith* (2014). For an analysis of these visual and cinematic tropes in Hindi cinema, see Chadha and Kavoori 2008.
54. For details of the recorded lives of the Gauḍīya *ācārya*s Rūpa Gosvāmin and Sanātana Gosvāmin, see *Caitanya Caritāmṛta* 1.7 and 2.1 (Dimock trans.), as well as Dimock 1999, 20.
55. This and following quotes are direct transcriptions from the English-medium production.
56. *Escape of Rupa and Sanatana* (2005).
57. For a broader history of the cow protection issue, see Pandey 1990.
58. See Ghassem-Fachandi 2012 for a full account.
59. *Life and Pastimes of Srila Haridas Thakur* (2002).
60. See Sarkar 1998 and 2001; Hasan 2007; McLain 2009; and Sippy 2012.
61. Chadha and Kavoori 2008.
62. Affiliated with the Cānd Qazi, grandson of Alauddin Hussein Shah of Bengal, r. 1494–1518. See Dimock 1999, 321.

63. Transcription of the dramatic performance, *Chand Qazi and Caitanya Mahaprabhu*, performed at ISKCON Chowpatty, Mumbai, January 19, 2014.
64. Scroll Staff, June 8, 2023, "Kolhapur violence: Five juveniles among 41 held for rioting, vandalism over social media posts," *Scroll.in*, https://scroll.in/latest/1050578/kolhapur-violence-36-arrested-for-rioting-vandalism-over-social-media-posts (accessed on July 11, 2023).
65. From the 2002 *Life and Pastimes of Srila Haridas Thakur*.
66. Particularly in relation to the "beef killings" of 2015 and 2016, in which Muslim and Dalit villagers were targeted by mobs who suspected them of consuming beef after a series of state bans had been instituted.
67. Bhaktivedanta 1956.
68. Drawn from interviews with Bhaktivedanta Hospital management. For details on this in the press, see: Chandrima S. Bhattacharya, "Sena attack forces hospital lock-out," September 19, 2003, *Telegraph India*, Mumbai, https://www.telegraphindia.com/india/sena-attack-forces-hospital-lock-out/cid/799430 (accessed on July 13, 2020).
69. The organizers of the "India Rising" festival continued to maintain social-media presence afterward, advertising follow-up events organized by the community. One October 2018 trip publicized on their Facebook page took a group to the forts of the seventeenth-century Maratha military leader Shivaji and included an enactment of the 1659 victory of Shivaji's forces over those of Azfal Khan, a Muslim military leader from Bijapur, at the Pratapgad Fort in Maharashtra—another performance of a Hindu victory over a Muslim threat.
70. See Sarkar 2001.
71. Jaffrelot in Zavos et al. 2004, 24, drawing from Halbfass 1990, 177.
72. Bhaktivedanta 1956.
73. Radhanath Swami, "A Memory from 1971 in Ayodhya," @radhanathswami, Instagram account, January 15, 2024.
74. My gratitude to Vineet Chander for informed and engaging conversations on these complex issues.
75. Nanda 2009. Although this trend extends to pre-Independence conceptualizations of Indian nationhood, as discussed by Khalidi 2008.
76. See Kaur 2007, 208ff. See also Hansen 2004; Kaur 2004; Ganneri and Sen 2012.
77. Breckenridge and Appadurai 1995.
78. Ramaswamy 2007, 33.

## Chapter 6

1. Khan 2004.
2. Appadurai 1996, 33.
3. Ong 1999.
4. I employ this term, drawn from the foundational work of Gilles Deleuze and Felix Guattari, in conversation with later studies, including Appadurai 1990, 1995, 2001; Casanova 2001, 2013; and van der Veer 1996, 2002a.

5. Appadurai 1990, 295.
6. Casanova 2001, 428.
7. For comparative analyses of culture and power, see Searle-Chatterjee 2005 and Said 1977, 20, 325–326.
8. See, for instance, Blank 2001 and Naim 2012, 196.
9. See Bhattacharya 2012, 28, for a discussion on the modern invention of the concept *saṁskṛti*.
10. See Penner and Yonan 1972; Williams 1984; Smith 1998.
11. See King 1999 for a genealogy of this trend.
12. For another salient example of this, see Karapanagiotis 2021, who discusses Hridayananda Das Goswami and Krishna West.
13. Bhaktivedanta Swami, lecture on Srimad-Bhagavatam 6.1.1-4, Melbourne, May 20, 1975 (Bhaktivedanta Archives 1978).
14. Bhaktivedanta Swami, lecture, Los Angeles, February 2, 1968 (Bhaktivedanta Archives 1978).
15. Satsvarūpa dāsa Goswami 1982–1983, vol. 5, chap. 37.
16. Tamal Krishna Goswami and Gupta 2005.
17. See, for instance, Mishra 2007.
18. See Srinivas 1956 for a now-classic consideration of the interrelation between Sanskritization and Westernization in modern Hindu communities.
19. Satsvarūpa dāsa Goswami 1982–1983, vol. 4, chap. 32.
20. Satsvarūpa dāsa Goswami 1982–1983, vol. 4, chap. 32.
21. Radhanath Swami, keynote speech at the Artha Conference in Govardhan Ecovillage, Wada, Maharashtra, December 9, 2012.
22. I analyze another vivid example of this, based on the film *PK*, in Robison 2019.
23. This is a Hindi-medium drama. Unless otherwise noted, all quotes are my translations of the Hindi dialogues.
24. *Oh My God! Returns*, video recording of the drama performed in Mumbai, January 2014.
25. As I have argued elsewhere (Robison 2016), although Bhaktivedanta was not brahmin, ISKCON's notion of authentic Indian culture is refracted through a brahmanical Vaiṣṇava lens.
26. Deadwyler 2007, 120, reports these details in relation to his meeting with the governor of Bihar.
27. See, for instance, the statements ISKCON Mira Road's temple president, Kamal Lochan Das, in Dhaval Kulkarni, "Vishwa Hindu Parishad Leaders Want Whole World Converted to Hinduism," *DNA India*, December 15, 2014, http://www.dnaindia.com/india/report-vhp-leaders-want-whole-world-converted-to-hinduism-2043938 (accessed November 23, 2018). While not representative of all ISKCON Mumbai members, these views parallel contemporary Hindu nationalist proclamations of *akhand bhārat*.
28. ISKCON's formulations of the *yuga* time frames are one of several contemporary conceptualizations of the *yuga* system. For a comparison of different models, see Gonzalez-Reimann 2014.
29. See Benhabib 2002.

30. Discussed at length in Pinch (1996), chap. 3. Pinch's historical analysis highlights how processes of Sanskritization through the adoption of brahmanical Vaiṣṇava identity—as I have found in my own research above—is in certain cases a multigenerational project, as in the case of the Yadav Vaiṣṇavas of Uttar Pradesh and Bihar.
31. Jaikishan and Shailendra, 1955.

## Conclusion

1. Srinivas 2015.
2. Appadurai and Breckenridge 1995, 16.
3. For a comparative analysis of the religious modernity of the Ramakrishna movement, see Beckerlegge 2012, 401.
4. Here again Grewal 2014 provides a salient instance of this dynamic.
5. Nandy 1988; Chakrabarty 2002.
6. Bhattacarya 1954.
7. Bhaktivedanta 1956.
8. Bilgrami 2015.
9. See Fernandes and Heller 2006.
10. My gratitude to Vineet Chander for suggesting these apt examples. Final reference from @gaurgopaldas, Instagram account, December 28, 2022, and @monkify.official.

# Selected Bibliography

## Sanskrit and Bengali Works (Including Translations)


Bhāgavata Purāṇa. 1996–2002. *Śrībhāgavatam: Śrīmad Bhāgavata Mahāpurāṇam*, edited by H. G. Shastri, Bharati K. Shelat, and K. K. Shastri. 4 vols. Ahmedabad, India: B.J. Institute of Learning and Research.

Bhāgavata Purāṇa. 1972–1977. *Śrīmad Bhāgavatam*, translated by A. C. Bhaktivedanta Swami. 12 vols. Los Angeles: Bhaktivedanta Book Trust.

*Bhaktirasāmṛtasindhu* of Rūpa Gosvāmin. 2003. *The Bhaktirasāmṛtasindhu of Rūpa Gosvāmin*, edited and translated by David L. Haberman. New Delhi: Indira Gandhi National Centre for the Arts; Delhi: Motilal Banarsidass.

*Caitanya Caritāmṛta* of Kṛṣṇadāsa Kavirāja. 1974. *Śrī Caitanya-Caritāmṛta of Kṛṣṇadāsa Kavirāja Gosvāmī*, translated by A. C. Bhaktivedanta Swami. New York: Bhaktivedanta Book Trust.

*Caitanya Caritāmṛta* of Kṛṣṇadāsa Kavirāja. 1999. *Caitanya Caritāmṛta of Kṛṣṇadāsa Kavirāja*, translated by Edward C. Dimock, Jr. Cambridge, MA: Harvard University Press.


## ISKCON Publications


*Back to Godhead*. Periodical Issues from 1944 to 2015. Alachua, FL, and Mumbai: Bhaktivedanta Book Trust International.

Bhaktivedanta Archives. Letters, Conversations, and Documents from 1965 to 1978. Sandy Ridge, NC: Bhaktivedanta Archives.

Bhaktivedanta Swami, A. C. 1956. "The S.R.C. Catastrophe." *Back to Godhead* 3, no. 1: 1–2.

Bhaktivedanta Swami, A. C. 1990. *The Journey of Self Discovery*. Los Angeles: Bhaktivedanta Book Trust.

Bhaktivedanta Swami, A. C. 1993. "Real Advancement of Civilization." *Back to Godhead* 27, no. 5: 23.

Bhaktivedanta Swami, A. C. 1995. *The Jaladuta Diary*. Sandy Ridge, NC: Bhaktivedanta Archives.

Giriraja Dasa Brahmacari. 1971. "Krsna Returns to India." *Back to Godhead* 1, no. 43: 23–28.

ISKCON Congregational Development Ministry. 2006. *Nectar of Congregational Preaching*. Mayapur, Bengal: Bhaktivedanta Book Trust.

ISKCON Congregational Development Ministry. 2012. *Bhakti Vṛkṣa Manual*. Mayapur, Bengal: ISKCON Congregational Development Ministry.

Jayadvaita Swami. 1975. "Conversations from India: A Senior Member of the Hare Krsna Movement Tells How Krsna Consciousness Has Gone from East to West and Back Again." *Back to Godhead* 10, no. 2: 7–14.

Kalanatha Das. 1998. "Krishna Consciousness Floods the Gateway of India." *Back to Godhead, Indian edition* 32, no. 4: 17–25.

Lokanath Swami. 1983. "Ox Cart Sankirtana." *Back to Godhead* 18, no. 12: 7–9.

Lokanath Swami. 2009. "Tukarama, Saint of Pandharpur," *Back to Godhead, Indian edition*, 43, no. 1: 5–8.

Radhanath Swami. 2008. *The Journey Home*. San Rafael, CA: Mandala Publishing.

Radha Gopinath Mandir. 2000 [1994]. *A Manual of Vaisnava Etiquette and Lifestyle*. Mumbai: Gopinath Books and Sri Tulasi Trust.

Radha Gopinath Mandir. 2003. *Grhastha Manual*. Mumbai: Sri Sri Radha Gopinath Mandir.

Radha Gopinath Mandir. 2012. "Model of a Spiritual Community." Unpublished document.

Radha Gopinath Mandir. N.d. "A Report on the Social Development Programme at Radha Gopinath Temple." Mumbai: ISKCON Chowpatty.

Rosen, Steven. 2003. *The Four Principles of Freedom: The Morals and Ethics Behind Vegetarianism, Continence, Sobriety, and Honesty*. New Delhi: Rasbihari Lal and Sons.

Rosen, Steven. 2012. *Bhakti Yoga in Business: The Spiritual Journey of N.D. Desai*. New York: Folk Books.

Sacinandana Swami. 2010. *The Gayatri Book*. Schona, Czech Republic: Vasati Publishers.

Satsvarūpa dāsa Goswami. 1982–1983. Śrīla Prabhupāda-Līlāmṛta. 7 vols. Los Angeles: Bhaktivedanta Book Trust. http://www.vedabase.com/en/spl.

Singh, T. D., Ravi V. Gomatam, and World Congress for the Synthesis of Science and Religion. 1987. *Synthesis of Science and Religion: Critical Essay and Dialogues*. San Francisco: Bhaktivedanta Institute.

Tattvavit Dasa. 2015. "Reflecting on Half a Century." *Back to Godhead* November/December 2015. http://btg.krishna.com/back-godhead-novemberdecember-2015 (accessed December 17, 2015).

## Audiovisual Materials and Dramatic Productions

"Mera Joota Hai Japani." 1955. Song composed by Shankar Jaikishan, lyrics by Shailendra. Mumbai: Saregama Productions.

*The Simple Temple*. 2002. Documentary directed by Arjuna Parker. Washington, DC: Innertain Films and Avatar Studios Productions.

Drama Festival Series produced and distributed by Radha Gopinath Media Services

*Bhatrol*. DVD, 2013.

*Blind Saint Bilvamangal Thakur*. DVD, 2012.

*Devastating Sacrifice*. DVD, 2013.

*Escape of Rupa and Sanatana*. DVD, 2012.

*Gauranga Takes Sannyasa*. DVD, 2012.

*Gauranga's Prophecy*. DVD, 2012.

*Jewel of Faith*. DVD, 2014.

*King of Devotion*. DVD, 2012.

*Legacy of Love*. DVD, 2012.

*Life and Pastimes of Narottam Das Thakur*. DVD, 2012.

*Life and Pastimes of Srila Haridas Thakur*. DVD, 2012.

*Lord Caitanya's Pastimes in South India*. DVD, 2012.

*My Sweet Lord: A Tribute to Srimati Yamuna Devi and Sriman George Harrison*. DVD, 2013.
*Ray of Vishnu*. DVD, 2012.
*Salted Bread*. DVD, 2012.
*Spiritual Renaissance: Viswanath Cakravarti Thakur*. DVD, 2012.
Dramas produced by ISKCON Pune Cultural Committee
*Oh My God! Returns: Battle for the All Glorious*. DVD, 2014.
*Bina PK: A Mega Drama*. DVD, 2015.
Dramas performed at ISKCON Chowpatty's weekly Sunday program
*Chand Qazi and Chaitanya Mahaprabhu*. Live dramatic performance. Mumbai, January 19, 2014.

## Scholarly Sources

Aligarh Historians Group. 1979. "The RSS Coup in the ICHR: Its First Fruits." *Social Scientist* 7, no. 11: 56–60.

Alter, Joseph. 2021. "Pahalwan Baba Ramdev: Wrestling with Yoga and Middle-Class Masculinity in India." *Modern Asian Studies* 55, no. 4: 1359–1381.

Anderson, Kenneth. 2007. "Spiritual Solutions to Material Problems: ISKCON and the Modern World." In *The Hare Krishna Movement: Forty Years of Chant and Change*, edited by Graham Dwyer and Richard Cole, 121–133. London: I.B. Tauris.

Anker, Elisabeth. 2014. *Orgies of Feeling*. Durham, NC: Duke University Press.

Appadurai, Arjun. 1990. "Disjuncture and Difference in the Global Cultural Economy." *Theory, Culture & Society* 7, no. 2–3: 295–310.

Appadurai, Arjun. 1996. *Modernity at Large*. Minneapolis: University of Minnesota Press.

Appadurai, Arjun. 2001. *Globalization*. Durham, NC: Duke University Press.

Appadurai, Arjun. 2006. *Fear of Small Numbers: An Essay on the Geography of Anger*. Durham, NC: Duke University Press.

Appadurai, Arjun, and Carol Breckenridge. 1988. "Why Public Culture?" *Public Culture* 1, no. 1: 5–9.

Appadurai, Arjun, and Carol Breckenridge. 1995. "Public Modernity in India." In *Consuming Modernity: Public Culture in a South Asian World*, edited by Carol Breckenridge, 1–22. Minneapolis: University of Minnesota Press.

Asani, Ali S. 2002. *Ecstasy and Enlightenment: The Ismaili Devotional Literature of South Asia*. London: I.B. Tauris.

Asher, Catherine. 1992. *Architecture of Mughal India*. Cambridge: Cambridge University Press.Asher, Catherine. 2020. "Making Sense of Temples and Tirthas: Rajput Construction Under Mughal Rule." *The Medieval History Journal* 23, no. 1: 9–49.

Asher, Catherine, and Cynthia Talbot. 2006. *India Before Europe*. Cambridge: Cambridge University Press.

Aukland, Knut. 2016. "The Scientization and Academization of Jainism." *Journal of the American Academy of Religion* 84, no. 1: 192–233.

Aukland, Knut. 2018. "At the Confluence of Leisure and devotion: Hindu Pilgrimage and Domestic Tourism in India." *International Journal of Religious Tourism and Pilgrimage* 6, no. 1: 4.

Baber, Zaheer. 1996. *The Science of Empire: Scientific Knowledge, Civilization, and Colonial Rule in India*. Albany: State University of New York Press.

Banerjee, Sikata. 2005. *Make Me a Man! Masculinity, Hinduism, and Nationalism in India.* Albany, NY: SUNY Press.

Barker, Eileen. 2013. *Revisionism and Diversification in New Religious Movements.* London: Ashgate Publishing.

Beckerlegge, Gwilym. 2000. *The Ramakrishna Mission: The Making of a Modern Hindu Movement.* New Delhi: Oxford University Press.

Beckerlegge, Gwilym. 2006. *Swami Vivekananda's Legacy of Service.* New Delhi: Oxford University Press.

Beckerlegge, Gwilym. 2012. "Media Savvy or Media Averse? The Ramakrishna Math and Mission's Use of the Media in Representing Itself and a Religion Called 'Hinduism.'" In *Public Hinduisms*, edited by John Zavos et al., 398–416. London: SAGE Publications.

Benhabib, Seyla. 2002. *The Claims of Culture: Equality and Diversity in the Global Era.* Princeton, NJ, and Oxford: Princeton University Press.

Bhagavan, Manu. 2013. *The Peacemakers: India and the Quest for One World.* London: Palgrave Macmillan.

Bhatia, Varuni. 2008. "Devotional Traditions and National Culture: Recovering Gaudiya Vaishnavism in Colonial Bengal." Ph.D. diss., Columbia University.

Bhattacarya, Krishna Chandra. 1954 [1931]. "Swaraj in Ideas." *Visvabharati Quarterly* 20, 103–114.

Bhattacharya, Sabyasachi. 2012. *Talking Back: The Idea of Civilization in the Indian Nationalist Discourse.* New Delhi: Oxford University Press.

Bialecki, Jon. 2017. *A Diagram for Fire: Miracles and Variation in an American Charismatic Movement.* Oakland: University of California Press.

Bilgrami, Akeel. 2015. "Mentalities of the Non-West as a Source of Swaraj: Lessons from Gandhi." Keynote Address, Rethinking Svaraj Conference, Manipal Centre for Philosophy and Humanities, New Delhi, January 17, 2015.

Blank, Jonah. 2001. *Mullahs on the Mainstream: Islam and Modernity Among the Daudi Bohras.* Chicago: University of Chicago Press.

Bloomer, Kristin. 2018. *Possessed by the Virgin: Hinduism, Roman Catholicism, and Marian Possession in South India.* New York: Oxford University Press.

Bose, Neilesh. 2014. *Recasting the Region: Language, Culture, and Islam in Colonial Bengal.* New Delhi: Oxford University Press.

Bromley, David G., and Larry Shinn, eds. 1989. *Krishna Consciousness in the West.* Lewisburg, PA: Bucknell University Press.

Broo, Mäns. 2003. *As Good as God: The Guru in Gaudiya Vaisnavism.* Turku, Finland: Abo Akademi University Press.

Brooks, Charles. 1989. *Hare Krishnas in India.* Princeton, NJ: Princeton University Press.

Brooks, Charles. 1990. "Hare Krishna, Radhe Shyam: The Cross-Cultural Dynamics of Mystical Emotions in Brindaban." In *Divine Passions: The Social Construction of Emotion in India*, edited by Owen Lynch, 262–286. Berkeley: University of California Press.

Brosius, Christiane. 2004. *Empowering Visions: The Politics of Representation in Hindu Nationalism.* London: Anthem Press.

Brosius, Christiane. 2010. *India's Middle Class: New Forms of Urban Leisure, Consumption and Prosperity.* London: Routledge India.

Brosius, Christiane. 2012. "The Perfect World of BAPS: Media and Urban Dramaturgies in a Globalised Context." In *Public Hinduisms*, edited by John Zavos et al., 440–462. London: SAGE Publications.

Bryant, Edwin F., ed. 2007. *Krishna: A Sourcebook*. New York: Oxford University Press.

Bryant, Edwin F., and Maria L. Ekstrand, eds. 2004. *The Hare Krishna Movement: The Postcharismatic Fate of a Religious Transplant*. New York: Columbia University Press.

Bubandt, Nils. 2014. *The Empty Seashell: Witchcraft and Doubt on an Indonesian Island*. Ithaca, NY, and London: Cornell University Press.

Burchett, Patton. 2019. *A Genealogy of Devotion: Bhakti, Tantra, Yoga, and Sufism in North India*. New York: Columbia University Press.

Busch, Alison. 2011. *Poetry of Kings: The Classical Hindi Literature of Mughal India*. New York: Oxford University Press.

Casanova, Jose. 1994 [1986]. *Public Religions in the Modern World*. Chicago: University of Chicago Press.

Casanova, Jose. 2001. "Religion, the New Millennium, and Globalization." *Sociology of Religion* 62, no. 4: 415–441.

Casanova, Jose. 2013. "Religious Associations, Religious Innovations and Denominational Identities in Contemporary Global Cities." In *Topographies of Faith: Religion in Urban Spaces*, edited by Irene Becci, Marian Burchandt, and Jose Casanova, 114–127. Leiden: Brill.

Chadha, Kalyani, and Anandam P. Kavoori. 2008. "Exoticized, Marginalized, Demonized: The Muslim 'Other' in Indian Cinema." In *Global Bollywood*, edited by Aswin Punathambekar and Anandam P. Kavoori, 131–145. New York: New York University Press.

Chakrabarty, Dipesh. 2002. *Habitations of Modernity: Essays in the Wake of Subaltern Studies*. Chicago: University of Chicago Press.

Chakravarti, Ramakanta. 1985. *Vaisnavism in Bengal, 1486–1900*. Calcutta: Sanskrit Pustak Bhandar.

Chatterjee, Partha. 1993. *The Nation and Its Fragments: Colonial and Postcolonial Histories*. Princeton, NJ: Princeton University Press.

Chidester, David. 2013. *Empire of Religion: Imperialism and Comparative Religion*. Chicago: University of Chicago Press.

Chryssides, George, and Margaret Wikins. 2006. *A Reader in New Religious Movements*. London: Continuum.

Cort, John E. 2000. "Defining Jainism: Reform in the Jain Tradition." In *Jain Doctrine and Practice: Academic Perspectives*, edited by Joseph T. O'Connell, 165–191. Toronto, Canada: University of Toronto Press.

Dalmia, Vasudha. 2001. "Forging Community: The Guru in a Seventeenth-Century Vaisnava Hagiography." In *Charisma and Canon: Essays on the Religious History of the Indian Subcontinent*, edited by Vasudha Dalmia, Angelika Malinar, and Martin Christof, 129–154. New Delhi: Oxford University Press.

Dalmia, Vasudha, ed. 2003. *Orienting India: European Knowledge Formation in the Eighteenth and Nineteenth Centuries*. New Delhi: Three Essays Collective.

Daner, Francine Jeanne. 1976. *The American Children of Krishna: A Study of the Krishna Movement*. Dallas: Holt, Rinehart, and Winston.

Das, Rahul Peter. 1997. *Essays on Vaisnavism in Bengal*. Calcutta: Firma KLM.

Das, Shukavak. 1999. *Hindu Encounter with Modernity: Kedarnath Datta Bhaktivinoda, Vaisnava Theologian*. Los Angeles: Sanskrit Religions Institute.

De, Sushil Kumar. 1986 [1961]. *Early History of the Vaisnava Faith and Movement in Bengal*. Calcutta: Calcutta Oriental Press.

Deadwyler, William. 1996. "The Devotee and the Deity: Living a Personalistic Theology." In *Gods of Flesh, Gods of Stone*, edited by Joanne Punzo Waghorne and Norman Cutler, 69–88. New York: Columbia University Press.

Deadwyler, William. 2007. "Bringing the Lord's Song to A Strange Land: Srila Prabhupada's Strategy of 'Cultural Conquest' and Its Prospects." In *The Hare Krishna Movement: Forty Years of Chant and Change*, edited by Graham Dwyer and Richard Cole, 103–120. London: I.B. Tauris.

Delmonico, Neal G. 1990. "Sacred Rapture: A Study of the Religious Aesthetic of Rupa Gosvamin." Ph.D. diss., University of Chicago.

Delmonico, Neal. 1993. "Rupa Gosvamin: His Life, Family, and Early Vraja Commentators." *Journal of Vaisnava Studies* 1, no. 2: 133–157.

DeNapoli, Antoinette E. 2014. *Real Sadhus Sing to God: Gender, Asceticism, and Vernacular Religion in Rajasthan.* New York: Oxford University Press.

Dimitrova, Diana. 2008. *Gender, Religion, and Modern Hindi Drama.* Quebec: McGill-Queens University Press.

Dimock, Edward C., Jr. 1989. *The Place of the Hidden Moon: Erotic Mysticism in the Vaisnava-Sahajiya Cult of Bengal.* Chicago: University of Chicago Press.

Dodson, Michael S., and Brian A. Hatcher, eds. 2012. *Trans-Colonial Modernities in South Asia.* Oxon: Routledge.

Dwyer, Graham, and Richard J. Cole, eds. 2007. *The Hare Krishna Movement: Forty Years of Chant and Change.* London: I.B. Tauris.

Dwyer, Graham, and Richard J. Cole, eds. 2013. *Hare Krishna in the Modern World: Reflections by Distinguished Academics and Scholarly Devotees.* London: Arktos.

Eck, Diana. 1979. "Krsna Consciousness in Historical Perspective." *Back to Godhead* 14, no. 10: 26–29.

Eisenstadt, S. N. 2000. "Multiple Modernities." *Daedalus* 129, no. 1: 1–29.

Elison, William. 2018. *The Neighborhood of Gods: The Sacred and the Visible at the Margins of Mumbai.* Chicago: University of Chicago Press.

Entwistle, Alan W. 1987. *Braj: A Centre of Krishna Pilgrimage.* Groningen: Egbert Forsten.

Eschmann, Anncharlott, Hermann Kulke, and Gaya Charan Tripathi, eds. 1978. *The Cult of Jagannath and the Regional Tradition of Odisha.* New Delhi: Manohar Press.

Fahy, John. 2019. *Becoming Vaishnava in an Ideal Vedic City.* New York and Oxford: Berghahn Books.

Fernandes, Jason Keith. 2020. *Citizenship in a Caste Polity: Religion, Language, and Belonging in Goa.* Hyderabad: Orient Blackswan.

Fernandes, Leela, and Patrick Heller. 2006. "Hegemonic Aspirations." *Critical Asian Studies* 38, no. 4: 495–522.Fernandes, Naresh. 2013. *A City Adrift: A Short Biography of Bombay.* New Delhi: Aleph Book Company.

Fernandes, Naresh, et al. 2012. *Taj Mahal Foxtrot: The Story of Bombay's Jazz Age.* New Delhi: Lustre Press, Roli Books.

Fletcher, John. 2013. *Preaching to Convert: Evangelical Outreach and Performance Activism in a Secular Age.* Ann Arbor: University of Michigan Press.

Flueckiger, Joyce Burkhalter. 2006. *In Amma's Healing Room: Gender and Vernacular Islam in South India.* Bloomington: Indiana University Press.

Freitag, Sandra. 2007. "More than Meets the (Hindu) Eye" The Public Arena as a Space for Alternative Visions." In *Picturing the Nation: Iconographies of Modern India*, edited by Richard Davis, 35–75. Hyderabad, India: Orient Longman.

Frykenberg, Robert Eric. 2001 [1989]. "The Emergence of Modern 'Hinduism' as a Concept and as an Institution: A Reappraisal with Special Reference to South India." In *Hinduism Reconsidered*, edited by Gunther Sontheimer and Hermann Kulke, 29–50. New Delhi: Manohar Publishers.

Fuller, C. J., and John Harriss. 2005. "Globalizing Hinduism: A 'Traditional' Guru and Modern Businessmen in Chennai." In *Globalizing India: Perspectives from Below*, edited by Jackie Assayag and C.J. Fuller, 211–234. London: Anthem Press.

Fuller, Jason D. 2003. "Re-membering the Tradition: Bhaktivinoda Ṭhākura's Sajjanaṭosanī and the Construction of a Middle-Class Vaiṣṇava Sampradāya in Nineteenth-Century Bengal." In *Hinduism in Public and Private: Reform, Hindutva, Gender, and Sampraday*, edited by Anthony Copley, 173–210. Oxford: Oxford University Press.

Fuller, Jason D. 2004. "Religion, Class, and Power: Bhaktivinoda Thakur and the Transformation of Religious Authority among the Gaudiya Vaisnavas in Nineteenth-Century Bengal." Ph.D., University of Pennsylvania.

Fuller, Jason D. 2009. "Modern Hinduism and the Middle Class: Beyond Revival in the Historiography of Colonial India." *Journal of Hindu Studies* 2, no. 2: 160–178.

Gandhi, Mohandas. 1997 (1910). "Hind Swaraj." In *Gandhi: "Hind Swaraj" and Other Writings*, edited by Anthony J. Parel. Cambridge Texts in Modern Politics. Cambridge: Cambridge University Press.

Gandhi, Mohandas K. 1965. *My Varnashrama Dharma*. Edited by Anand T. Hingorani. Bombay: Bharatiya Vidya Bhavan.

Ganneri, Namrata, and Atreyee Sen. 2012. "From Jauhar to Jijabai: Samiti and Sena Women in Mumbai, and the Reconfiguring of 'History.'" In *Public Hinduisms*, edited by John Zavos, et al., 283–302. London: SAGE Publications.

Ghassem-Fachandi, Parvis. 2012. *Pogrom in Gujarat: Hindu Nationalism and Anti-Muslim Violence in India*. Princeton, NJ: Princeton University Press.

Gold, Daniel. 2005. "Epilogue: Elevated Gurus, Concrete Traditions, and the Problem of Western Devotees." In *Gurus in America*, edited by Thomas A. Forsthoefel and Cynthia Ann Humes, 219–226. Albany: State University of New York Press.

Goldberg, Philip. 2010. *American Veda*. New York: Harmony Books.

Gole, Nilufer. 1996. *The Forbidden Modern: Civilization and Veiling*. Ann Arbor: University of Michigan Press.

Gonzalez-Reimann, Luis. 2014. "The Yugas: Their Importance in India and Their Use by Western Intellectuals and Esoteric and New Age Writers." *Religion Compass* 8, no. 12: 357–370.

Gooptu, Nandini. 2017. "Religious Myths Retold: Masters and Servants in India's Corporate Culture." In *Religion and the Morality of the Market*, edited by Daromir Rudnyckyj and Filippo Osella, 72–93. Cambridge: Cambridge University Press.

Gottschalk, Peter. 2013. *Religion, Science, and Empire: Classifying Hinduism and Islam in British India*. New York: Oxford University Press.

Green, Nile. 2004. "Oral Competition Narratives of Muslim and Hindu Saints in the Deccan." *Asian Folklore Studies* 63, no. 2: 221–242.

Green, Nile. 2013. *Bombay Islam: The Religious Economy of the West Indian Ocean, 1840–1915*. Los Angeles: University of California Press.

Greenough, Paul. 1995. "Nation, Economy, and Tradition Displayed: The Indian Crafts Museum, New Delhi." In *Consuming Modernity: Public Culture in a South Asian World*, edited by Carol Breckenridge, 216–248. Minneapolis: University of Minnesota Press.

Grewal, Zareena. 2014. *Islam is a Foreign Country: American Muslims and the Global Crisis of Authority*. New York: NYU Press.

Gupta, Ravi. 2007. *The Caitanya Vaisnava Vedanta of Jiva Gosvami*. Oxford: Routledge.

Gupta, Ravi, ed. 2014. *Caitanya Vaisnava Philosophy: Tradition, Reason and Devotion*. Burlington, VT: Ashgate Publishing.

Haberman, David. 1994. *Journey through the Twelve Forests: An Encounter with Krishna*. Oxford and New York: Oxford University Press.

Haberman, David. 2001 [1988]. *Acting as a Way of Salvation: A Study of Rāgānugā Bhakti Sādhana*. Delhi: Motilal Banarsidass.

Halbfass, Wilhelm. 1990 [1988]. *India and Europe: An Essay in Philosophical Understanding*. Delhi: Motilal Banarsidass.

Hancock, Mary. 2002. "Modernities Remade: Hindu Temples and Their Publics in Southern India." *Environment and Planning D: Society and Space* 20: 693–718.

Hancock, Mary. 2008. *The Politics of Heritage from Madras to Chennai*. Bloomington and Indianapolis: Indiana University Press.

Hansen, Thomas Blom. 1996. "Globalisation and Nationalist Imaginations: Hindutva's Promise of Equality through Difference." *Economic and Political Weekly* 31, no. 10: 603–616.

Hansen, Thomas Blom. 2004. "Politics as Permanent Performance: The Production of Political Authority in the Locality." In *The Politics of Cultural Mobilization in India*, edited by John Zavos, Andrew Wyatt, and Vernon Hewitt, 19–36. New Delhi: Oxford University Press.

Hardy, Friedhelm E. 1983. *Viraha-Bhakti: The Early History of Krishna Devotion in South India*. Delhi: Oxford University Press.

Hasan, Mushirul. 2007. "The BJP's Intellectual Agenda: Textbooks and Imagined History." In *Hindu Nationalism and Governance*, edited by John McGuire and Ian Copland, 226–252. Delhi: Oxford University Press.

Hatcher, Brian. 1999. *Eclecticism and Modern Hindu Discourse*. New York: Oxford University Press.

Hatcher, Brian. 2007. *Bourgeois Hinduism, or Faith of the Modern Vedantists: Rare Discourses from Early Colonial Bengal*. Oxford: Oxford University Press.

Hatcher, Brian. 2020. *Hinduism Before Reform*. Cambridge, MA: Harvard University Press.

Hawley, John Stratton, with Shrivatsa Goswami. 1981. *At Play with Krishna: Pilgrimage Dramas from Brindavan*. Princeton, NJ: Princeton University Press.

Hawley, John Stratton. 2015. *A Storm of Songs: India and the Idea of the Bhakti Movement*. Cambridge, MA: Harvard University Press.

Hawley, John Stratton. 2020. *Krishna's Playground: Vrindavan in the 21st Century*. New York: Oxford University Press.

Heehs, Peter. 2003. "'The Centre of the Religious Life of the World': Spiritual Universalism and Cultural Nationalism." In *Hinduism in Public and Private: Reform, Hindutva, Gender, and Sampraday*, edited by Anthony Copley, 66–83. New Delhi: Oxford University Press.

Heifetz, Daniel. 2019. "Religion, Science, and the Middle Class in the All World Gayatri Pariwar." *International Journal of Hindu Studies* 23, no. 1: 27–42.

Heifetz, Daniel. 2021. *The Science of Satyug: Class, Charisma, and Vedic Revivalism in the All World Gayatri Pariwar*. Albany: SUNY Press.

Held, David, et al. 1999. *Global Transformations: Politics, Economics, and Culture*. Stanford, CA: Stanford University Press.

Hess, Linda, and Richard Schechner. 1977. "The Ramlila of Ramnagar." *Drama Review* 21, no. 3: 51–82.

Holdrege, Barbara A. 1999. "What Have Brahmins to Do with Rabbis? Embodied Communities and Paradigms of Religious Tradition." *Shofar: An Interdisciplinary Journal of Jewish Studies* 17, no. 3: 23–50.

Holdrege, Barbara A. 2003. "From the Religious Marketplace to the Academy: Negotiating the Politics of Identity." *Journal of Vaishnava Studies* 11, no. 2: 113–142.

Holdrege, Barbara A. 2015. *Bhakti and Embodiment: Fashioning Divine Bodies and Devotional Bodies in Krishna Bhakti*. London and New York: Routledge.

Hopkins, Thomas. 2007. "ISKCON's Search for Self-Identity: Reflections by a Historian of Religions." In *The Hare Krishna Movement: Forty Years of Chant and Change*, edited by Graham Dwyer and Richard J. Cole, 171–192. London: I.B. Tauris.

Horstmann, Monika. 2001. "Charisma, Transfer of Charisma, and Canon in North Indian Bhakti." In *Charisma and Canon: Essays on the Religious History of the Indian Subcontinent*, edited by Vasudha Dalmia, Angelika Malinar, and Martin Christof, 171–182. New Delhi: Oxford University Press.

Hughes, Stephen. 2007. "Mythologicals and Modernity: Contesting Silent Cinema in South India." *Journal of Sacred Texts and Contemporary Worlds* 1, nos. 2–3: 207–235.

Iwamura, Jane Naomi. 2011. *Virtual Orientalism: Asian Religions and American Popular Culture*. New York: Oxford University Press.

Jaffrelot, Christophe. 2004. "From Indian Territory to Hindu Bhoomi: The Ethnicization of Nation-State Mapping in India." In *The Politics of Cultural Mobilization in India*, edited by John Zavos, Andrew Wyatt, and Vernon Hewitt, 197–215. Oxford, New York: Oxford University Press.

James, Paul, and Manfred Steger. 2014. "A Genealogy of 'Globalization': The Career of a Concept." *Globalizations* 11, no. 4: 417–434.

Janson, Marloes. 2014. *Islam, Youth, and Modernity in the Gambia: The Tablighi Jama'at*. New York: Cambridge University Press.

Jordens, J. T. F. 1978. *Dayananda Sarasvati: His Life and Ideas*. Delhi: Oxford University Press.

Judah, J. Stillson. 1974. *Hare Krishna and the Counter Culture*. New York: John Wiley and Sons.

Juergensmeyer, Mark. 1991. *Radhasoami Reality: The Logic of a Modern Faith*. Princeton, NJ: Princeton University Press.

Kamdar, Mira. 2000. *Motiba's Tattoos: A Granddaughter's Journey Into Her Indian Family's Past*. New York: PublicAffairs.

Kanungo, Pralay. 2011. "Marginalised in a Syncretic City: Muslims in Cuttack." In *Muslims in Indian Cities: Trajectories of Marginalization*, edited by Laurent Gayer and Christophe Jaffrelot, 237–262. London: Hurst.

Karapanagiotis, Nicole. 2021. *Branding Bhakti: Krishna Consciousness and the Makeover of a Movement*. Indianapolis: Indiana University Press.

Karlekar, Malavika. 2005. *Re-visioning the past: early photography in Bengal, 1875–1915*. New York: Oxford University Press.

Kaur, Raminder. 2003. *Performative Politics and the Cultures of Hinduism: Public Uses of Religion in Western India*. New Delhi: Permanent Black.

Kaur, Raminder. 2004. "Fire in the Belly: The Mobilization of the Ganapati Festival in Maharashtra." In *The Politics of Cultural Mobilization in India*, edited by John Zavos, Andrew Wyatt, and Vernon Hewitt, 37–70. New Delhi: Oxford University Press.

Kaur, Raminder. 2007. "Spectacles of Nationalism in the Ganapati Utsav of Maharashtra." In: *Picturing the Nation*, edited by Richard Davis, 207–241. New Delhi: Orient Longman.

Kaur, Ravinder. 2020. *Brand New Nation: Captialist Dreams and Nationalist Designs in Twenty-First Century India*. Stanford, CA: Stanford University Press.

Kent, Alexandra. 2000a. *Ambiguity and the Modern Order. The Sathya Sai Baba Movement in Malaysia*. Göteborg: Department of Social Anthropology, University of Göteborg.

Kent, Alexandra. 2000b. "Creating Divine Unity: Chinese Recruitment in the Sathya Sai Baba Movement of Malaysia." *Journal of Contemporary Religion* 15, no. 1: 5–27.

Khalidi, Omar. 2008. "Hinduising India: Secularism in Practice." *Third World Quarterly* 29, no. 8: 1545–1562.

Khan, Aisha. 2004. *Callalo Nation: Metaphors of Race and Religious Identity among South Asians in Trinidad*. Durham, NC: Duke University Press.

Khan, Dominique-Sila, and Zawahir Moir. 1999. "Coexistence and Communalism: The Shrine of Pirana in Gujarat." *South Asia* 22, Special Issue: 133–154.

Khanduri, Ritu. 2012. " 'Does This Offend You?' Hindu Visuality in the United States." In *Public Hinduisms*, edited by John Zavos et al., 348–364. London: SAGE Publications.

Khilnani, Sunil. 1997. *The Idea of India*. New York: Farrar, Straus, and Giroux.

Kim, Hanna. 2009. "Public Engagement and Personal Desires: BAPS Swaminarayan Temples and Their Contribution to the Discourses on Religion." *International Journal of Hindu Studies* 13, no. 3: 357–390.

King, Anna S. 2007. "For Love of Krishna: Forty Years of Chanting." In *The Hare Krishna Movement: Forty Years of Chant and Change*, edited by Graham Dwyer and Richard Cole, 134–170. London: I.B. Tauris.

King, Anna S. 2013. "Interview with Dr. Anna S. King." In *Hare Krishna in the Modern World: Reflections by Distinguished Academics and Scholarly Devotees*, edited by Graham Dwyer and Richard J. Cole, 36–57. London: Arktos.

King, Richard. 1999. *Orientalism and Religion: Postcolonial Theory, India and "the Mystic East"*. London: Routledge.

Knott, Kim. 1986. *My Sweet Lord: The Hare Krishna Movement*. Wellingborough: Aquarian.

Knott, Kim. 1993. "Contemporary Theological Trends in the Hare Krsna Movement: A Theology of Religions." *ISKCON Communications Journal* 1, no. 1: 44–51.

Knott, Kim. 2000. "In Every Town and Village: Adaptive Strategies in the Communication of Krishna Consciousness in the UK, the First Thirty Years." *Social Compass* 47, no. 2: 153–166.

Koch, Ebba. 1991. *Mughal Architecture: An Outline of Its History and Development, 1526–1858*. Munich: Prestel.

Koch, Ebba. 2006. *The Complete Taj Mahal*. London: Thames & Hudson.

Krishnan, Prabha. 1990. "In the Idiom of Loss: Ideology of Motherhood in Television Serials." *Economic and Political Weekly* 25, nos. 42–43: WS103–WS116.

Kurien, Prema. 2012. "What Is American about American Hinduism? Hindu Umbrella Organizations in the U.S. in Comparative Perspective." In *Public Hinduisms*, edited by Zavos et al., 90–111. London: Sage Publications.

Larios, Borayin. 2019. *Embodying the Vedas: Traditional Vedic Schools of Contemporary Maharashtra*. Warsaw and Berlin: De Gruyter Open Ltd.

Lee, Joel. 2021. *Deceptive Majority: Dalits, Hinduism, and Underground Religion*. Cambridge: Cambridge University Press.

Lorenzen, David. 2004. "Bhakti." In *The Hindu World*, edited by Sushil Mittal and Gene Thursby, 185–209. New York: Routledge.

Lucia, Amanda. 2014. *Reflections of Amma: Devotees in a Global Embrace*. Berkeley and Los Angeles: University of California Press.

Lucia, Amanda. 2020. *White Utopias: The Religious Exoticism of Transformational Festivals*. Berkeley and Los Angeles: University of California Press.

Lutgendorf, Philip. 1991. *The Life of a Text: Performing the Ramcaritmanas of Tulsidas*. Berkeley: University of California Press.

Lutjeharms, Rembert. 2018. *A Vaisnava Poet in Early Modern Bengal: Kavikarnapura's Splendour of Speech*. New York: Oxford University Press.

Manring, Rebecca. 2011. *The Fading Light of Advaita Acarya: Three Hagiographies*. New York: Oxford University Press.

Masuzawa, Tomoko. 2005. *The Invention of World Religions: Or, How European Universalism Was Preserved in the Language of Pluralism*. Chicago: University of Chicago Press.

Mayaram, Shail. 2004. "Hindu and Islamic Transnational Religious Movements." *Economic and Political Weekly* 39, no. 1: 80–88.

McCartney, Patrick. 2011. "Spoken Sanskrit in a Gujarat Ashram." *Journal of the Oriental Society of Australia* 43: 61–82.

McGuire, M. L. 2011. "How to Sit, How to Stand:" Bodily Practice and the New Urban Middle Class." In *A Companion to the Anthropology of India*, edited by Isabelle Clark-Decès, 117–136. Oxford: Wiley-Blackwell.

McKean, Lise. 1996. *Divine Enterprises: Gurus and the Hindu Nationalist Movement*. Chicago: University of Chicago Press.

McLain, Karline. 2009. *India's Immortal Comic Books*. Bloomington and Indianapolis: Indiana University Press.

Mehta, Uday, and Akshayakumar Ramanlal Desai. 1993. *Modern Godmen in India: A Sociological Appraisal*. Bombay: Popular Prakashan.

Melton, J. Gordon. 1989. "The Attitude of Americans toward Hinduism from 1883 to 1983 with Special Reference to the International Society for Krishna Consciousness." In *Krishna Consciousness in the West*, edited by David G. Bromley and Larry Shinn, 79–101. Lewisburg, PA: Bucknell University Press.

Menon, Dilip, ed. 2006. *Cultural History of Modern India*. New Delhi: Social Science Press.

Menon, Kalyani. 2012. *Everyday Nationalism: Women of the Hindu Right in India*. Philadelphia: University of Pennsylvania Press.

Michael, R. Blake. 1989. "Heaven, West Virginia: Legitimation Techniques of the New Vrindaban Community." In *Krishna Consciousness in the West*, edited by David G. Bromley and Larry Shinn, 188–214. Lewisburg, PA: Bucknell University Press.

Miller, James William. 2005. "Wellness: The History and Development of a Concept." In *Spektrum Freizeit 1*, 84–102. Universität Duisburg Essen Publications.

Mishra, Pankaj. 2007. *Temptations of the West: How to Be Modern in India, Pakistan, Tibet, and Beyond*. New York: Picador.

Moodie, Deonnie. 2019. *The Making of a Modern Temple and a Hindu City: Kalighat and Kolkata*. Oxford: Oxford University Press.

Moodie, Deonnie. 2021. "Corporate Hinduism: An argument for attention to sites of authority in a nascent field of research." *Religion Compass* 15, no. 2: 1–9.

Mukherjee, Tarapada, and Irfan Habib. 1987. "Akbar and the Temples of Mathura and its Environs" *Proceedings of the Indian History Congress* 48: 234–250.

Mukherjee, Tarapada, and Irfan Habib. 1988. "The Mughal Administration and the Temples of Vrindavan During the Reigns of Jahangir and Shahjahan." *Proceedings of the Indian History Congress* 49: 287–300.

Naim, C. M. 2012. "Interrogating 'The East,' 'Culture,' and 'Loss,'" in Abdul Halim Sharar's Guzashta Lakhna'u." In *Indo-Muslim Cultures in Transition*, edited by Alka Patel and Karen Leonard, 189–204. Leiden: Brill.

Nanda, Meera. 2003. *Prophets Facing Backwards: Postmodern Critiques of Science and Hindu Nationalism in India*. New Brunswick, NJ: Rutgers University Press.

Nanda, Meera. 2009. *The God Market: How Globalization Is Making India More Hindu.* Gurgaon, India: Random House India.

Nandy, Ashis. 1988. *The Intimate Enemy: Loss and Recovery of Self under Colonialism.* Delhi: Oxford University Press.

Napolitano, Valentina. 2016. *Migrant Hearts and the Atlantic Return: Transnationalism and the Roman Catholic Church.* New York: Fordham University Press.

Naregal, Veena. 2002. *Language Politics, Elites, and the Public Sphere: Western India Under Colonialism.* London: Anthem Press.

Nicholas, Ralph W. 2001. "Islam and Vaishnavism in the Environment of Rural Bengal." In *Understanding the Bengal Muslims: Interpretative Essays*, edited by Rafiuddin, Ahmed, 52–70. New Delhi: Oxford University Press.

Novetzke, Christian Lee. 2008. *Religion and Public Memory: A Cultural History of Saint Namdev in India.* New York: Columbia University Press.

Nye, Malory. 2001. *Multiculturalism and Minority Religions in Britain: Krishna Consciousness, Religious Freedom, and the Politics of Location.* Richmond Surrey: Curzon Press.

O'Connell, Joseph T. 1993. *Religious Movements and Social Structure: The Case of Chaitanya's Vaisnavas in Bengal.* Shimla: Indian Institute of Advanced Study.

O'Connell, Joseph T. 2018. *Caitanya Vaiṣṇavism in Bengal: Social Impact and Historical Implications*. Oxford: Routledge.

Okita, Kiyokazu. 2012. "Who Are the Madhvas? A Controversy over the Public Representation of the Madhva Sampradaya." In *Public Hinduisms*, edited by John Zavos et al., 210–223. London: SAGE Publications.

Okita, Kiyokazu. 2014. *Hindu Theology in Early Modern South Asia.* Oxford: Oxford University Press.

Olivelle, Patrick. 2005. *Manu's Code of Law.* Oxford: Oxford University Press.

Oliver, Paul. 2014. *Hinduism and the 1960s: The Rise of a Counterculture.* London: Bloomsbury Press.

Ong, Aihwa. 1999. *Flexible Citizenship: The Cultural Logics of Transnationality.* Durham, NC: Duke University Press.

Oommen, T. K. 1986. "Insiders and Outsiders in India: Primordial Collectivism and Cultural Pluralism in Nation-Building." *International Sociology* 1, no. 1: 53–74.

Orsi, Robert A. 1985. *The Madonna of 115th Street: Faith and Community in Italian Harlem, 1880–1950.* New Haven, CT, London: Yale University Press.

Pandey, Gyanendra. 1990. *The Construction of Communalism in Northern India.* New Delhi: Oxford University Press.

Penner, Hans H., and Edward A. Yonan. 1972. "Is a Science of Religion Possible?" *Journal of Religion* 52, no. 2: 107–133.

Pérez, Elizabeth. 2016. *Religion in the Kitchen: Cooking, talking, and the Making of a Black Atlantic Tradition.* New York: NYU Press.

Pinch, William. 1996. *Peasants and Monks in British India.* Berkeley and Los Angeles: University of California Press.

Poling, Tommy H., and Frank Kenny. 1986. *The Hare Krishna Character Type: A Study of Sensate Personality.* Lewiston, NY: Edward Mellen Press.

Poonam, Snigdha. 2018. *Dreamers: How Young Indians Are Changing Their World.* Gurgaon: Penguin Random House India.

Prakash, Gyan. 1999a. *Another Reason: Science and the Imagination of Modern India.* Princeton, NJ: Princeton University Press.

Prakash, Gyan. 1999b. "The Image of the Archaic." In *Social History of Science in Colonial India,* edited by S. Irfan Habib and Dhruv Raina, 252–290. New Delhi: Oxford University Press.

Prakash, Gyan. 2010. *Mumbai Fables.* Princeton, NJ: Princeton University Press.

Pranskeviciute, Rasa, and Tadas Juras. 2014. "Acting in the Underground: Life as a Hare Krishna Devotee in the Soviet Republic of Lithuania (1979–1989)." *Religion and Society in Central and Eastern Europe* 7, no. 1: 3–22.

Puttick, Elizabeth. 1997. *Women in New Religions: In Search of Community, Sexuality, and Spiritual Power.* New York: St. Martins Press.

Raina, Dhruv, and S. Irfan Habib. 2004. *Domesticating Modern Science: A Social History of Science and Culture in Colonial India.* New Delhi: Tulika Books.

Raj, Kapil. 2007. *Relocating Modern Science: Circulation and Construction of Knowledge in South Asia and Europe, 1650–1900.* New York: Palgrave Macmillan.

Rajagopal, Arvind. 2001. *Politics After Television: Hindu Nationalism and the Reshaping of the Public in India.* Cambridge: Cambridge University Press.

Ramanujan, A. K. 1989. "Classics Lost and Found." In *Contemporary Indian Tradition: Voices on Culture, Nature, and the Challenge of Change,* edited by Carla Borden, 131–148. Delhi: Oxford University Press.

Ramaswamy, Sumathi. 1997. *Passions of the Tongue: Language Devotion in Tamil Nadu.* Berkeley: University of California Press.

Ramaswamy, Sumathi. 2007. "Body Politic(s): Maps and Mother Goddesses in Modern India." In *Picturing the Nation: Iconographies of Modern India,* edited by Richard Davis, 32–50. Hyderabad, India: Orient Longman.

Ramberg, Lucinda. 2014. *Given to the Goddess: South Indian Devadasis and the Sexuality of Religion.* Durham: Duke University Press.

Ramey, Stephen. 2008. *Hindu, Sufi, or Sikh: Contested Practices and Identifications of Sindhu Hindus in India and Beyond.* New York: Palgrave Macmillan.

Ray, Sugata. 2012. "In the Name of Krishna: The Cultural Landscape of a North Indian Pilgrimage Town." PhD diss., University of Minnesota.

Rich, Adrienne. 1972. "When We Dead Awaken: Writing as Re-Vision." *College English* 34, no. 1 (October): 18–30.

Robbins, Thomas. 2001. "Introduction: Alternative Religions, the State, and the Globe." *Nova Religio: The Journal of Alternative and Emergent Religions* 4, no. 2: 172–186.

Robison, Claire. 2014. "Bhaktivinoda Ṭhākura's Nāma Haṭṭa System: Community Development and the Modern Missionary Roots of a Gauḍīya Vaiṣṇava Community." *Journal of Vaishnava Studies* 23, no. 1: 109–136.

Robison, Claire. 2016. "Daiva Varṇāśrama Dharma and the Formation of Modern Vaiṣṇava Subjects in ISKCON Mumbai." *Nidan: The Journal for the International Study of Hinduism* 28, no. 2: 69–87.

Robison, Claire. 2019. *PK Hamara Hai*: Religious Nationalism and the Defense of *Dharm* in Media Counterpublics." *Studies in South Asian Film & Media* 9, no. 2 (January 2019): 143–157.

Robison, Claire. 2021. "ISKCON-Christian Encounters: A Story in Three Acts." In *The Handbook of Hindu-Christian Relations*, edited by Michelle V Roberts and Chad Bauman, 193–205. New York: Routledge.

Robison, Claire. 2023. "Urban Devis: Fashioning Lay Women's Holiness in Krishna Bhakti Networks. *Religions* 14, no. 6: 786.Rochford, E. Burke. 1985. *Hare Krishna in America*. New Brunswick, NJ: Rutgers University Press.

Rochford, E. Burke. 2007. *Hare Krishna Transformed*. New York: New York University Press.

Rochford, E. Burke. 2013. "Sociological Reflections on the History and Development of the Hare Krishna Movement." In *Hare Krishna in the Modern World: Reflections by Distinguished Academics and Scholarly Devotees*, edited by Graham Dwyer and Richard J. Cole, 11–35. London: Arktos.

Rochford, E. Burke. 2018. "Aligning Hare Krishna: Political Activists, Hippies, and Hindus." *Nova Religio* 22, no. 1: 34–58.

Rochford, E. Burke, and Kendra Bailey. 2006. "Almost Heaven: Leadership, Decline and the Transformation of New Vrindaban." *Nova Religio* 9, no. 3: 6–23.

Rook-Koepsel, Emily. 2021. *Democracy and Unity in India: Understanding the All India Phenomenon, 1940–1960*. London and New York: Routledge.

Rosen, Steven. 2007. "1965 was a Very Good Year and 2005 Is Better Still." In *The Hare Krishna Movement: Forty Years of Chant and Change*, edited by Graham Dwyer and Richard Cole, 11–25. London: I.B. Tauris.

Rosen, Steven. 2012. *Bhakti Yoga in Business: The Spiritual Journey of N.D. Desai*. New York: Folk Books.

Roy, Srirupa. 2007. *Beyond Belief: India and the Politics of Postcolonial Nationalism*. Durham, NC: Duke University Press.

Said, Edward. 1977. *Orientalism*. London: Penguin Books.

Salomon, Richard, ed. and trans. 1985.*The Bridge to the Three Holy Cities: The Sāmānya-praghaṭṭaka of Nārāyaṇa Bhaṭṭa's Tristhalīsetu*. Delhi: Motilal Banarsidass.

Sanford, A. Whitney. 2005. "Shifting the Center: Yakṣas on the Margins of Contemporary Practice." *Journal of the American Academy of Religion* 73, no. 1: 89–110.

Sardella, Ferdinando. 2013. *Modern Hindu Personalism*. New York: Oxford University Press.

Sarkar, Tanika. 1998. "Orthodoxy, Cultural Nationalism and the Hindu Right." In *Nation, Empire, Colony: Historicising Gender and Race*, edited by Ruth Roach Pierson and Nupur Chaudhuri, 166–181. Indiana: Indiana University Press.

Sarkar, Tanika. 2000. "A Shudra Father for Our Lord: Balakdashis and the Making of Caste, Sect, and Community." *Studies in History*, 16, no. 1: 41–73.

Sarkar, Tanika. 2001. *Hindu Wife, Hindu Nation*. Bloomington and Indianapolis: Indiana University Press and Permanent Black.

Sarkar, Tanika. 2006. "A Book of Her Own, A Life of Her Own: The Autobiography of a Nineteenth-Century Woman." In *Cultural History of Modern India*, edited by Dilip M. Menon, 32–64. New Delhi: Social Science Press.

Sarkar, Tanika. 2011. "Holy infancy: Love and Power in a 'Low Caste' Sect in Bengal." *South Asian History and Culture* 2, no. 3: 337–351.

Sassen, Saskia. 1998. *Globalization and Its Discontents: Essays on The New Mobility of People and Money*. New York: The New Press.

Sassen, Saskia. 2001. "Spatialities and Temporalities of the Global: Elements for a Theorization." In *Globalization*, edited by Arjun Appadurai, 260–278. Durham, NC: Duke University Press.

Saunders, Jennifer. 2019. *Imagining Religious Communities: Transnational Hindus and their Narrative Performances*. New York: Oxford University Press.

Schechner, Richard. 1985. *Between Theater and Anthropology*. Philadelphia: University of Pennsylvania Press.

Scott, J. Barton. 2016. *Spiritual Despots: Modern Hinduism and the Genealogies of Self-Rule*. Chicago: University of Chicago Press.

Searle-Chatterjee, Mary. 2005. "'World Religions' and 'Ethnic Groups': Do these Paradigms Lend Themselves to the Cause of Hindu Nationalism?" In *Defining Hinduism: A Reader*, edited by J. E. Llewellyn, 151–166. New York: Routledge.

Sen, Amiya. 2001. *Hindu Revivalism in Bengal c. 1872–1905: Some Essays in Interpretation*. New York: Oxford University Press.

Shankar, Shobana. 2021. *An Uneasy Embrace: Africa, India, and the Spectre of Race*. Oxford: Oxford University Press.

Sharma, Krishna. 1987. *Bhakti and the Bhakti Movement: A New Perspective*. New Delhi: Munshiram Manoharlal.

Shinn, L. 1987 *The Dark Lord: Cult Images and the Hare Krishnas*. Philadelphia: Westminster Press.

Singh, Kavita. 2010. "Temple of Eternal Return: The Swāminārāyan Akshardhām Complex in Delhi." *Artibus Asiae* 70, no. 1: 50.

Sinha, Ajay. 2007. "Against Allegory: Binode Bihari Mukherjee's *Medieval Saints* at Shantiniketan." In *Picturing the Nation: Iconographies of Modern India*, edited by Richard Davis, 66–91. Hyderabad, India: Orient Longman.

Sippy, Shana. 2012. "Will the Real Mango Please Stand Up? Reflections on Defending Dharma and Historicising Hinduism." In *Public Hinduisms*, edited by John Zavos et al., 22–44. London: SAGE Publications.

Smith, Brian K. 1998. *Reflections on Resemblance, Ritual, and Religion*. New Delhi: Motilal Banarsidass.

Spivak, Gayatri Chakravorty. 1988. "Can the Subaltern Speak?" In *Marxism and the Interpretation of Culture*, edited by C. Nelson and L. Grossberg, 271–313. Basingstoke: Macmillan Education.

Squarcini, Federico, and Eugenio Fizzotti. 2004. *Hare Krishna: Studies in Contemporary Religion*. Salt Lake City, UT: Signature Books.

Srinivas, M. N. 1956. "A Note on Sanskritization and Westernization." *The Far Eastern Quarterly* 15, no. 4: 481–496.

Srinivas, Smriti. 2001a. *Landscapes of Urban Memory: The Sacred and the Civic in India's High-Tech City*. Minneapolis: University of Minnesota Press.

Srinivas, Smriti. 2001b. "Advent of the Avatar: The Urban Following of Sathya Sai Baba and its Construction of Tradition." In *Charisma and Canon: Essays on the Religious History of the Indian Subcontinent*, edited by Vasudha Dalmia, Angelika Malinar and Martin Christof, 292–309. New Delhi: Oxford University Press.

Srinivas, Smriti. 2008. *In the Presence of Sai Baba: Body, City, and Memory in a Global Religious Movement*. Leiden: Brill.

Srinivas, Smriti. 2015. *A Place for Utopia: Urban Designs from South Asia.* Seattle: University of Washington Press.

Srinivas, Tulasi. 2009. "Building Faith: Religious Pluralism, Pedagogical Urbanism, and Governance in the Sathya Sai Sacred City." *International Journal of Hindu Studies* 13, no. 3: 301–336.

Srinivas, Tulasi. 2010. *Winged Faith: Rethinking Globalization and Religious Pluralism through the Sathya Sai Movement.* New York: Columbia University Press.

Srinivas, Tulasi. 2018. *The Cow in the Elevator: An Anthropology of Wonder.* Durham, NC: Duke University Press.

Srivastava, Sanjay. 2017. "Divine Markets: Ethnographic Notes on Postnationalism and Moral Consumption in India." In *Religion and the Morality of the Market*, edited by Daromir Rudnyckyj and Filippo Osella, 94–115. Cambridge: Cambridge University Press.

Steger, Manfred. 2009. "Globalisation and Social Imaginaries: The Changing Ideological Landscape of the Twenty-First Century." *Journal of Critical Globalisation Studies* 1: 9–30.

Stewart, Tony K. 2010. *The Final Word: The Caitanya Caritāmṛta and the Grammar of Religious Tradition.* Oxford: Oxford University Press.

Subramaniam, Banu. 2000. "Archaic Modernities: Science, Secularism, and Religion in Modern India." *Social Text* 18, no. 3: 67–86.

Subramaniam, Banu. 2019. *Holy Science: The Biopolitics of Hindu Nationalism.* Seattle: University of Washington Press.

Sud, Nikita. 2012. *Liberalization, Hindu Nationalism, and the State: A Biography of Gujarat.* New York: Oxford University Press.

Sugirtharajah, Sharada. 2003. *Imagining Hinduism: A Postcolonial Perspective.* London: Routledge.

Tamal Krishna Goswami. 2012. *A Living Theology of Krishna Bhakti: Essential Teachings of A.C. Bhaktivedanta Swami Prabhupada.* New York: Oxford University Press.

Tamal Krishna Goswami and Ravi M. Gupta. 2005. "Krishna and Culture: What Happens When the Lord of Vrindavana Moves to New York City." In *Gurus in America*, edited by Thomas Forsthoefel and Cynthia Ann Humes, 81–95. Albany: State University of New York Press.

Thapar, Romila. 1997 [1987]. "Syndicated Hinduism" (reprinted). In *Hinduism Reconsidered*, edited by G. D. Sontheimer and H. Kulke, 54–81. Delhi: Manohar.

Thomas, Renny. 2020. "Brahmins as Scientists and Science as Brahmins' Calling: Caste in an Indian Scientific Research Institute." *Public Understanding of Science* 29, no. 3: 306–318.

Thomas, Rosie. 1995. "Melodrama and the Negotiation of Morality in Mainstream Hindi Film." In *Consuming Modernity: Public Culture in a South Asian World*, edited by Carol Breckenridge, 157–182. Minneapolis: University of Minnesota Press.

Tkatcheva, Anna. 1994. "Neo-Hindu Movements and Orthodox Christianity in Post-Communist Russia" *India International Centre Quarterly* 21, no. 2/3: 151–162.

Tweed, Thomas. 2006. *Crossing and Dwelling: A Theory of Religion.* Cambridge, MA: Harvard University Press.

Upadhyay, Surya Prakash. 2016. "Neoliberal Capitalism and the Emergence of Corporate Hinduism in Urban India." In *Religious Activism in the Global Economy: Promoting, Reforming, or Resisting Neoliberal Globalization?*, edited by Sabine Dreher and Peter J. Smith, 91–108. London: Rowman & Littlefield International Ltd.

Valpey, Kenneth. 2006. *Attending Krishna's Image: Caitanya Vaisnava Murti Seva as Devotional Truth.* Oxford: Routledge.

Vande Berg, Travis, and Fred Kniss. 2008. "ISKCON and Immigrants: The Rise, Decline, and Rise Again of a New Religious Movement." *Sociological Quarterly* 49, no. 1: 79–104.

van der Veer, Peter. 1996. *Conversion to Modernities: The Globalization of Christianity.* New York and Abingdon: Routledge.

van der Veer, Peter. 2002a. "Transnational Religion: Hindu and Muslim Movements." *Global Networks* 2, no. 2: 95–109.

van der Veer, Peter. 2002b. "Colonial Cosmopolitanism." In *Conceiving Cosmopolitanism*, edited by Robin Cohen and Steve Vertovec, 165–179. Oxford: Oxford University Press.

Varma, Rashmi. 2004. "Provincializing the Global City: from Bombay to Mumbai." *Social Text* 22, no. 4: 65–89.

Varma, Rashmi. 2012. *The Postcolonial City and its Subjects: London, Nairobi, Bombay.* New York and London: Routledge.

Vaudeville, Charlotte. 1976. "Braj, Lost and Found." *Indo-Iranian Journal* 18, nos. 1–2: 195–213.

Vaudeville, Charlotte. 1996. *Myths, Saints, and Legends in Medieval India.* New York: Oxford University Press.

Versluis, Arthur. 2014. *American Gurus: From Transcendentalism to New Age Religion.* Oxford: Oxford University Press.

Vertovec, Steven. 2000. *The Hindu Diaspora: Comparative Patterns.* London: Routledge.

Vivekananda. 1992–1994. *The Complete Works of Swami Vivekananda.* Calcutta: Advaita Ashrama.

Vrajaprana, Pravrajika, ed. 1994. *Living Wisdom: Vedanta in the West.* Hollywood, CA: Vedanta Press.

Waghorne, Joanne Punzo. 2013. "Global Gurus and Third Stream Religiosity." In *Gods in America: Religious Pluralism in the United States*, edited by Charles L. Cohen and Ronald L. Numbers, 228–250. New York: Oxford University Press.

Wallace, Gary. 1981. "A Review to Make Everybody Happy." Review of *Sri Caitanya-Caritamrita*, vol. 1, by Krsnadasa Kaviraja Gosvami. *Social Science* 56, no. 1: 53–56.

Warrier, Maya. 2003. "Processes of Secularization in Contemporary India: Guru Faith in the Mata Amritanandamayi Mission." *Modern Asian Studies* 37, no. 1: 213–253.

Warrier, Maya. 2005. *Hindu Selves in a Modern World: Guru Faith in the Mata Amritanandamayi Mission.* London: Routledge.

Warrier, Maya. 2012. "Engaging the 'Practitioner': Boundary Politics in the Academic Study of Hinduism" and "Krishna Consciousness, Hinduism and Religious Education in Britain." In *Public Hinduisms*, edited by John Zavos et al., 45–54. London: SAGE Publications.

Washbrook, David. 1993. "Economic Depression and the Making of 'Traditional' Society in Colonial India 1820–1855." *Transactions of the Royal Historical Society* 3: 237–263.

Watanbe, Chika, Levi McLaughlin, Aike Rots, and Jolyon Thomas. 2020. "Why Scholars of Religion Must Investigate the Corporate Form." *Journal of the American Academy of Religion* 88, no. 3: 693–725.

Weiss, Richard S. *The Emergence of Modern Hinduism: Religion on the Margins of Colonialism.* California: University of California Press.

Williams, Raymond Brady. 1984. *A New Face of Hinduism: The Swaminarayan Religion.* Cambridge: Cambridge University Press.

Wuaku, Albert Kafui. 2009. "Hinduizing from the Top, Indigenizing from Below: Localizing Krishna Rituals in Southern Ghana." *Journal of Religion in Africa* 39: 403–428.

Wuaku, Albert Kafui. 2013. "Exploring the South-South Trajectory of Global Religious Flows: The Origins of Ghana's Hinduism." In *Religion on the Move*, edited by Afe Adogame and Shobana Shanker, 133–158. Leiden: Brill.

Wulff, Donna. 1985. *Drama as a Mode of Religious Realization*. Chico, CA: Scholars Press.

Zarrilli, Phillip. 1999. *Kathakali Dance-Drama: Where Gods and Demons Come to Play*. Oxon: Routledge.

Zarzosa, Agustin. 2013. *Refiguring Melodrama in Film and Television*. Lanham: Lexington Books.

Zavos, John. 2000. *The Emergence of Hindu Nationalism in India*. Delhi, Oxford: Oxford University Press.

Zavos, John. 2001. "Defending Hindu Tradition: Sanatana Dharma as a Symbol of Orthodoxy in Colonial India." *Religion* 31: 109–123.

Zavos, John. 2009. "Negotiating Multiculturalism: Religion and the Organisation of Hindu Identity in Contemporary Britain." *Journal of Ethnic and Migration Studies* 35, no. 6: 881–900.

Zavos, John. 2012. "Hindu Organisation and the Negotiation of Public Space in Contemporary Britain." In *Public Hinduisms*, edited by John Zavos et al., 70–89. London: SAGE Publications.

Zavos, John, et al., eds. 2012. *Public Hinduisms*. London: SAGE Publications.

Zeller, Benjamin. 2010. *Prophets and Protons: New Religious Movements and Science in Late Twentieth-Century America*. New York: New York University Press.

# Index

*For the benefit of digital users, indexed terms that span two pages (e.g., 52–53) may, on occasion, appear on only one of those pages.*

Figures are indicated by *f* following the page number


Adivasis (indigenous people), 216, 263–64
Agarwal, Anil, 184–85, 286 n.60
Akbar (Mughal ruler), 109–10
Akhil Bharatiya Vidyarthi Parishad (student organization), 20
All-India Management Association (AIMA) World Marketing Congress, 107–8
Ambedkar, B.R., 50, 276 n.102
Americanized Hinduism, 61–63
Anand, Dev, 61–62
Annamrita Midday Meal program, 183
Āṇṭāḷ (poet), 39, 190
Appadurai, Arjun, 228–29, 232–33, 261–62
Artha Forum, 107
Ārya Samāj, 46–47, 268 n.25
Asad, Talal, 189–90
Association, Books, Character Building, Diet (ABCD), 173–74
Association of Medical Consultants, 107–8
Aurangabad, ISKCON temple in, 30–31, 94
Aurangzeb (Mughal ruler), 219–20, 221, 223
Australia, ISKCON in, 60–61
Azfal Khan (Muslim military leader), 290 n.69

Babri Masjid (Muslim holy site), 225–26
Bachchan, Amitabh, 170–71
Bakshi, G.D., 212
Bhagavad Gītā (Hindu text)
  generally, 114–15
  *bhakti* and, 102–3, 104
  business ethics and, 107
  central Vaiṣṇava status of, 41
  counselling and, 132
  five systematic topics, 164–65
  instruction in, 153–54, 155–58, 160–61, 164–66, 174–77, 178–79
  promotion of, 23–24
  translations of, 59–60, 102–3
Bhāgavata Purāṇa (Hindu text)
  central Vaiṣṇava status of, 41
  instruction in, 155–56, 158–59, 160, 164–65, 180
  plays based on, 217
  translations of, 51–52, 59–60
*bhakti* (devotion)
  Chowpatty community, in, 81–82, 102–9
  cultural orientation and, 231–32
  education and, 179–82
  Gauḍīya Vaiṣṇava tradition, in, 5, 16–17, 20–21, 48
  ISKCON and, 66
  plays and, 198–203, 199*f*
  Radhanath Swami and, 103–9
Bhakti Hṛdaya Bon Mahārāja (Swami), 51–52
Bhaktirasamrita Swami, 161
Bhakti Rasamrita Swami, 107
Bhakti Śāstrī (ISKCON course), 156–57
Bhaktisiddhanta Sarasvati
  generally, 88–89
  Chowpatty community and, 81–82
  culture and, 236
  Gauḍīya Vaiṣṇava tradition and, 47–52, 53–54
  media and, 59–60
  mission and, 48–52, 53–54
  science and, 172

Bhakti Tirtha Swami, 254
Bhakti Vaibhāva (ISKCON course), 156–57
Bhaktivedanta Academy of Culture and Education (BACE), 96–97, 110–11, 156–57
Bhaktivedanta Book Trust, 59–60
Bhaktivedanta Hospital, 30–31, 89–90, 91–92, 96–97, 160–61, 168, 183, 225
Bhaktivedanta Hospital Youth Foundation, 173–74
Bhaktivedanta Institute, 172–73
Bhaktivedanta Swami
 generally, 2–3, 51, 83, 100–1
 Americans in India and, 61, 62–67
 Bhakti Śastri course and, 12–13
 books of, 102–3
 caste and, 50–51, 248–49, 280 n.31
 culture and, 35–36, 233, 236–37, 240–41
 death and succession of, 87–88
 education and, 12–13, 155–57, 158–59, 160–61, 176
 Gauḍīya Vaiṣṇava tradition and, 267
 "Hindu," critique of term, 267 n.4
 Hindu traditionalism and, 9
 ISKCON and, 5–7, 22, 33–34, 38, 51–56
 mantra of, 160, 181
 mission and, 51–56, 66
 nationalism, on, 226
 plays and, 198–99, 200–2
 politics, on, 224–25, 226–27
 Radhanath Swami and, 63–64, 88–89, 98–100, 108–9
 "re-importation" of Gauḍīya Vaiṣṇavism, 68
 religious revision and, 11–12
 revivalism and, 11–12
 science and, 172–73
 training and, 94
 United States, in, 38, 51–52, 53–54, 57–58
 "universal religion" and, 243
 *varṇāśrama* and, 282 n.6
 Western culture and, 56–61
Bhakti Vikas Swami, 68–69
Bhaktivinoda Ṭhākura (Gauḍīya figure)
 counselling and, 133–34
 Gauḍīya Vaiṣṇava tradition and, 46–49, 50, 53, 57
 mission and, 46–49, 50, 53
 science and, 172
Bhanu Swami, 68–69
Bharatiya Kamgar Sena, 225
Bhārata Mātā (national image), 228–29
Bharatiya Janata Party (BJP)
 generally, 19–21, 189, 203–4, 211–12, 224–26
Bharatiya Vidya Bhavan, 209–10
Bhatia, Varuni, 46–47
Bhattacharya, Krishna Chandra, 263
Big Brother and the Holding Company, 55
Birla, Yash, 105
BJP. *See* Bharatiya Janata Party (BJP)
Bollywood, 24, 105
Bombay Public Trusts Act of 1950, 64
Bosnia, ISKCON in, 22–23
Bourdieu, Pierre, 135–36
*brahmacaris* (monastic model)
 generally, 29, 34–35, 132
 Chowpatty temple, *brahmacaris* in, 85, 102–3
 Counselling System and, 136–37
 *gṛhasthas* compared, 136–39
 Westerners as, 97–98
Brahmacari Training Academy, 156–57
Brahmo Samaj (modern Hindu group), 45, 268 n.25
"brand India," 232–33
Brazil
 ISKCON in, 5–6
 revivalism in, 8
Breckenridge, Carol, 228–29, 261–62
Brooks, Charles, 53, 136
business ethics (in ISKCON's persona), 107–8

Caitanya Bhāgavata (Gauḍīya text), 40–41
Caitanya Caritāmrta (Gauḍīya text), 40–41, 43–44, 79, 194–95, 221–22, 224, 267
Caitanya
 debate with *qazi*, 222–23
 *harināma* chanting and, 66
 Gauḍīya Vaiṣṇava tradition, in, 39–40, 41, 42, 43–44, 282 n.3
 influence on early Gauḍīya *gosvāmins*, 39–40, 42–44, 220
 ISKCON tracing roots to, 38

in relation to Jagannath, 202–3
in relation to Tukārām, 191, 199–200
Radha Gopinath Temple *mūrti*s and, 76–77
*Śikṣāṣṭaka* prayers of, 79
travels in South India, 194–95
Caṇḍidāsa (poet), 39
caste
Chowpatty community and, 81–82, 83–85, 125–27, 130–32, 139–40, 248–50
Gauḍīya Vaiṣṇava tradition and, 40–41, 44–45, 50–51
Catholics
ISKCON, joining, 114–15, 116–17, 122
in Mumbai, 116
Chaitanya Das, Krishna, 172–73, 187, 211, 213–14
chanting
Chowpatty community, in, 77, 80–81, 91, 120*f*, 147–48, 181
counterculture and, 55
Gauḍīya Vaiṣṇava tradition, in, 53–54, 243
ISKCON and, 61–64, 66
Character, Competence, and Devotion (CCD), 173–74
Charan, Chaitanya, 241–42
Chawla, Juhi, 105, 204–5, 214–15
Chetana programs, 85–86, 193, 237, 238*f*, 241
Chisthi Sufism, 224–25
Chowpatty community
generally, 4, 34, 71–75
alternative social structures in, 90–91
*bhakti* in, 81–82, 102–9
BJP and, 226–27
*brahmacari* model and, 136–39
brahmins and, 125–28, 130–32
bridging Mumbai's cultural divides, as, 29
caste and, 83–85
clothing in, 71–73, 81–82, 87–89, 252, 255–59
Counselling System, 92–97, 131–37, 139, 142–49
countercultural status of, 118
cultural orientation (*see* cultural orientation)
demographics of, 82–87
devotional dancing and chanting, 120*f*
devotional family (*see* devotional family)
dietary restrictions, 124–25, 128–30, 147–48
donations to, 90, 102–3
dual names, 279 n.16
education (*see* education)
financial services, 111–12
Flower Festival, 80*f*, 254
formation of community, 87–92
Govardhan Ecovillage, 18–19, 30–31, 84–85, 94, 129–30, 210–11, 254, 264–65
*gṛhastha* model and, 136–37, 139–41
Hindu nationalism and, 189–90, 224–25, 226–27
humanitarian activities, 183, 205–7, 210–11
India Rising Festival, 187, 203–15, 206*f*, 225, 227–28, 290 n.69
kinship model and, 142–49
Marriage Board, 34–35, 128, 139–41, 283 n.15, 283 n.23
media and, 18–19, 85, 183–84, 262
Mentorship System, 279 n.18, 282 n.12
mission and, 81–82, 84–85, 96–97, 102–3, 245–46
Modi and, 224–25, 226–27
national orientation (*see* national orientation)
ordered atmosphere of, 81
pilgrimages, 191–98, 287 n.6
plays and, 198–203, 199*f*, 217–24
Radha Gopinath Media Services, 80–81
Radha Gopinath Temple, 75–82 (*see also* Radha Gopinath Temple)
social media and, 264–65, 290 n.69
temple, 75–82 (*see also* Radha Gopinath Temple)
Vaiṣṇava Training Academy (VTA), 137, 156–57
*varṇāśrama* and, 132–33
*yātrās*, 191–98, 287 n.6
Counselling System, 12–13, 19, 34, 91–97, 131–37, 139, 142–49
*brahmacari* model and, 136–37
devotional family and, 34–35, 132–36, 142–49, 150–51

Counselling System (*cont.*)
meetings, 134–35, 142–46
subcommittees, 283 n.15
training, 94, 135
wellness paradigm, 94–96, 280 n.26
women in, 146–48
Covey, Stephen, 19
"crossing and dwelling"
devotional family and (*see* devotional family)
religious revision as, 14–17
Cross Maidan festival, 63–65, 88–89, 99–100
cultural orientation
generally, 35–36, 230–34
*bhakti* and, 231–32
caste and, 248–50
clothing and, 252, 255–59
dance and, 235
festivals and, 235
film and, 239, 241–42, 256–57
gender roles and, 251–53
"ISKCON culture," 248
"Krishna culture," 236–37
lifestyle regulations, 235, 239, 253–57, 259
music and, 235
plays and, 241
pop culture and, 244
religious revision and, 234–37
revivalism and, 10, 246
saris and, 252, 255–57, 258
television and, 239, 256–57
tensions in, 254–55
"universal religion" and, 243–50
Vedic-Vaiṣṇava cultural worldview, 232–37, 243–45, 248, 262, 263–64
Western modernity, opposition to, 237–43
whiteness and, 252–54
women and, 237, 238*f*

Dalmia, Vasudha, 208
dance, 208, 235
Dayananda Sarasvati (Hindu intellectual), 46, 50
Deadwyler, William H., 58, 243
Debi, Rashsundari, 50–51
Desai, Dharmsinh, 63
Desai, Narendra D., 63, 89, 100–1, 105
*Devastating Sacrifice* (play), 217, 218–19
Devī (deity), 218–19
devotional family
generally, 34–35, 114–15
*brahmacari* model and, 136–39
brahmins and, 125–28, 130–32
Counselling System and, 34–35, 132–36
dietary restrictions and, 124–25, 128–30, 147–48
*gṛhastha* model and, 136–37, 139–41
kinship model and, 142–49
Marriage Board and, 128, 139–41
realignment of religious identity regarding, 36
rejection of traditional family practices and, 3, 124–25, 133, 150–51
revivalism and, 10
*varṇāśrama* and, 132–33
diaspora, 69–70, 268 n.28, 271 n.84
dietary restrictions, 53–54, 86, 91, 92–93, 110, 126, 127–30, 131–32, 144, 197, 232, 251. *See also* vegetarianism; *specific restriction*
Drama Festival, 198, 199*f*
dramatic productions, 198–203, 199*f*, 217–24, 241

East India Company, 45
education
generally, 35, 150–52
*bhakti* and, 179–82
Bhakti Śastri course, 12–13
Bhaktivedanta Academy of Culture and Education (BACE), 96–97, 110–11, 156–57
Brahmacari Training Academy, 156–57
Gita Champions League (GCL), 12–13, 160, 174–77, 183, 184–85, 224
Gopal's Fun School, 85–86, 110–11, 156
Gopal's Garden, 156, 246
ISKCON Desire Tree, 158, 241, 283 n.2
Journey of Self Discovery (JSD), 160–63 (*see also* Journey of Self Discovery (JSD))
media and, 18–19, 159–60
multilingual nature of, 158–59
*paramparā*, 165

religious practices and, 168–72, 284 n.24
science and, 163–74
scientism, 150–74
social media and, 158
Vaiṣṇava Training Academy, 156–57
Vrindavan Institute for Higher Education (VIHE), 156–57, 285 n.42
Elison, William, 27
*Escape of Rūpa and Sanātana* (play), 220–21
ethnoscapes, 232–33
"eutopias," 261

Fahy, John, 270 n.56
Favors, John E., 254
feminism, 237, 238*f*
Fernandes, Naresh, 25–26, 110
festivals, 235. *See also specific festival*
Festivals of India, 187, 208, 209–10, 288 n.28
film, 222, 239, 241–42, 256–57
Flower Festival, 254
Food for Life Midday Meal programs, 183
Ford, Alfred, 184–85
Fuller, Jason D., 44–45

Ganatra, R.K., 66–67
Gandhi, Mohandas K., 50, 51–52, 57, 58–59, 263
Gaṇeśa (deity), 170, 211–12
Ganesh Chaturthi (festival), 74
Gauḍīya Mission, 48–49, 53–54
Gauḍīya Vaiṣṇavism tradition
generally, 3, 5–6, 33–34
*bhakti*, 5, 16–17, 20–21, 48
British rule and, 45–46
early history, 33–34, 39–44
gender in, 40–41
ISKCON and, 38–39
Krishna in, 39–40, 41–42
Krishna revival and, 2–3
mission and, 43, 46–52
*sanātana dharma*, 46
*varṇāśrama*, 40–41, 50
Gay and Lesbian Vaishnava Association (GALVA), 259
gender
Chowpatty community in, 79, 85–86, 138–42, 146–49
clothing and, 255–59
cultural orientation and, 237, 238*f* 251–53
Ghai, Subhash, 187
Ghana, ISKCON in, 20–21, 23
Ghosh, Sishir Kumar, 46–47
Ginsberg, Allen, 55
Giridhārī (name of Krishna), 200
Giriraja Swami, 65–66
Gita Champions League (GCL), 12–13, 160, 174–77, 183, 184–85, 224
globalization
Hindu traditionalism and, 19–20
religious globalization, 21–24
Gopāla Bhaṭṭa Gosvāmin (Gauḍīya figure), 41, 42–43
Gopal's Fun School, 85–86, 110–11, 156
Gopal's Garden, 156, 246
Goswami, Tamal Krishna, 9, 54, 236–37
Gottschalk, Peter, 163–64, 172–74
Govardhan Ecovillage, 18–19, 30–31, 84–85, 94, 129–30, 210–11, 254, 264–65
Govinda's Vegetarian Restaurant, 110
Grateful Dead, 55
Greenough, Paul, 209, 288 n.31
Grewal, Zareena, 97–98
*gṛhasthas* (marriage model), 136–37, 139–41
Gupta, Ravi, 236–37
gurus
generally, 6–7, 40–41
ISKCON and, 55–56, 68–69, 280 n.33

Haberman, David, 181–82
*habitus* (practice), 135–36, 181–82
Hansen, Thomas Blom, 207
Hanson, Mark, 97–98
Hare Krishna mantra, 181, 191
Haridāsa Ṭhākura, 221–22, 272 n.15
Harivaṃśa Purana, 39
Harrison, George, 55, 200–1, 288 n.19
Hawley, John Stratton, 215–16
Hindu nationalism
Hindu traditionalism and, 225–26
ISKCON and, 189–90, 224–25, 226–27
religious diversity versus, 189
revivalism and, 263–64

Hindu traditionalism
  education and, 150–51
  globalization and, 19–20
  "Hindu," critique of term, 267 n.4
  Hindu nationalism and, 225–26
  migration and, 17–18
  revivalism and, 8–14
  urban areas, in, 17–21
Hirschkind, Charles, 159–60
Hopkins, Thomas J., 23
Hungary, ISKCON in, 276 n.106
Hunger Free Mumbai, 205–7, 210–11
Husain Shah (Sultan of Bengal), 220, 224

India Rising Festival, 187, 203–15, 206*f*, 225, 227–28, 235, 290 n.69
INSPIRO Youth Festival, 230–31
International Monetary Fund (IMF), 269 n.46
International Society for Krishna Consciousness (ISKCON)
  Americans in India and, 61–67
  anti-American suspicions of, 62, 276 n.111
  branding and, 90, 232–33, 279 n.17
  development in India, 56, 64, 65–70, 182–86
  Devotee Care Committee, 93–94
  diaspora and, 69–70
  foundation of, 5–6, 52–54
  Gauḍīya Vaiṣṇavism tradition and, 38–39, 41, 47–48, 50–52, 284 n.24
  Governing Body Commission (GBC), 6–7, 55–56, 87–88
  gurus and, 23–24, 55–56, 68–69, 280 n.33
  "Hinduization" and, 69–70
  Hindu nationalism and, 189–90, 226–27
  institutionalization of, 55–56
  Krishna, preeminence of, 41, 54
  literary focus of, 59–60
  media and, 18–19, 32–33, 277 n.132
  mission and, 51–56, 66, 245–46
  pilgrimages (*yātrās*) and, 68, 191–98
  religious globalization and, 21–24
  religious life in, 54–55
  shared devotional culture and, 190–92
  suspicious attitudes toward, 116–18, 185
  trajectories of influence and, 19
  transnational development of, 60–65
  Western culture and, 56–61
  Youth Services (IYS), 85, 192–93
Irani, Smitri, 211–12
ISKCON. *See* International Society for Krishna Consciousness (ISKCON)
"ISKCON culture," 248
ISKCON Desire Tree, 158, 241, 283 n.2
Iwamura, Jane Naomi, 108

Jackson Brand Paper Products, 287 n.2
Jaffrelot, Christophe, 225–26
Jagannātha (deity), 43–44, 200, 202–4, 218–19
Jāhnavā Devī (Gauḍīya figure), 43–44
Jains
  ISKCON community, in, 110–11, 114–15, 116–17, 122–25, 150–51, 153
Janmohamed, Zahir, 270–71 n.73
Jan Sangh Party, 66–67
Jayadeva (poet), 39
Jayadvaita Swami, 65–66
Jayapataka Swami, 68–69
*Jewel of Faith* (play), 217, 218–19, 221
Jhūlelāl (deity), 195–96, 287 n.9
Jīva Gosvāmin (Gauḍīya figure), 40, 41, 232
*The Journey Home* (Radhanath Swami), 102, 103–7, 281 n.41
Journey of Self Discovery (JSD), 153–54, 160–74, 176–77, 178–79, 182, 183
Juhu, ISKCON temple in, 30–31, 61–62, 65–68, 111*f*, 158, 183–84, 185–86

Kabir (poet), 224–25
Kaikini, Jayant, 271 n.78
Kalaa Raksha Scheme, 211
Kali Yuga ("age of darkness"), 246
Kamdar, Mira, 274 n.70
*Kanji Viruddh Kanji* (play), 241
Kapoor, Sonam, 183–84, 230–31
Kaur, Raminder, 228
Kazakhstan, ISKCON in, 276 n.106
Kenya, ISKCON in, 5–6
Keśava Caitanya (guru), 191, 199–200

Khan, Aisha, 232–33
Khanna, Mukesh, 207
Khilnani, Sunil, 25
Khurrana, Ayushmann, 204–5, 214–15
King, Anna, 57
King, Martin Luther, 30
Kirtanananda Swami, 87–90
Kirtan Dubai, 264–65
Kirtan Mumbai, 264–65
Krishna. *See also specific topic*
  *bhakti* and, 179–80
  ISKCON, preeminence in, 41, 54
  revival and, 2–3
  Supreme Personality of Godhead, as, 5, 176
  transregional worship of, 191
"Krishna culture," 236–37
Kṛṣṇadāsa Kavirāja (hagiographer), 40

Lady Northcote Hindu Orphanage (LNHO), 89
Lakṣmaṇa Sena (Bengali ruler), 39
Lal Beg, 200, 218–19
Le Mark Institute of Art, 207–8
*The Life and Pastimes of Srila Haridas Thakur* (play), 221–22, 223–24
lifestyle regulations, 235, 239, 253–57, 259. *See also specific regulation*
Lion's Club, 66–67
Liss, Gary, 99–100
Lithuania, ISKCON in, 276 n.106
Locana Dāsa (hagiographer), 42
Lorenzen, David, 40–41
Lutgendorf, Philip, 42

Madhavas (band), 230–31
Mafatlal, Hrishikesh, 105
Mahābhārata (Hindu text), 39
Mahajan, Poonam, 211–12
Mahindra (company), 24
Makar Sankranti (holiday), 207
Malhotra, Manish, 183–84
Malini, Hema, 183–84
mantras, 53–54, 58, 159–60, 181, 191
Marriage Board, 34–35, 128, 139–41, 283 n.15, 283 n.23
Mata Amritanandamayi Mission, 4–5
Mayaram, Shail, 15–16
McKean, Lise, 79
media, 18–19, 159–60, 183–84, 262, 277 n.132
mediascapes, 232–33
Mentorship System, 279 n.18, 282 n.12
Mercy, Austerity, Thoughtfulness, Cleanliness, and the Holy Name (MATCH), 173–74
micropractices, 31–32
Midday Meal programs, 183
migration, 15–16, 17–18
Ministry of Education, 211–12
Ministry of Textiles, 207–8, 288 n.31
Mīrābāī (saint), 200
mission
  Chowpatty community and, 81–82, 84–85, 96–97, 102–3, 245–46
  Gauḍīya Vaiṣṇava tradition, in, 43, 46–52
  ISKCON and, 51–56, 66, 245–46
Moby Grape, 55
modernity, 9, 36, 237–43, 261–65
Modi, Narendra, 7–8, 20, 117, 174–75, 189, 211–12, 224–25
Moodie, Deonnie, 11–12
Mukherjee, Rani, 183–84
Müller, Max, 45–46
Mumbai
  cosmopolitanism of, 24–25, 27–29
  cultural tensions in, 25–26, 27–29
  economic disparities in, 26–27
  Hindu traditionalism in, 27–29
  migration and, 15–16
  Radha Gopinath Temple, 75–82 (*see also* Radha Gopinath Temple)
  religious attitudes in, 115
Munshi, K.M., 209
Muslims
  alterity in Hindu-oriented nationalism, 115, 216, 219–24, 228–29, 263–64
  targeting of, 26, 116, 221–22, 223, 224
  temple media depictions of, 218–24
  post-colonial dymanics and, 8, 97–98

Nanda, Meera, 19–20
Narahari Cakravartin (Gauḍīya figure), 43–44
Nārāyaṇa Bhaṭṭa (Gauḍīya figure), 43–44

Narottāma dāsa Ṭhākura (Gauḍīya figure), 43, 218
Nashik, ISKCON temple in, 30–31
National Handicrafts and Handlooms Museum, 288 n.31
national orientation
  generally, 35, 187–88
  alterity and, 215–16, 218–24
  armed forces and, 212
  crafts and, 209, 211
  India Rising Festival and, 187, 203–15, 206*f*, 225
  performative displays and, 198–203, 199*f*, 208, 209–10, 217–24
  pilgrimages (*yātrās*) and, 191–98
  post-colonialism and, 211, 212–13
  religious revision and, 213–15
  rural ideal and, 210–11
  Sanskritic Hindu model of, 209, 211–12
  shared devotional culture and, 190–92
Navi Mumbai, ISKCON temple in, 30–31
Nehru, Jawaharlal, 189
New Religious Movement (NRM), 5–6, 7–8, 22, 151, 261–62
Newton, Isaac, 165–66
New Vrindavan, 93–94
Niebuhr, H. Richard, 236–37
Nigdi, ISKCON temple in, 30–31, 94
Nityānanda (Gauḍīya deity), 76–77
Nṛsiṃha/Narasimha (avatar), 222–23
Nye, Mallory, 69–70

Obama, Barack, 101–2
O'Connell, Joseph, 40
*OMG: Oh My God!* (film), 241–43
Ong, Aihwa, 23–24, 232–33
Other Backwards Caste (OBC), 215–16, 218–24, 248–49

Padnavis, Devendra, 211–12
Panda, Ram Kumar, 208
Paramahamsa Yogananda (guru), 46
*paramparā* (lineage of gurus), 5, 108, 149, 166–65
PARTH Seva Department, 111–12
Pārvatī (deity), 217
Pattanaik, Devdutt, 19
Pérez, Elizabeth, 31–32
pilgrimages, 191–98, 287 n.6
Piramal, Ajay, 105
Piramal, Swati, 105
plays, 198–203, 199*f*, 217–24, 241
polytheism and monotheism, 168–72, 284 n.24
Prabhupāda Swami, 66, 225–26
Prakash, Gyan, 25
Prerna programs, 85, 172–73, 189–90, 193, 211, 213, 241, 256
proselytizing. *See* mission
Protestants, 19, 167–68
Pune, ISKCON temple in, 94, 188–89, 209–10
Puri, Vibhu, 214–15
Puṣṭimārgis (religious sect), 218, 237–38

race and ethnicity 22–23, 61–66, 97–98, 108, 231–34, 248, 251–54
Rādhā (deity), 39–40
Radha Gopinath, 162, 164–66, 168–71
Radha Gopinath Media Services, 80–81, 158
Radha Gopinath Temple, 75–82
  architecture of, 75–77, 89
  *brahmacaris* in, 85, 102–3
  environs of, 73–74
  photographs, 28*f*, 31*f*, 76*f*, 78*f*
  security at, 77, 81
  visitor experience, 76–79
Radhanath Swami, 29, 30–31, 97–102, 110, 184–85, 186
  autobiography, 102, 103–7, 281 n.41
  *bhakti* and, 103–9, 180–82
  Bhaktivedanta Swami and, 63–64, 88–89, 98–100, 108–9
  business ethics, on, 107–8
  caste and, 84–85
  Counselling System and, 92–94, 149
  culture and, 35–36, 231–32, 233–34, 241, 252–55
  leadership of Chowpatty community, 4, 7, 34, 68–69, 88–91, 137, 140–41
  pilgrimages (*yātrās*) and, 192–93, 197
  politics, on, 226–27
  public figure, as, 101–2, 105–8, 157–58
  *varṇāśrama* and, 132–33
  Westerner, as, 97–98, 108, 251–54
Rāghava Caitanya (guru), 191, 199–200

Rāma (deity), 172, 189–90, 192–93
Ramakrishna Mission, 48–49
Rāmānandīs (religious group), 218
Rāmānuja (medieval theologian), 191
Ramanujan, A.K., 38
Ramaswamy, Sumathi, 228–29
Ram Lila (festival), 74
Rasamrita, Bhakti, 190, 194–95
Rashtriya Svayamsevak Sangh (RSS), 20, 227–28, 278 n.6
Rath-Yātrās. *See also* India Rising Festivall-2, 43–44, 201–15, 225–26
Republic Day, 189
research methodology, 30–33
religious revision, 8–17
  ISKCON and, 229
  cultural orientation and, 234–37
  education and, 150–51, 155
  national orientation and, 213–15
"re-visioning," 13–14
revivalism, 8–14, 246–48, 262
Rich, Adrienne, 13–14
Rochford, Burke E., 55, 69–70, 269 n.53, 283 n.1
Roy, Srirupa, 287 n.2
Rūpa Gosvāmin (Gauḍīya figure), 40, 41, 42–43, 54–55, 176, 180, 220
Russia, ISKCON in, 5–6, 60–61

*sādhana* (practice)
  Chowpatty community, in, 80–81, 91–92, 112–13, 144, 147–49, 197
  Counselling System and, 135–36, 137–38
  education and, 152, 177–78, 181–82
  Gauḍīya Vaiṣṇava tradition, in, 3, 41, 43, 47–48, 50–51, 53–55
Sadhguru, 261 65
Sadhvi Bhagwati Sarasvati, 280 n.30
Sagar, Ramanand, 217
Śaivas (Hindu tradition), 216, 218–19, 228–29
Śāktas (Hindu tradition), 216, 218–19, 228–29
Sal Beg (devotional figure), 200, 218–19
*sanātana dharma*, 46, 127–28, 235, 267
Sanātana Gosvāmin (Gauḍīya figure), 220
Sanford, A. Whitney, 48
*saris* (clothing), 53, 243, 252–53, 255–58
Sathya Sai International Organization, 4–5
Satsvarūpa (biographer of Bhaktivedanta Swami), 240
science, education and, 163–74
scientism, 150–74
Scientology, 22
sexual orientation, 259–60
Shahjahan (Mughal ruler), 109–10
Shivaji (Maratha military leader), 290 n.69
Shiv Sena (political organization), 25–26, 27–29, 66–67, 74, 201–2, 225
Shukla, Umesh, 241
Siddiqui, Maryam, 174–75, 224
Sikhs, 114–15, 216
Singhania, Nawaz Modi, 105
Sītā (deity), 192–93
Śiva (deity), 217, 218–19
Slavin, Idelle, 100–1
Slavin, Jerry, 100–1
Slavin, Larry, 99–100
Slavin, Richard. *See* Radhanath Swami
Smith, Will, 264–65
social media, 32–33, 158, 264–65, 290 n.69
Societies Registration Act of 1860, 64
Somaiya College, 203
South Africa, ISKCON in, 5–6, 60–61
Soviet Union, ISKCON in, 22–23, 60–61
*Spiritual Renaissance* (play), 217, 221
Spivak, Gayatri, 18
Śrī Gopāla (deity), 76–77
Srinivas, M.N., 53
Srinivas, Smriti, 112
Srinivas, Tulasi, 11–12
Sri Rama Ramanuja Achari, 280 n.30
Sri Sri Ravi Shankar, 17–18, 152–53, 264–65
Stallone, Sylvester, 239
"state-temple-corporate complex," 19–20
Steger, Manfred, 270 n.63
Stewart, Tony K., 43–44
Subramaniam, Banu, 163–64
Swetshop Boys, 22
Swift, Taylor, 244

Taiwan, ISKCON in, 23
Talpade, Shivkar Bapuji, 214–15

Tandon, Raveena, 183–84
Tata Group, 24
television, 222, 239, 256–57
Thackeray, Bal, 66–67
3HO International, 17–18
Tilak, Bal Gangadhar, 2
Tipu Sultan (ruler of Mysore), 223
Transcendental Meditation, 17–18
transnational religious organizations, 4–5, 15–18, 21–22, 74–75, 261–62, 264
Tukārām (poet), 191, 199–200, 201–2
Tweed, Thomas, 14–15, 16, 31–32, 34–35, 104, 118

Udaan (holiday), 207
Ukraine, ISKCON in, 5–6, 20–21, 23, 60–61
United Kingdom
  East India Company Ac t 1813, 45
  ISKCON in, 23, 69–70
United States
  counterculture in, 55
  Great Awakenings, 8
  Hindu traditions and, 61–63, 97
  ISKCON in, 2–3, 20–21, 23, 59, 69–70, 87–88

Vaiṣṇava Purana (Hindu text), 39
Vaiṣṇava Training Academy (VTA), 137, 156–57
Vallabhācārya (historical Hindu figure), 282 n.3
van der Veer, Peter, 8–9, 27–29
Varma, Rashmi, 210–11
*varṇāśrama-dharma* (social system), 40–41, 50, 132–33, 228, 282 n.6
*varṇas* (social classes), 40–41
Vedas (Hindu texts), 155–56
Vedic Planetarium (proposed), 184–85
vegetarianism
  BJP and, 20–21
  Govinda's Vegetarian Restaurant, 110
  ISKCON and, 53–54, 91, 124–25, 127–28, 130, 131–32, 155, 185, 203
  pilgrimages (*yātrās*) and, 197
  and politics, 20–21, 185, 222–23, 226–27
Vidyāpati (poet), 39
Vilas, Shubha, 105, 156–57, 281 n.41
Vishva Hindu Parishad (VHP), 66–67, 209
Viṣṇu (deity), 190, 218–19
Viśvanātha Cakravartin (Gauḍīya figure), 217
Viśva Vaiṣṇava Rāja Sabhā (World Vaiṣṇava Association), 47, 48–49
Viṭṭhaldev (deity), 201–2
Vivekananda (Hindu intellectual), 46, 48–49, 58–59, 283 n.24
Vrindavan Chandrodaya Mandir (proposed complex), 184–85
Vrindavan Institute for Higher Education (VIHE), 156–57, 285 n.42
Vṛndāvana Dāsa (hagiographer), 42

Washbrook, David, 8–9
Weber, Max, 6–7
Wordsworth, William, 59, 275 n.100
World Bank, 269 n.46

Yadav, Akhilesh, 174–75
Yamuna Kinara, 111–12
*yātrās* (pilgrimages), 191–98, 287 n.6
Yogananda, Paramahamsa, 103–4
Yusuf, Hamza, 97–98

Zavos, John, 18, 225–26